VICTORIAN

KENILWORTH

and its

PEOPLE

R D Leach

Robin D. Leach

Published by Rookfield Publications

2006

www.Victoriankenilworth.co.uk

By the same author:

Kenilworth's Railway Age (1985)	The complete story from early plans to the station's demolition, including industrial usage and some aspects of how the town developed due the railway's arrival. 92 A5 pp including 12 pages of illustrations. (Out of print)
Kenilworth's Engineering Age (1995)	The rise of engineering firms as they replaced established industries, such as brick-making and animal skin processing. Of particular note are their origins in stables, outbuildings and sheds and the subsequent transition to purpose-built industrial estates. 64 A5 pp including 20 illustrations. £3.95.
Rails to Kenilworth and Milverton (1999)	A more detailed look at the origins and early days of Kenilworth's branch-line, the 150th anniversary celebrations, rail-workers' reminiscences, newspaper reports of incidents and a detailed account of the origins of the rail system of Leamington and Warwick to which the branch was joined. 88 A4 pp 50 illustrations and 3 layout plans. £7.95.

The above titles published by The Odibourne Press.   www.Odibournepress.co.uk

Front cover illustration: *This photograph surfaced in 1985 when it was published in the Kenilworth Weekly News. It had been found in a Somerset manor house and appears to be one of a pair of photographs presented to Captain Ernest Trepplin in October 1883, Trepplin later moved to Somerset.*
At the time, the fire-station was opposite the thatched cottage (extreme right-background) and within months of the presentation the cottage was demolished to make way the Local Board of Health's offices. By the following summer, the brigade had a new engine-house, it was a little way down Savage Lane, protected by the gate (extreme left-background), and was in a converted carpenter's shop. The building to the left still stands.
The photograph is reproduced with the permission of Kenilworth's modern brigade. (See p107)

Back cover illustration: *The new Bowling Green Hotel, later the Abbey Hotel, is Kenilworth's most impressive Victorian structure. It has been tastefully refurbished into apartments, The Abbey.*

Published by Rookfield Publications

Printed by Warwick Printing Company Limited

ISBN: 0-9552646-0-X
       978-0-9552646-0-3

Contents

Kenilworth is run by leading ratepayers at meetings held in the vestry at St.Nicholas church. The major industry is in decline, one in seven of the population are officially paupers. A railway line is built. The inhabitants struggle through the hardships; an Institute is formed for the educated, a working man's club for the less so. A series of farm fires instigate moves to form a fire-brigade. Industry begins to flourish, a fellmongers at Mill End, and then new brickworks. A gas company is formed.
The Queen visits the town.
Entertainment is provided by steeple-chase meetings, the annual statute fair and travelling shows, all of which induce visitors by the thousand. The cricket club provides sporting opportunities.
The Warwickshire Constabulary build their headquarters in Albion Street.
Bad times return, the farm-workers rise up against their masters, many emigrate, and a Co-operative is started.

Poor sewerage disposal results in a Local Board of Health being formed, and a sewerage system being built. A water company is formed, and there is a promise of swimming baths.
The cemetery needs extending, the Abbey Fields are acquired, the railway system is extended. A convalescent home is built.
New roads are built, as is a new hotel. The tannery closes unexpectedly. The cricket team plays Warwickshire.
The fire brigade moves to a new station, and deals with a major town-centre fire.

Trade slumps, hundreds emigrate, but the Co-operative flourishes. The town recovers once-more, another new brickworks is opened. The Local Board is replaced by an Urban District Council bringing political parties to the fore. A political club is formed. Football clubs begin to flourish alongside the Cricket clubs. A golf club is started on a farm. The swimming pool is built.
The fire brigade gets a steam-powered engine. Cars appear on the roads and cause accidents.
Kenilworth soldiers and volunteers leave for the wars in the Sudan and Africa. Flooding engulfs Mill End.

Personal and place names are contemporary spellings, and thus liable to variation. Modern place names are occasionally added in brackets to help the reader identify a location.

Numbers in brackets after a person's name give their age. It should be noted that ages were not always accurately kept, so someone who is 30 in one year may ten years later be only 38!

Quotes from newspapers are in italics, quotes from other sources are not.

Photographs, except where stated, are by the author and taken within the last two years.

Acknowledgements and Sources

The major sources of information for this work were the newspapers of the day, in particular the *Kenilworth Advertiser* held at Kenilworth Library, where the staff, particularly Carole Kelly, Linda Young and Tracey Brown, have been ever courteous and helpful for the duration of the 20 year project. The census returns and directories held at the library were also studied. Extracts from the library's map collection were copied, and are reproduced with permission, and courtesy, of the Ordnance Survey.

For the years prior to Kenilworth having its own newspaper, the *Leamington Chronicle, Leamington Courier* and *Warwick Advertiser* were studied at the County Records Office, Warwick, where other documents consulted included the minutes of Vestry meetings, the Local Board and Kenilworth Urban District Council; various legal records such as wills, probate, deeds and property reports; and other papers including planning applications. Particular thanks are due to Caroline Sampson, Head of Archive Service, for granting permission for the reproduction of several documents.

I am especially grateful to Leonard Stickley for allowing me access to his family's collection of documents, dating back almost 200 years, relating to the Woodmill Meadows site at Mill End, formerly Henry Street's fellmongers. Phillip Street too has provided much useful information concerning his ancestors and their business affairs.

Due to the efforts of Keith Hughes, I was allowed access to Kenilworth fire brigade's collection of memorabilia. The front cover, and credited photographs elsewhere are the result.

Through Richard Levitt and Roy Ablewhite, I was allowed access to the records of the Kenilworth Tennis Club, which provided details of the site's previous use as a brickworks.

A chance meeting with John and Valerie Holland from Lincolnshire at Kenilworth Library, resulted in a splendid exchange of information concerning Dr John Clarke and his son John Henry Grayson Clarke.

Jill Prime provided some details of her ancestors in the Adams and Newton families.

The internet has provided a large number of contacts throughout this and other countries who have added valuable information. Some of these are included below:

Innes Sloss provided information about the early life of PC James Sloss, and the current occupiers of Newbold House, Harley and Cally Miller, sent details of Captain John Woodcock's time in Scotland.

Georgia Slaughter, of the Kansas City Library, provided all the details regarding John Boddington's life in Kansas. Jane Cox, of Hereford Library, and Melissa Sedon, Sites and Monuments Records Officer for Herefordshire Council, between them uncovered details of the Reverend Barker and his South Bank House. Michael Speak provided additional information.

Amongst the many who contributed to the life of the Trepplin family outside Kenilworth, Elizabeth Boardman, Brasenose College archivist, and Maureen Church, Sidmouth Museum, made notable contributions.

I am grateful too, for the efforts of Sam Leach and Matt Iggo in producing the website, www.VictorianKenilworth.co.uk.

The final layout and setting was performed by Denise O'Malley, and as in my previous books, sound advice and invaluable editorial work was by Richard Storey.

Finally, particular thanks to Sue for her support and assistance whilst I indulge in my hobby.

Bibliography

A.T.Andreas, *History of the State of Kansas* (1883)
R.W.Brunskill, *Brick Building in Britain,* Victor Gollancz, Ltd. (1990)
D.J.Mitchell, *A History of Warwickshire County Council 1889-1989,* Pub by WCC (1988)
Joyce Powell, *Kenilworth at School,* Odibourne Press (1991)
Michael Speak, *Victorian and Edwardian Buildings in Hereford, 1837-1919.* Unpublished (2006)
P.F.Speed, *Social Problems of the Industrial Revolution* (1975)
Rob Steward, *The Inns and Roads of Kenilworth,* Odibourne Press (2000)
Memorials in the Churchyard of St.Nicholas, Kenilworth History and Archaeology Society (repr.2005)

Further details of some subjects covered in this work can be found in articles submitted by this author to the Kenilworth History and Archaeology Society which have been published in their annual booklet *Kenilworth History.* These include:

A Station for Kenilworth (1992 edition)
The Tale of The Two Virgins - and a Man who was Abel (2002-3)
The Engine, The Wyandotte and Four Boddingtons (2003-4)
Kenilworth's Sporting Victorians (2004-5)
On the Trail of the Trepplins (2005-6)

The reader will find many related and additional articles of interest in these and other editions. Kenilworth is blessed with a surprisingly large band of historians, dedicated to researching and publishing a wide range of subjects, and a visit to Kenilworth Library's reference section by the curious will be well rewarded.

Preface

"Her most gracious Majesty, Queen Victoria. May she long reign on the throne of these realms, happy in the affections and obedience of a brave, loyal and devoted people. May she preserve inviolate the civil and religious institutions of this free and mighty empire. May she administer the laws with strict justice and impartiality. Above all, may God give her grace to promote His honour and glory, and thus bring down his blessings on her native land."

The shouts and cheers from the assembled crowd that followed this powerful speech by attorney Robert Poole in the Castle grounds on 28th June 1838 *"...literally rent the air, the venerable ruin that stood towering beside them took up the cry, and its ruined walls, its deserted rooms, echoed the burst of universal attachment which pervaded the numerous throng."*

From an early hour, the inhabitants of Kenilworth had been astir, looking forward to celebrating the coronation of their new Queen at Westminster Abbey. The morning had seen the Parish church filled to witness a *"...discourse of much eloquence..."* by the Reverend H M Villiers, reading from the First book of Kings, Chapter 1, verse 9. At about 5 o'clock the festivities proper were under way with a major procession starting at The Kings Arms, led by the general inhabitants parading a silk banner displaying a crown. The Kings Arms Benefit Club and The Castle Benefit Club followed with their banners and the throng made its way along Abbey Hill, Bridge Street and High Street on its way to the Castle. A feast was laid out on the lawn for 1,500 people; the old and infirm were conveyed in carriages paid for by Thomas Cotton. £150 had been raised to provide school children with roast beef, plum pudding and ale on Castle Green.

After eating, the two parties combined then split into large groups around the Castle grounds. Some were dancing to music from a band in the Castle ruins, others took part in rural sports and other entertainments and it all concluded with a firework display, donated by Robert Poole, *"...which had a very splendid effect, lighting up the hoary towers of the Castle, and showing with its brilliancy the rents that time and weather had effected in this once impregnable fortress."*

"Aspiring to no higher rank than a populous country village, Kenilworth has in the festivities shown itself fully to take a place with the larger towns in its neighbourhood, in the demonstration of all that loyalty and affection to our lovely monarch. It was a peculiarly gratifying spectacle to observe the reciprocity of good fellowship which existed among all parties present. Rich and poor, old and young, the grave and the gay, all united together in harmony."

No one who was present could possibly have imagined the changes that would take place in Kenilworth in their new Queen's lifetime.

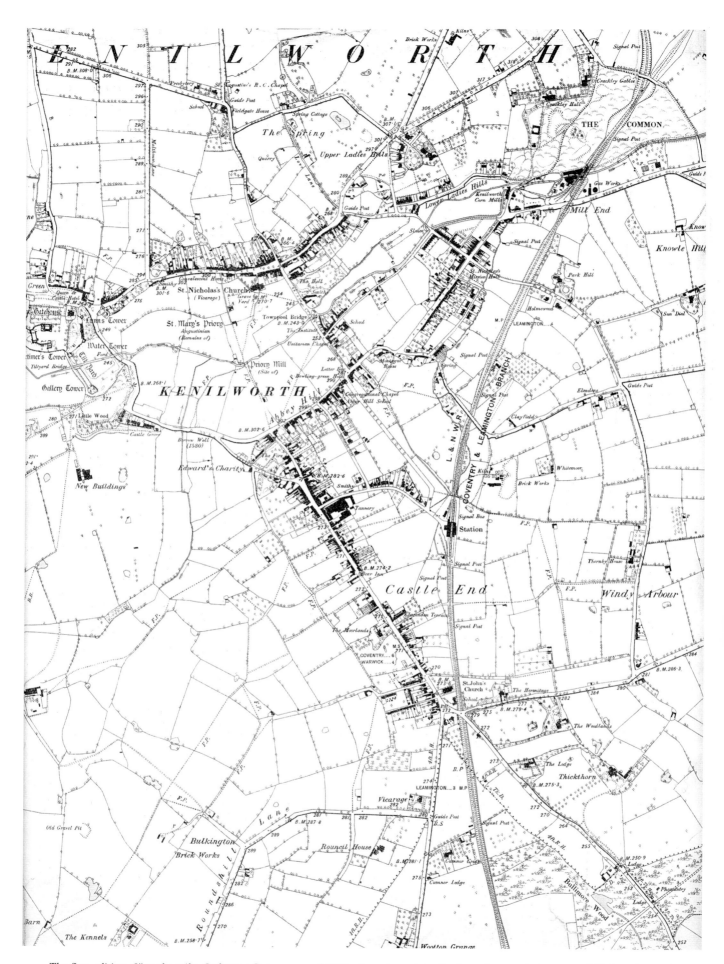

The first edition, 6" to the mile, Ordnance Survey map of 1885, shows how virtually the entire population was still living alongside the major route roads.

6

Part One

"A populous country village ..."

Decisions for the running of the parish were taken at Vestry Meetings. The most important of the Vestry's functions were the upkeep of the roads and the administration of the Poor Law Act of 1601. Village Vestries had become controlled by land owners and Kenilworth was no different; not only did farmers dominate numerically but due to the rates they paid most were entitled to additional votes as the make up of the Vestry of 1839 show:

Thomas Tidmarsh (38)	3 votes	Farmer, Villiers Hill
Robert Boddington (38)	3 votes	Farmer, Chase Lane
William H Butler (43)	2 votes	Land Steward
Robert Draper (31/60)	2 votes	Tanner
George Blundell (35)	2 votes	Farmer, Chase Lane
Thomas Handley (29)	2 votes	Farmer, Redern Farm
Thomas Ward (44)	1 vote	Farmer, Grounds Farm
Thomas Fraser (38)	1 vote	Grocer, Castle End
Robert Poole (?)	1 vote	Attorney
Charles Quarterley (23)	1 vote	Curate

Farmers were thus entitled to a total of eleven votes whilst the rest of the group could only muster seven, including two for a land steward. In addition, Fraser and Blundell were Overseers of the Poor, and Tidmarsh and Draper were Churchwardens.

The vestries were not particularly well equipped to cope with the economic situation of the early part of the nineteenth century and the Poor Law Amendment Act of 1834 had instigated the grouping of local vestries into Unions and Kenilworth became part of the Warwick Union. One outcome of this was that each Union could build its own central workhouse, closing smaller Parish workhouses. It is not known for certain exactly when Kenilworth's own workhouse in (Upper) Rosemary Hill closed, but the new workhouse in Warwick was opened by the Union in late 1838 or early 1839 giving the Union three (including the old Warwick one). Not surprisingly, the two old houses were no longer required and were put up for sale and that in Rosemary Hill, complete with half an acre of land, was sold by auction in October 1839. In High Street was a School of Industry set up with charitable donations for the benefit of thirty poor girls. Originating in the late 18th century, it is likely to have become linked with the workhouse and closed at about the same time.

The most powerful of the local authorities were the County Magistrates at the Quarter Sessions. They had to approve the poor rate settled upon by the Vestries, but also decided the County Rate out of which the upkeep of county bridges, the police force and prosecutions were financed.

The poor were categorised as either "indoor" or "outdoor". Paupers who had to leave home to work in a workhouse for example, were classed as "indoor". Ratepayers had to take on paupers who went to them

for work but overseers often favoured people, thus a landowner could favour his tenants; these were forms of outdoor relief. Unhappy paupers who were not favoured were known to take "revenge" by setting fire to hay-ricks etc. In Kenilworth, the indoor poor totalled 38, but the outdoor totalled 372 of whom half were children. The relief paid to these totalled under £300 for the first quarter of 1839, about 1s 3d per person per week.

Running a business in such a depressing situation was clearly difficult; one victim of the times was stonemason Edward Price who was discharged as an insolvent debtor. Others turned to crime - John Mayho was charged with stealing about half a hundredweight of coal from Charles Adams' brickworks near Rouncil Lane. One of Adams' employees saw the incident and recognised Mayho as he knew him well. Found guilty, he was sentenced to one month with hard labour.

Doubtless contributing to the situation was the appalling springtime weather. Regular frosts and occasional snow flurries during May limited available agricultural work, both then and later in the year due to the subsequent poor crop yields. Particularly badly affected was the town's major manufacturing industry, the making of combs from horn. The origins of the industry are obscure, but it had existed in Kenilworth for at least a century, possibly due to the Warwickshire long-horned cattle; there was a ready supply of raw material from the farms and tanneries. It cannot be said for certain whether its decline was a significant cause or effect of the town's problems, but it was certainly causing great hardship; one comb-maker, 60 year-old Joseph Arnold, arose at 5.00 one morning in March 1840, and hanged himself. Alfred Arnold (72) and David Arnold (25) were also comb-makers at the same address. "Many persons in this Parish, owing to the declining trade, are unable to provide for themselves and families by following the trade of combmaking, and from their long sedentary habit by applying themselves to that occupation they are physically incapable of earning sufficient for their maintenance by agricultural work. It therefore appears necessary that some provision should be made to meet the cause of distress." It became clear what this "provision" was to be twelve months later when comb-makers began applying for poor relief. John Newey, was sent to the workhouse, Joseph Aitken was sent to work on the town's roads, and Thomas Colin was taken on by Joseph Jaggard at his Rounsell Farm. All local farmers had been contacted to see how many labourers they could take on, but this is the only known success. Thomas Betty, along with rake-maker William Webb, applied to be excused rates but was not successful. Mr Weale of the Poor Law Commission was invited to see "...the peculiar distresses which now exist..." with the intention that he could persuade the Warwick Union to help the town financially, but instead he reported that the town's expenses were only a trifle more than when they joined the Union and were thus not entitled to any more. At the next Vestry meeting, it was decided to apply to Parliament to release occupiers of small tenements from the payment of rates and charge them instead to the owners, and William Butler, John Cave Brown Cave and Thomas Cotton were assigned to find the best way forward in this.

Attempts continued to find employment - in the Autumn of 1841 a new gravel pit was opened at Park Hill purely for the employment of the poor, and others were opened at Knowle Hill and at the Poor's Piece (the Common). The distress in the comb industry continued - in January 1842 of the fourteen men who applied for poor relief, ten were comb-makers, a tenth of the entire combmaking workforce. (Of the other four applying, two had known occupations, general labourers.) Occasionally men were sent to work in another part of the Warwick Union, James Hales was sent to the Mill in Warwick for example, but alternative employment in Kenilworth was the norm. James and Thomas Colin, along with William Cotton, (the last two being comb-makers) were amongst those sent to work for Joseph Lidzey repairing the roads, but now there were over thirty working for Lidzey, against the usual five or six. The funding for the roads ran out by the end of 1842 and an extra rate had to be collected to pay the men.

Due to particularly severe winter conditions in February 1841, individuals responded generously to a collection amongst the town's respectable inhabitants. The money was spent on coal and clothing which was distributed to the families that were in the greatest need. There was always one place of refuge from this despair - public houses were the only places of entertainment and additionally they were warm and well lit, and the beer could be less damaging to drink than the local water. In the 1830s all that was needed to start a beer-shop was to pay £2 excise duty, and it was known for poor-law guardians to buy them on behalf of widows, paupers, etc. One person known to have changed his trade from comb-maker to beer seller is Edward Boddington at Mill End.

Even during these desperate times there was a memorable event. Kenilworth's history has been littered with Royal visits and the first of the Victorian era took place in late October 1839. The Queen Dowager was being escorted from Coventry to Warwick Castle by the Earl of Aylesford troop of the Warwickshire Yeomanry when they were met at Gibbett Hill by Lord Leigh and nearly a hundred of his tenants, all on horseback, who joined the parade through Kenilworth and on to Guys Cliffe.

*   *   *

In 1840, the Earl of Clarendon gave some land to allow the church graveyard to be extended. The new area stretched southwards over an area believed to contain remnants of the Abbey and associated buildings, and as soon as digging began in July the area was found to contain a large amount of loose stonework. It was therefore decided to carry out a large scale clearing operation to a depth of nine feet to ensure future grave digging would be trouble free and, due to this, it very quickly became a significant archaeological excavation. Serious digging began at the end of August and within days the Calvary (Abbey burial ground) was found and at the full depth of nine feet were several sepulchral slabs, 6ft by 2ft, either decorated with ornamental crosses but otherwise plain, or rib-backed. The crosses varied in design but were not particularly well executed. Only two were taken up, one of each type, and 3ft below that with a cross was found a skeleton with arms folded and its fingers under its armpits. Probably buried without a coffin, Dr William Boddington suggested an age of about sixty or seventy years at the time of death. Beneath the other slab was a skeleton without its arms folded. Part of a floor of enamelled tiles was uncovered as was the basement of a "semi octagonal building." Also found were window traceries including a circular one dating from the time of Edward the first or second, as well as a square Norman doorway capital. As the excavations continued into September, more Norman stones were found in the Priory foundation walls and it was concluded that the Priory was built on the site of a Norman construction.

Digging at the 25ft wide semi-octagonal building revealed what was thought to be the Chapter house but the experts were baffled as to why the foundation walls were twelve feet thick at the base, an extraordinary thickness for the size of building and vaulted ceiling they would have supported. Four external and three internal walls were in perfect condition. Also found were walls connecting the Chapter House and gatehouse, and a fireplace complete with ashes and animal bones. More sepulchral slabs were found, including two that had been made into a drain, and two which were smaller than the others which were presumed to be from the acolytes of the Convent. A number of circular stones, still rough hewn on the back but having crosses on the front, were assumed to be head or footstones. The first burial in the new extension was of Mary White in 1842.

*   *   *

Kenilworth was at the crossroads of the local toll-road system. On the Kenilworth to Stonebridge toll-road towards Birmingham, there were gates at Redfern and Red Lane which in the late 1830s were let for about £120 a year, and another at Mouldings Gate which was let for just under £70. By comparison, on the busier Coventry to Warwick road, the gate at Stivichall was let for £558, and that at Guys Cliffe for £351.

In November 1840, plans were deposited by the trustees of the Coventry to Warwick and Leamington Turnpike Roads for major improvements to the road to Leamington. "Parts of the present turnpike road leading through Kenilworth are narrow and incommodious for travellers' carriages." Included in the plans, drawn by a Mr George, were a couple of short cuts including the demolition of Samuel Burbury's Bridge House on the corner of New Street and Warwick Lane (Bridge Street), and Thomas Birch's house where Abbey Hill turned into Castle End, but these options were not taken up. The road from the Horse and Jockey Inn down to the Chesford Bridge was to be improved, including a new cutting and the building of a new bridge. From Lea's Cottage a new road was planned to Binswood Terrace giving a straight, level approach to Leamington avoiding the existing route via Sandy Lane.

It was suggested that Samuel Burbery's Bridge House should be demolished to ease the corner of the toll road.

"*Considerable sums of money have been borrowed on the credit of the tolls authorised to be taken...*" by the trustees who included William Butler, Thomas Cotton, John, Robert and William Boddington, Samuel Burbery, Francis and Richard Robbins, Robert Draper all of Kenilworth, and Dr Edmund Bourne of Coventry. In May 1841, the Leamington Commissioners attempted to ensure there was a tollgate no closer to Leamington than Chesford Bridge, but the Bill was already before Parliament.

Only two full tolls were allowed to be taken from the same vehicle in any twenty-four hour period, and a return trip was free through the same gate, as was passing through a second gate once a fee was paid. Tolls taken were to be re-invested in the upkeep of the road. The Act was passed on 18th May 1841 and was valid for 31 years.

The tolls on the turnpike road from Warwick to Coventry, were available for letting each June; that at Stivichall was let for £805 in 1840 and Guys Cliffe for £382. The gates at Redfern and Red Lane, on the Kenilworth to Stonebridge toll road which started at the Kenilworth guide post, were let together.

A year after the Act was passed, the work had yet to begin, and the road from Leamington to Kenilworth was as bad as ever: "*A most disgraceful state...scarcely passable.*" It was suggested that the opponents of the proposed railway scheme, joining Leamington with Coventry, should contribute funds for the turnpike improvements and "*...all occasion for a railway would be obviated.*"

In the fourteen weeks from 27th December 1841 to 4th April 1842, the following passed through the Guy's Cliffe gate. All of this would have passed through Kenilworth, plus of course, more traffic from Leamington.

Coaches with 4 horses	28
Coaches with 3 horses	181
Coaches with 2 horses	1211
Gigs	2163
Wagons and carts	928
Horses, asses and mules	1759
Oxen and cows	485
Sheep and pigs	1413

Eight coaches ran between Leamington and Coventry and "*...the amount of money received during the year 1841...*" was as follows:

Mail	once each way	£328	15s	7d
Warwick Coach	twice each way	£505	1s	6d
Slater	twice each way	£811	1s	3d
Sibley	once each way	£363	9s	11d
W.Hunt	once each way	£565	7s	4d
Luck	twice each way	£810	5s	2d
Pilot	once each way	£312		
Price	3 coaches	£900		

A further £1,095 was taken from "cars", and £1,642 from posting.

One well established carrier was Crowley, Hicklin and Batty, who in 1841 carried luggage and parcels in their fly van between a canal wharf on the Tachbrook Road and Coventry Railway station, calling at the Kings Arms in Kenilworth.

In March 1842, advertisements were placed in the *Leamington Courier* for tenders to construct the new length of road from Binswood Terrace to Lea's Cottage. The road was open by the summer and from June 1842 to January 1843, the new Chesford Bridge Bar was let for £110. The trustees' meetings took place at the Kings Head in Coventry.

The area at Chesford was prone to flooding. In 1848, the water reached up to the toll bar and the road was impassable. It "*...ought to have the attention of the proper authorities.*" "*Many and loud are the complaints made about the road from this bridge to the toll-gate, being impassable during wet weather to foot passengers.*" Within weeks the floods were back; from the bridge to the toll house was knee-deep with water after rain the night before.

At the start of 1867, the Warwick County Magistrates were discussing the abolition of the county's toll roads.

* * *

In June 1841, the first census of the Victorian era was taken. Under Registrar, George Lampray (53), whose drapery business was now carried on by his daughter Hannah (25), the town was divided into five districts, the enumerators being William Sutton (24, gardener), Mr Robbins, Thomas Fraser (40, grocer), William Hopkins and George Heathcote (30, baker).

Kenilworth, still uncertain as to whether it was a village or town, was straggly, and covered a large area when compared to its population of a little over 3,000. The vast majority of the inhabitants lived along the sides of the route roads.

Clinton Lane was one end of the major route through the town linking Birmingham and Coventry, but being on the extremity it is not surprising that half the residents were involved in agricultural work; one,

George Satchwell, was a farmer and thirteen others were agricultural labourers. Joseph Smith was one of four carpenters and had three sons; William a bricklayer's apprentice, Joseph jnr a comb-maker's apprentice and ten-year-old Edward. It is possible that William was apprenticed to near neighbour Henry Joyce, the only other bricklayer in the area. John Evetts, a solitary shoemaker, and three elderly gentlemen of independent means, complete the list.

Around the corner in Castle Green there was a small change in employment with eleven agricultural labourers out of twenty-seven occupations. Six of the others were comb-makers, all from different families. The average age of the agricultural workers was 52, whilst those employed in the less physical comb industry was 35. A father and son, John and George Harris, were tanners whilst 37 year-old Job Satchwell was a builder, possibly employing his son David, one of two joiners. Thomas Walker was the publican at the Castle Inn (Queen and Castle) whilst there was one entry each for independent means, labourer, dressmaker and gamekeeper. At Little Virginia, seven of the eleven occupations were agricultural labourers, the others being a gardener, nurse, cordwainer and comb-maker.

From here along New Row (Castle Hill) and High Street, the occupations change dramatically with thirty-three employed in combmaking and just four as agricultural labourers. This is the area where combmaking in Kenilworth is thought to have started, but it is difficult to know precisely how many comb factories there were. Although George Tandy, Joseph Littleton and John Jervis (Jarvis?) were certainly three, there were likely to be smaller family concerns such as the Freeman family, which included John (72), James (45), William (35), John jnr (24), and Robert (20) who were all comb-makers or horn-pressers and lived with or near each other. Thomas Pell Marston, and John Taylor, bricklayer, represented the building trade, but as one would expect there was also a number of shops. James Drury was a grocer in New Row and probably did good trade as he was the nearest for residents of Castle Green and Clinton Lane, but 23 year-old George Church was quickly establishing himself in High Street. Other trades included Joseph Betty, butcher and farmer; David Fancott, a baker established in 1825 and possibly employing 17 year-old Edward Rice; William Rollisson, tailor; William Browitt, draper; Samuel Boddington, chandler; Ann Rice (45), a shoemaker with her son John assisting; and Charles Jackson and his son who were watchmakers. Charles was also an excise officer. He was one of a number of professional people in the road, others being Obadiah Ayton, Surgeon; Robert Poole, Attorney and living at The Priory with his office next door; William Butler, land steward, and Luke Sturley, Parish Clerk. Amongst the duties to be performed at the church was the ringing of the bell at 4 o'clock in the morning and 9 o'clock in the evening during the summer, and 5 o'clock and 8 o'clock in the winter. Another manufactory was rope-making, with Thomas Brookes and 60 year-old Thomas Burbidge involved. Five female members of the Littleton family, Hannah, Sarah, Ann, Charlotte and Francis, were all living off independent income. Being an important route, it is not surprising that there

were two inns, the Red Lion run by John Freeman and the Castle Tavern (Virgins and Castle) owned by Birmingham-born Abel Miles. Miles had first become licensee of the inn in 1826 when it was owned by William Ball and known as The Two Virgins, a name it had carried already for perhaps 300 years. It was then in "...a very ruinous state..." and Ball borrowed several hundred pounds to carry out extensive renovations. It was at this time that the name changed to the Castle Tavern. In 1831 the inn was conveyed to Miles and it then boasted a coach-house, piggery and garden ground, and a brew-house including brewing equipment that Miles had bought for £290. Miles also took on the debt William Ball had incurred for the extensive renovations. Miles must have been successful as he later bought five cottages across the road, alongside the vicarage, and a field at Whitemoor. Miles had married Kenilworth girl Sarah Lenton on Boxing Day 1826, spinster Mary Betts was his live-in employee.

Beyond the crossroads with Hogg Lane (Fieldgate Lane) and Warwick Lane (Bridge Street), in New Street, was another inn, the Coventry Cross. The Coventry Cross had been for some years, certainly before 1830, the town's Post Office, probably due to its location on the road to Coventry from where the horse post was sent and received. Mary Morris was both licensee of the inn and Post Mistress until her death aged 65 in 1832, at which point butcher John Manton, aged just 22, took on both the inn and post. Soon after his early death just six years later, the two concerns split; John Manton's widow Elizabeth continued as postmistress and William Freeman became the inn licensee. For the time being the two shared premises and neighbour William Holmes, not born until 1844, later recalled knocking on a small door in the wall of the Coventry Cross to buy a stamp. In 1841, letters from Coventry and parts of the north and east arrived at six every morning with a second delivery at 2.30 p.m., and despatches to the same places at 7.45 a.m. and 9.45 a.m. The post from Warwick and the south and west was less regular, arriving at 10.00 a.m. and despatched each morning at 6.00. It cost 10d to send a letter to London by coach, and by rail was "...almost as dear..." until the uniform "Penny Post" was introduced in 1840.

Nearby, 69 year-old Elizabeth Brown was a beer-house keeper, (at premises later to be called the Royal Oak) and 52 year-old Sarah Richards was a publican at The Barrel. Combmaking was again a leading occupation, with six involved including two each from the Tandy and Perkins families, jointly with six butchers, but of these there were only two businesses. There was a much greater mix of businesses and occupations including the town's youngest cooper, Richard Jones (20), a fishmonger, cordwainer, attorney, two shoemakers, corn dealer, two cattle dealers, two gardeners, a miller, smith, watchmaker, coachman, and tailor.

Just at the end of the buildings on the north side of New Street was Love Lane which led across to The Spring. Alongside its northern half was a stone quarry on one side and a small group of cottages on the other. These, and other cottages at The Spring housed four combmakers and several carpenters, as well as half a dozen labourers.

Hogg Lane was sparsely populated with just a few working men including a combmaker, a couple in the building trade and labourers.

At the other end of the town, approaching along the Leamington Road, the first sign of habitation was Thickthorn Lodge, occupied by wine and spirit merchant William Snewing. The Reverend John Wilson lived at Thickthorn itself, built in 1830 on the site of a farm house. A little further along on the other side of the road was a small brickworks owned by James Arnold, but operated by James Manton. The brickworks had been in operation at least since 1830. At the northern end of the brickfield, at the point where the road from Warwick formed a junction, was another James Arnold business, the Horse and Jockey Inn, but after his wife died in 1842, it seems he gave up the inn, with first William Smith and then Ebenezer Lynes becoming the licensee. In 1847, it was put up for sale and became Camden House. There was another road at this junction, an undeveloped lane heading eastwards known as Stoneleigh Road (Birches Lane). The Reverend Charles Twistleton lived along the road at Woodlands.

Just across the road from the Horse and Jockey was John Hopper's (45), Malt Shovel Inn. This was alongside a blacksmith's, a common occurrence as a traveller could take refreshment whilst the farrier did his work.

The Malt Shovel Inn (right), was alongside a blacksmith's, (left).

At this point was the start of the town's main thoroughfare, Castle End (Warwick Road), and as one might expect where three main roads meet there were other businesses including yet another inn, Christopher Botterill's Green Man, and carter Joseph Hopkins. In the vicinity of the Malt Shovel and Green Man were two unmade trackways; one led to Rawlins Row, White's Row, and Parish Row, which were a collection of poor quality houses, and the other was Joseph Jaggard's occupation road, known in part as Greaves Row, which led to Bulkington and Oaks Farm.

Castle End stretched for almost a mile and accounted for over a quarter of all addresses. Despite having many gaps between buildings along its length, particularly at its southern end, there were no side roads except for footpaths and trackways to farms. It contained an array of interesting businesses, and of course, inns and public houses. Thomas Smith's, The Bear, (Bear and Ragged Staff) had been put up for sale in 1840; it had stabling and outbuildings and a *"...ten-quarter malthouse with iron kiln..."* and an attached 1½ acre pasture, known as the Bear Field. It was advertised for

sale again sixteen months later, describing the malt-house as recently erected and the tenant as *"respectable."* Other inns were 70 year-old Ann Betty's White Lion, shoemaker John Dormer's Boot Inn, Jeremiah Mayhew's Rose and Crown and Henry Bursell's Kings Arms Hotel. Henry Bursell snr and his wife Mary had been proprietors of the Kings Arms since 1819. They had two sons John and Henry. Upon Henry snr's death in 1834, the inn became Mary's alone, and she also inherited a cottage and land across the road, and several areas of land in the south and east of the town. Although jointly owned, Henry jnr took over the running of the inn in 1839. Not far from the Kings Arms was the well-established business of chemist and druggist John Newton. Amongst his stocks could be found Pickstock's Astorian Powder which had been proved by "...*the American and Russian fur companies as an infallible preventative of Moth in furs and woollens...*", Manby's Fever Powder which helped relieve children suffering from small-pox, measles, relaxation of the bowels, chicken-pox, teething and colds, and *"Captain Pidding's Howqua Small Leaf Gunpowder...the purest and most wholesome Green Tea imported from China."*

John Dormer's, the Boot Inn.

Alongside the Boot Inn, to the south of it, was James Heritage, a 60 year-old pumpmaker and repairer. This was a vital occupation as so much of the town's water supply came from wells. The sort of work he undertook is demonstrated by a receipt from the Castle Tavern where in 1843 Heritage opened up a well, took out and repaired the pump, replaced 21ft of oak lining, repaired or replaced some of the iron work, rods and bucket, and then re-assembled it for £5. Next door to Heritage was Henry Adams' boys school, started in about 1825, although by 1841 it was his son Richard (30) who was the master, and he had a baby son, Charles. Richard's wife, Caroline, and John Newton's wife, Mary, were sisters in the Olerenshaw family. Annual fees were 20 guineas for pupils under ten years of age, and an extra 2 guineas for those over. The school had 21 pupils aged between eight and fourteen. Nearby, but on the opposite side of the road, was a school for young gentlemen between the ages of four and ten run by Charlotte Richards (35). Her fees were 25 guineas per annum, and an extra 10s for washing. Admitting no more than twelve pupils *"...in order to secure select and respectable association..."*, she advertised the benefits of an extensive playground in an attached field, a separate bed for each child, instruction in both French and Latin, and two holidays a year - a month at Christmas and five weeks in the summer. At the time of the census, Miss Richards had her full quota of twelve pupils, aged between six and nine.

The largest place of employment was undoubtedly Henry (26) and Robert (33) Draper's tannery, continuing a business which had occupied the site since about the turn of the century. Not surprisingly, there was also at least one comb factory, in the name of William Turner (44), Joseph Pace (40) and John Webb (33), and although it is not possible to know the number of employees, 20 occupants along the road recorded their occupations as combmaker, including William Turner's two teenage sons. The works were just opposite the entrance to Borrowell Lane and were owned by Mary Pope, widow of Thomas Pope who had the works previously. Nearby was Charles Bliss (25), with the unlikely combination of draper and Bank Manager.

Outside Turner, Pace and Webb's factory, about 200 yards from its end, the road divided to pass around the Abbey Fields Estate, a group of fields rented to farmers and others by Lord of the Manor, Lord Clarendon. The westbound lane passed the Edwards School and the Borrow-well, from which the lane took its name, and continued to pass the Castle, but the main road continued in almost a straight line uphill. This last length of road included John Richards' (82) Crown and Horseshoes Inn, surgeon William Boddington (50), cab proprietor John Matthews (25), and gardener William Sutton (24). Sutton was also a rate collector; in February 1840 he had replaced John Squires who was very inefficient. Squires was sacked and had his salary withheld until all outstanding rates had been collected. William Sutton also lays claim to introducing strawberry growing to Kenilworth in the early 1840s. One June at that time he won a prize in Birmingham for a dish of 60 *"...with a special flavour..."* which he attributed to the Kenilworth soil. They were grown from Keen's seedlings which were *"unsurpassed"* for quality and flavour, but they were delicate and did not travel well to market. At its summit, Castle End met the Abbey Fields and a sharp right bend took the road along Abbey Hill. Charles Draper (25), surgeon, practised here. Jane Blair had a boarding school for young ladies; there were five teachers, including two of her daughters, for 21 pupils, mostly 14 or 15 years old but some as young as six. Wheelwright John Clarke (50) and cabinetmaker Richard Barran were amongst the tradesmen. Abbey Hill ended at Peter Heynes' (60) well established Bowling Green Inn, his two sons Luke and Henry were combmakers. The inn was well known for its pleasure grounds which included a bowling green, quoits and skittles amongst

its attractions. In 1841 it held its first Carnation Show.

From the Bowling Green Inn, running alongside the Abbey Fields to the High Street/New Street junction was Bridge Street, a name becoming more widely used for Warwick Lane. The most important manufactory here was Samuel Burbery's tanning business, close to the bridge over Finham Brook. John Collins and John Honey were likely employees living nearby. John Bryan(t), a carrier, lived here too, but it is difficult to see how he made a living from his only advertised run - a Thursday trip to Birmingham. Nearby, James Russell was a painter/decorator/glazier and James Elkington a grocer, but the most important resident was Sir John Cave Brown Cave at Kenilworth Hall. Set back from the road, near its junction with Pepper Alley, was the National School, a two-storey brick building built in 1836, with mixed infants downstairs and junior girls upstairs. Miss Sarah Insell (30), was a school mistress and was paid £26 a year for her efforts. The school building was in the northeast corner of "The old messuage and tenement and premises theretofore in the occupation of Jacob Arlidge Deceased, and afterwards of Joseph Brooks, Samuel Turner, Thomas Wright, William Townsend and John Kepputt." The entrance was to Warwick Lane, but there was also a "...right of barrow way from and to the said road called Pepper Alley to the back of the said premises for the purpose at all seasonable times of taking coals or other material and taking out ashes and night-soil only to and from the said premises."

Pepper Alley was a narrow lane from Bridge Street, following the course of Finham Brook to Washbrook. It housed another comb factory but this may have been just a father and son team Edward Dunn (55) and his son Charles. James Swain (35) was a carrier based here, taking goods to Coventry on four weekdays and Warwick on three. With two bricklayers, a sawyer and a carpenter, construction was well represented, but a more unusual resident was William Malpas, an engineer.

The occupants of the two large houses in (Upper) Rosemary Hill, (Rosemary and Hill House) were Phillip Carmouls (40), and tannery proprietor Robert Draper (respectively). Carmouls, of independent means, had a talent for painting in water colours and his paintings adorned a number of local sitting rooms. Also along the short road were a gardener, rake-maker, tailor and grocer. Almost opposite the two large houses lived John Savage, a carpenter and builder, and he had a workshop at the rear of his premises accessed by a small road known as Savage Lane (Richards Close).

The continuation of (Upper) Rosemary Hill became Albion Row (Street) at an 'S' bend. At this point was the site of the closed workhouse. It was demolished and in its place was built Montague House, its first occupant became surgeon William Boddington. Albion Row, the road taking its name from a row of terraced houses, was an important route to Stoneleigh and as a result had a well-established degree of development. Again, the major occupation was comb manufacturing with at least two businesses, Joseph Drury and Thomas Hornidge, and twenty-four employees. In a road of only 10 labourers or agricultural labourers out of 63 workers, there was a great variety of occupations including carpenters and sawyers, shoemakers, smiths, a cooper, coal dealer, cabinetmaker, and the more interesting ribbon weaver and two parchment makers, the only ones in town. There was also a publican, 70 year-old Catherine Ballard.

Albion Row continued into Mill End where a sharp right turn took the road parallel to Finham brook and on to Stoneleigh - straight ahead at this bend was the mill itself, and a trackway across a ford in the brook, across Poors Piece (the Common), and on to Coventry. From the late 1830s, the water-powered mill had been owned by John Boddington; this is likely to be the John Boddington who was a farmer and lived at the Castle gatehouse. Nephew Thomas Robbins, who was a miller, was staying with him in 1841 and within a few years Boddington leased the mill to two other nephews, Francis and Richard Robbins. Three millers are listed at Mill End in 1841, including William Green (38) and John Barran (40). Edward Boddington (60) was a comb manufacturer at Mill End alongside a small stream that fed the Finham Brook, and the four other comb-makers in the area are likely to have been his employees.

Southwards from the aforementioned 'S' bend in Albion Row ran Tanhouse Lane, the name coming from at least two and possibly three tanneries which existed at one time, but now there was just one, Joseph Ball's tan-yard, towards the far end of the lane. With two members of the Hornidge family amongst four comb-makers, and also four shoe-makers (including three from the Eggerton family), in the same road, there are signs of inter-related businesses - a sawyer, carpenter and labourer are the only other listed occupations.

In February 1838, James Arnold, owner of the Leamington Road brickworks, had taken over a small brickworks to the south of Tanhouse Lane. The lease of possession lists a number of people including three builders from Leamington suggesting these were the previous operators. Described as "A cottage and dwelling house, brick-yard sheds, hovels and other erections", the works was less than five years old. Arnold had an arrangement with the builder William Robbins. Just three years later, Arnold sold the works to James Manton for £400; the years Arnold owned the works were those when the future of his Leamington Road works was in doubt due to the impending construction of the railway.

The town's financial well-being was largely reliant upon the surrounding farmland, which started from the rear of the properties along the roads. Larger farms, such as The Chase, were split into smaller, more manageable affairs, and smaller farms existed, such as that at Whitemoor. Innkeepers and others owned or leased land for the grazing of their horses; the Bursell family, for example, owned several fields immediately behind the Kings Arms. There was a variety of cattle, dairy and crop farming, and the livestock helped to sustain the two significant town industries - horn comb manufacture and tanning.

There was only one notable industry in Kenilworth that was not in some way directly involved with farming - brick and tile making. Brickworks were often set up just to produce bricks for particular building projects and were thus short-lived; their existence was often recorded in field names such as Brick Kiln Close alongside Park Hill Road and Brickfield nearby at Crewe

Farm. The fuel was normally furze or gorse. Clay was dug in the autumn and heaped up to five or six feet high and the stones picked out. In winter, the rain and frost broke the clay down and then in spring, the clay was turned over and beaten and more stones removed. Further tempering was done by the clay being trampled by men and horses, sometimes it was passed through rollers. Bricks were then made from late spring through to early autumn to coincide with the building season. Three cubic yards of clay made about a thousand bricks.

In April 1841, more than one in ten of the town's 666 houses were unoccupied and as only one was being built, it was unlikely that there would be much work for brick makers. Despite this, there were operational brickworks in the early years of Victoria's reign. One was Charles Adams' works described as being in Roundsell Lane, this may have been an early reference to the works at Oaks/Bulkington; others were those already mentioned at Whitemoor and Leamington Road.

Of the 650 or so occupations listed at the time of the census, no fewer than 117 were involved directly with the comb industry. Farmers, 25, and agricultural labourers, 58, form the next largest group although there would obviously be seasonal fluctuations. Tannery and fellmonger workers totalled 24. Those supplying clothing numbered 55: the number of shoemakers, 31 and 4 apprentices, may suggest these were supplying more than just local needs, and of tailors and drapers there were 20, including 7 apprentices. There were 72 general labourers who would have boosted numbers working at any of the manufactories. The population was 3,149.

* * *

The building and repair of bridges within the Union district was the responsibility of the County Bridgemaster, Mr Kendall, and the cost of the work was paid by the Union, the local Parish, or both. In 1841, Kenilworth's Barrow Bridge was "...very decayed and dangerous." Indeed, its condition was so poor that the Parish started legal proceedings against the Union. Parish Clerk Luke Sturley (86), had lived in Kenilworth all his life and produced documents regarding the repair of the bridge from as far back as 1777, proving it was the responsibility of the County, and they were indicted at the 1841 Easter Quarter Sessions. This led to a meeting of Sir John Cave-Brown-Cave, William Henry Butler, the Parish Solicitor, Robert Poole, and two representatives of the County, at The Kings Arms Hotel on 4th May. An agreement was signed as to the necessary repairs. The bridge's six feet-wide arch over the water was believed to be centuries old but was sound enough - much of the work to be done involved widening the bridge from 13ft to 18ft, with new parapets and wing walls and an improved road surface of stone and gravel. It was agreed to split the costs evenly between the Union and Parish and the job was let to a Kenilworth stonemason for £70. No sooner had work started than William Henry Butler, acting on behalf of the Parish, said that the Parish would not pay its share unless the arch was increased from 6ft to 7ft to improve the flow of water under it. The matter was discussed at the

Summer Quarter Sessions where the question was asked, "Should Magistrates be involved in pulling down an ancient and curious arch?" It was agreed that the water always flowed through the arch and that an increase in size was not necessary, and work proceeded as originally agreed. The date of the work was carved into the stone, and at Easter 1843 Mr Kendall reported that the substantial rebuilding work was complete.

* * *

Formed as assistance to the local police force was the Kenilworth Association for the Prosecution of Felons. It consisted of some wealthy locals and business people including Mrs Amherst, George Blundell, Samuel Burbery, William and Robert Boddington, Henry Bursell, J R B Cave, Thomas Cotton, David Fancott, Joseph Jaggard, William Randle, Joseph Littleton, Elizabeth Manton, John Hopkins and Thomas Handley of Redfern. In 1838, their annual meeting was held at midday on Wednesday 13th June at the Coventry Cross. This resulted in the publication of a list of "...*rewards paid to any person or persons who shall apprehend and deliver into the custody of the law any offender or offenders...which shall afterwards be convicted.*"

These included: "*Murder of any member of this association or any of his or her family or domestics £20*"; maiming or disfiguring a horse, £5; breaking into a house with intent to steal, £5; embezzlement, stealing corn (thrashed or un-thrashed), "*Damaging or destroying any implements of husbandry, iron work, notice board or fence, £2*"; wilfully leaving open a gate, stealing growing corn, vetches or hay etc., stealing turnips, carrots or "*...robbing fishponds or milking any cow...*", £1. The head police officer into whose custody the offenders would be taken was Samuel Dingley who lived in Bridge Street. In 1841 he was only 23.

In 1839, the Quarter Sessions appointed a committee to instigate the implementation of the newly passed Constabulary Act. The outcome was that Leamington, Southam, Bedworth, Rugby and Kenilworth each received an Inspector, with a Superintendent installed at Woolston - he was former Royal Navy Commander, Captain George Baker. The appointment was made by the Magistrates who were also responsible for the collection of the Police Rate. Baker did not last long in the post as he was "palpably inefficient" and was replaced at the Easter 1841 sessions by James Isaac who had earlier been appointed Kenilworth's Inspector.

A constable's pay was 15-22s a week. They were given all clothing, a staff and a cutlass, the latter to be used at night-time only or at other times as decided by two justices. The *"Superior constable"* stationed at Kenilworth earned 30s a week. The annual clothing allowance was 6 guineas a man. The intermediate officers, one for each division, were appointed at £75 per annum.

In 1842, the number of Constables for the area was increased by seven to a total of forty six. Constables were drawn from the local community and amongst those applying for the five vacancies in Kenilworth in 1842 were baker David Fancott, brazier Thomas Finnemore,

and carpenter Job Satchwell. Others included a saddler, farmer, grocer and tailor.

In 1848 each of the five towns mentioned above were provided with a lock-up for the temporary detention of prisoners, but the location of that at Kenilworth appears not to be recorded. In the summer of 1849, perhaps unwisely, the Churchwardens decided to make better, alternative, use of the lock-up, and it became "...the site of some small dwelling houses ..." probably Clifton Terrace. Around Christmas time that year, a man was found insensible near the Crackley milepost but with no official accommodation for villains available, Constable Makepeace had to shut him in a stable at the New Inn overnight. It was normal for a person taken into custody to be taken to Coventry or Warwick.

In the summer of 1850, new fixed stocks were provided at the "...*end of Randle's malthouse...*" and not surprisingly the Parish was investigating having a new lock-up; William Robbins went to Foleshill to look at one there. There was certainly a great need for one; in August the same year a disturbance took place but the "actors" had to be let go as to detain them overnight would, by having to keep watch over them, take the police officers away from other duties.

* * *

The London and Birmingham Railway was built on the Kenilworth side of Coventry in the latter half of the 1830s. It is probable that few locals watching its construction had experienced a railway journey; traders were well practised in receiving goods by horse-drawn vehicles or fetching loads from the canal basins of Leamington, Warwick and Coventry, and perhaps even Stratford and Birmingham. However the new railway cut the journey time to London: a typical coach took almost eleven hours to reach the capital from Leamington. In 1836, a proposed branch from the new railway line, through Kenilworth to Leamington, had been defeated in Parliament, mainly by the opposition of landowners but also by traders who could see no benefit. However in 1839, soon after the opening of the new railway at Coventry, plans were once more drawn up for a branch through Kenilworth; again opposition was quickly mustered and the venue for a protest meeting was the Kings Arms. The Assembly Room was on the first floor of the main building and was just 17ft by 45ft and had folding doors across the middle. At this stage, little parliamentary progress was made, but the following year, with the scheme gathering momentum, another meeting was called at the Kings Arms that was attended by the Lords Leigh, Clarendon and Aylesford, Sir John Cave-Brown-Cave and the Hon Charles Bertie Percy. This meeting, held in the same Assembly Room, resulted in a list of over 160 opponents being published early in 1840, but less than a quarter of these appeared in the Kenilworth census of the following year, suggesting there was much opposition from the outlying districts covered by other parishes such as Stoneleigh and Leek Wootton. Just twelve signatories were women. Amongst the opposition from Kenilworth were those whose livelihoods would be threatened by the railway, such as carter Joseph Hopkins and coachman George Slater. Also

Abel Miles and Sarah Bursell, as the only publicans on the list, of the Castle Tavern and the Kings Arms respectively, suggests a dependency upon coaching traffic. A quarter of Kenilworth's opposition came from Mill End, including blacksmith Isaac Jones. Also, market gardener William Penn had his cherry orchard on the railway's route. Other Kenilworth opposition came from butchers, rope-makers, comb-makers, farmers, an attorney, chandler, book-keeper and draper.

One major point of opposition was the claim that no public necessity existed for the railway and from Kenilworth's point of view it was unlikely that it could, for example, sufficiently revive the flagging horn-comb industry. On the other hand, the town used 15,000 tons of coal annually and an increase of available varieties coupled with a reduction in prices was likely. There was also clear trading potential for the tannery and it is notable that nobody known to be from either the coal or animal-skin processing businesses appeared on the list of opposition.

The campaigners in favour began to exert their influence and when Lord Leigh signed away 26 acres of his land to the railway company in April 1842, the opposition quickly collapsed. The scheme was well supported by the businessmen of Leamington and this is indicative of the different status and ambitions of the two towns. Leamington's population had grown from 315 in 1801 to almost 13,000 in 1841, whereas Kenilworth's population, being agricultural-based, was more stable.

The Bill became an Act of Parliament on 18th June 1842. A railway office was established in Kenilworth; the landlady was Catherine Harriss who ran a lodging house, probably alongside the Kings Arms. In mid-1843, Highway Surveyor Joseph Lidzey contacted the railway company to see if any of the struggling townspeople could be employed building the railway but the reply is not known.

Several possible sites for a station at Kenilworth had been investigated, but that chosen was in three fields owned by Thomas Cotton, a few hundred yards behind the Kings Arms, at a point where the line was to run almost north-south. On the town side of the line was Long Meadow, earmarked for the station yards, whilst an acre of two fields known as the Forces and Fetts Grove was where the line itself was to be. The western boundary was defined by a small brook and, at the northern end of the site, this was crossed by a bridge at a point where three pathways met; the railway was planned to cross the brook at that point. Thomas Cotton wanted a bridge to carry his track-ways over the railway or be paid compensation for a level crossing. The eventual agreement was for a level crossing and an improved trackway alongside the railway yard for Cotton's access, the upkeep of which was to be shared. Cotton received £1,428 for his four acres of land and inconvenience. To the south of the station site, the same brook needed to be diverted alongside the railway to help drainage through the clayfields.

Once the site for the station had been agreed, there arose the matter of building a road from the town to serve it. It was probably not too difficult a decision to route it to the main road in the town and alongside the town's premier hotel, the Kings Arms, and negotiations began with the proprietor, Henry Bursell. A narrow access road to the stabling at the rear of the hotel had to be widened, necessitating the demolition of a building fronting onto Castle End, and two further buildings on Bursell's land at the rear of his hotel had to be carefully taken down and their materials stacked for re-use, and another taken down and re-erected. The new road was to cross the field used by the Kenilworth Cricket Club and the railway company authorised a compensation payment of £10, but not knowing this the club only applied for £7 10s and were duly paid! The road was to be thirty feet wide between the fences with a 5ft wide footpath raised 6ins on either side. The construction of the road was "...fagots of brushwood, made of gorse or other durable material, the covering to be of six inches in thickness. Upon this is to be laid a coating of good gravel, one foot thickness, properly formed and rounded from the centre to the sides." The whole length of the road was to be fenced and four field gates, costing £2 each, were included, as was a drainage system. The contract went to Rugby man Joseph Chambers for £524 2s 6d and he was given just six weeks to complete his task from the day the contract was signed, 20th February 1844. The new road was named Clarendon Street.

As construction of the railway progressed, Lidzey reported in April 1844 that the "...Public Highways of the Parish be very much injured by the heavy carts and carriages employed by the servants of the railway..." and he was directed to instruct the company to have them repaired.

The new line opened on a bitterly cold Monday 9th December 1844, the first train arriving at Kenilworth from Leamington at about 8.30 a.m. The feeling of agitation towards the scheme locally had begun to dispel and a celebration meal was held at The Kings Arms "...well attended by the friends of the undertaking in the neighbourhood." Many of these were local tradesmen, and it was held in the same assembly room as the protest meetings. The railway was rated at £800 a mile on the Poor Rate. This was reduced to £600 but the railway company protested at the excessiveness of the assessment and offered £300 a mile whilst discussions took place, but the town demanded £450 as a temporary measure.

It did not take long for the railway to have an impact on local commerce. Within fifteen months of it opening, a meeting was held to discuss the re-establishment of the weekly market originally granted by charter in the reign of Elizabeth I. The reasons given for the successful resolution were clear cut: "*From the central position of the town of Kenilworth, being in an agricultural neighbourhood, and in the locality of populous towns, and in so immediate conjunction with the London and Birmingham Railway, with the great facilities now afforded by low fares and day tickets, added to the reduced rates charged for the conveyance of grain &c., by the luggage trains, the Market will afford peculiar advantages, not hitherto possessed.*" The provision market started at 11.00 a.m., the corn market at 3.00.

The railway also boosted pleasure-seekers and the Bowling Green Inn was a favourite haunt, being a short walk up a footpath across fields from the station. In August 1846 130 employees from Messrs Carpenter in Birmingham had a dinner and tea at the inn and the following week 300 Leamington schoolchildren arrived by train to have a "...*pleasant tea on the beautiful bowling green at the back of the house.*" "*There is a large tent constantly upon the Green in the summer months.*" The following month a group of Warwick Sunday School children came by rail to visit the new, nearly complete, chapel, which was being built to commemorate the passing of the Dissenters Chapels Bill. They also visited the Castle.

In 1846, a passing place for trains was installed at the station, giving separate platforms for passengers travelling to either Leamington or Coventry.

* * *

The popularity of steeple-chasing descended upon Kenilworth in March 1841 when Kings Arms landlord John Bursell and Mr Littleton challenged each other for a £20 prize. The start was by the Castle and the pair headed off on a three-mile route across Chase Meadows. Mr Littleton on Emma was leading by a clear field when the pair fell in a brook allowing Bursell on Matilda to catch them. In a close finish, both managed to pass the wrong side of the finishing post, and so the race was run again! Bursell won the re-run with ease and, not surprisingly, the event was followed by a celebratory meal at his inn.

Kenilworth was known for its Easter festivities, and steeple-chasing became an annual event, held on Easter Monday. In 1843, the course started at the rear of the Bowling Green Inn from which almost the entire 3-mile course across meadowland could be seen. There were two races. For the April 1848 event, extra trains were arranged to boost the expected large crowd. The course was laid out over the Thomas Tidmarsh's Villiers Hill farm and a farm belonging to Mr Harbourne; the best vantage point was the summit of Villiers Hill. The longest race was over four miles with 25 leaps of "...*trying fences and rotten brooks.*" The course went down the hill into meadows then along the field "...*at the bottom of the hill, leading to Dalehouse Lane.*" The highlight was the race for military officers, and their mounts, based in Coventry, but their arrival was delayed due to a Chartist meeting. Once underway the race provided a real spectacle, as every horse but the winner fell at some point, most were re-mounted and finished. "*After a whole series of misfortunes, more laughable than serious, Maid Marion won in a common trot.*" Its rider was Wharton Wilson of the 11th Hussars. A celebration evening meal was held at the King's Arms, where the only injured rider was still being treated the following week.

There were other events connected with horseracing; nearly a hundred took part in the 1841 "...*annual St.Leger dinner, of the members of the Castle Tavern Lottery.*"

A well-established annual event, held each September, was the Statute Fair, the purpose of which was the hiring of servants and other employees for the forthcoming year. Although the original concept remained, it was in decline and had recently become overshadowed by the accompanying sideshows and amusements that stretched along Castle End, at least as far south as the Bear Inn, and spilled over into the fields alongside. It was not just an event for Kenilworth, but for the whole district to celebrate "...*the terminating of twelve months servitude of the labouring classes in this county, and many domestic servants engaged in the neighbouring towns have begged permission from their master or mistress to attend this village gathering - albeit many miles distant - in order that they might gain the chance of letting themselves.*" In 1846 there was about an average attendance of both male and female servants and "...*hiring went on with briskness.*" The weather was good and crowds arrived by train from Coventry, Warwick and Leamington for "*a day's recreation*" and there was plenty of "*merry making*" and "*lively parties*" at the Castle. In 1848 the weather was not so good and in consequence little business was done despite there being a good number of female farm servants present. Obviously, the inns did particularly well this day, with food displayed in their windows to attract customers, and dancing until late in those that had ballrooms.

By 1850, there were scarcely any candidates for hire, little business was done, and the fair had "...*merged into one of mere pleasure...*" with plenty of sideshows and "...*incitements for juveniles to spend a penny or more.*" There were no arrests by the police that year despite "...*the usual attendance of riff-raff.*" More than 2,500 visitors arrived by train alone and in the evening there was a great crush at the station, causing delays. George Henwood, the Station Master, was credited with his actions for ensuring there were no casualties. The significance of the event to those outside Kenilworth was demonstrated the following year when the ribbon manufacturers of Coventry shut at midday and at least 1,800 arrived by train from the city. Doubtless many more came on foot and horse-drawn vehicles so the total number of visitors can only be guessed at.

* * *

On the last Sunday of September 1848, the town was visited by a black and white rabid dog of "*moderately large size.*" It caused "*considerable excitement*" as it went along Coventry Road and New Street "...*biting at everything that came its way.*" In High Street it "...*seized a cat which it picked up and shook...*" and at Castle Green "...*upset a lad named Barber, and bit his trowsers.*" Then, going back along High Street, it entered Mr Betty's yard where it fought with the house dog, but then tired and lay down. Mr Betty, a butcher, shut it in a passageway. "*Mr Jackson, watchmaker, brought a loaded gun and pointing the weapon through a chink in the door, the dog was immediately shot.*" The town crier went around town ordering dogs to be kept inside, and several animals with which the dog had been in contact, had to be destroyed. An explanation for the dog's behaviour was provided: "*In connection with this subject it may be mentioned that among dogs employed for drawing carriages, many go mad. The police should use every means to put down this cruel custom.*"

* * *

The position of County Coroner was prestigious. In April 1851, there were two contenders for the vacancy, R Smith and William Savage Poole (34), solicitor of Kenilworth and son of attorney Robert Poole. Voting was in Warwick over two days and those eligible to make judgement arrived by train and carriage, some were entertained by bands of musicians, and generally the scene was of great excitement. Poole addressed his supporters from the window of his hotel, The George in Warwick Square. His supporters wore crimson favours, Smith's wore white. The ballot resulted in Poole's favour by 1112 votes to 811.

* * *

In the summer of 1851, Castle Tavern landlord Abel Miles became ill and on 3rd September he agreed to let the inn at the rate of £50 a year for a minimum of three years to Thomas Pettifor who had married one of Miles's nieces, Keren. Within five days of this agreement, Miles died aged 52. His wife's health was also frail, her condition deteriorated rapidly, and she died just twelve days after her husband.

The grave of Abel and Sarah Miles.

The couple had no children, and despite Miles having six living brothers he had chosen two of his neighbours, butcher Joseph Roberts and grocer George Church, as his executors. Under the terms of his will, all his assets were to be sold and split various ways, but before the auction took place in May 1852, Thomas Pettifor also died, leaving the Castle Tavern in the hands of Keren. It was her bid of £700, which was successful at the auction. The legal documents referred to the inn as the "Castle Tavern, formerly the Two Virgins" but the sale notice for the first time combined the two names to "The Virgins Inn and Castle Tavern."

Miles's five cottages alongside the vicarage, occupied by Thomas Constable, Richard Holmes, Thomas Dutton, Alfred Spiers and Robert Freeman, were bought by the Reverend Edward Revell Eardley-Wilmot for £390, but he sent Charles Bliss to do his bidding. Edward Draper bought Miles's field at Whitemoor for £260. After all his debts had been cleared, there remained £529 to split between all his nephews and nieces, each receiving a little under £20.

The title, Virgin's Inn and Castle Tavern, an amalgam of two of its former names, was first used in 1852.

* * *

On 21st July 1846, a meeting was held at the vicarage for the purpose of *"...considering the necessity of making some provision for the education of the boys of the lower class in the parish."* The Chair was taken by the vicar, the Reverend Edward Eardley-Wilmot. Also present were C J Wheler, T Cotton, W Boddington, J E Barker, Reverend W Hayward and the churchwardens - R Boddington and T Fraser. *"The important subject was judiciously discussed and the following resolutions unanimously adopted: 1) That there being no National Boys School in the Parish, and consequently a very large number of children being totally without the blessing of a Christian education, it is desirable to take steps for building and endowing a School for this purpose on some appropriate site, to be obtained at the further end of the Parish called Castle End. 2) That considering the great want of accommodation for the Poor in the Parish Church, and the distance of the part of the parish in question from the church, it is desirable that the building to be erected for this purpose, be of such a style as to become the chancel of a church, should such an arrangement at any time become necessary."* All eight present formed a committee to carry out the objects and collect subscriptions, and the resolutions were printed and circulated around Kenilworth and the neighbourhood. *"We cannot but hope and believe that the great object of the meeting will be fully and most advantageously accomplished. The education of the children of the poor is, indeed, desirable, as the foundation of their moral rectitude, and in connection with the divine precepts of the Gospel of Christ, the best preparation for their usefulness in this Life and their happiness thereafter."*

In addition to the need for the new school, it had long been realised that the Parish Church of St.Nicholas could no longer support the spiritual needs of the entire sprawling community. Of the 886 persons it could seat there was provision for only *"...189 poor persons (to) enjoy the inestimable privilege of free sittings..."* and additionally many of the poorest faced a long walk from the southern extremities of the town. Led by the Reverend Edward Eardley-Wilmot, a campaign was started to provide a church in that area and, at an early stage, the name St.John was chosen. The intention was eventually to split the town into two parishes. The new church now took priority over the new school. The southern area of the town was the poorest district. Just south of The Green Man was a trackway, leading to farms, alongside which was built Greaves Row; Greaves was a builder and perhaps built the houses. Behind them was Parish Row and White's Row and, starting at Beck's smithy, was Rollins Row. In this small area almost 20 listed their occupations as pauper, many of the rest were just labourers. The roads were the worst in town with little or no material on the surface.

The Building Committee responsible for the scheme consisted of the Reverend Edward Eardley-Wilmot, Lord Leigh, churchwardens Robert Boddington and Thomas Fraser, E Wheler, Thomas Cotton, William Boddington, William Poole, Robert and Edward Draper and Charles Bliss. The necessary funds were raised by donation alone and by April 1851 £2,300 had been raised. The cash was paid into the Church Account at the Leamington and Warwickshire Bank, or the branch bank in Kenilworth run by Charles Bliss. (Living next door to the bank were bank accountant, Walter T Parsons (26), and his wife Caroline.)

The chosen design for the church was by Ewan Christian of London and the contracted builders were the firm of Lilley from Measham, Leicestershire. The church was to have a nave 25ft by 75ft with a south aisle 16ft 6ins wide and would sit 532. A tower at the west end formed a porch on the ground floor and had an organ gallery above. It was designed so that a north aisle could be added, if required, to provide another 310 seats. The stone used in construction was red rag with Wootton white sandstone dressings, of which the whole of the interior walls were to be made. The stonework was entrusted to a Mr Elliott. The siting of the building on the chosen plot of land was such that the spire was directly in line with the roads leading to both Warwick and Leamington, and also left enough space for the planned school on one side and a parsonage on the other.

There was little doubt as to who was mainly responsible for the scheme: *"Through the devotedness and zeal of the Reverend Eardley-Wilmot...an effort which will secure to the poor of Kenilworth a place of public worship where they can all conveniently attend."*

The ceremony to lay the foundation stone was arranged for 19th August 1851. It was a cloudless day and from 6.00 a.m. flags and bunting were being hung out. Three union flags were hung from St.Nicholas' church and Miss Blair's girl-school made displays of evergreens. William Poole, *"...no man is more respected in the parish..."*, threw across High Street a pole decorated with laurels and flowers. In Castle End Charles Bliss and Walter Parsons had flags in their windows and the inns, notably the Kings Arms and Rose and Crown were splendidly decorated. The event began with a service at St.Nicholas at 7.00 a.m., but there were *"...throngs across the Abbey Fields before that time..."* and not surprisingly the church was full. Amongst those in attendance were Lord Leigh, Charles Bertie-Percy, Henry Wise and an estimated 40 clergy in full regalia. At the end of the service, a collection raised £93 for the building fund.

The service was followed by a parade led by the building committee, then the architect and builders. Next came *"...a beautiful canopy of crimson velvet embodied with gold, surmounted by a silver spear to which was appended a royal standard and which opened beautifully in the breeze."* Behind were nine boys carrying the flag of St.George and Miss Blair's girls carrying a union flag, the churchwardens and then Lord Leigh, attended by a man carrying a mallet and silver trowel. The parade ended with the vicar and schoolchildren.

A spacious platform had been built to the eastern side of the site for the benefit of ladies to view the ceremony; this too had been decorated with banners and evergreens. The ceremony began with a hymn and prayer after which a leaden box containing a scroll parchment was put in the cavity under the foundation stone by Charles Bliss. On it was written the details of the occasion. The stone was then *"...slung in the usual way and having been properly adjusted..."* Lord Leigh made a brief blessing. There followed a speech by the Reverend Mr Bull of Birmingham, a hymn, and a speech by Leigh who led three cheers for the Reverend Edward Eardley-Wilmot, after which the procession reformed for the return trip. Fifty of the more important people only made it as far as the Kings Arms where a meal was provided. The silver trowel used in the ceremony was made by Mapplebeck and Lowe of Birmingham and was inscribed with details of the occasion. It was presented to Lord Leigh by the building committee for his generosity and assistance; he had given the largest donation, £200. The children of the parochial schools all received a medal to mark the occasion.

As building work progressed, the funds were used up and in June 1852 Eardley-Wilmot made an appeal to raise £200 more: *"To raise this small sum of £200 has become a work of great difficulty..."* due in part to the generosity that had gone before. By October 1852, just fourteen months after the laying of the foundation stone, the church was ready for its opening ceremony. *"Innumerable flags and banners bearing suitable mottoes and devices, were displayed in all parts of the town which was full of animation."* The sermon was preached by the Bishop of Winchester, a native of Kenilworth, and prayers were taken by Eardley-Wilmot. A collection at the close raised an astonishing £280, including £50 from Lord Leigh, that met all outstanding costs; this suggests that the poor for whom the church was provided were not largely in attendance. Another dinner at the Kings Arms followed and 150 poor children were given a tea.

Having provided a church, principally for the poor at the southern end of the town, the original proposal, to provide a school, was instigated and in August 1854 a small area of land to the south, enclosed by the church, railway and two roads, was bought from Edward Draper for £80. The school was intended to serve the *"...children of the labouring, manufacturing and other poorer classes in the ecclesiastical district of St.John's."* As with the church, the school was paid for by voluntary contribution. It cost £700 and was built of red and blue bricks, the windows being cased with stone. The schoolroom was 48ft by 18ft, the adjoining classroom 18ft square, and this was to provide accommodation for between one and two hundred poor children. Lord Leigh laid the foundation stone, an occasion he described as being a proud privilege. The school was built by E Matthew of Coventry and designed by Ewan Christian, then of Coventry, the same architect as for the church. It opened on Thursday 12th July 1855. The gates and rooms were decorated with evergreens, flowers and ribbons, arranged by the Misses Unett, Buck, Draper and Gibbon. The celebrations started with a service at the church at 11.30 by the incumbent Reverend Frederick Kite, followed by a meeting in the schoolroom. Lord Leigh occupied the chair and was supported by Thomas Cotton, W Boddington, Reverends Frederick Kite and Edward Eardley-Wilmot, other churchmen including visitors from Coventry, and the churchwardens.

In the afternoon, the children of the parochial schools walked in procession through the town to a field alongside St.John's church "...where they partook of their annual festivities in a tent, erected for the purpose. The older villagers had tea provided in the new School-room." The Reverend Frederick Robert Kite had been assistant minister at Abbey Hill church. To commemorate the events, Greaves Row was renamed St.John's Street.

St.John's church was aligned so that the spire was visible from a distance along the roads from Leamington and Warwick.

*   *   *

In September 1853, the Queen and Prince Albert were scheduled to travel north from Windsor and so at some point had to transfer from the broad gauge Great Western Railway to a standard gauge line. The place chosen for this was Leamington where a wooden platform with a canopy was constructed by Branson and Gwyther, railway contractors, at a point where the different gauges were adjacent. Two hundred invited guests were allowed onto the platform. From here, her London and North Western Railway train, with James McConnell the company's locomotive superintendent at the controls, headed up the branch to pass through Kenilworth at about half past one. Although it was known that the train would not be stopping, it was decided to "...make a demonstration as would testify the loyalty of Her Majesty's subjects at Kenilworth." Arches of evergreens were erected over the line, and the station was decorated with banners and flags. The children of the National School attended with a banner bearing the inscription "Welcome Victoria", and as the train passed the "...most hearty of cheers rent the air." After the schoolchildren had sung the national anthem, they were "plentifully regaled" with wine and buns bought with contributions from well-wishers. Charles Bliss and Mr Fraser made all the arrangements.

This event was obviously exciting enough, but just five years later Her Majesty was to return, and this time she was to travel through town by carriage to board her train. At the vestry meeting of 25th March 1858, the Reverend William Bickmore, William Poole and Charles Bliss, in their capacity as churchwardens, along with Thomas Cotton, William Henry Butler, Joseph Burbery and Charles and Edward Draper, became responsible for making the arrangements for Her Majesty's visit scheduled for 15th June. The first task was to contact Lord Leigh, with whom she was to stay, to discover the precise itinerary and whether an address would be required. It transpired that the Queen was to leave Stoneleigh Abbey, where she would be staying overnight, southwards, and enter Kenilworth along the Leamington Road, travelling up Castle End and turning down Clarendon Street to meet up with her awaiting train. Progress in making the arrangements was slow and just two weeks before the visit, a public meeting was held to speed matters up. It was decided to split the town into districts so that one or more of the committee could collect subscriptions to offset the costs. William Boddington was appointed treasurer. With twelve days to go, three of the committee were designated to obtain tenders for the construction of a stand to seat 600 schoolchildren, but ultimately three such stands were built. William Poole suggested a tea be provided in the evening, free for children under fourteen and at a cost of sixpence for adults; tickets were to be issued to ensure that only parishioners took part. £10 was allocated to Reverend Frederick Kite to decorate the Castle End part of the route.

As preparations progressed, there was doubtless great excitement on the Saturday preceding the visit when in the midst of a thunderstorm a detachment of the Royal Horse Artillery, comprising fifty men, three brass cannons and ammunition carts, arrived and camped in a field belonging to Mr Boddington. They remained until Monday at 4 o'clock when they moved to

Stoneleigh Abbey to mark the Queen's arrival with a 21-gun salute. She had travelled from Euston to Coventry by rail, and from there to Stoneleigh in a carriage by way of Baginton.

The following day, all was ready for the Queen's procession through town. Three stands had been erected in Kenilworth; one was at St.John's for the schoolchildren of that area, another with 700 seats for pupils of all other denominations was "...*by the side of the road immediately leading to the station...*" and the third had a large platform and was near the station itself. This one, constructed by a Coventry builder, had a poor attendance upon it. In addition, many wagons had been decorated and drawn up along the route to provide vantage points.

Swain and Long, two Kenilworth carpenters, constructed at least three triumphal arches. Canvas was stretched over a wooden framework and painted to represent granite. These were decorated with "V R", "Long may she Reign" and the Royal Coat of Arms, which were framed with laurel leaves. These were sited at Stoneleigh, Ashow and St.John's. All buildings on the route were decorated. The King's Arms was "...*profusely ornamented with banners and evergreens...*" whilst clearly visible to Her Majesty as she travelled along Clarendon Street, were at least thirty union jacks covering the immense tannery bark-rick, and others upon the adjacent chimneys.

The county constabulary, boosted by twenty members of the Coventry force, kept the roads clear and the Warwickshire Yeomanry Cavalry, including the Stoneleigh Troop, escorted Her Majesty. An unexpected addition to those in attendance was 'H' Field battery under the command of Captain Leslie who diverted their march from Nottingham to Woolwich to salute the queen in Kenilworth. Part of the station booking office was partitioned off to form an entrance, the floor was covered in crimson cloth and the walls hung with alternate flutings of pink and white calico. Great quantities of flowers supplied by Mr Perkins of Leamington were arranged on either side of the passage and the doors were fitted with fancy trelliswork.

Amongst those privileged to be on the station platform were Mr Amherst, William Boddington, Reverend William Bickmore, William Butler, Henry Draper and Walter Congreve with their wives, Thomas Cotton JP with his daughter, and Miss Hyacinth Cave-Brown-Cave who presented Her Majesty with a bouquet. Her train left the station to deafening cheers at 11.05, with Mr McConnell again at the controls.

During the day over 2,000 people, mostly the poorer families and children, were treated to a meal of meats and plum pudding in one of the Abbey Fields rented by William Poole. A gaily-decorated steam engine belching smoke, indicating the site, was used to heat water. There was also a temporary pantry and dairy erected for the occasion. Draper, Sutton and Elsworth were responsible for these arrangements.

The purpose of Her Majesty's journey was to open the new pleasure grounds at Aston Hall, and she returned to Kenilworth at about half past four. By her command, Lord Leigh directed her escort to the Castle ruins, but as no suitable reception had been arranged

she headed back to Stoneleigh, leaving Prince Albert to wander the ruins with Lord Leigh.

The following day, the Royal Party went by carriage to Leamington and Warwick, for the Castle, before boarding the Royal train at Warwick for the journey home. That evening, Lord Leigh gave a special dinner for his tenants and the Stoneleigh Troop at the Kings Arms in a 120ft long room, capable of seating 400 people, which Henry Bursell had just added to his premises. This was a new building fronting onto Station Road and was a great improvement on the Assembly Room on the first floor of the main building.

The day after the Queen's visit, the town was hit by a terrific evening thunderstorm. The first casualty was a young child apparently struck down by lightning near St. Nicholas Church. A carpenter, Job Satchwell, was some sixty yards away and rushed to assist the child just as a second bolt hit the church spire and sent masonry falling onto him. He made it back to his house alongside the church whereupon "...*he became insensible and remained so for an hour.*" "*The electric fluid struck the steeple dislodging some of the large stones a few feet below the vane. The vestry chimney was at the same time thrown down damaging the roof in its fall.*" Churchwarden William Boddington barricaded the church off as it was considered unsafe, a wise move: "*About eleven p.m., the storm returned in all its former fury and recommencing its attack upon the steeple displaced other large stones which fell among the bells.*" The lightning had struck the south angle of the spire and carried away masonry about 12ft in height and 4ft in width weighing about two tons. "*The fluid took a downwards direction inside the spire, passed out at the east side and forced away another mass of masonry leaving an opening between the belfry and the first great fracture. The opening thus made was like an inverted cone with the apex on the inside.*" All the bell wheels were broken but the bells themselves were unharmed. Damage to the spire was so great that about 32ft of masonry had to be taken down. By late August the rebuilding work was nearly complete, the last few stones being put in place before the vane was at last returned to its spot. Job Satchwell was only then just well enough to return to work, the child he rescued was apparently unharmed, but its mother "...*was so frightened by the storm that she died a few days afterwards.*"

* * *

Henry Street was born in Market Bosworth in 1825, but within months the family moved to Coventry where his father traded as a baker and flour dealer in Gosford Street. After his father had died and the family had moved again, Henry, still only sixteen, set himself up in business at Balsall as a fellmonger, a business that took animal skins freshly cut from carcases and processed them ready for supplying to tanneries. Four years later, in 1844, Henry moved his business to Kenilworth, to existing skin-working buildings in Tanhouse Lane, not far from where the new railway line was being constructed and near the point where the Tanyard Stream passed under the road. Flowing water through the site was vital for the processes. At about this time he was also recorded as a currier, a trade that improved the properties of leather. By 1851, he was a Master Fellmonger employing nine men and two boys. It is probable that Street lived on site at this time. Soon after his move to Kenilworth, Street married Sofia Thompson.

The watercourse that ran through the works drained into Finham Brook at Mill End and in 1854 problems were encountered here, as effluent from the works caused a blockage and a subsequent unhealthy nuisance at the point where the stream passed under the road. The solution appears to have been to widen the entrance of the conduit "...at the corner of Mr Boddington's house...", the corner of the Engine Inn.

Business was obviously going well for Street as in May 1855 he bought part of one of two Mill End fields known as the Woodmill Meadows to build a larger works. The field, owned by William Henry Butler, had been cut in two by the building of the railway giving a high embankment to the east of the site. Along the northern edge was Finham Brook and on the other side of this was a small plantation that was included in the sale. Street paid £335 for his one and a half acres and soon began erecting buildings along the southern edge of the brook.

In Spring 1856 whilst walking along Albion Row, in all probability on the way to or from his works, Street noticed smoke coming from the house of an elderly couple called Brittain. Mrs Brittain was in the habit of carrying some fire from her kitchen to the bedroom each night, but on this occasion the coals set fire to her nightclothes. Her husband was unable to help due to "age, infirmity and fear." Street rushed in and saw Mrs Brittain prostrate on the floor and with help managed to extinguish the flames, but she died the following day.

Alongside his business success, Street was becoming influential in town affairs. In 1860, he was appointed as a rate collector and this was followed two years later with his appointment as an Overseer of the Poor. He was now 35 years old, living on Abbey Hill and could afford several servants.

Henry Street's house on Abbey Hill.

Street siting his works alongside a constant supply of water was obviously advantageous but it did also bring its hazards. In March 1867, the town was "quite inundated" after a severe storm and the works was particularly badly hit by flooding. Many skins were washed away but most were recovered some distance downstream.

Samuel Burbery originally had his tanning business in Hogg Lane (Fieldgate Lane) in 1835, but moved to a site alongside Townpool Bridge before 1841. At this time he moved into Bridge House on the corner of New Street and Warwick Lane (Bridge Street), but after starting an additional tannery in West Street, Warwick, he moved to Northgate Street in the County Town by 1850. By the early 1860s he is no longer recorded in Kenilworth.

* * *

The precise origins of the gas company are unknown, but on 18th January 1853 William Henry Butler, Henry Draper and Charles Bliss signed a conveyance agreeing to form a company to supply and convey "...inflammable air or gas..." for lighting the streets and houses etc., and the company was provisionally registered on 12th March. Long before this, meetings had been held, financial arrangements made and contracts signed as the gasworks themselves were completed by the end of March. "Every arrangement dependant upon the practical skill and workmanship of the contractor and builder was well and satisfactorily carried out." A celebratory dinner was held at the King's Arms on the last day of March, at which Edward Draper took the chair. The company had a working capital of £3,000.

During the following months, detailed rules governing the operation of the company were drawn up and signed by William Butler and Henry Draper in the presence of Mr Blakiston of Poole and Son, Solicitors of Abbey Hill. The company could now be fully registered and was so on 22nd August. The Directors were listed as Draper, Butler, Bliss, (who were also the Trustees), William Boddington (surgeon), Henry Bursell (hotel proprietor), Francis Robbins jnr (miller), and Charles Lowe, a miller of Sheepy Mills, Leicestershire. Other shareholders included William Allen - a Warwick solicitor who was allocated the shares numbered 1 to 10, Thomas Finnemore - a Kenilworth brazier who could look forward to increased business, and Thomas Jeacock, a Kenilworth blacksmith,

It would appear most sensible to have positioned the works reasonably centrally in the town. This would keep the length of mains pipe required to a minimum, which in turn would diminish the number of gas escapes in joints, and reduce the difficulty of maintaining pressure. Placing the works, for example, near the railway station would also have made coal deliveries easier. The site chosen for the works might therefore seem surprising at first, but by positioning them at one of the town's extremities at Mill End, on the opposite side of the railway embankment to Henry Street's skinworks, had two advantages. The first was that the field chosen, the meadow split in half by the construction of the railway, was owned by William Butler and was doubtless available to the company on good terms. The second was that the railway embankment alongside would provide a barrier in the event of an explosion, a perceived risk rather than an actual one. The gasholders, of 9,000 and 15,000 cu ft capacity, were fed by two retorts.

The precarious nature of night-time manoeuvres by pedestrians and vehicles was highlighted by the claims that Clarendon Street, now becoming known as Station Road, was "...difficult to trace..." on dark nights, and so the lighting of the busier roads was becoming desirable. Thomas Harding, who lived in the road at Sussex Villa, was at his own expense, vigorously persistent in canvassing ratepayers to have a district of the town lit by gas, and on 30th September 1853, a public meeting was held at the National School to discuss lighting the streets by the new supply. The Reverend Frederick Kite took the chair and the adoption of the motion was carried with only one unnamed dissentient. Five gentlemen were appointed as Gaslight Inspectors as required by Act of Parliament.

Despite this eagerness, nothing of any substance materialised for reasons that became apparent two years later at a meeting at the National Girls School. The Reverend Edward Eardley-Wilmot took the chair and much of the meeting was taken up by a lengthy speech by Dr William Boddington of Montague House, in favour of lighting the streets. He refuted the suggestion that as a shareholder he was solely interested in profit, and claimed that investors would "...not get a single sixpence, if indeed they cleared their expenses..." by the scheme. He argued that lighting the town would make it as attractive as possible and that the current increase in visitors drawn by the "...salubrity of the place and picturesque neighbourhood..." would continue to rise due to the benefits of them being able to "...find their way around at night." The growth would be a boost to trade and give extra sales from farm produce. The argument against revolved around the rateable value of property. The relevant Act of Parliament required that the cost of lighting should be split 3/4 on houses and 1/4 on land, but Kenilworth's rateable value was £6,000 for houses and £7,000 for land, thus producing an unfair burden. Remarkably, it was William Butler, the Gas Company chairman, who eventually proposed that the "...measure is uncalled for and unneeded..." and this motion was carried on a show of hands.

It seems extraordinary that six years after gas became available, agreement had still not been made as to lighting the streets. It was expected at the Annual General meeting of gas company shareholders held in July 1859, that an attack would be made on the existing board members due to "...the antagonism the Directors had evinced towards the promotion of the scheme for lighting the streets." With Henry Bursell retiring by rotation but not offering himself for re-election, and Francis Robbins having to stand down due to him no longer being a shareholder, the unusually large attendance could have produced a particularly rough ride for the remaining Directors. "Considerable animation characterised the proceedings..." yet once the Board's attempts at studying the interests of the town were revealed along with its financial position, there was the "greatest unanimity." Mr Jakeman of Warwick and Edward Draper were voted to the Board, Thomas Kemp of Warwick and Kenilworth schoolmaster Walter

Congreve were not.

By September, the difficulties must have been largely overcome with the decision that the Gas Company and the town would split the cost of laying the pipelines. The chosen course of the lighting, Station Road, up Castle End and along Abbey Hill as far as Montague House, reflects the importance of the roads. By the end of October the first lamps were alight, but only then because of the generosity of some townsfolk. Two ornamental lamps, one in Castle End and the other on Abbey Hill, were presented to the town by Henry Draper, and another outside the Bowling Green Inn was donated by Thomas Harding. It was Thomas Finnemore who had been entrusted with the task of erecting the lamps and for one he "...furnished an iron pillar for the lamp at the corner of Abbey Hill at his own expense, in lieu of a projected wooden one." The gas appeared "very excellent in quality."

At the first meeting of the Kenilworth Gas District Ratepayers held in the vestry on the last Monday of 1859, £50 was voted for expenses in the ensuing year for lighting the town and it was intended that this would not only cover the cost of gas, but would also enable two more lamps to be erected "...in places where they are much needed."

*　　*　　*

During the summer of 1848, a Reading Society was established with the object of "The Diffusion of General Knowledge." With no bookseller or library in Kenilworth it had the potential to be well patronised. Those involved with setting up the society, with the exception of W Harding, are unknown. The membership subscription was just 2d a week to be paid weekly, monthly, quarterly or annually in advance. The intention was to establish a library devoid of all political and theological books "...and on no pretence whatsoever shall any immoral book be introduced." Even political discussions were banned, but history, travel, arts, sciences, poetry, etc., were obviously welcome. Members defacing a book were fined 2s 6d in addition to paying for its repair. The constitution stated that the book collection could never be divided or disposed of in any way so long as three members remained, but should this fall to two the remaining members had to hold the property in trust for the people of Kenilworth until the society could be re-formed under the same constitution. The laws were drawn up on 30th October and the society was constituted on 24th November. It also became known as the Book Society, and was based at the girls' national schoolroom on Rosemary Hill. Within two years it boasted three hundred volumes. The reading room was open on Monday, Tuesday, Thursday and Friday evenings from 6 o'clock for three hours. Periodicals and daily newspapers were available in addition to books. Visitors too could make use of the facilities for 4d a week, but only by leaving a deposit of the full cost of a volume they wished to borrow. By 1854, surgeon George Ayton was its secretary.

The Kenilworth Mutual Improvement Society (KMIS) was probably formed in 1849 and the two societies to some degree overlapped. The Reverend

Edward Eardley-Wilmot was heavily involved in the KMIS, which succeeded in spreading knowledge throughout all classes of Kenilworth's townsfolk. This is perhaps best demonstrated in January 1855 at the height of the Crimean war when Eardley-Wilmot, himself a former Royal Artillery Captain, invited his brother Lt Col Eardley-Wilmot of the Royal Military College at Woolwich to deliver a lecture explaining the siege of Sebastopol. He brought along a number of models of cannons, mortars, shells, etc., and explained in detail their effectiveness during the siege. The room, decorated with banners and Union Jacks, was crowded to excess long before the start, and many were unable to obtain admission. After his brother's departure the following day, the Reverend Mr Eardley-Wilmot decided to repeat the two-hour lecture himself the following week, and included in it the current positions as displayed on the latest maps published by the Admiralty. He also explained the *"...justice which animates us to fight against Russian aggression and tyranny."* He had specifically made the effort for the benefit of the town's less fortunate, and the audience was composed entirely of poor men who *"...showed their respect for the vicar, by the most marked attention and decorum. Those of them who read the newspapers will now understand what they read better, while those who cannot read will not be wholly ignorant of the nature of our military operations in the Crimea."* Two months later he made efforts to set up premises for the treatment of Crimea wounded. The Society was thus established as an important source of information for the whole town and by the mid-1850s was taking a little over £30 a year in subscriptions, sale of newspapers, entrance to lectures and tickets for its annual tea party.

The opportunity to borrow books was a vital addition to a town devoid of bookshops; the only attempt to fill the gap, by a Mr Claremont, had failed some years before. That was to change by 1854 due to former bank accountant, Birmingham born, Walter T Parsons. Across the road from his former place of employment, he opened The Library and in addition to books he sold stationery, and stocked a large range of photographs, including stereographs *"...comprising every view of the Castle that has hitherto been taken."* Photographs were for sale costing from 3s to 10s 6d, and stereoscopic slides were 1s each or 9s a dozen, rising to 1s 6d and 14s if coloured. Lithographs could be bought for 1s each or up to 10s a set and these were designed to *"...enable tourists and visitors to purchase accurate representations of the principal parts of the ruins."* The variety of items for sale obviously boosted trade, but his chance of success as a bookseller was made more likely by literary interest created by the Book Society, and the introduction of compulsory schooling in 1846 which meant that for the first time a whole generation was growing up having been taught to read.

Kenilworth had not been well covered by local newspapers. The weekly *Leamington Courier* and *Warwick Advertiser* gave little coverage until the 1850s when an almost weekly paragraph appeared. The Coventry papers did not usually carry even this amount, and often just copied those same reports. Each had occasional advertisements inserted, usually for property

sale. These papers were available for members of the Reading Society and KMIS, and were available for purchase in town, the aforementioned Mr Claremont had been an agent for the *Leamington Courier* for example. Walter Parsons, though, saw the potential for Kenilworth to have its own newspaper and on Thursday 19th August 1858 he published the first *Kenilworth Advertiser,* price 1d. The four pages carried little local news, just a few lines announcing the Gas Company was to pay a dividend of 3% to its shareholders, and an announcement that the Coventry Band of Hope was to give a concert in the Albion Chapel, but true to its name, it carried a large number of advertisements for local shopkeepers and businesses. For the first time these could now appear together in one publication instead of several. Examples include R W Hubbard selling *"Pure drugs and chemicals; Fine fresh Hamburg Leeches...",* chimney sweep George Golder (29) thanking patrons of his eight years in business and reminding them that he also repaired clocks and bottle-jacks, and of course the largest advert was for Parsons' business itself - *"Printseller by Appointment to the Queen."* His first editorial concluded with the paragraph: *"Our first word is an appeal to the indulgent forbearance of a discerning, and we hope, friendly public, in their judgement of this our first attempt to inaugurate a new era for Kenilworth. But while thus anxious to disarm unfriendly criticism, by a candid confession of our misgivings, we will not allow a spurious humility to deter us from taking credit for having brought to the work considerable labour, zeal and attention. The omission of the active exertion of qualities such as these, which are within the compass of every intellect, would justly expose us to the censure of those whose patronage we seek, and whose indulgence for many other shortcomings, we shall oftentimes have to entreat."* The *Kenilworth Advertiser* was printed by Alfred Connop in Smithford Street, Coventry.

At around this time, Parsons also sold a recently published tourists guide to Kenilworth and district, which included views of the Castle *"printed in Oil colours."* In a partnership, Parsons started a popular monthly magazine called *The Geologist* but sold his half of the copyright for £50. It ran from 1858 to 1864 when it was incorporated with *The Geological Magazine.*

Only seventeen months after starting the newspaper, Walter Parsons died at The Library, aged just thirty five, but the *Kenilworth Advertiser* survived, continued together with The Library, by his wife Caroline. She retained her husband's name for the business.

In late 1858, within months of the *Advertiser* appearing, moves were afoot to set up an Institute under the Literary and Scientific Institute Act of 1854, which would undermine the existing KMIS and Reading Society. Early discussions had led to three of the promoters, schoolmaster Walter Congreve, the Reverend John Button and Charles Bliss, to seek the opinions of Reverend W Bickmore, by now the President of the KMIS, but found him *"...unable to co-operate with those who wish to have an Institute on a wholly secular basis (and) after due consideration he was unable to coincide with their views."* Undaunted, a meeting was arranged at Congreve's house, probably at his Abbey

The Library, where the Kenilworth Advertiser was founded by Walter T Parsons.

Hill school, for 3rd December in order to "...take into consideration the desirableness of having in Kenilworth a Literary and Scientific Institute on a free and independent basis." At the meeting, having first resolved to call itself "The Kenilworth Literary and Scientific Institute", the second resolution declared that it should be "...free from all party politics and religious differences..." and twenty of the thirty present declared themselves to be a provisional committee. At the second meeting a week later, which just sixteen of the committee attended, the aims of the institute were declared as to be "...the promotion of self-culture and the acquisition of useful knowledge...", and the all-important question of premises was discussed. It was hoped that the society, as it still referred to itself, would accumulate sufficient funds to build its own, but in the meantime there were hopes that a room could be found for its members to use as a library. Four days later the third meeting attracted only ten committee members, but rules were made as to the appointments of a treasurer, secretary etc., and the arrangements for general meetings. The wording of some of these provisional rules became protracted when additional phrases were included in attempts at clarification, and so a sub-committee of Dr George Ayton, William Butler, Boddington and Walter Congreve was given the task of simplifying the wording. By the time the regular meetings had reached the 8th February 1859, the society had decided upon shortening its name to "The Kenilworth Institute" and had set a date for 1st March, and a venue of the Assembly Rooms at the Kings Arms, for the public meeting required under the terms of the Act of Parliament. The last private meeting, a week before the Kings Arms date, saw a dozen present discussing the arrangements for the presentation to the public and the necessity of financing the project. Fees

were suggested of 10s 6d for an honorary member, 1s a quarter and 1d a week, and "...most of the gentlemen present promised to give certain sums annually to the building fund." Present at this decisive meeting were Ayton, Walter Congreve, Thomas Finnemore, J Brown, Reverend John Button, Walter Parsons, Henry Street, F Robbins, Emery, Harding and G Boddington.

After an opening address by Congreve, the public meeting on a Tuesday afternoon quickly descended into confusion. When came the time to vote on the formal proposal that it was expedient to form a society based upon the provisional rules then circulating the room, the Reverend Frederick Kite suggested an amendment simply proposing that the vote should be whether it was expedient to have a Literary and Scientific Institute. This amendment was carried by a majority, but then several of those present stated that "...they did not understand the subject and did not know what they were voting for." After further discussion, the original proposal was put to the vote and was carried "on a division." The Reverend John Button then proposed "...that a Society be now formed in accordance with the preceding resolution and to begin it existence today...and that the name of this society shall be the Kenilworth Institute..." and this was duly carried. The first meeting of the Institute proper was set for Wednesday 9th March at 7.00 p.m. in the Girls National School building near the Town Bridge. It was here that the general public had their first chance to enrol, in fact it was necessary to do so to make possible the voting for the committee proper that evening. Interestingly, amongst those present were the Reverend William Bickmore and many other members of the KMIS and, after a show of hands, these too were allowed to vote. Under the Chairmanship of Edward Draper (50, solicitor, living at The Hermitage), Walter Congreve was duly appointed as Treasurer and G Boddington as Secretary, thus allowing the voting for the other eleven committee members to begin. Each member wrote a short list of those he wished to elect and gave it to one of two tellers, Draper and Boddington, who had both been sworn to secrecy. Those who were duly elected were the Reverends Bickmore, Button, Kite and Clay; George Church, Charles and Edward Draper, Mr Poole, Henry Street and James Rae. Subsequent committee meetings were limited to the formal adoption of the revised and simplified rules. One amendment was particularly interesting as it increased the committee to thirteen members with the stipulation that "...four shall be working men in receipt of daily wages." It was at this same meeting that it was first suggested that the KMIS should amalgamate with the Institute and, not surprisingly, it was the Reverend William Bickmore, being the President of one and Committee member of the other, who was to take a leading role in the discussions of both parties. It appears that it was the KMIS that initially suggested the amalgamation, and it was they that put forward the terms, including the honouring of their own commitments for the rest of the year. The KMIS's General Meeting of 7th May voted through the conditions and two weeks later the two became one on the result of a unanimous vote of Institute members. All "...funds, chattels, books and effects..." which included just £6 1s 6d in cash, were handed over, and Mr Evans of the KMIS continued in his position as subscription collector for the new body.

All these meetings, of both societies, took place in the upper room of the Girls' National School and often on the agenda was a motion for Institute members to "...ascertain the probability of obtaining an eligible site for a building." The only site to be mentioned was a proposed new road by Mr Cotton "...about to be cut from the Station Road to Abbey Hill...in the ensuing autumn..." but no favours were about to be performed as Cotton said a "...site could be purchased under the same conditions to be laid down for all the sites..." and this option does not appear to have been followed up.

One necessity was the appointment of trustees. These were decided upon at a meeting in May 1859. Three ordinary members along with three committee members retired to the lower schoolroom for discussions and later returned with seven acceptable nominations. These were Thomas Emery (draper), Edwin Fraser (grocer), Robert Hubbard (druggist), Walter Parsons (bookseller and Kenilworth Advertiser proprietor), Edward Smith (stonemason), William Webb (letter carrier) and Thomas Hennell who had a ribbon manufactory in Coventry and lived on the Leamington Road at Kenilworth Lodge. The appointment of Thomas Emery necessitated his resignation as a committee member. There were now 124 members registered and it was estimated that these would produce about £44 a year in subscriptions.

The National Girls' School which became the home of the Reading Society and The Institute.

The Institute was now in a position to become registered and so contact was made with Mr John Tidd Pratt, the barrister appointed to certify institutes, and the paperwork required under "...an Act to exempt from County, Borough, Parochial and other local rates, land and buildings occupied by scientific or literary institutes..." was duly signed on 7th September 1859. The immediate impact of this was that the rules had now to be fully implemented and thus the provisional committee had to be replaced by one that included "...four working men." This election eventually took place at the Girls' School on 11th October; with voting between 7 p.m. and 8 p.m. by which time all completed papers had to be placed in a hat on a table. The votes were then split in two with Congreve and Elsworth counting one pile, Ayton and Finnemore the other. The voting separated those classed as "working men" and the two lists of results were as follows:

Henry Street	33	*W M Berry*	39
Reverend Button	33	*Robert Swain*	34
Joseph Hancox	32	*William Turner*	32
John Brown	32	*Henry Evans*	24
Edward Draper	29	Henry Heritage	15
Reverend W Bickmore	27	Edward Manley	11
Luke Heynes	25	Clifford James	9
Reverend Clay	25	George Lidzey	8
J R Rae	24	Thomas Neale	3
G M Boss	22		
Charles Jackson	21		
William Boddington	20		
Thomas Dickenson	18	*(Those shown in*	
Reverend Kite	16	*italics were duly*	
William Poole	15	*elected.)*	
Samuel Boddington	9		
Henry Thornett	8		
G Evans	4		
William Walton	2		

With winter approaching, it was time to organise a series of lectures and it was decided to hold these in the upper room of the Girls' School as investigations at several sites still produced "...nothing of a definite nature..." in the search for a permanent home. It was intended to hold a lecture every Tuesday evening at 7.30. Appropriately, the subject of the first, held on 25th October, was "Military Architecture, Illustrated by Kenilworth Castle." Subsequent lectures included Hamilton Davies "Golden Words", Mr Temple "The Study of History" and John De La Fraime "How to get on in the World." The Reverend William Bickmore had obtained a couple of written lectures on the subjects of "Fungi" and "Health and How to Preserve It" and it was suggested that an Institute member could volunteer to read these.

*   *   *

G Page was the Chairman of the Kenilworth Friendly Insurance Society that had been established in 1839 after a series of meetings at the Castle Tavern which then became its base. There were several similar societies in Kenilworth and each enjoyed social events. In July 1846: *"On Monday last, 20th, members of the National Insurance Society, with their wives and friends, totalling 70, had a tea provided by the committee at the National School Room. They walked in procession preceded by* the Town band. Through the kindness of John Boddington they were allowed into the Castle ruins where they "tripped it on the light fantastic toe" till night began to fall, when they returned to the schoolroom for supper." The evening ended with the national anthem.

In the summer of 1848: "On Monday last, members of the Kenilworth Mutual Insurance Sick Society celebrated their anniversary. Members and friends assembled at the National School room in the afternoon and had a cup of tea after the "usual business" had been done. After tea "the whole party formed into processional order and, as is their custom, the married members with their wives, and "ribless" ones with their "sweethearts" preceded by a band of music, with flags and banners fluttering in the breeze marched away to the Castle." They entertained themselves with country dancing and other amusements until evening, and after the national anthem they returned to schoolroom for supper.

Early June 1859 was a particularly busy time: "Local Benefit Societies - On Whit Monday the Kenilworth Union Benefit Society which numbers nearly one hundred members, assembled at the Clarendon Arms, Castle Green, whence they proceeded accompanied by a band of music down High Street, New Street and Albion Row where they were met by the Rev J P Wallis (late curate of the Parish Church) and conducted to his chapel which was densely crowded on the occasion. After the service the procession was re-formed and returned to the Inn where an excellent dinner was provided by Mr Osborne the worthy host. The chair was taken by the Reverend Mr Wallis and the vice chair by Mr Thomas Eaves. The usual loyal toasts were given and heartily responded to. - The Kenilworth Friendly Society met the same afternoon at the Girls' National School Room where they partook of tea and afterwards adjourned to the ruins. A merry dance and an excellent supper concluded the evenings enjoyment. - The Kings Arms Union Benefit Society also assembled on Monday morning and went in procession to the Parish Church where an excellent sermon suitable for the occasion was preached by the Reverend W Bickmore. The members afterwards partook of a superior dinner provided for them at the hotel. The customary loyal toasts were given and the health of several gentlemen, supporters and patrons of the society were proposed and received in the most cordial manner. - The financial statements of each society appeared to be of a very satisfactory nature."

* * *

In 1851, Thomas Walker of the Castle Inn on Castle Green advertised that "...in consequence of extensive alterations, he has erected a splendid new tent capable of accommodating 150 persons...", but within a year the inn had a new owner, Joshua Blackwell. The Castle Inn was in a prime position to attract visitors; just two weeks apart in the summer of 1857, Blackwell catered first for a party of 500 from Birmingham, and then 300 from a Birmingham saddle manufacturer. He soon set about making numerous improvements and additions, and one of these was a spectacular new room decorated by T Manning of Leamington, "...a young artist of considerable merit. The paintings on the various panels are in oil and the subjects are illustrative of Queen Elizabeth's visit to Kenilworth. The first represents Amy Robsart's escape from Cumnor Hall, with Wayland Smith leading her charger, the second, old doctor Alesco in his laboratory preparing a sleeping mixture for Amy to prevent her visiting the Revels at Kenilworth Castle, the third Amy's escape from the grotto from Tressillian's lodgings with Lawrence and Michael Lambourne in her company; the fourth, the duel by moonlight between Leycester and Tressillian supposed to have been fought by a large oak tree at the back of Kenilworth Castle; the fifth the meet in the grotto at the Pleasaunce between the Queen and Amy Robsart; sixth, Lord Leycester owning his marriage to the queen and begging her pardon; seventh, Blount and Flipperty Gibbet with the Countess's casket of jewels, and next poor Amy's fall through the trap at Cumnor Hall. Over mantle pieces at each end are representations of Kenilworth Castle as it was in its days of prosperity, Queen Elizabeth entering it with her attendants and nobles, and as it is at present times with groups of visitors to the interesting ruins." The room was known as the clubroom and adjoined the main hotel. At this time, Blackwell amended the name of his premises to The Queen and Castle Hotel. Its popularity continued, particularly amongst manufactories. In the summer of 1859, two separate parties of 100 and 350 were catered for simultaneously, but visitors were not limited to the summer months; in October 1859, Coventry ribbon manufacturer Mr Hart treated his workforce of 240 to refreshments after a trip to the Castle. In 1862, a party of 4-500 workers from Watkins and Keen were dined, having travelled from Birmingham by rail.

* * *

Railway-related incidents were inevitable; in 1851 at the junction of the roads to Leamington and Warwick, a horse was startled by a train going under the bridge and two people were injured in separate vehicles, one of which almost went over the parapet. In early 1853 there was a potentially disastrous accident one night when a wagon rolled out onto the main line from a station siding to one mile north of station, apparently blown by high wind. A goods train ran into it, and the man responsible for not ensuring the wagon was secure, John Robertson, was jailed for a month.

John Aldridge (41), lodged in town while he worked "...attending a steam thrashing machine." On 16th May 1863, he set off in the morning for Coventry to meet his wife, carrying two watches and £1 11s 6d in cash. Nothing more was known of his movements until he was escorted back to Coventry station, by two men, in a state of intoxication. He left Coventry on the 9.15 p.m. train having failed to meet his wife as arranged, and arrived back at Kenilworth at 9.30. He gave up his ticket, wished the collector good night, and walked with apparent ease in the direction of the Kings Arms. "A few minutes later, the driver of a Leamington goods train which was just coming to standstill felt a sudden jerk. As soon as the train had completely ceased its motion, *he alighted, called to a policeman, borrowed his lamp, and endeavoured to discover the cause of the interruption. On directing the ray of light under the engine, a horrible sight met his view. The body of the deceased was lying across the line, the head completely severed, and the hands crushed and one of them hanging on by a few shreds of skin."* Aldridge now only had one watch and 1¹/₂d on him. Police were unable to find out what happened to the money or watch. The inquest was held at the Boot Inn by Deputy Coroner Burkitt, standing in for William Poole, and a verdict of accident was returned.

In January 1864, there was a near-fatal accident to a passenger at the railway station. A lady arriving on the 4.15 p.m. train from Coventry astonishingly got out the wrong side of the coach and fell onto the other line. The only explanation can be that she saw the station building and got out that side, not realising that the single line divided into two at the station for trains to pass. As luck would have it, this was one of the times during the day when trains did pass, and the 4.15 p.m. from Leamington was approaching. Two quick-thinking passengers jumped down onto the rails and literally threw the lady onto the platform then leapt clear with seconds to spare. Five months later, the railway company made efforts to increase the comfort of passengers on the platform for Leamington trains: *"The down platform, formerly a rude wooden structure, has been replaced by a more commodious one, the facing being of stone and when completed the pavement will be of coloured bricks. The alteration will greatly enhance the appearance of the station."*

An even more extraordinary railway accident happened in October the same year on the 9.00 p.m. mail train from Leamington, crewed by driver William Makepeace and stoker George Fell. As the train left Kenilworth station, Makepeace shouted *"look out mate"* to Fell who took it to mean he had to look out for the signals whilst his driver was engaged on some other matter concerning the engine. However, as the train approached Coventry, Fell suddenly realised he was alone on the footplate. He reported this to the Coventry Station Master who despatched PC Sayes and two porters on a trolley up the line to search for Makepeace, finding him near the Park Hill bridge, quite dead with a massive head injury. He was loaded onto the trolley and taken to Kenilworth station where his body was examined by Dr Wynter. The inquest was held at the Kings Arms in front of Alexander Carter, and it was supposed that Makepeace climbed upon the tender of the locomotive and was hit by the bridge, but there was no attempt to explain why Fell was alone for so long without realising. Makepeace had been a driver for eighteen years, mostly on the L&NWR, and left three children for his widow to support.

A local man stated that in 1868 Kenilworth station had two signalmen, one or two platform porters, a youth as a booking clerk, a station master and James Beaton to superintend the goods department. Beaton was still there 25 years later. One of the porters, Mr Paxton, became a guard on the line.

*   *   *

Due to a new Police Act in 1856, each county had to provide a police force in all its divisions by the end of the year. Chief Constable James Isaac drew up plans for Warwickshire's suggesting an increase in personnel from 70 to 135, including one office clerk, and a doubling of expenditure, a quarter of which was to be provided by the treasury. As part of this county-wide restructuring of the police force, Kenilworth was one of five towns (the others being Henley in Arden, Polesworth, Kineton and Nuneaton) to have new police stations, the one in Kenilworth replacing the latest lock-up which was probably at Washbrook. Plans for each were drawn by the county surveyor, Mr Kendalls, and submitted on 16th October 1857, and that for Kenilworth was the largest as it was to become the County Constabulary headquarters. An impressive building with three front entrances, seven upstairs bedrooms, four cells on ground level and a walled prisoner's yard 31ft 6ins by 16ft were proposed, but unfortunately the plot of land it was intended for could not be acquired. On 3rd April the following year, Kendalls' revised plans were submitted for a smaller site, fronting onto Albion Street on its corner with Park Road. The new plan was a cleverly reduced version of the original - now there were only two entrances, six upstairs bedrooms, the four cells were now two above each other, the prisoners' yard was now smaller, 18ft by 13ft, but its retaining wall was not reduced, remaining at a daunting 15ft high. Two kitchens and sculleries were provided at the rear, a strong-room and offices were in the main building, and so was a heating and ventilation system for the cells, each of which included a w.c.

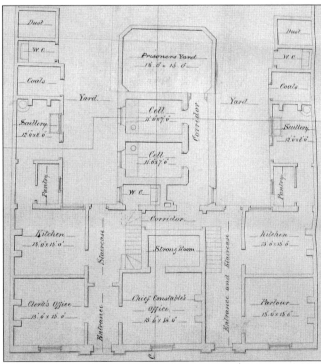

The ground-floor plan of the building shows the Chief Constable's office between the two front doors, the clerk's office to the left, and full kitchen facilities.
(Warwick County Records Office, QS 24/624)

Tenders were invited for its construction. Only one Kenilworth builder was attracted sufficiently and R Swain's letter, post marked "South Kenilworth" on 9th June, applied for the contract at £1,162 16s 10d. The following day he wrote again to correct an error and increase his estimate to £1,375! The lowest tender was now for £1,170 from John Dutton of Coventry. He had additional distinct advantages in that he had recently completed the construction of the Coventry Police Station, and his father Charles lived in one of his houses, Spring Cottage, in Ladies Hill. It was probably a straightforward decision by the Police Committee, chaired by Lord Leigh on 28th June, to accept Dutton's tender.

The contract was signed on 17th July and from that date, Dutton had six months to complete the project. The money was to be paid in three equal amounts at pre-agreed stages of completion. The first was paid on 8th October when the roofing had been finished, the second on 27th December when the whole of the works were complete, and the third two months later when it had been established that all was well. Building work was actually finished on Christmas Eve, but after that Dutton was involved in a separate arrangement in fitting out the Chief Constable's office. By 11th March 1859, the station, still referred to occasionally as "the new lock-up", was considered ready for immediate occupation. The front pieces of the two entrances were made of Bath stone, as were the front windowsills but all other window sills were of cheaper Kenilworth stone. The steps to the front entrance were of Yorkshire stone and the doors and their frames were of varnished oak. The roofs were made of 20ins by 10ins Bangor slates. Each cell included a wooden bench, 2ins thick and 2ft 6ins wide. All the drains were connected to one of two main pipes that ran under the front doors and downhill to drain directly into the nearby brook. Also included in the contract, but not shown on the plan, was a four-foot wide well of an expected depth of 35ft. By the conclusion of the countywide improvements, the force consisted of the Chief Constable, five superintendents, ten inspectors, a hundred and fifty four constables and one clerical officer.

The Warwickshire Constabulary Headquarters.

As a deterrent, the old stocks in Kenilworth were still in use; William Bartlett, convicted of drunkenness six weeks previously, remained in them from 1 o'clock until 6 o'clock one September Thursday in 1859, under the surveillance of a policeman.

* * *

The Kings Arms proprietors, Henry and John

Bursell, bought land either side of Station Road from Thomas Cotton on 22nd March 1850; the area behind the Kings Arms was called Little Broad Meadow. Henry Bursell was also a small-time sheep breeder. His prize assets were two long-woolled Leicester ewes which were claimed in 1851 to have produced 40 lambs between them in 6 years.

Henry Bursell was a Corporal in Lord Leigh's Troop of the Warwickshire Yeomanry Cavalry and each September he made his premises available for a gathering. In 1855, the event started with a shooting competition on Bushy Common at which the thirteen competitors shot four rounds each at a target 60yds away. Bursell himself and a man named Smith were the only ones to score four hits and Bursell allowed Smith to carry off the £5 prize. Next was a sword-handling competition held on the bowling green at the Kings Arms and William Haddon of Maxstoke was the victor from the fourteen entrants. After their exertions, the troop and other yeoman sat down to a meal at the Kings Arms where the chair was taken by Lord Leigh.

In the late 1850s, Bursell began a series of improvements at the Kings Arms. A banqueting hall was added in 1858 - fronting onto Clarendon Street it was in the upper storey of a building previously used either as stabling or carriage storage. Then, in the summer of 1859, Henry had a new bowling green laid out at the rear of the hotel and marked the occasion with a special dinner with more than twenty guests, but tragedy struck the family just weeks later whilst John Bursell and his family were on holiday in the Channel Islands. The steamship 'Express' that they were on ran into some rocks as it approached Jersey harbour. As the passengers were being transferred to the safety of other vessels, John fell between the two boats and drowned. His body was not found for several weeks when it was recovered by the steam-tug 'True Briton' whilst it was laying a cable from Guernsey to Jersey. His remains were returned to Kenilworth, and he was buried at St.Nicholas church on 10th October.

Soon after the tragedy, it seems that Henry Bursell decided to take up farming full-time and took up Long Meadow, about 200 acres, in the vicinity of Red Lane. William G F Bolton took over at the Kings Arms as a yearly tenant. An 1861 advertisement declares *"...Bolton's hotel is within two minutes walk of the Turkish bath, which is daily open to visitors of this neighbourhood."*

In May 1862, John Bursell's moiety came up for auction under the terms of his will. The sale posters included a detailed description: The ground floor had four parlours, bar, smoke and tap rooms, two kitchens, scullery, dairy, laundry and storerooms. On the first floor was the old assembly room, 45ft by 17ft and divisible by folding doors, two private sitting rooms, seven "airy" chambers and a w.c. The second floor had eight chambers. There was also large cellaring. At the rear of the hotel and fronting onto Station Road were the wine and spirit vaults, the banqueting room 104ft by 18ft, a large billiard room and ale and porter stores. There was also stabling and loose boxes for 40 horses, large carriage-houses and the *"tastefully laid out"* bowling green. The hotel was well lighted with gas and had hand pumps of soft and hard water. The sale was subject to the lifetime interest of an 83-year-old lady, Mary Bursell.

In June 1862, Henry Bursell was declared bankrupt with a deficiency of £3,800. He had lost a lot of money on building speculation and a large part of these losses was £1,600 he paid to William Savage Poole in 1857 as a mortgage on a freehold estate. The sum was missing and this was the public start of the sad decline of solicitor and County Coroner, William Poole.

It all unravelled in the case of John Howes, an uneducated farmer who could write only his name, read only a little printed material but not understand writing. He had William Poole as his solicitor and, not surprisingly, Howes trusted Poole implicitly. Poole had become an attorney in Kenilworth in 1844, first in partnership with his father Robert until 1850, and then with his brother until 1857.

Howes had been in the habit of giving Robert Poole money to invest on his behalf, and this continued with William Poole as soon as he took up his position. The first investment was £1,000 to pay off a mortgage on some property in Leamington, including the Greyhound Inn, with Poole paying Howes 4% interest, and Robert Poole and a Mr Patterson making themselves liable to indemnity against any loss. However, in 1849 the value of the property was only £700 and so William Poole transferred the property into his own name, (to relieve his father and Patterson from liability), and paid Howes the £300 difference, but purely in his accounts, no money changed hands. Poole never told Howes any of this. In December 1855, Poole exchanged the property for five Westminster Improvement bonds, which Poole believed to be worth £200 each but were actually five times that amount, and again failed to tell Howes. Poole made other investments for Howes, including giving money to his own brothers-in-law, Thomas and James Boddington, solicitors, but these became insolvent in August 1857. Poole suggested an investment in a building project in Balsall in December 1861, which was due to be completed in March 1862, but each time Howes quizzed him on his investment Poole became evasive. Howes eventually discovered the property had been put up for re-sale and asked Poole for his money back only to be told that he did not have it. Howes employed another solicitor to investigate and very quickly William Poole's affairs began to unravel. It was discovered that he had been insolvent for some years and that his books had been kept in such a way as to show that it was Howes' and other clients that had lost money. In addition, the Westminster bonds once valued at £5,000 were now worthless. Poole was not only declared bankrupt with debts of over £24,000 above the value of his entire estate, but he was also accused of fraud and misappropriation of funds, as shown by the Westminster Bonds initially being for his benefit on a client's investment. The conduct of Poole was described in this case as "*not as it should be*" but not actually fraud. Other cases, however, were called "*...express misrepresentation...gross misconduct as an attorney...and on other cases...guilty of fraud and misconduct.*" The final hearing when he was struck off the Roll of Attorney was on the first Tuesday of June 1863. Although his conduct as Coroner had never been questioned, he had to be relieved of this position as well because one of the conditions of his position was that he could afford any possible fine imposed, somewhat ironically, for malpractice as a Coroner. As a bankrupt, of course, he failed this stipulation.

The fallout continued. Thomas and S Boddington of Birmingham became bankrupt, with a debt of about £9,000, due largely to being sureties for Poole: they owed nothing on their own account. The local press claimed that Poole was given £3,000 by the Boddingtons to pay some off his creditors, but it was never handed on; Poole refuted this and threatened legal action, which prompted a public apology. It is likely that miller Francis Robbins' bankruptcy the same year was connected.

Probably in late 1861, just before his affairs became known, Poole had entered into a partnership with Mr Burkitt, a young solicitor in Kenilworth. This partnership too became the subject of a bankruptcy action - there was a deficiency of over £2,179. Transactions with the Reverend G A Poole, Howe and Reverend John Craig, amounting to £789, were unknown to Burkitt as Poole acted on his own. Poole kept no proper account books, just papers amounting to petty cash spending and memorandums. Mr Burkitt on the other hand kept good records of his affairs, balancing his account every month and making deposits and withdrawals at the bank. The amount due to Leamington Priors Bank was £1,437 but, since the commencement of the partnership, Poole had drawn £6,200 and Burkitt just £605. The partnership started about two years previously when Poole knew he was already insolvent. The first lengthy hearing was mostly legal arguments over whether Burkitt could be separately discharged as a bankrupt whilst investigations into Poole's affairs continued. It was decided that he could be.

Henry Bursell, despite being recorded in the bankruptcy court in June 1863 as a "*...former hotelier and coal merchant, now a farmer...*", under unknown circumstances managed to remain at the King Arms. In 1866, it was described as a "*Family and Commercial Hotel, Posting House and Inland Revenue Office*". It had also undergone "*...considerable repairs and alterations...*" which were likely to have included the addition of the Portico at the front.

The following year, in July, Mary Bursell died and three years later, in July 1870, the freehold was advertised for sale using the same description as that in 1862; it was still in the occupation of Henry Bursell and his family. Bursell, now 57, had again decided to take up farming full-time and took on a lease at Grounds Farm, and gave up another area of land for renting, 40-acre New Field, which he had had for 22 years. A farewell dinner was held in February 1871, a sad occasion for Bursell as he was born in the Kings Arms and had lived nowhere else. The event also welcomed the incoming tenant; George Bundock Dempster was a solicitor and advertised himself as such throughout his brief stay in charge.

A year after he arrived, Dempster held a supper for tradesmen and 30 attended. The event had been delayed by the "*...serious indisposition of Mr Dempster...and the various repairs necessary to the Hotel.*" Dempster missed the evening completely as he was "*upon a tour*" for his health but Mrs Dempster more than ably coped, as she was effectively running the hotel due to her husband's illness. He died soon after. In the summer of 1875, Mrs Dempster put a stop to rumours that she was selling the Kings Arms by advertising that she fully intended continuing the business, including the carriage hiring for so long associated with the hotel. It was probably during the Dempster's time that "Castle Hotel" was added to the name.

Bursell's venture into full-time agriculture did not last too long; in September 1876 his property at Grounds and Castle farms was valued, and auctioned off the following month.

Edward Draper bought Whitemoor Farm from Thomas Cotton on 10th May 1866 when James Betty was the tenant; Joseph Betty (43), probably his brother, was a butcher. In September that year, James gave up farming and went into the butcher's business with Joseph. However, a double tragedy was about to strike the family. Joseph died on the 18th August 1867 and within days James Betty bought himself a new horse, but the first time he rode it he was thrown near his house and received what was thought at the time to be a minor head injury but within days, he died. The horse was destroyed.

William Poole, having recovered financially in unknown circumstances, bought Whitemoor Farm from Draper on 22nd March 1870, and soon afterwards named the house Elmdene. He soon found work as the Secretary of the Kenilworth Gas and Coke Company and by 1873 had regained his position as Coroner, but he did not practise as a solicitor again.

Dudley House.

* * *

Thomas Skeffington Bourne was born in 1824, the third son of Edward (Edmund?) Bourne MD of Coventry. He was apprenticed with Mr R Power, surgeon, at Atherstone and after completing his articles he became a student at Kings College, London, from where he graduated with an MRCS Diploma in 1846. That year he came to Kenilworth to assist Dr William Boddington at Montague House, eventually leaving to start his own practice in Nuneaton, but in 1860 he returned to partner Dr George Boddington. This same year his wife gave birth to a son, named Edmund Kemp Bourne. When Boddington left for Sutton Coldfield, Bourne was left in charge of an extensive practice on Abbey Hill. His mother Jane and his three sisters, Charlotte, Margaret and Lucy, moved in to Holme Rock in Station Road.

On 9th June 1852 surgeon Obidiah Ayton died suddenly of apoplexy, aged 72, whilst crossing the road to see a patient in Stoneleigh. He had served the rich and poor equally in Kenilworth for 45 years. His practice was continued by his nephew George, but he died aged just 41 in August 1865. Ayton's accounts had been done by Overseer and Parish Clerk William Sutton who now moved on to be a rate collector. To fill the vacant practice, Dr Daniel Robert Wynter (25) and his brother Dr Hugh Bold Wynter (28) moved into Dudley House with their mother Francis. She was the widow of Captain Wynter of the 11th Madras Infantry and both sons had been born in India.

* * *

How stressful life could be, even for those with work, is shown by a series of incidents in 1864 and 1865. One October 1864 day, tanner George Ryley came home for his dinner. Quite often, he had to do with dry bread but this day he asked his wife Emma for some of the mutton broth she was serving to their children, but she refused. Emma was known to be quarrelsome, George was a good hardworking man and gave his wife 15 to 17s a week for food and he expected more. On this occasion, he lost his temper and assaulted her, ending up in front of Mr Cotton JP. Cotton agreed that Ryley had been severely provoked but added *"...these assaults are of frequent occurrence in Kenilworth where there is a great deal of very gross and immoral conduct going on."* Ryley was bound over to keep the peace. Just the following week Phoebe Newey was in court charged with assaulting Ann James, wife of comb-maker Edward James, her neighbour in New Row. Phoebe was a *"...quarrelsome and violent woman...none of her neighbours live in peace with her."* Due to the high costs against her, £1 13s, Phoebe was fined only 6d or, upon default of payment, twenty one days hard labour on only bread and water. The same day saw James Atkins in court charged with assaulting his sister in an argument about his wife.

It was not just the adults that had problems. Stone-throwing by schoolchildren was becoming a great nuisance in 1864, particularly at St.John's where it was eventually decided to stop the schoolchildren going outside at playtime in an attempt to bring an end to the problem. The school decided to make an example of the next offender and after throwing a stone at schoolmaster James William's daughter Frances, George Mountford "*...a lad whose head was just visible above the top of the dock...*" was that example. His mother, who had only 6s to pay his fine and expenses of double that amount, said "*Do what you like with him...I wouldn't mind him going to gaol*" and he was duly sentenced to one month.

The 1864 case of miller's daughter and Mill End resident, twenty five year-old Ann Barran, was one that left more questions than it answered. She worked at "*...the bugle or gimp factory.*" At one time she was engaged to sailor James Ward, but this was broken off some two years previously and she was now set to marry miller Thomas Haynes of Northamptonshire - but Ward was about to return. She had a four year-old daughter by an unnamed father, and was now four months pregnant again. One night in mid-June, after going to bed at 9.00 p.m. following a supper of bread, cheese and porter, she had a very disturbed night, calling out at three o'clock. This was not unusual as she often suffered from nightmares. At 6.00 a.m. she was found dead in her bed by her mother, with her daughter fast asleep at her side. An enormously detailed autopsy report by Police Surgeon John Clarke and Dr Wynter could find no obvious cause of death. Death by natural causes was the verdict but only as this was the most likely rather than certain cause. The inference that she had taken her own life due to her circumstances could not be substantiated. The County Coroner, William Poole, was at this time suspended from duties and so the inquest was conducted at the Bowling Green Inn by Magistrate Alexander Carter of Coventry.

Twenty seven year-old Amelia Betts still lived with her father on Castle Green and had been in regular trouble with the police for heavy drinking. One particular night in April 1865, she did not get home until four in the morning. Her father found her later in a very poor state and, believing that she had taken poison, sent for Police Inspector Gallaway. Gallaway found a bottle in her pocket containing a substance of the same peculiar colour as her vomit. It was only now that a doctor was sent for, Dr Clarke the Police Surgeon, and his treatment soon began to work. Gallaway asked Betts to take care of his daughter but he refused saying he had "*...already enough to put up with from her.*" Gallaway remonstrated with Betts and his inhuman conduct but on the advice of Dr Clarke, she was taken to the police station to sleep in an especially prepared cell.

Just a few months later, a Mrs Power was trying to gain a divorce from her husband on the grounds of adultery and cruelty. Both were originally from out of town, he from Bath, she from Atherstone, and they had two children. He was still only twenty two but had developed an uncontrollable drinking habit, often coming home late and threatening his wife. She had left several times but always returned, believing he could mend his ways. The final split had come in June 1864 after he had been with local prostitutes but, perhaps surprisingly, no final decision was given in court. The following month, two sixteen year-olds from the Black Country eloped to Kenilworth where astonishingly it was reported that they were married at St.Nicholas. They

were discovered by their pursuers at The Bear Inn whereupon the groom was literally carried away by his friends. He was taken back home by them, his wife travelling on the same train.

At an inquest at the Virgins Hotel and Castle Tavern in 1866, the death of miller James Grant was declared "*a supposed suicide*" after he was found in a pool in Crackley Wood, but there was no evidence as to how he fell in. A far more tragic inquest was held the following month at the Coventry Cross, following the discovery of a baby's body in the earth below a water closet. A servant to Miss Langley, Elizabeth Alexander, was the mother and much of the evidence of the sequence of events came from her live-in friend Sarah Jones and neighbour Maria Harris. The post-mortem revealed that the child was born alive and suffocated in the earth, but it was possible that the child was born unexpectedly and fell to earth by accident. There was not enough evidence to charge Elizabeth with murder so she was given concealment of birth charges. The circumstances of the pregnancy were not even discussed.

In the first week of June 1869, the body of a young girl was found in the river 50yds from the Chesford Bridge on the Leek Wootton side. It was that of 19 year-old Emma Varnham from Knowle who was working at The Globe as a domestic servant. She was apparently driven to it over a young man named Tom. The Globe was the former Crown and Horseshoes, the name was changed by new licensee Samuel Harding in about 1850.

*   *   *

The game of cricket had been long established in Kenilworth. A flourishing club had some notable players: "*The celebrated Box practised the manly game here before he became known as belonging to all England.*" The cricket ground had been lost by the building of Clarendon Street in 1844 and it was to be four years before games were once again played when a new field was found in August 1848. The new pitch was used for ten years when another move took the club to The Spring Farm and Captain Grayson's field. The club had two secretaries, T Harding and R C Adams, practised twice a week, on Tuesdays and Thursdays at 4.30., and held fortnightly meetings into October.

Matches against Welford, Barston and Stoneleigh were played, as were some matches against local schools. The cricketers at Walter Congreve's boys' boarding school at The Abbey's on Abbey Hill beat a town club team as often as they lost. A game at Captain Grayson's The Spring in 1859 saw the Kenilworth Club bowled out for just 19 in its first innings with the school managing 35. The club did better second time around, scoring 52, but the school scored enough runs to win with the loss of only two wickets. Walsh, Paget and Toppin were the star pupils. Congreve's boys were aged up to only fifteen and this suggests there was a junior side at the town club.

On Wednesday 21st May 1862, the cricket club were invited to play Oxford University at Parr and Wisdens ground. The start was delayed until 1 o'clock due to rain. Kenilworth batted until nearly 6 o'clock, just an hour before the scheduled finishing time, for their 225 all out. It was agreed to continue the match an extra half hour by which time the University had reached 79 for 6 at close. The Kenilworth team was: T E Cobb, G C Greenway, B Smith, Captain Gowan, T Ratliff, T O Raey, W Ratlif, R T Fetherstone, E Johnson, T Ivens and T W Andrews. Raey top scored 43.

In 1864 the club played against Southam at the County Ground in Warwick. The recorded scores were Southam 76 and 37 for 4, and Kenilworth 148. Kenilworth's runs were scored by C Smith 0, T Arnold 0, B T Fetherston 68, G Carter 6, C Colbeck 32, H W Draper 10, A Hardwin 12, P Behrens 1, F C Walsh 4, W Perry 0, and J Rae 0. The side included three young gentlemen from Leamington College, and Arnold who was a professional; although his batting does not appear to be notable, his bowling was, taking 9 of the 14 Southam wickets.

A meeting was held at the Bowling Green Inn in early 1866 to re-organise the club; Mr Hubbard presided, and an agreement was reached with John Phillips, the innkeeper, for use of his field at the rear of the inn. In July 1867 the team of W Elers, H W Draper, G Boxall, C Smith, A Moore, E Hill, W Pennington, A O'Brian, R Bill, C Crossley and H Moore lost to Southam by 2 runs. H Draper became secretary but the club seemed to be in decline.

The Bowling Green Field or Piece, became the home of Kenilworth Cricket Club for almost twenty years.

The new Bowling Green Inn licensee had arrived in 1859. *"An advertisement announces that this old-established hostelry has been taken to by Mr John Phillips and there is no doubt that under his spirited management the undertaking will be a successful one. The green has a very beautiful appearance being ornamented by a profusion of shrubs and flowers, grottos, arbours, etc., there is also a large covered tent lit with gas, for the convenience of the votaries of Terpsichore, and of visitors in general."*

John Phillips, of honest memory, spared neither time nor money to make the Bowling Green Inn attractive, but its low and gloomy rooms, narrow and dark passages, made the work almost an impossibility. The bowling green itself was immediately behind the inn and extended down to a field boundary where there was a footpath. On the other side of this path was the Bowling Green Piece, the field used by the cricket club.

Charles Snewing was born on August 1st 1817 and was brought up by his parents, wine and spirit merchant William and his wife Ann, at The Lodge on the Leamington Road. After leaving school, Charles studied as a veterinary surgeon at The Royal College in London and through his career came into contact with horseracing and training establishments and eventually owned a few horses; one of these was 'Caractacus', a fine bay colt, bought as a yearling from William Blenkiron of Middle Park, Eltham. In 1862, despite not winning a race until the Somersetshire Stakes at Bath, 'Caractacus' was entered for the Epsom Derby. His stable attendant, John Parsons, asked Snewing for the ride to which he agreed. The jockey wore a light blue jacket and white cap. The favourite for the race was 'Marquis' at 3-1, with 'Buckstone' 7-2 and 'Caractacus' an outsider at 1000-15.

For much of the race 'Caractacus' was not in contention. Upon entering the old course the two favourites came on with a clear lead, 'Caractacus' was 8th. As 'Marquis' entered the straight, his lead had increased with 'Caractacus' 4th; but then the four leading horses were running almost in a line.

"On they came, the favourite leading by a clear length. Nearing the grandstand a desperate effort was made...a struggle, a rally, a final burst, and the three leading horses went past the post in a hard knot. A pause of a few moments and the telegraph spoke; the winner was, not the 'Marquis', not 'Buckstone', but 'Caractacus', against whom the odds had been as great as 40-1. A novel feature in connection with this race was that it was timed by Mr Bennett's new chronograph dial clock by which the second hand records even tenths of a second, which was employed for the first time."

'Caractacus' had won the event by a neck in a time of 2 minutes 45 and five-tenths seconds, the third fastest time there had been. Two Derby records were set that day - the largest-ever field at 34, and the youngest ever winning jockey, John Parsons was just 16. *"A sensation which will long be remembered."* It must have been a quite extraordinary time for Snewing as his wife Maria died the year before and just five weeks after the Derby, it was announced that his mother Ann had died on 18th July, *"...at the residence of her only daughter, St.Lukes Vicarage Bilston, age 68, Ann Snewing widow of William Snewing esq., of Kenilworth Lodge."* 'Caractacus' was not fit enough to take on the Saint Ledger that year, a race he may well have won as the first two horses home were those he beat into 2nd and 3rd place at Epsom.

*　　*　　*

Possibly encouraged by the successful construction of the new school at St.John's, it was decided in late 1857 to replace the National girls' school building near Townspool Bridge with a new building for educating the poor of the town. The finances were to involve the sale of the old school but at vestry meetings, all were agreed that this should not happen until the new was open. A building committee was appointed consisting of the Reverend William Bickmore, his curate the Reverend Mr Clay, William and Samuel Boddington,

Charles Bliss, John Spencer, William Newbery, Edward Draper and solicitor William Poole. Architect Henry Bradley was employed and from 2nd to 16th May 1859 his designs were on display at the bank, courtesy of Charles Bliss, and tenders were invited. The successful applicant was Mr Marriott of Coventry.

The site chosen for the new school was just around the corner from the old in Pepper Alley and the land was generously given by the Earl of Clarendon. Funds were raised entirely by donation and one contribution in June 1859 was from the Coventry Church Extension Society for £60, which left a shortfall of about £200.

Work was by now under way and in the first week of August the laying of the foundation stone was marked by a parade through town. It was headed by the town band with the schoolchildren three-abreast behind. Next came the architect and builders, Edward Draper carrying the all-important trowel and mallet on a blue cushion, followed by the building committee and clergy, and finally a carriage conveying Mrs Bickmore and Mrs Butler. They all passed through a triumphal arch at the end of Pepper Alley to the site. After hymns, prayers and a blessing, the stone was lowered and laid by Mrs Bickmore. Deposited in the stone were silver and copper coins, a copy of the Kenilworth Advertiser and a scroll that recorded the occasion. The trowel and mallet were presented to Mrs Bickmore.

The new school was in two parts; accommodation for the girls was 55ft by 18ft with a single classroom 15ft by 16ft, and the infant school was 36ft by 16ft with a classroom 16ft by 16ft. There was also a *"commodious teacher's residence"* and a large playground. The style was modern gothic and it was built of brick with Kenilworth stone dressings. It opened in the summer of 1860.

The school was, according to inspectors, performing well. It was receiving government grants; in 1859 this amounted to £53 10s that included £42 for the wages of the mistress and two pupil teachers for a year. The remainder was a capitation grant. The children of the poor had to pay 1d a week to attend, tradesman's children 2d and those of master tradesmen 4d. The infant school was for the children of St.Nicholas parish but the girls could come from St.John's as well.

The condition of St.Nicholas church became a matter of some concern and was first raised as an issue in 1850. It is probable that the arrival of the Reverend William Bickmore in early 1856 was instrumental in what was to follow. He said that he moved from a London church that was *"...clean orderly and decent, to that of Kenilworth which was foul and green with age and damp, and in which the poor were thrust into corners."* At a service to commemorate the ending of the Crimean War in early 1856, Charles Bliss began a collection towards restoration and collected £26. From the *"...sale of ladies' work and other sources..."*, the fund steadily rose to several hundred pounds.

The church had other problems, notably in 1859. The clock was regularly inaccurate but thanks to the attentions of a *"...clever chimney sweep..."* its consistency improved, but it was set differently to the "railway time" at the station. Then in July the choir refused to sing as its members were not being given their usual remuneration, and within weeks a new choir was in rehearsal.

But by 1863 the building's situation was becoming serious. *"The galleries are dilapidated and the church presents a miserable appearance."* Removal of the galleries was suggested as they were *"...excrescences...greatly instrumental in making the church damp, cold and unwholesome. For as long as the north and south galleries remain it will be impossible for light and air to penetrate into and circulate freely."* Reverend William Bickmore commented on the *"...lumbering ugly gallery which is not fit to put a human being in."* In the galleries *"...the pews are broken away, they are the most miserable places I have seen in a Parish Church."* It was suggested that the lighter west gallery could be retained for the accommodation of schoolchildren, but the other three, including one above the organ, should go. The north wall was damp as the outside soil was three feet above floor level. The floor itself was *"...damp, not to say wet."*

The pews were inconvenient and badly arranged; it was thought that extra space could be made to accommodate the poor, allocated just 130 places, *"...who at present are ill provided for...almost all of which seats are unfit for use."* The existing pews should have sat 6 or 8 worshippers but were so small most could only have four kneeling with comfort. Many were in a ruinous state, some were *"...not fit to put a dog in."* The Earl of Clarendon had recently visited Kenilworth and was astonished; he had *"...no idea it as so bad."*

A committee was formed to look into restoration of the church and to invite architects to provide solutions. Eight different plans were submitted to be discussed at a later meeting. W Smith of Adelphi Chambers, London, drew the chosen designs; he had experience of similar projects, notably in Norfolk.

The proposed re-arrangement of the pews began a series of discussions, as many were paid for and had belonged to families or households for years. This had started about 80 or 90 years previously, the last time the pews were re-arranged, and it was quickly revealed that the system was completely illegal. It had been over fifteen years since a pew had been sold to a parishioner and the remnants of the custom were to be done away with, but it was decided that seating was to be allocated to those who had claim to pews. The number of houses occupied by parishioners using the church, *"...exclusive of non-conformists..."*, was 160 of which 83 had no place in church despite paying about £10 a year to the parish rates.

Churchwarden W Boddington prepared a report concerning the seating and presented it to a meeting on the morning of Tuesday 3rd February. Exclusive of the Parish of St.John's, there were 618 houses inhabited by 2,514 persons and on the previous 7th September, the churchwardens had counted *"...a very good average congregation..."* and they numbered 520 inclusive of children. *"The boys school were absent from their usual place..."* but some were present in other parts of the church. It was suggested that the alterations should provide comfortable kneeling accommodation for not less than 700 people - Charles Bliss stated that at best it could currently accommodate 630 as it was so poorly laid out. Mr Smith's plan allowed for 792 sittings, and Boddington proposed these were arranged as 383 allotted seats, 100 for children, and 309 for the poor. A similar project, galleries removed, new and re-arranged pews, had recently been carried out at Knowle Church, which was similar to but smaller than St.Nicholas, and it was considered a great success.

Due to the chosen renovations and extensions of the seating, the "...*proposed memorial chapel to the Bishop of Durham which was arranged for 85 persons, has been abandoned.*" This was to have been in the Chancel aisle. There were 50 monumental stones in the church, including blue flagstones, which would have to be covered. Alternatively, it was suggested that they could be put in one aisle, in the churchyard or on the walls.

The initial estimate for the work was £2,050. In case not all of it could be raised, it was decided that the seating would be the priority. It was intended to raise the money by subscription and a bazaar at the Castle. At this time there was £400 to £500 in hand. By 20th June, the Earl of Clarendon had donated £300, Lord Leigh £105, E H Woodcock £50 and he promised £50 more if enough seats are provided for the poor, and Reverend William Bickmore, T Cotton and E Wilkinson gave £50 each. £1,400 had now been raised. It had to be established that it was legal to take away seats from the parishioners of St.John's, but it was still decided to collect contributions from them as the poorer parishioners were indebted to those of St.Nicholas for the building of their own church. The bazaar at the Castle was on 25th and 26th, Tuesday and Wednesday, of August. and contributed another £600, taking the funds past the total required to allow work to start.

The builder engaged was Mr Marriott of Coventry, and by the summer of 1864 work was well under way. In August, one of Marriott's workman, a man named Batchelor, fell about three feet and injured himself, not too severely it was thought, but by the time Dr Clarke arrived, Batchelor had died. The inquest revealed that it was not the fall that killed him, but "*ossification of the heart.*"

By late September it was reported that "...*Mr Marriott is making rapid progress with the work. The old red tile roof has been removed and a slate one put in its place. Internally, the woodwork of the roof, composed of deal and oak, is almost completed and other portions of the work are in a forward condition.*"

Despite the progress, it was not until Tuesday 18th July 1865, that the official re-opening took place. "*Flags, flowers and bunting meeting the eye in every direction.*" At 11 a.m., a service was held by the Bishop of Winchester, with the choir of St.Michael, Coventry, attending. Lunch was then provided in a tent for the "...*large and respectable company of ladies and gentlemen who sat down together.*" Lord Leigh presided, and on either side of him sat the Bishops of Worcester and Winchester. In the afternoon, the Bishop of Worcester held another service.

The whole of the old box-like pews had been removed and replaced with 800 open sittings. Carvings on the pulpit, stalls, communion rails etc., were by T H Kendall of Warwick and Leamington. A stained glass window, placed in the south chancel by Mr Holland of

Warwick, contained the arms of the Bishop Villiers, Durham and Carlisle, with appropriate mitres, an ornamental background, and monograms in the border. This was a substitute for the previously planned memorial chapel.

The renovation of St.Nicholas Church included the roof-tiles being replaced by slate, and the ground level on the northern side being lowered to stop the floor from becoming wet.

Much of the work still had to be paid for. The collection taken after the re-opening service was £105, taking the total to over £2,500, but the final cost was now estimated between £3,000 and £4,000. It was thought that the "...*deficiency will be made up with little difficulty.*"

The poor condition of much of the stonework of the town's première tourist attraction, the Castle, was also causing concern. In early 1867, work started on the repair of Leycester's buildings, and Mr Joyce, a Kenilworth builder, spent several months at work on Caesar's Tower. It had been decided by the Earl of Clarendon to renovate many parts of the Castle over a period of time at a cost of thousands of pounds. Unusually large numbers of visitors were reported at times during the year, perhaps boosted by those curious to see the work in progress. The Castle was open every day, except Sundays, from 8.00 a.m. to 8.00 p.m. even during the winter. Admission was 3d for adults and 1d for children.

* * *

As the new National school was being built in Pepper Alley, the sale of the old was being considered. The most likely buyer was its part-time occupant, the Institute. Discussions were held in January 1860 with Edward Draper and an agreement was quickly reached. The need to raise the necessary funds resulted in four options: a) donations, b) 1,000 lots of 2s, c) penny subscription, and d) by circulating all known Institutes in the Kingdom. A building fund account book was started. With the children safely moved into their new building, the Institute bought the old for £350 in August 1860. Not surprisingly, the Reading Society, which for all of its fifteen years had been based in the old schoolroom, had by 1863 become obsolete. Its trustees were approached by representatives of the Institute with a view to an amalgamation, mainly so that the Institute could add several hundred books to its collection. The Reading Society was down to just three members, Bliss, Hicks and Robbins, but under its rules this needed to drop to two before its assets could be disposed of. The solution was simple, Robbins resigned allowing the merger to proceed. A public meeting was needed for the merger to be formally discussed and this was held at the Institute on Thursday 24th September. The motion was proposed and carried, the books became the property of the Institute and the Reading Society ceased to exist.

The now fallen gravestone of Walter and Caroline Parsons who were responsible for starting Kenilworth's first newspaper.

Caroline Parsons continued to publish the *Kenilworth Advertiser,* still just four pages and costing 1d, until the end of 1870. The new owner announced his arrival in the first edition of 1871; *"The public is respectfully informed that the business lately carried on under the style of Walter T. Parsons will in future be conducted by Charles R. Adams, Castle End."* This included both The Library and the copyright to the newspaper. Adams was a schoolmaster - he had taken on his father Richard's boys' school in Castle End, close to the Boot Inn. The school was in 1871 described as a "Gentleman's Boarding School" and was soon in the charge of Charles' wife and daughter. Charles (30), employed a man and a boy to help him run his newly-acquired business. Caroline Parsons lived for only another twenty months, dying after a short illness at the home of her brother-in-law, C Purdy. She was buried in the same grave as her husband Walter, and their two children who had died in infancy.

In October 1873, Adams took over the short-lived business of William Wilson in High Street. In addition to books and stationery, Wilson had sold music and pianos, and it seems that Adams quickly closed this shop but continued the music business in Castle End, hiring and selling pianos and selling the latest sheet music at half price. He also now operated a circulating library *"in connection with Musie's."*

In May 1874, Adams increased the size of his four page newspaper to accommodate more local news. The publishing day was changed from Thursday to Saturday but its price remained at 1d. He promised *"...a local story of a laughable nature..."* for juvenile readers had been written and would soon appear. He naturally advertised various aspects of his own business and during the autumn proclaimed he had *"...playing cards, and all the new card games for winter evenings..."* including Snap, Zoo, Cinderella, Bezique and Bijou in a selection of twelve at 6d each. Also for sale was a range of artists materials.

Soon after the death of his mother Caroline, Adams put the school, abutting the main road, up for sale in February 1875. It was described as having two acres of land at the rear and a large frontage suitable for building on. It was well suited to continue as a school as it had been for about fifty years. In total, the whole covered three acres. The plans were available from Charles who now also advertised himself as a surveyor. It was bought at auction for £950 by Mr Elworthy, the head gardener for Lord Leigh at Stoneleigh.

As with all newspapers, the *Kenilworth Advertiser* was not without its occasional errors: *"We are sorry that due to an oversight at the printers, the resolution passed at the Conservative meeting on Wednesday February 4th, appeared at the end of the Liberal meeting in our paper last week."*
(Kenilworth Advertiser, 12th February 1874)

*   *   *

The tannery in Castle End was founded in about 1800. It had a reputation for producing some of the best sole and strap leather on the market as well as "...all classes of leather suitable for modern requirements." It was ideally placed in the centre of a good hide and bark district, and had access to the established leather and boot-making centres at Walsall, Birmingham, Northampton and Leicester. It was capable of turning out over 800 hides a week.

The use of a steam-powered bark grinder was obviously beneficial, but in August 1848 it was to prove disastrous. At about midday on Thursday 10th, fire was seen to fall thirty yards from the chimney of the boiler house onto the straw thatch of the 130-ton bark-rick that had been collected that spring and piled up in a field at the rear of the tannery. A man called Gumley raised the alarm, and dozens of men from the tannery and around raced to the scene. There was a good supply of water to hand from the tan-pits and reservoirs, and with ladders placed against the rick, the flames were quickly being tackled. The fire was kept confined by the external drenching, but the interior could not be controlled and soon new fires were burning through. After an hour, two fire engines arrived from Warwick but the combined efforts were having little effect. It was decided to pull down and drag away any of the unburnt bark in an attempt to save some of the store and this took priority over fighting the fire, with everyone assisting. Fortunately, the weather was calm and the little wind there was blew away from the nearby buildings. At 10 p.m. the remaining rick, still some twenty feet high, was a mass of flames. A number of people received burns, two of them seriously. The fire engines remained at the scene all night, but the following morning there was still little sign of it dying down - it was expected to carry on burning for several days. Only a small portion of the rick, which was worth £450, was saved. All those that assisted were paid for their efforts, and all clothes, buckets, etc., damaged in the fire were replaced by the Drapers. Amongst those seen to be helping were Thomas Fraser - Churchwarden, Charles Bliss - Overseer; and Mr Roby the Superintendent of the Leamington Police, who had seen the fire from a passing train and interrupted his journey.

Despite this major conflagration, the most regularly occurring fires were those on farms. In 1856, a straw stack and 160 bags of wheat were destroyed at John Ward's Chase Farm by a fire that was started by children playing with Lucifer matches in the rick-yard. The estimated damage of £240 was paid in full by the Birmingham Fire Office, one of seven insurance companies that had agents in town, six of which specifically included the word "fire" in their title. Three years later a fire was started at a farm near Leek Wootton by a steam engine not being shut down properly. Then, in the summer of 1861, William Mander lost a barn and a considerable amount of valuable materials at Oaks Farm in a fire that was considered to be the work of an arsonist, but more was to come for him just a few months later. At about midnight on Saturday 12th October, four men were walking home from Castle Green to their homes near St.John's church when they saw an unusual light in the direction of Oaks Farm. Once they realised they were looking at a fire they hurried to the farm and awoke Mander and his family. With the alarm raised, soon the church bells were ringing and dozens of people rushed to the scene. On fire were two hay-ricks, one clover-rick, a pea-rick and two stacks of straw. Despite strenuous efforts, it was soon obvious these could not be saved and so attention was turned to the prevention of the fire spreading. Initially wetted blankets and rugs protected a bean-rick nearby, but it was soon decided to pull it to pieces and remove it to a safe distance. The farm buildings were doused copiously and sustained no damage. One of the four discoverers had gone to Woodcote to call Richard Hicks, brother-in-law to Mander, and he rode to Warwick for the fire engine. A delay ensued in arousing the inmates of the Warwick Arms where the horses for the engine had to be procured. Mr Bolton of the Kings Arms sent another messenger to Coventry and the fire engine of the Sun Office arrived at the same time as that from Warwick, two and a half hours after the alarm was first raised. Mr Elvins of the County Fire Office accompanied the Warwick engine. About an hour later, a second engine arrived from Coventry attended by the City's Volunteer Fire Brigade,

claiming it would have arrived earlier if they *"...had been able to procure more than two horses or better horses than those they were supplied with."* It appears to have been overlooked that Leamington not only possessed the most powerful engine in the district, but also had *"...unusual facilities for despatching an engine very quickly..."* and this engine, the fourth on the scene, finally arrived after the fire had been subdued. The only aid provided by Kenilworth, apart from manpower, was a solitary water-cart owned by Mr Draper that was in use before any of the engines had arrived, and was then used to great effect replenishing them with water.

Fires in ricks at Oaks Farm led to meetings intended to form a fire-brigade.

There was no doubt that both Oaks Farm fires were the work of an arsonist and indeed, there were *"...strong suspicions as to the author of this dreadful act and a reward is offered for his capture."* It was not unknown for disgruntled agricultural workers who had been dismissed to seek revenge on their former employers and as there was a specific suspect, this could have been such a case. The reward was quite substantial, being £50 from the County Fire Office and another £50 from Mander himself, but such was the sympathy for him that a dozen or more, including William Butler, Charles Bliss, Edward and Charles Draper, William and Samuel Boddington, and Walter Congreve, collectively vowed to pay his part of the reward. The damage done was estimated at £325 and the insurance payout included £14 paid to *"all parties assisting at the fire."*

Just three days after the fire, the Roads Committee met in the Vestry and, not surprisingly, it was unanimously agreed that it was "...desirable that a fire engine should be kept at Kenilworth..." and a committee was appointed to carry out the resolution. Those involved were Mander himself, Edward and Charles Draper, Samuel and William Boddington, Charles Bliss, Samuel Burbery, William Poole, William Butler and Spencer, Bolton, Ward, Isaac, Newbury and Arnold, and just two days later they passed three resolutions. The first was for the formation of the "Kenilworth Association for the Preservation of Property from Fire" and that an engine and other property required for its purposes were vested in Trustees on behalf of the subscribers. The second was the recommendation of the formation of the "Kenilworth Volunteer Fire Brigade", and the third was the purchase of an engine and equipment as soon as funds could be raised. Charles

Bliss, Charles Draper, Samuel Boddington and Mr Bolton were appointed as a sub-committee to collect subscriptions and to ascertain the likely costs involved, including finding a suitable location to keep the engine. Within a week, there was already a list of over thirty volunteers to form a brigade.

At a meeting of the fire brigade committee on 1st November, it was reported that the Warwick Fire Office had contributed £25 towards the fire engine fund, but that the Earl of Clarendon had not yet replied to an earlier communication, presumably a request for a donation. Mr Beaumont, the Fire Office's secretary, also mentioned that he could probably find a suitable second-hand engine in London.

Despite all this early effort and optimism, nothing of any substance seems to have been achieved, and almost a year later, the inevitable happened. On the second Sunday in October 1862, at about 10.15 p.m., a horseman galloped into Warwick with news of another farm fire in Kenilworth, this time at Mr Reynold's Dunspit Farm. At once Mr Elvins despatched the County engine, horsed again by Mr Baldwin of the Warwick Arms, and it was the first to arrive on the scene. It was quickly followed by the Sun and Rifle Brigade engines from Coventry, and the Leamington engine accompanied by Mr Lund the Police Superintendent. Despite this faster response, a wheat-rick and hay-rick were destroyed and it was not until 4.30 a.m. that the fire was finally extinguished. Once more arson was suspected, and the damage this time was estimated at up to £200. The property was insured at the Birmingham Fire Office.

A month later, on 25th November 1862, a ratepayers meeting was called to "...take into consideration the desirableness of establishing a Fire Engine in Kenilworth." The meeting was called by William Boddington and Charles Bliss in their capacity as churchwardens. The minutes of the various meetings of the Fire Brigade Committee were read and Joseph H Burbery reported that donations recently received included £20 from Lord Clarendon, £10 from Lord Leigh, and a number of smaller amounts, which produced a total of £80 when added to the earlier offerings of £38. Having established that there were now sufficient funds to proceed, it was proposed and carried unanimously that, once obtained on behalf of the Parish, the engine and appliances were to be vested in the hands of five trustees, two of whom should always be the churchwardens. Charles Bliss, Henry Street and Joseph H Burbery were selected to serve alongside churchwardens Boddington and Draper.

The local press was not impressed with the speed of developments: *"Procrastination amongst those whose duty it is to provide a Fire Engine seems to have been the order of the day. There would be no difficulty in forming an efficient fire brigade - a great desideratum - from the ranks of the volunteers, who being accustomed to act upon the word of command would work steadily together. The plan has already been tried, and proved successful in many towns; the volunteers being found to be more fitted for the work than the generality of the men who compose fire brigades. The confusion which is always conspicuous amongst untrained men is avoided in the case of volunteer brigades, who, as long as they are of any service, use their utmost endeavours to save property and to subjugate the devouring element."*

Finally, in June 1863, twenty months after the first Vestry meeting: *"We are glad to be able to inform our readers that at last a fire engine, in every way adapted to the wants of the Parish, has been provided, and is lodged in a place which has been prepared for it on the Abbey-hill. There is, however, something more to be done before the engine can prove to be of any material service, and that is to get a thorough good fire brigade. There are many young men in Kenilworth who, after a little training under an experienced "chief", would be able to work the engine in such a manner as to make it do good service in time of need. We therefore hope that no time will be lost in securing the services of those who may be relied upon to do their duty, should a fire at any time break out."* Surgeon Charles Draper, in his late forties, was voted to the position of brigade Captain. Premises were sought to house the manual-pump engine, and outbuildings belonging to Sarah Ryley on (Upper) Rosemary Hill, between the two large houses occupied by Phillip Carmouls and Dora Hill, were chosen, for which she was paid a rent of about £3 annually. Sarah Ryley owned a number of properties in town, including several in High Street where she, and brigade Captain Draper, lived.

The fire engine-house was on (Upper) Rosemary Hill in an outbuilding, belonging to Sarah Ryley, between two large houses.

Although set up initially with donations and operated by the Trustees, the continuing financing of the volunteer brigade had to be taken up by the town. At the Vestry meeting in March 1864 it was proposed and carried that the engine and brigade should be a burden upon the Highway rate.

The first annual dinner in July 1864 was always likely to be a grand affair and the brigade did not disappoint - parading through town in full uniform with the engine gaily decorated with flowers and with the Temperance Drum and Fife Band in front. The Coventry Volunteer Brigade also made a spectacular appearance with their decorated engine drawn by four horses. Seventy sat down for a meal at which Captain Draper took the chair.

The earliest account of the brigade in action was published in January 1866. A young boy foddering the horses in an outhouse at Joseph H Burbery's Chase Farm carelessly upset his lantern and set fire to the hay. Burbery sent for the fire brigade but it was now that the problems began. No horses could be found to pull the engine and so the brigade members decided to pull it themselves, an astonishing effort considering the state of the roads and the hills negotiated. The brigade must have been exasperated upon arrival at the farm to discover the flames had already been extinguished. It is not known if Burbery supplied horses for the return trip or whether the brigade was then faced with a repeat of their exertions! George Dempster at the Kings Arms and John Phillips at the Bowling Green Inn, just yards from the engine-house, later volunteered to have horses available for the engine and the two became staunch supporters of the brigade.

By the summer of 1867, the brigade had a new Captain, it was Dr Daniel Wynter, the second surgeon to hold the prestigious position. Captain Wynter took the chair at the brigade's 1868 annual dinner held at the Kings Arms. The Reverend William Bickmore announced that *"...the expenses of cleaning and repairing the engine had heretobefore been defrayed by the highway rates but in consequence of the auditor having disallowed this item it was thrown back on the members of the brigade..."* but now an Act of Parliament allowed costs to be taken against the poor rate. Bickmore had made a collection to defray current costs so that the brigade should *"...not pay a single sixpence...and should be kept clear of all expense save for their private delectation and amusements."* In his speech, Captain Wynter stated: *"When the Kenilworth brigade was established, it was at first of course, ignorant of their drill, but from the kind assistance received from (the Coventry brigade) must be attributed to their success and present position."*

At the July Vestry meeting, it was formally agreed to take the expenses from the poor rate, although typically it took a year to be implemented. The same meeting saw permission given for the purchase of *"...two jumping sheets, suction hose, tank, drag, lamp and other adjuncts..."* and two "extincturs." On 1st April 1869, a meeting was called specifically to deal with the brigade as it had been realised that the resolutions of the previous year were not sufficient under the Act. In addition, despite the acquisition of the listed equipment, no monies had been spent from the rates. The Trustees now had a bill from Merryweather's for £26 for which they had funds of only £11 2s 4d. The meeting was deferred for three weeks and when it resumed the Trustees suggested "selling" the brigade to the town for the amount that it was currently in debt, £14 17s 8d, and this was adopted.

The formal takeover of the brigade by the town took place at a special vestry meeting on Tuesday 20th May 1869, and remarkably that night, or possibly the following one, there was a fire in one of the bedrooms at the Kings Arms. Henry Bursell and his employees managed to put the flames out before the brigade arrived, but there was much damage to the furniture in the room.

From the beginning, the brigade had been under the watchful eye of the Coventry volunteer brigade, under the command of Captain Lovett, to whom they were indebted *"...for the kind manner in which they came forward when they were first established and drilled them, and also for the hints they had given them."* Lovett himself was *"...at all times ready to assist them in any way..."* and at the Kenilworth Brigade's annual dinner

in 1869, he declared that his own brigade *"...is so mixed up with the Kenilworth that he as Captain hardly knew one from the other, in fact, he took as much interest in the latter as he did his own."* It is fortunate that Kenilworth had not sought help from the Leamington brigade; after a fire at the house of one of its leading patrons, at which the brigade did more damage than the fire, the *Leamington Courier* said of its own volunteers *"...the town is prone to boast of its fire brigade, but without a practise drill of engines, ladders and men, they are worse than useless."* The Kenilworth brigade were, in comparison, much better drilled but perhaps not so well equipped; they did not even have boots and Mr Nicks (Hicks?) started a fund by doubling his own annual subscription.

At the annual brigade dinner in August 1870, it was remarked how few of the gentry turned up, and only one farmer - not surprisingly William Mander! *"The inhabitants of Kenilworth are not treating (the brigade volunteers) with the respect they merit, and the people of Kenilworth need a thorough good fire before they appreciate their services."*

Much of the brigade's funds did not come from the rates. By 1871 honorary members subscriptions totalled just £6 14s for the year with fines paid for non-attendance at drill amounting to 14s 6d. Expenditure of £2 17s 6d suggested a lack of investment in equipment from these funds, it was more likely to be for the events such as the annual dinner. Captain Wynter was, as expected, re-elected for a fifth year and the four lieutenants, Heritage, Hailstone, Berry and Overton retained their positions, as did treasurer Henry Street and secretary Mr Jackson. There were though two or three vacancies in the brigade itself.

*   *   *

At the Institute's general meeting held on 22nd November 1870, it was proposed to enlarge the reading room and to alter the entrance to the building. In connection with this its neighbours were approached, Mr Pratt to the north and Mr Heatley who was "contiguous", with a view to purchasing their property, but both these declined to agree terms, and the plans were held in abeyance.

With H E Barton in the chair, Secretary Dr Thomas Bourne read the Institute's 1871 annual report. There had been an upturn in the Institute's finances during the year, with the 1870 deficit of £2 17s becoming a profit of £14 9s. The major difference was an increase in subscriptions, although membership stood at just 81. There had been a minor revolt amongst weekly members with a few refusing to pay the increased subscription of $1\frac{1}{2}$d a week, asking the librarian to accept the old cost of 1d or they would leave, as some did. In addition, the takings from the annual concert had continued to decline until 1870s' was run at a loss, and so no concert was arranged for 1871. In contrast, the four penny-readings brought in £7 5s against £2 12s the previous year.

The Institute was restricted by its surroundings and had two options, and Charles Adams was involved in both. One was to sell the premises for £400 and re-locate and Adams said that he knew someone who was interested; the second was alternative alterations to the existing buildings which Adams had drawn up, and it was these that it was decided to proceed with. Adams' plan was to build a porch on the north end of the west front and a 4ft wide arcade along the whole length of the west side. The main building would be lengthened by 8ft at the southern end and the existing reading room extended over the space now gained. The cost was estimated at £350, but once more nothing came of the plans.

Towards the end of 1874, the Institute was falling into disarray. Takings were well down and an attempt to re-introduce entertainments failed due to the school manager not allowing the use of a school room; the library was out of order and needed to be re-arranged, volumes were missing, and no new books had recently been added. The £5 that was available was spent on a new bagatelle table. An unsuccessful application had been made to Reverend Joseph Barker for a plot of land in his new road (Southbank Road) for the Institute to build its own new premises. The number of people who actually came and read the newspapers, periodicals and large amount of available literature was described as *"few."* It was agreed that the current committee was as good as any it had had but that the whole Institute movement was now *"a retrograde one."* With an income of around £40 a year it was never likely to be able to fulfil its targets and there were already suggestions that it should be replaced by, or merged with, a free library.

The Institute accounts for the year ending 22nd October 1875 show that it was down to just 58 subscribers, and no "visitors"; there was still a balance in hand of £6 for the year.

*   *   *

In 1848, George Summers had a brick, tile, drainage tile and pipe works at Oaks Farm and made tiles and pipes by *"...Swain's registered machine...".* George Summers died age 38 in 1857. When William Mander died in 1858, Oaks Farm passed to his son, also William - it was three years after this that the Oaks Farm fires were started. At this time, the brick-yard and its equipment were listed, the presence of *"...faggots of firewood..."* suggesting a recent or intended firing. In 1861 Joseph Burgess, who ten years earlier was a brick maker employing four men at The Chase, was at the Bulkington brick-yard. He was still there, with his son Thomas, in 1871. In 1873, 5 acres of oats were sold at Bulkington brick-yard for £2 2s 6d.

In about 1865, William Mander's brother Edward, seven years his junior and in his mid-30s, set himself up as a wine and spirit merchant in one of Mrs Pope's houses alongside Anstey's yard; William Anstey was on one side of the yard entrance and Mander on the other. He advertised for sale "Kinhan's LL, the very cream of Irish Whiskey." In 1871, Mander employed his 50 year-old sister Mary as housekeeper.

In 1851 James Arnold employed 3 men at the Leamington Road brickworks, one of whom was Thomas Arnold, possibly his son. Ten years later, Arnold (now 72), employed two men and two boys. By 1866, it seems that James had died and the business of brick and

tile making was in Thomas's name.

In 1878, under the will of a Miss White, Camden House (formerly the Horse and Jockey Inn) and St.John's Lodge, came up for auction, or "public competition" as it was called. In close proximity to this, a brick-yard was also for sale and this would have been the former Arnold works fronting the Leamington Road. It was said that it could be *"...most profitably worked for many years in the manufacture of bricks of the finest quality..."* and all the machinery and shedding on the site was included in the sale. It was also suitable for building a country residence and a lodge was already under construction. There is no record of the works being in use after this date.

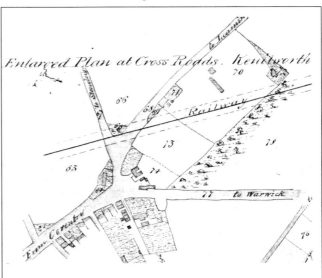

The junction of the roads to Coventry, Leamington and Warwick. The Arnold brickworks was in field 70, and Camden House, the former Horse and Jockey, in field 74.
(Warwick County Records Office QS111/114)

In 1851, Edward Kimberley was a Brickmaker Master living in Castle End and employing four men, but at which works remains a mystery. By 1861, he was a brick and tile maker living in New Street, and later Coventry Road. At this time, and not far away, Tentor's Close and Three Corner Field were being used for clay extraction and the nearby New Inn was owned by Thomas Arnold, possibly James Arnold's brother, who was also listed as a brickmaker. He died in 1856 and the New Inn, and his other property in Albion Street and New Row, were sold.

Little is known of the early days of the brickworks at Crackley and it is possible that either Arnold or Kimberley, most likely the latter, was in operation there. It appears to have been an advanced works, as in 1868 the *"steam clay machine"* at the brickworks merited interest even whilst it was out of order; when coal merchant George Godfrey paid a visit on business, his curiosity got the better of him and whilst inspecting the lifeless apparatus, he became wedged between the main shaft and its framework. He sustained severe bruising.

Whilst living at Crackley Cottage in 1871, Kimberley employed two men and two boys at his works. In 1874, Kimberley is recorded for the last time as having his own business and, possibly not coincidentally, by the end of the year builder Edward Smith for the first time advertised himself as a brick and tile maker.

Edward Smith (born 11th July 1827), was the son of Clinton Lane carpenter Joseph. By 1866, Edward was established as a builder with premises fronting onto School Lane on the corner with Rosemary Hill. Originally named Rosemary Lodge, Edward and his wife Rebecca changed the name of their home to Kenilworth House, and in it she opened a millinery establishment, selling "...straw and fancy hats, French and English gloves, feathers, flowers, falls and velveteen jackets. Also a choice assortment of Ladies pelerines and corsets, winsey skirts...". In addition to his brickworks, Edward was extracting stone from the nearby quarry off Love Lane, and his son, Joseph Lawrence (born 1853) was his assistant.

In 1851 James Manton (56), was employing two men plus Jenny Batchelor as a maid at his Whitemoor brickworks. The two men are likely to have been James Batchelor (51) and William Batchelor (22) listed as brick-makers at Tanhouse Lane.

Manton took out a mortgage of £600 on the property in 1853 but within three years he had to sell up to pay off his debts, including £60 to Henry Bursell. There followed a succession of owners tied in with mortgages and several bankruptcies over a period of about ten years. The brickworks became occupied by Henry Hicks who in 1861 employed four men and three boys. James Batchelor and his son were still brick-makers living at Whitemoor and it is likely that these were two of them, particularly as they were now related by marriage to its earlier occupier, Manton. Manton's own son Charles, just 10, was a brickmaker's assistant. The works had two large kilns and a drying shed, together with four substantially-built cottages with washhouse and other conveniences. The clay was of excellent quality and the kilns were constructed to burn 34,000 bricks each. It was let at the yearly rental of £50 with a royalty of 2s per thousand upon all bricks made above 200,000. Hicks, only 26 and the son of Richard Hicks, was also farming 77 acres at New Woodcote, employing five, and running a coal merchant business employing another two.

In June 1863, the brickworks came up for sale: "All that valuable freehold brick-yard situate at the Whitemoors Kenilworth, in the occupation of Henry Hicks and his sub-tenants, containing 3 acres 2r or thereabouts. An extensive business is being carried on upon the premises there being a great demand for bricks in the locality." Despite being in the middle of proceedings against him, William Poole was involved in the sale. A year later the property was conveyed to Henry Street and was then described as "Four messuages,

outbuildings and gardens, all that ground lately occupied as a brick-yard with Kilns etc..." and still occupied by Henry Hicks. As Street paid only £300, against the £600 mortgage Manton took out, it is possible that it was no longer a going concern.

Walter John Lockhart, originally from Dunstable, established himself as a coal merchant in Clarendon Street in 1865, the same year he married Julia Piggot in Luton. To coal he soon added lime, salt, stone and bricks - his father had a long-established similar business in his home town. His merchandising was based at the station where he had an office, built before 1870, just outside the station entrance on 100 sq yds of land owned by the Bursells and rented by Lockhart for £5 per annum. In 1871, Lockhart was employing four men, and had also established himself as an agent, for both the Leamington Priors Bank and London and North Western Railway, in The Square. The Lockharts had no children, but in 1871 they were involved, with others, in providing a tea for 200 schoolchildren.

On 2nd March 1872, Walter Lockhart took on a lease for land adjacent to the brickworks at Whitemoor, owned since the 1780s by successive members of the Hawkes family of Stoneleigh. Lockhart took the lease for four fields, three were pasture and the other had two brick kilns and hovels used as drying sheds, but it is not clear if Lockhart built these himself: they appear to be quite separate from those built on the adjacent non-Hawkes-owned land. He was allowed to take clay, loam and sand from the site, but only for the making of bricks, tiles and pots and not for re-sale. Being a dealer in coal, he was well placed for getting fuel for the works. The lease was for twenty years with an annual rent of £171 12s which included a royalty of £80 for the first 800,000 bricks; any extra incurred an additional payment of 2s per 1,000 bricks. To produce a million bricks an acre of a clayfield needed to be dug to a depth of about two feet. Lockhart could set up any buildings associated with the works at his own expense and also had to preserve the topsoil to put back after the pits had been filled in.

He soon set about building the town's second mechanised brickworks, using both wire cutting and pressing techniques and produced frogged and lettered bricks, inscribed simply "W J LOCKHART KENILWORTH" - the first to include the town's name.

Just a month after he signed his lease, Lockhart had plans drawn up for a railway siding into his works, and construction was completed that June. On Monday 13th July, Lockhart treated his workforce, and those who

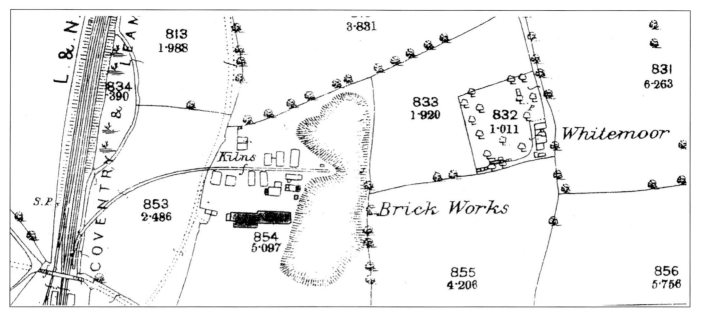

The brickworks at Whitemoor as it was when occupied by Walter Lockhart. The buildings next to the word Whitemoor, were those bought by Henry Street and described as "Four messuages...lately occupied as a brickyard" which had been occupied by Henry Hicks.

had been building the new siding, to a supper at the Rose and Crown. *"A capital repast was provided and the invited seemed heartily to appreciate the hospitality of their entertainer."* Lockhart's health was proposed and received, and a very convivial evening spent. The siding, however, was not brought into use until the Board of Trade inspector authorised it in August.

In the autumn of 1873, Walter Lockhart placed an advertisement in the *Kenilworth Advertiser: "Wanted at once, a man thoroughly conversant with the making and burning of bricks, to superintend the Whitemoor Brick-yard."* The response is not known, but by 1880 Walter's younger brother by ten years, Edgar, was the works foreman and living in Park Road.

In the summer of 1879, Lockhart was reported by the Inspector of Nuisances for the excessive smoke coming from the brickworks chimney. He was ordered to solve the problem by either better stoking or extending the chimney to take the smoke away; which solution he chose is not known. On May 2nd 1880, the landowner Richard Hawkes died and left the works to one of his three sons, Henry, who lived at Warwick New Road in Leamington.

The comb factory of Turner, Pace and Webb was the largest such establishment in the town, and the last stronghold of the industry. In 1851 they were employing 21 men, 2 women and 2 boys but its best days were behind it. In 1858 John Webb left the firm to become both a tax collector and involved with the gas company. Then in 1864 the owner of the premises, Mary Pope, died aged 90, and her property was put up for sale. It comprised the dwelling house she had occupied, the adjoining grocers shop in the occupation of Mr Anstey, and the rest of the site that was described as a *"...dwelling house and extensive range of Warehouses, now used as a comb manufactory; together with a large yard with buildings thereon and gardens at the rear thereof; the whole containing 3,300 sq yds of thereabouts."*

The firm continued in the name of Turner and

Pace but in about 1870 Pace died, his wife Elizabeth (63) continuing to live at Anstey's yard. By now it was only a small affair and William Turner (74) was employing just two men. He died at his home, Grove Cottage, Castle Terrace, aged 84 in 1880. Anstey's Yard for a while became an accepted address, cordwainer Thomas Buswell was there as was agricultural labourer Henry Overton who took in lodgers.

In 1851, tannery proprietors Robert Watts Draper (43), and Henry Draper (36), both lived at Rosemary Hill and they employed 38 people, but later in the year Robert, a long-time resident, left town. At a private function at the Kings Arms he was presented with a silver salver worth £40. Henry was now sole proprietor.

The acquisition of oak bark was obviously paramount to the operation. In the summers of both 1856 and 1859 the company advertised that one of its representatives, either Henry Draper or his clerk, would be at the Warwick Arms each Saturday between 2 and 3 p.m. to treat all those who could supply bark.

In 1858, a new chimney was erected at the tannery by H Price of Coventry. It reached a height of 222ft and had a large base with a gradual reduction of diameter relative to its height. It was noted for its elegant proportions.

By 1862, Henry Draper was in financial difficulties and had a debt of £14,000 to the bank Greenway, Smith and Greenway of Warwick. Kelynge Greenway was involved in liquidating Draper's affairs and in doing so introduced to the tannery his own cousin, Phillip Newman, a schoolmaster with no knowledge of tanning, as a partner. Newman put in £1,800 of his own and Kelynge Greenway invested £26,000, some of which he borrowed from his sisters. The new partnership, Draper and Newman, lasted five years but was dissolved in 1867 when Draper (51) retired. He did not receive a payment. Newman *"...received a salary and acted as traveller..."* and was the proprietor although in reality the business belonged to Greenway. Also installed in the firm during this time was William Clarke, already working for one of the Greenways, who was sent to the tannery as book-keeper (replacing the clerk and cashier William Sutton) to *"...represent the whole family who had lent money to Mr Newman."* William Clarke was the man who drew all the cheques and made all the financial arrangements of the company, but only *"partially"* received his instructions from Newman; many discussions were had directly with Greenway when Newman was not present, purely to *"safeguard family affairs."*

At the dissolution of the Draper-Newman partnership, the whole premises were valued and described. Just to the left of the main gateway in Castle End was the men's dinner room - actually part of Mr Draper's house. There were also two offices and a w.c. nearby. Near the entrance was a large shed with a slated roof, supported by pillars, covering eighteen wooden pits and eight brick pits. The brick pits were four yards by five yards and six feet deep. More pits were in a shed with iron pillars supporting a corrugated iron roof, and alongside this was a former blacksmith's shop now used as a storeroom. The lower yard had twenty brick-built pits with a corrugated iron roof supported on pillars, but this roof had many broken windows. Other pits were described as *"...covered with corrugated iron."* The bark-yard at the rear had an entrance leading onto Clarendon Street, and this rear yard seems to have been the location for another fourteen pits, a covered reservoir, a lime store with three lime pits, an open shed and other storerooms. The largest building was the three-stories-high drying shed which also housed the "striking and rolling" rooms and yet more pits. Another yard to the south had gates leading to one of Edward Draper's fields. There was a two-storey shed with no use recorded. Another small yard had five further lime pits. The boiler shed housed two boilers - these fed a 12hp horizontal engine, apparently about twelve years old, and a smaller 8hp engine apparently in use for about thirty years. A barn was used for preparing and feeding the bark to the mills. Across Castle End was a three-acre field, part used as a garden, in which a reservoir was situated.

The whole of the tannery was valued at £4,436; Mr Draper's house and the offices at £900 and the three acre field across the road with right of easement to the use of the reservoir £500. Alongside the tan-yard entrance was a house, valued at £280, divided into three for the use of tan-yard workers, the occupants then being Brown, Sheldon and Faxon. Alongside this was

another house, with stables and outbuildings, occupied by Simms, Moss and Paxton, but it is not clear if this was also for the exclusive use of tannery workers. Adjacent to the tan-yard, and fronting onto Station Road, was a piece of garden ground totalling 1,700 sq yds. The total value of all these properties was estimated to be £6,776.

The new accountant, William Clarke, suffered the tragedy of his wife Martha (nee Oakley) dying in 1870 aged 39. He was left with a family of George (11), Charles (8), Hubert Edward (6) and Laura (3). His sister-in-law, Mary Oakley (21), came to help with the children, and at this time he also employed two domestic servants, Elizabeth Underhill and Elizabeth Rainbow.

In 1873, the Tannery workforce formed a branch of the London and Liverpool Tannery Union. Their produce was displayed at exhibitions and at the 1873 Northampton Leather exhibition, Phillip Newman won a medal for *"...best foreign butt - a Buenos Ayres butt of extraordinary quality."*

On Christmas Eve 1874, George Dencer, aged 46, a long serving and much-respected employee, was helping a boy operate a small leather-rolling machine when Dencer's hand was drawn under the roller and badly crushed. Joseph Faxon, who was working nearby, heard his scream and threw off the driving strap to stop the machine, but it took some time for the roller to be prised from the bed to free his hand. All the fingers and part of the hand were amputated but mortification set in. He had seemed well on the way to recovery but, despite a later amputation of the arm, he died on 29th December. His funeral took place at St.John's with more than ninety men from the tannery present. No one could understand how he came to have such an accident with machinery he was so familiar with, nor could they have expected such an accident to have such a sad consequence.

The water system for the mill at Mill End began alongside the town bridge, where a plate with nine holes fed the mill-race which, about half-way to Washbrook, turned and ran alongside Pepper Alley (School Lane). At Washbrook, the bridge over the mill-race was known as Woodmill Bridge, that over the brook as Allibone or Odiborne bridge; between the two was a sluice system. From here, the mill-race continued to the mill and the water returned to the brook via an underground channel. By 1847, Francis Robbins (27) had added steam power to waterpower. By 1854 he had acquired the windmill

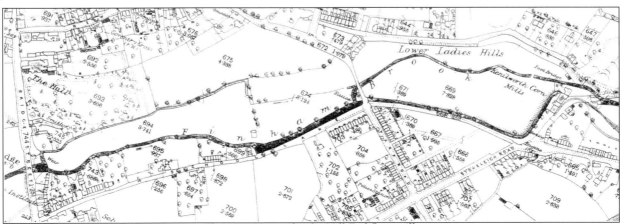

The water system for the Mill End flour mill.

on Tainters Hill, and converted it to steam. In 1861 he employed only four men, a drop of three in ten years. In May 1862, Francis Robbins was declared bankrupt with a deficiency of over £3,000, and at about this time he began to concentrate on farming and the mills were taken on by his brother Richard, initially on his own, but within a few years in partnership with John Powers.

One Mill End family involved with the mill started their own business. Miller William Green and his wife Sarah had nine children. The eldest, Helen (b.1823), was just twelve years younger than her mother - perhaps William had re-married. Other children were William jnr (b.1829) and Emma (b.1836). Another son, Thomas (b.1850) died aged 10 on 11th August 1860. By 1851 William jnr was working with his father at the mill but in 1854, the heirs of Charles Chaplain sold some nearby premises to William snr for £180, and he started selling beer there, probably around 1861. Carpenter Thomas Johnson of Mill End, bought the beerhouse two years later for the same price and it is probable the name the Cottage Inn first appeared at this time. Within three or four years, William Green jnr took over the license and his father was once again working at the mill.

In 1871, William Green jnr (41) was head of the house, but both he and his father William snr (68) were recorded as beerhouse keeper and engine driver at the mill; it seems their jobs were interchangeable. Sarah was now 58 and two of her daughters, Helen (47) and Emma (33), were a dressmaker and barmaid respectively.

Miller William Green began selling beer at what became the Cottage Inn.

In June 1865, Robbins and Powers treated their entire workforce from their three mills at Kenilworth, Stoneleigh and Coventry, to a day's entertainment and fun at Stoneleigh Deer Park. The party of over 170, including friends, met at the Stoneleigh mill at 11.00 a.m. and travelled to the park where they played skittles, quoits and cricket. Lunch was provided in a spacious tent after which Mr Robbins addressed the workers in *"very affectionate terms."* A further selection of rustic games was followed by tea, before the gathering broke up at 9.30.

No doubt one of those taking advantage of his employers hospitality was 24-year-old waggoner Joseph Hobbs who had worked at Mill End for about two years. He was responsible for delivering many thousands of sacks of flour a year, and simultaneously collecting empties, paying 1d a sack, which he recorded in his disbursements book along with any tolls and replacement horseshoes that he had to pay for. Hobbs himself could not write and so family members or friends filled in the book for him. These expenses he then claimed back from mill manager Richard Limbrick. Hobbs was only allowed to pay out sack allowance at two customers, the Workhouse in Warwick and the Lunatic Asylum at Hatton, which took about eight sacks of flour a week. He duly made entries in his book and was paid back by Limbrick, until it was discovered that Asylum rules forbade anyone there to accept any monies. Hobbs was charged with fraudulently obtaining from his employer the sum of 1s 10d, but other offences totalling over £1 were listed. Limbrick claimed Hobbs was a good man and that the charges had been *"got up"* by Robbins and the prosecutor Haymes because they were both members of the Association for the Prosecution of Felons. The Asylum's baker claimed that Hobbs had never paid him a single penny, and Hobbs agreed, saying he had in fact given the money to a man named Voss, the baker's assistant and a patient at the asylum. When the case was heard, there were long discussions deciding if Voss should be brought to court or if the court should adjourn to the asylum, and whether Voss could even be proved to be a reliable witness. It turned out that seven years previously, Voss had been charged with murdering his own daughter but on grounds of insanity he never stood trial. He was eventually cleared to testify against Hobbs, subsequently assuring the court that Hobbs was the most generous man he had ever met, often giving him sixpence or a shilling to buy tobacco, and he assumed that since he was not allowed any money that it was simply a succession of gifts. Hobbs was defended by Honorable E Leigh who argued that Limbrick had paid the money willingly and if Hobbs had not passed it on it was only due to Asylum rules. It was dishonest, but fell outside the Act of Parliament under which the case was brought. The court was ordered to return a verdict of not guilty, Hobbs was acquitted and fifteen years later, he was still working as a waggoner at the mill.

When John Boddington died in 1869, his two nephews benefited; Francis Robbins became custodian of Kenilworth Castle and Castle Farm, and Richard Robbins was left "...the water and steam flour mills including all machinery and fixtures." Two years after his uncle's death, Richard (43) was employing ten men and two boys in the mills, including Richard Limbrick, now described as a cashier and salesman. On 7th November 1874, the foreman at the mill was moving flour in a barrow on the second floor when he passed the trap door. He missed his footing and fell to the floor below sustaining severe head injuries.

Mill operators Robbins and Powers continued to treat their employees well: in July 1878, they took their entire workforce out on a trip to Manchester. In 1881, 8 men and 2 boys worked the two Kenilworth mills.

At the Cottage Inn, in early September 1875, William Green snr complained of feeling unwell and went upstairs to lie down, leaving the rest of the family busily brewing. Quite late in the day, one of his daughters went to check on him only to discover that he had died. He had been suffering for some time from asthma and other maladies.

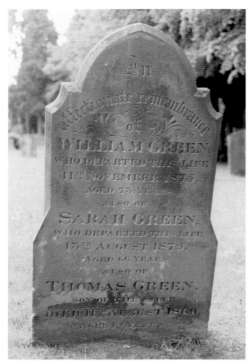

The gravestone of William Green, miller and founder of the Cottage Inn, and his wife Sarah.

*   *   *

In 1869, it was believed that just 50 gas-lamps would light the whole town, yet there were only 19 in place. The same argument about the way the rates were split was holding up progress; there were 341 houses in town above an annual rental of £6 and 560 small tenements, and it was finally suggested that those in tenements more than 50 yards from a lamp should not have to pay the rate for it. By the summer of 1869 all necessary agreements had been reached and work commenced, first in laying the pipes to a larger area of the town and then the necessary enlargement of the works itself.

Secretary and Treasurer of the Lighting Committee, John Webb, placed notices in newspapers stating that on the first Monday of each month the Lighting Inspectors would be in the upper room of the Institute to hear any complaints regarding the street lighting scheme. The July 1869 notice added that he would accept any tenders, by the first Monday of August, for all or part of the work of erecting the lamps and posts.

A Vestry meeting was held in September to make a final agreements as to the contributions to the lighting rate. The outcome was that the £150 needed to light more districts would be raised on housing not exceeding £6 rateable value, exempting small tenements altogether, and all houses more than 90 yards from a light. The rate had been fixed at 4½d in the £1 at an earlier meeting. On 7th September 1869, the whole of Castle End was lit for the first time. There had also been other progress; *"The lamplighter's ladder is becoming a thing of antiquity, and the nimble servitor is now burdened only with his rod and torch, containing an oil-light in a perforated tube, with a tap key attached."*

It was hoped that by the time of the next full moon, all 52 public lamps would be alight for the first time, but this was dependant upon expansion being carried out at the gas works. In May, the gas company had contacted W Cotton, engineer of the Warwick Gas Company who detailed the improvements necessary to cope with the increased demand. He was retained as a consulting engineer and allotted the contracts. The following month it was agreed to raise £1,000 by issuing 100 new shares at £10 each and offering them to existing shareholders at the rate of one new share per three existing shares. All but five shares were taken up by existing shareholders.

Whilst on some fronts all was progressing well, there were two problems. Firstly, the resident stoker, James Love, had to be warned about neglecting his work and turning up drunk. This coincided with millers Robbins and Powers complaining about a lack of gas pressure. More complaints were considered the following month and Love was sacked. He was replaced by Daniel Lawrence in whose hands, literally, the success or otherwise of the company rested, and for this he was paid 18s a week. The other problem was that the lighting committee was having difficulty collecting the rate and it wanted to come to a different arrangement with the company. The committee said that they would pay up until the end of December 1869 and wait for the outcome of a Parish meeting. This problem was overcome the second week in of the new-year and it was probably then that all of the extended lighting system was lit for the first time. The lighting now covered the main road from St.John's church to the Ladye's Hills, Clarendon Street, Albion Street, Oddibourne Bridge, High Street, Castle Hill and Castle Terrace. *"Every inhabitant must feel thankful that the hours of darkness will now be safely penetratable, who has occasion to be abroad at night for business or pleasure, at a private or public entertainment." "We congratulate the promoters of this great public work, and do apprehend that any who doubtfully consented will have cause to grumble, but will one and all in future vote for anything that is wanted to make perfect, but for nothing that is calculated to hinder, whatever tends to promote health, safety and comfort."*

Restructuring of the works continued until the summer of 1871. A small amount of land had to be obtained from the railway company, J H Clark built a new tank and boundary walls for £301, J and S Roberts installed mains, sockets and pipes for £70, and R Dempster installed the a gasholder for £279.

The summer also saw the end of an era for the company with its chairman from its inception in 1853, William Boddington, standing down but remaining a Director. Edward Draper took his place. The company was very sound and a dividend of 6% was announced at the same meeting.

In 1869, Henry Street had made it known that he intended to install a railway siding to his works, but such were the concerns of the locals that a Parish meeting was organised in November that year. The plan was changed to avoid crossing Mill End on the level and so the siding entered the works from the Common side - raised on piers to cross the brook - and giving a steep decline into the yard. One of the piers was partly across the pathway that went under the main railway bridge, bringing an observation that it was "ugly and awkward."

A new building was built alongside the siding to use as a despatch and delivery shed.

The siding was built by the railway company, but at Street's expense who claimed "...*the parish will be more profited by its use than myself, for I don't think it will ever pay me interest on the outlay.*" The siding extended to the nearby mill. Just before Christmas 1869, Street's neighbours, the Kenilworth Gaslight and Coke Company, received a suggestion from him that their coal could be unloaded in his yard instead of at the station. As the gas company's output was rapidly expanding, any savings or improved convenience was welcome. An agreement was reached whereby Street received 1s for each truck that was received in his yard, plus another 9d if his employees unloaded it and delivered its contents to the gas company. The probable contributory effect of the new arrangements can be seen in the gas company's accounts - the year up to July 1870, £328 of coal cost the company £50 in carriage, but by 1873, £469 of coal cost just £35 in carriage.

Across the brook, Street used his plantation for storing old machinery and his carts, and the edge of the Common for wool drying, for which he paid the tenant, Mr Roberts. In 1871, the business was flourishing enough for Street to extend his works and he chose to do so on his plantation on the northern side of the brook. In addition, drying sheds were built under the railway arches after an agreement was made with the railway company. He took the opportunity to improve the Common pathway that ran past the new buildings and under the railway, levelling the "...*mass of ruts and obstacles...*" as well as laying down "...*a very large quantity of turf...and herbage...*" to improve the general appearance of the area. There were concerns that Street was encroaching upon common land, but it was easy to prove that all the development was taking place on his, or the railway company's, property. In addition, Clarendon's agent, Humbert, had been involved with the alterations to the pathway. Despite this, nearly three years later Street was threatened with legal action for encroaching upon the Common, but Humbert wrote a letter confirming all was in order.

The building of Street's siding and its use by the gas company was quickly seized upon by Reverend Edward Knowles. In 1870, he wrote to the gas company suggesting that "...*a reduction in freight charges...will bring an increase in profits...*" and these would be further boosted by the building of the extra or improved retorts. This, he then suggested, should produce a decrease in charges. Accompanying his letter was a petition, "...*not for our benefit but for that of our neighbours...*" signed by many industrialists involved with the brickworks, tannery and fellmongers, clergy and other leading citizens, asking for a reduction from 6s to 5s per 1,000 cu ft. The reply from Secretary William Poole claimed the gas company were "*most desirous*" of reducing the price but explained that they had a duty to shareholders and suggested that the current price compared favourably with other similar companies. He also stated the obvious in saying that the company was currently outlaying a quarter of its capital in providing the town with lighting, but he hoped that a reduction could one day be made.

In February 1871, a meeting between the Lighting Committee and the gas company failed to give an expected reduction in the cost of street lighting, but it was agreed that savings could be made by reducing the brightness during full moons when less light was needed. The Reverend Edward Knowles was now part of a movement to have St.Nicholas church lit with gas, at a cost of £70, so that evening services could be held on Sundays. This was seen in some quarters as an unnecessary extra service and implied a "*spirit of rivalry*" with St.John's where such services were already held.

By 1874, the three original gas retorts had been increased to eight. William Poole was Secretary, John Webb Manager, Daniel Lawrence Working Manager, and the office was in New Street near the Post Office.

In January 1872, heavy rain again caused the brook to swell and Mill End was once more the worst affected. Early in the day a young girl, Caroline Simmonds, fell off a plank placed across the brook near the mill and was swept away, only to be rescued at Street's works. Later Thomas Jeffs, employed by Coventry coal dealer Benjamin Causen, decided to take the shortcut across the Common ford to the gas works to pick up a load of coke. The stream "...*took down the horse and immersed the man...*" but luckily the struggling horse kicked Jeffs towards the bank and he survived relatively unharmed. The horse drowned. Just before Christmas the same year, the heavy rains returned. "*Water never known so high by the oldest inhabitant.*" "*The lower part of Messrs. Robbins and Powers mill was flooded, and at Mr Streets works operations were suspended from a like cause.*"

The ford at Mill End on the road to Coventry, was the scene of several accidents.

Henry Street's wife Sofia died on 30th January 1873, aged 49, and just six months later, Street entertained his workforce, their wives and a few chosen friends, totalling upwards of 60 people, at the works. He provided a *"capital spread"*, his health was drunk and songs and music continued until dusk.

His successful business enabled Street to buy property. At a sale at the Kings Arms at the end of July 1876, Lot 1 was Crew farm which *"...afforded a capital site for a residence."* The buildings and 68 acres of land were knocked down to Street for £3,890. The same week saw a "Perpetual injunction" issued against Street from the claims of Lord Leigh, restraining him or any of his workmen from discharging from the works any *"...solid refuse or any liquid refuse or water..."* which was below the standard set by the rivers pollution committee. Street was not however liable for anything which might be discharged into the stream through the iron pipe on the south side of his works. The stringent standard included *"...2 parts of organic carbon or 0.3 parts weight of organic nitrogen in 100,000 of liquid."* To give Street time to comply, the injunction was suspended until May 1877.

Henry's nephew by marriage, Dathan Brown, was responsible for the Mill End works from the mid-1860s: in 1869, Henry Street appealed against the rate assessment for the skinworks, coal wharf and siding, but as the works were by then occupied by Brown the rate was simply divided. The siding by now extended to the mill and Robbins and Powers also appealed against their rate for the siding. In about 1875, Brown took over Samuel Burbery's tannery in West Street, Warwick, and ran it as a fellmongery. On 31st May 1880, he suffered an unfortunate accident. He was working with Joseph Lapworth on the mangle, a pair of steam-driven rollers used to squeeze water out of washed wool, when he inexplicably tried to remove by hand wool that was stuck to one of the rollers. His hand was drawn into the rolls and despite the efforts of Lapworth to stop and reverse the machine, the flesh had been torn off the four fingers of Brown's right hand. Dr Tibbits was sent for and he later amputated much of the hand but left the undamaged thumb and *"...enough of the stump of the hand to make it as useful as a limb as possible under the circumstances."* Brown had lost a finger on his other hand in a previous accident. His recovery was going well but a week later tetanus set in and despite the efforts of Tibbits and several colleagues, Brown died on 13th June. He had been well enough to be up and about just the day before but his will was written on 10th June so the worst was obviously expected. Brown was buried in Kenilworth. His widow Sarah received an immediate payment of £1,000 from his will, all his assets were sold, and the proceeds put in a trust for her. The executors were Sarah, and Henry Street who took over the West Street works. Henry installed his brother Thomas, who worked for him at Mill End, as manager of the West Street site. Sarah bought a house in Lower Ladies Hill.

In time, Sarah Brown re-married, a Meriden farmer, Mr Pearman, being her second husband, but disputes arose between her and Henry Street as to the disposition of Dathan's assets - ultimately the Court of Chancery was involved. Sarah claimed that Street was supposed to pay her interest on £2,000 every six months but, when he stopped paying her, she went to his office on several occasions and caused a scene. She would stand at the door for an hour at a time and both William Henry Walmsley and his wife Jane saw and heard altercations; Street saying, *"You have struck me twice with the door..."* and *"...you have struck me in the face with the door."* It was Street however, that was taken to court by Sarah for assault, saying she had been kicked and had bruises to prove it. Street claimed he did no more than put his hands on her shoulders and that one of the Walmsleys would have seen an assault. The bench decided that Street had exceeded the law, but upon taking into account the provocation, fined him only 6d. Sarah was told that if she had any grievances as regards to her husband's trust she should pursue it through a solicitor.

By 1881, the two sons of Henry's brother Thomas, Henry Louis (20) and Arthur William (17), were working at West Street and Mill End respectively.

* * *

From its inception, the fire brigade's Annual Dinner had been held at the Kings Arms, but fireman Swain suggested that in 1871 it was the turn of the Bowling Green and a deputation was sent to discuss the matter with licensee John Phillips, but the Kings Arms remained the venue. After the previous year's disappointment, all the town's leading figures attended; Reverend William Bickmore, former Captain Charles Draper, Richard Robbins, Edward Draper, Henry Bursell, Samuel Boddington, Henry Street, George Church, Walter Lockhart, Luke Heynes, *et al.*, and in all fifty or so sat down to a splendid feast. Amongst the usual toasts and complimentary backslapping were a number of interesting comments. The Reverend William Bickmore, for example, revealed that the reason he was such a strong supporter of the brigade was that he had had a fire at his own residence, and seen several calamitous conflagrations in London. It was suggested that an alarm bell should be erected at the engine-house but this was countered by the claim that the church bells were more than adequate. It was then recommended that there should be a public demonstration of the jumping sheet to improve public confidence in it, and so the brigade announced it would provide a demonstration at the house of anyone willing to jump into it! The Reverend William Bickmore was the first to volunteer, and he duly launched himself into the air from the top storey of the vicarage to be safely delivered to the ground. Barton, Anstey, George Dempster of the Kings Arms, Bury and J F Taylor also bravely leapt from their highest floors. Wynter used the publicity as a recruitment drive, and to carry out a variety of drills and demonstrations around the town to accustom the onlookers to the brigade's methods so that they could provide assistance in times of need.

In 1872, the annual dinner was arranged for 3rd June at a time, 4.00 p.m., specifically to tempt farmers. Tickets were 3s each. Wynter remained as a popular Captain, Henry Street as treasurer and C Jackson as Secretary. During the speeches, grocer George Church, representing traders and lamenting the decline in trade, remarked that the good communications with neighbouring towns *"...induced people to make purchases elsewhere."* It was also commented that the engine needed repainting.

The Reverend William Bickmore launched himself from the upper floor of the vicarage, in the town's first jumping-sheet demonstration.

If a letter written anonymously by a brigade member in late 1872 is to be believed, morale was falling due to poor or lacking equipment. Some of the straps connecting the horses to the engine needed replacing and this would obviously produce difficulties in getting the engine to all but the most local of fires. Replacements had been promised but were not forthcoming. There was also a shortage of boots, which of course put member's safety at risk. There was much dissatisfaction at the drills and talk of experienced members leaving. The letter obviously stirred a few consciences, as within a couple of weeks it was announced that there was to be a concert at the Institute to raise brigade funds. Reserved tickets were 2s 6d each and unreserved 1s. The attendance was described as scanty but the concert was a very enjoyable one. Local artiste Miss Sutton could not appear due to illness, but her replacement Miss Morris from Coventry was a regular performer in Kenilworth and was well liked. Mr Hollis from Northampton also took part. Although the concert proceeds were spent on "undress caps", within a week the new strapping was ordered, and boots and other equipment were soon to follow.

When the new equipment was available for use, it was decided to hold a public inspection of the Brigade by the Parish Overseers. Mr Fancott's Lower Abbey Field was arranged as the venue and the occasion set for 10th March 1873 at 6.30 p.m. The Brigade assembled at the engine-house for preliminaries at 6.00 p.m. and two horses were collected from the Bowling Green. The new harnesses were tested by a drive around the principal streets of the town before the brigade arrived in the Abbey Fields where *"...a numerous concourse of inhabitants were awaiting them."* The engine was positioned alongside the brook, the horses detached, and all the equipment laid out for inspection. The brigade was then put through a drill with its various appliances and the overseers were entirely satisfied with what they saw. All the equipment was under the supervision of Senior Lieutenant Heritage.

There appeared to be a new urgency about making the brigade more proficient. Drills were arranged for the second Monday of every month and numerous rules had been drawn up for the efficient operation of the brigade; Dr Wynter introduced a new rule that any member not attending eight of the monthly drills would be asked to resign. The Brigade had seventeen working members, four Lieutenants and the Captain; their names and addresses were printed for circulation for easy contact in case of fire.

Possibly because of the public drill in early March, Dr Wynter believed something similar but on a larger scale would be advantageous. In early May, he brought together the Captains of the Coventry, Leamington, Warwick, Banbury and Stoneleigh Abbey Brigades for a meeting at the Kings Arms to discuss his suggestion of a major fire brigade demonstration in June. After some preliminary discussion, Wynter proposed Kenilworth as the venue and 10th June as the date, but the Banbury Captain explained the difficulties of getting his brigade to the town. The Warwick Captain said he thought that the County Town was the obvious place to hold the event, but if not either Leamington or Coventry. When put to the vote, the host won the day and Kenilworth was chosen. It was also expected that the brigades from Coleshill, Bilton and Nuneaton would attend.

Perhaps surprisingly, it was a Tuesday that was chosen, but the people of Kenilworth made arrangements for it to be a general holiday and streets were decorated with bunting. By around midday the brigades had assembled at the junction of the Warwick and Leamington roads ready for the parade through town. It was led by a posse of police under the command of Deputy Chief Constable Jervis on horseback, the Leamington Hungarian Band, The Kenilworth Drum and Fife Band and the Kenilworth Brigade with its engine. This was followed by the Coventry steam fire engine accompanied by an old stagecoach. The Leamington brigade, the Warwick with its steamer, then the Coleshill, Nuneaton and Stoneleigh Abbey brigades with their engines followed. At the rear was the Banbury brigade on foot - it seems the difficulties in bringing their engine could not be overcome. The chosen route was Castle End, Abbey Hill, Albion Row, Park Road, New Street, High Street and into Francis Robbins's Castle Meadow under the Castle walls where the demonstrations took place. First to display were the manual engines and the Leamington brigade were the first to get water through their jet. The two steamers were put into action and that from Warwick took just seven minutes to get steam up. Other drills were planned, but the weather became so unfavourable that the procession re-formed and headed for the Kings Arms where about 165 brigade members and their friends sat down to a sumptuous meal. There was, of course, a whole series of speeches by those involved. The Reverend William Bickmore proposed the toast to the Kenilworth Brigade to whom he was particularly grateful as they had once rescued him from a fire and Dr Wynter stated the obvious in saying he believed that the people of Kenilworth had not before seen anything quite like they had that day. The Coventry Captain believed it should become an annual event with Coventry, of course, being the next hosts.

On occasions, the brigade paid visits to other local brigades' events. In November 1873 for example, Captain Wynter and firemen Vincent, Brown, Manton and Hughes attended the Coventry Volunteer Brigade annual dinner at the Craven Arms. The same year was a busy one for the brigade. In April a fire in the hayloft at Joshua Blackwell's Castle Inn was spreading to adjoining buildings despite the efforts of an enthusiastic public; the arrival of the brigade soon had matters under control and the fire was put out. However, the uncertainties of fighting fires at farms remained. Just two days after the Castle Inn blaze there was a similar fire in a barn at Leek Wootton and messengers were sent to the Warwick and Kenilworth brigades. At Kenilworth, there was a great deal of difficulty in assembling enough members, as it was a Sunday afternoon with pleasant sunny weather. This also meant that due to hiring out, John Phillips at the Bowling Green had only one horse available and so a second had to be procured from the Kings Arms. The fire was reached as quickly as possible under the circumstances, but had been subdued before the brigade's arrival. The following month at about 2 a.m. on a Saturday morning, an unnamed police officer in Bridge Street saw a fire in the direction of Hatton and at once alerted Captain Wynter. He, though, was reluctant to call out his brigade until he knew the fire's location as they had several times been called to fires outside their district. The police officer himself then set off to find where the fire was and discovered several ricks alight at Banner Hill farm and the occupants unaware. The officer raised the alarm and then helped to tackle the fire whilst a messenger was sent to fetch the Warwick engine. As a result, Wynter never received a request for help.

Following the death of its occupant, Dora Hill, in about 1874, fire brigade captain Dr Wynter and his mother moved conveniently into the house alongside the fire engine-house. It was during the Wynters' residency that the name Hill House is first recorded. In the summer of 1874, the volunteers were invited to take part in a fire brigade competition held in Banbury. Leaving confident of putting on a good show, they returned having been well beaten into last place. Captain Wynter complained that his brigade were dressed and prepared for fighting fires, not lightly equipped for competition as the others were!

It was decided in 1875 to have a picnic instead of an annual dinner, and so on the last Saturday in June the brigade set out for a day of boating and other amusements in Stratford. By coincidence, the Kenilworth brass band had a day out to the same place the same day. The brigade had gone a year without a single call-out.

At the AGM at the engine-house in 1876, the brigade was saddened at the resignation after nine years of its Captain, Dr Wynter. He recommended Mr Soars as his replacement and he was duly elected. Henry Heritage was retained as vice-captain, and other members were Hatwood, William Riley, W Berry, J Poole, E Heritage, Thomas Plumbe, C Robbins and J Smith.

The same year, a grand fete at the Castle was planned to raise funds for the brigade; extra trains from local towns were arranged and full column advertisements appeared in local newspapers. The high points were the appearance of the Band of the Grenadier Guards, songs by prize-winner F H Smith of Coventry, gymnastics by Turle and Sovoni, and the band of the 2nd Warwick Militia. Unfortunately, it rained all day, keeping visitor numbers to a minimum. Many tried their best and dancing took place with couples carrying umbrellas, *"...a novel appearance, and was the source of some amusement."* A somewhat dampened and restricted firework display started at 8 o'clock in a brief lull *"...illuminating the Castle ruins by means of coloured lights and the affect was beautiful, as far as could be seen."* Financially it was a disaster, the brigade lost £25 and a plea was sent out for donations to cover the losses; *"Many of our sympathetic townspeople will not withhold assistance under such circumstances."*

The following year, the brigade held its annual dinner at the Kings Arms and Mrs Dempster provided an excellent dinner for sixty-five persons. *"Nothing was wanting either in the excellence of the viands or attendance."* The efficiency of the brigade under Mr Soars was praised, and he in turn praised the men under his command.

For a time, the two Dr Wynters lived separately, Hugh moving to his own accommodation with his wife and two children, but both could afford to employ a cook, housemaid and groom. The practice had been at Dudley House on Abbey Hill, which the Wynters leased, and it was its sale in July 1873 that prompted the move to Hill House on Rosemary Hill, but at about this time, Hugh left the practice. In 1880, Daniel Wynter suffered another blow when his mother died. Daniel had been romantically linked in his early days in Kenilworth but the lady *"...declined to complete the engagement..."* and so he was now alone, in a solo practice, save for his servants. Within months of his mother's death, he moved again, this time to Hyde House in Station Road.

Dr Wynter moved into Hyde House.

*　　*　　*

Kenilworth was developing a reputation for market gardening. Land in Pepper Alley (School Lane), for sale in the summer of 1859, was used by Mr Whateley as a market garden and Henry James, a New Street greengrocer, grew strawberries on the Ladies' Hills and sold the plants in his shop. In 1875, he won first prize at Aston Lower Grounds Horticultural Show for 25 strawberries of any type; the varieties he exhibited were British Queen and Dr Hogg.

Some of the market gardens were small affairs and other ways had to be found to make money. In March 1871, market gardener William Sutton (54) bought a *"commodious wagonette"* and a *"pony carriage"* and made them available for hire from his premises just north of the Globe Hotel.

Sometimes called the May Fair, and often held in late April, a cattle-fair was held annually. In 1865 there was a very small amount of fat stock but it sold very quickly; beef for about 7½d a pound and mutton 8½d.

In 1868, a twelve year-old boy called Pettifor, employed at Mr Burbury's Wootton Grange farm, was in charge of two horses and a wagon during a storm. The horses were startled by thunder and the wagon ran over the boy and broke his leg - probably a lucky escape. In another horse accident the same year, two vehicles collided on Crackley Bridge, one horse falling over the side and breaking its neck, but it was perhaps farms where the most danger was, if only due to the age of the employees.

In August 1875, there was a severe outbreak of foot and mouth disease in Warwickshire. After about five weeks there were 8,000 infected cattle, an increase of 2,000 in a week, of which 490 cases were in Kenilworth. It was thought that the disease was being spread through the markets and rather belatedly, an appeal was made to close them. Edward Branston, a Kenilworth butcher who owned several fields, was fined £5, or given the alternative of two months jail, for not reporting cases. By mid-October the disease was on the decline and Kenilworth's cases were down in a week from 584 to 481 out of the county total of 7,200.

The produce of Kenilworth farms was of great variety. 1878 saw particularly fine growth upon pastures and of corn. There was a *"...big yield in strawberries, large quantities of which have found their way to other towns, raspberries, currants and cherries are more or less abundant."* A good crop of plums was expected, and *"...potatoes are turning up nicely..."*, but the yields of apple and pear trees were uncertain, as were those of beans and peas.

*   *   *

Upon a recommendation, Thomas Howcott, who had been out of work for some time, was in 1871 taken on by John Phillips as head carman at the Bowling Green. Whilst there, Howcott had complained that he could not trust his memory, he feared he was not strong enough for the work and was unacquainted with the area, but Phillips was satisfied and urged him to do his best. Then, on 28th August 1871, Howcott arose at his usual time, opened the street gates to allow his fellow workmen in, and then went back to his room. For no discernible reason, he slit his throat then tied his neckerchief tight around his throat in a determined attempt at suicide. He was found by Walter Freeman who raised the alarm. Dr

Wynter succeeded in resuscitating him, but Howcott became desperate and tried to rip open his wound with his bare hands; police officers who had arrived on the scene managed to restrain him. He was eventually taken in a cart to Warneford Hospital under the care of two police officers. It was decided that money could not have been the cause as he had as much as 30s on him, but it was believed his brother had committed suicide just ten months previously.

It was inevitable that there would eventually be an accident in Kenilworth involving gas and that simple lack of experience with the new power source was likely to be a contributory factor. A couple of days after Christmas 1864, the Chief Constable's clerk, Mr James Jervis, and PC Savage awoke and rose in the living accommodation at the Police Station. Having gone downstairs they entered the kitchen where they could both smell gas and sensibly opened a window. Believing the source of the leak to be *"...the waterslide in the chandelier..."*, Jervis climbed onto the table and inspected it - whilst holding a light. Inevitably, there was an explosion. Jervis's face was badly burned and all of Savage's hair blown away. The door was slammed shut by the blast and the two had to fumble around in the flames and debris to find their way out. Upstairs, Mrs Savage and her young child were in a bed that was lifted off the floor by the blast whilst nearby the solitary prisoner *"...was almost frightened out of his senses."* The ceiling of the passage leading from the kitchen to the yard was completely blown up. Inspector Gallaway was in a bedroom in the upper floor and initially believed there had been an earthquake. Jervis was in the most intense agony and was treated by the Constabulary surgeon Dr John Clarke, but it was always thought his injuries were not life-threatening. The following year there was another explosion, this time at the gasworks itself. There were no injuries but there were a number of broken windows and other damage.

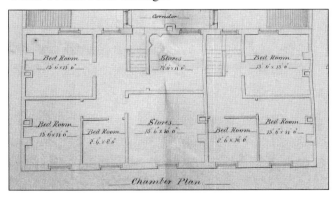

The first floor living accommodation at the Police Head Quarters. The two kitchens were below the back bedrooms.
(Warwick County Records Office, QS 24/624)

Jervis had not long begun work at the Chief Constable's Office, arriving with the highest testimonials from the West Yorkshire Constabulary where he had held a similar position in Wakefield. Jervis established a library at the Police Station for the use of officers, and he took it upon himself to keep it in order. Serving under Chief Constable Isaac and his Chief Clerk Jervis, were two Inspectors, John Moth and John Lapworth, 18 officers and 177 sergeants and constables.

In November 1867, Isaac received 100 colt six-chamber revolvers for issuing to constables on night duty. There were not enough for all officers and so the rest were issued with cutlasses and the entire force was to be trained in swordsmanship.

On 16th April 1873, James Jervis, who had recently been promoted to Deputy Chief Constable, was thrown from his horse near Gibbett Hill and was subsequently attended to by Dr Joseph Morris of Leamington. Morris advised him to rest but just two days later Jervis was seen in Stratford. As time went on, Jervis was diagnosed as suffering from cerebo-spinal irritation. In October, Jervis was seen at Kenilworth railway station acting in a peculiar manner resulting in him being reported for being drunk and facing an inquiry at Shire Hall. It did not take long for Dr Morris and Dr Alfred Baker of the Birmingham General Hospital, to convince the Committee that Jervis's actions were the result of his fall earlier in the year and not through drink. It was decided that Jervis should take a complete break for three months after which he would be able to resume duties but, in the event, it was only a month before he was back at work as his condition had much improved. He was however soon to move to Rugby to head that division and continue the same role of deputy chief.

The grave of Chief Constable James Isaac, who was responsible for the Constabulary Headquarters being built in Albion Street.

The problem of juvenile crime was highlighted by twelve-year-old William Hemmings. He constantly refused to go to school and his father had had a great deal of trouble with him despite *"beating him severely."* Late in 1874, Hemmings was caught with David Hancox stealing nine lockets and a tape measure from shopkeeper Mr Summerfield in Bridge Street. Hancox was *"generally*

respectable" but had been led into trouble by Hemmings. Both boys were sent to the County jail to receive twelve strokes of the birch rod; Hancox was then to be discharged but Hemmings was imprisoned for two weeks and then sent to the county reformatory at Weston for five years.

The Chief Constable's *"...indifferent health and advancing years..."* brought about his resignation after almost twenty years in office in October 1875. He had lived at The Spring but saw out his final years at The Yews in Castle End. James Isaac died in 1877 aged 65. His deputy, Jervis was the obvious replacement, but he was now based in Rugby.

* * *

In 1851, eight houses were being built near John Dormer's premises - this was probably Clarendon Terrace, it certainly existed just a few years later. Built on the site of John Burbury's malthouse, the address was given as Castle End despite the terrace fronting onto a made up road, historically Stockdale Lane. The houses were numbered, 1-8.

Clarendon Terrace was built on the site of a malthouse.

Almost on the corner of this lane and Castle End, were the premises of John Dormer who was a boot and shoemaker by trade, but he increased his income by utilising the building as the Boot Inn, a license he had held since 1830. Dormer had become a minor celebrity in 1851 when a five year-old pig of his grew to an astonishing size - it was 9ft 6ins long, had an 8ft girth, stood 3ft 10ins high and weighed *"sixty seven score."* All the local gentry came to admire it and Dormer having *"...challenged the world to produce a bigger one..."* intended to exhibit the animal at The Great Exhibition. However, his plans came to nothing due to potential transport problems - the pig's fate was inevitable.

By 1861, John Dormer (63), was widowed. Employed by him was 18 year-old Mary Lenton and at some time the two married. When Dormer died, aged 72, in April 1870, The Boot was continued for a while by his young widow Mary. She was the daughter of house painter John Lenton who, for unrecorded reasons, repeatedly threatened to kill her. The matter eventually ended up in court in July 1872 at which Lenton was bound over to keep the peace for six months. Just two months later, and with the connection to shoemaking ended and Mary no longer in residence, Mr L A W Cook was advertising the premises as The Earl Clarendon Inn, promoting its skittle and quoits ground and closeness to the railway station. Cook's stay was brief as by the end of 1873, George Tarry, a farmer, had taken over.

*   *   *

Borrowell Lane was in a cutting and very narrow, just 14ft wide in places, and it was normal for pedestrians to have to scramble up the bank to avoid vehicles. It was virtually impossible for vehicles to pass one another. The Edwards Charity trustees owned the land on one side and agreed that they would give up enough land to allow the road to be widened to 22ft on the condition that a stone wall was erected. The cost of the wall was estimated at £70. Mr Wallington further suggested that the future ought to be considered, that at least a 30ft wide road was required, and that the landowner on the other side should also give some land up. It was decided to have the area properly surveyed to achieve accurate costing and then to advertise for tenders for construction work.

At a Vestry meeting in June it was agreed to widen the road on just the Edwards Charity side and John Swain's tender of £67 3s was accepted. Within weeks work was started. One obvious problem was the Borrowell itself, much celebrated by its supposed use by Queen Elizabeth some three hundred or so years before, as it had to be moved due to the widening. The opportunity was taken to build a suitable structure around the water source: *"The drinking fountain and place for the supply of water known as the Barrow Well, adjoining the road where the above improvement is to be effected, was decided to be removed further back from the road on land given by the trustees of the Edwards charity. The fountain is to be enclosed with small iron gates and the whole of this work was proposed to be done by voluntary subscription."* Mr Heathcote of Warwick donated a drinking ladle to be used at the fountain. As the work was nearing completion, part of the new wall collapsed on two men working on the road. One, John Payne, was buried and received severe bruising but no breakages. Whilst the work was going on, another of Mr Swain's employees, Thomas Hudson, drowned whilst swimming in the Avon at Ashow, the second drowning at that spot within a couple of weeks.

The Barrow Well was moved and enclosed when the new retaining wall, allowing the road to be widened by 8ft, was built.

In early 1872, Road Surveyor William Evans asked for a pay rise as, an extra two miles of road were now under his command, some of the parish tools were kept at his house and the accounts had become complicated and took up a great deal of his time. He was granted an extra 2s a week, provided the parish road equipment continued to be stored in his hovel. The equipment owned was basic, the town hired a horse and cart for road maintenance for £95 a year.

An explanation of the care of Kenilworth's main thoroughfare, Castle End, was given in a letter in early 1873. The writer complained that the stones were too large and scattered and were easily loosened by passing hooves and wheels. This in turn made holes that were eroded further by rainwater, eventually followed by more stones being scattered and deep ruts appearing due to carts following the worn course which gave a smoother ride. The only maintenance appeared to be on alternate days when a man with a rake or shovel attempted to level stones but normally succeeded in only loosening some. A roller was rarely used. By comparison, Leamington used smaller stones, then rolled them flat, to produce a smooth surface which lasted longer. The writer was particularly concerned for the welfare of horses and suggested that those responsible for the road surface should spend a few hours pushing a wheelbarrow up and down the road. It was subsequently suggested that the town should invest in a horse and cart and this it did. It was further agreed that an iron roller would be beneficial.

> **The Reverend Joseph Henry Barker...**
> ...attained a BA and MA at St.John's College, Cambridge in the 1830s and was appointed to the Church of St.Peter in Hereford (1834-49). He was Chaplain to Hereford Infirmary (1843-64) and its County Gaol (1849-75). By 1871 he was a widower with a daughter and three sons; Edwin, an architect, Charles, a surveyor, and Albert. The family lived in Southbank House on Aylestone-hill, Tupsley, in Hereford, that had been designed by Edwin as a 20 year-old in 1859. It was described as "not particularly attractive with an awkward two-storey bay window." It seems that Reverend Joseph Barker and his family were regular visitors to Kenilworth and were on occasions described as "living" in the town.

In March 1873, the Reverend Joseph Barker made it known that he intended to build a new road across his land from Station Road, not far from the Kings Arms, to join into a short lane, Upper Hill Close, which in turn joined Abbey Hill. Upper Hill Close was part of Dr Wynter's rented property, Dudley House. Barker was, at the time, staying with Wynter. It was intended to build houses along the new road with a value of not less than £400. A Vestry meeting was called at which the plans were explained and discussed and ultimately passed. The new 600-yard road replaced an existing footpath running from the corner of the Kings Arms to the rear of the Chapel on Abbey Hill. As part of the new arrangements, the footpath running along the back of the Bowling Green Inn to the Chapel was extended into the new road.

At the end of 1873, a ratepayers' meeting was called to discuss the drainage arrangements of the new road, but with only five people attending it was adjourned to a more convenient time. The difficulty was that the drainpipe in Station Road was inadequate to take the extra drainage from the new road, now named Southbank Road after Barker's house in Hereford. Henry Street suggested that two thirds of the £112 the new drain would cost should be paid by Station Road residents and one sixth each by Barker and the parish, but Barker refused to contribute more than £10, saying that unless that was accepted he would use cesspools instead, making a new drain unnecessary. There was also a watercourse that Barker could use. It was not even clear at the meeting whether the existing drain in Station Road was the property of the residents or of the parish, but all agreed that since the building of the new road, the Station Road cellars had been flooding, although this may have been due to poor construction of the drains.

It was finally agreed that as Barker was to gain most from a new drain being constructed, he should pay the most and so his proportion should increase. The meeting ended harmoniously, with John Judd promising to consult all the residents of Station Road and the Parish agreeing to take over the new road once the problem was sorted.

Whilst inspecting a new house being built for him in Southbank Road in early 1876, H Page managed to fall into the cellar but he was not seriously injured. In 1877, W Balcombe advertised for sale both building plots and finished villas in the new road.

Albert Morris...

...was a well-known and respected businessman who had served his apprenticeship in Kenilworth before setting himself up as a commercial traveller in the fruit trade. In 1874 he was living at 7, Clarendon Terrace. He was successful enough to start building his own villa in the "Abbey Hill building Estate", Southbank Road. On Christmas Eve 1874 he set out for home from a trip south by the Great Western Railway on a double-headed sixteen coach train. It left Oxford at 11.40 a.m. but just before reaching the canal bridge at Shipston a tyre came off the wheel of the leading coach. Most of the train subsequently derailed, and three coaches rolled down the embankment. Albert Morris was alive but badly injured when removed from the wreckage, and he died on the way to a hospital in Oxford. Only 34 years old, Albert left a widow, Susanna, and a daughter. Susanna died 14 years later at Fern Hill.

Obviously, roads could only be lit with gas if the gas company had laid mains along the road. Southbank Road was one without and in 1878 William Lett held the contract for lighting the petroleum street-lamps for £10 a year. This was seen as excessive and contract fell to 5 guineas. Borrow-well Lane also had no gas and once three lamps were erected in 1880, Lett secured the contract for those as well. The renewal of his licence to store 50 gallons of petroleum on his premises was always passed by the Board without query.

Lett had been in business as a general ironmonger since the late 1860s. His premises, probably formerly occupied by Thomas Finnemore, were in Castle End almost opposite the Rose and Crown. He advertised for sale lawnmowers, which could "...be easily managed by ladies..." for as little as 25s and as much as 45s, and "garden engines" which were foot-operated pumps for watering, which weighed only 12lbs and cost 25s. At other times, he advertised tin baths for hire and fishing tackle for sale.

By the end of 1881, Lett had been succeeded in his business by William Shard, who also took the contract for lighting the Borrow-well Lane and Southbank Road lights. The Board however were perhaps not quite as sure of his integrity as he was issued with a licence for storing only 40 gallons of petroleum.

*   *   *

The soup kitchen for the benefit of the poor was re-instated in 1868 by Lady Catherine Cave-Brown-Cave, although it was actually run by Mrs Bryan at Town Pool Bridge. The soup itself consisted basically of meat and peas, but additional ingredients, including more meat, carrots and onions, were continually requested to be donated to improve its quality. It was sold at the rate of 2d a quart, or in exchange for a ticket acquired in advance from Mrs Bryan or George Church the grocer. The kitchen was open three days a week from 12.30 to 1.00 p.m. for fourteen weeks starting on the first Thursday in December. The winter of 1869-70 saw 739 gallons sold, an average of about 57 servings per session, and total takings of £24 12s 8d.

1874 closed with some appallingly cold weather. Before Christmas £20-worth of bread, amounting to about a thousand 4lb loaves, was distributed from the Duchess of Dudley's Charity, and clothing was distributed the following week. The supply of gas was at the same time very poor, the Christmas congregation at St.Nicholas Church was in virtual darkness.

Lighting a house by means other than gas was hazardous. In 1874 William Webb's widow Elizabeth, an inebriate and in need of constant care, lived in Albion Street. Jane Gibbs had been looking after her for over three months when one night at 3 a.m., Mrs Webb called to Jane asking her to trim her lamp. As she was doing so, for some reason the benzoline in the bottle she was using ignited, some of it spilt and set fire to the carpet. Jane ran to the door and threw the burning bottle down the stairs, but in doing so set her nightdress alight - she rushed out of the house and into the garden completely engulfed in flames. A neighbour, Mr Lewis, heard her screams and smothered the flames with a blanket, but despite being attended to by Dr Wynter she died in less than half an hour. Elizabeth Webb herself died just a few weeks later, but it is not known if this was due in any way to the fire.

*   *   *

It appears that by 1871, there was no cricket club with the town's name, but there was an Abbey Hill Cricket Club. On Thursday 29th June, they played a match against Priory Hill of Wolston at the Abbey Hill ground and beat them comfortably. R S Mort 25, W H Draper 20, and F C Wilson 22 scored most of the Abbey Hill's 113 runs before Priory Hill were bowled out for just 9. A second innings saw the visitors score a further 50 runs. Wilson took ten wickets over the two innings. The following week the team played against a side from Coventry and scored 62 but their innings was followed by a heavy thunderstorm, which made bowling difficult, and the visitors scored 116.

It is not known who called it, but a meeting was arranged at the Institute on Tuesday 4th June 1872 at 7.00 p.m., to consider the steps required to re-establish a Kenilworth Cricket Club. The Reverend Clifford Rickards was voted to the chair and he quickly established the general feeling that it would not prove too difficult to form a club or to find a suitable ground on which to play. Upon the suggestion of William Clarke, a committee was appointed to set out club rules and to seek a playing field. Reverend William Bickmore was appointed President, Reverend C Rickards Honorary Secretary, with William Pennington, S W Smith, Rodwell, R Newman, Shepherd, Lett, William Clarke and Adams making up the committee. Thirty names of potential members were collected at this first meeting; honorary members' annual subscriptions were set at 10s and playing members 5s.

The newly-formed club's first practice was in the Abbey Fields at 6.00 p.m. on Saturday 22nd, with a second a few days later, probably in a field leased by Joshua Blackwell. Negotiations were in hand with Blackwell to use a field at The Spring to play matches, but despite this, the practice ground was the venue on the 29th for a match between North and South Kenilworth, with Abbey Hill being the dividing line. In a thirteen a side match the South batted first with William Pennington top scoring with 7 (if the 8 extras are discounted) in a total of 36. The North had two stars in H and J Smith who added 28 runs between them, Rodwell scored 5, but the other ten batsmen totalled just 2. The South's second innings saw Spicer top score with 14 in a total of 68 and chasing 57 to win the North were 36-2 with S Smith on 10 not out when the match ended.

Secretary Rickards said that when he helped form the club that it was not intended to play any matches in the first year, but challenges were made and the last week in June saw the first match proper, again in the Abbey Fields, against a Leamington X1. The Kenilworth team included eight players from the practice match, five from the South and three from the North, but neither of the free-scoring Smiths appeared. Shepherd scored 20 and Adams 10 as the home side were all out for 67, but the innings had barely finished when a very heavy thunderstorm blew up and lasted two hours. When play resumed, conditions were so slippery and spongy that it was almost impossible to bowl, the visitors being 54 for five when play stopped.

Playing matches attracted new subscribers and attendance at practices was on the increase. It was hoped that this would result in better performances, but the next match brought another defeat. Played in fine weather, again in the Abbey Fields, Hatton scored 124 in their two innings against the home side's 108. On 10th August, another home match against Hatton produced the club's first victory. Kenilworth's first innings 66 included 18 extras and a top score of 10 by Brett. Hatton's reply was hampered by having only ten players, who managed only 21 runs, but following-on with a full team they scored 67. The 22 Kenilworth needed to win was achieved with the loss of only one wicket. Two days later saw another home victory, this time against St.Marys of Warwick. Over these two matches, Kenilworth appears to have used only two bowlers, Wilson taking 16 wickets and Shepherd, soon to leave the club, 21. The season produced six wins and five defeats, and by its end, there were 33 honorary members, 30 active members and *"eight players nominated at 2s 6d."* The driving force of the club was its captain, William Pennington of Thickthorn, who was always available for matches and practices, and having such a man of influence at its head was credited for its initial success. However, many of the players came from outlying districts rather than Kenilworth itself.

The end of season dinner was held at the Kings Arms with the President, Reverend W Bickmore, in the chair, and George Dempster provided an excellent dinner. Bickmore said that when he first came to the town in the 1850s there was a flourishing club with Mr Fetherstone and R Poole at its head, but it had the greatest difficulty in finding a playing field close to the town centre. During his own speech, Mr Rickards suggested the formation of an under-15 team. It turned out to be one of his last contributions to the club; the Reverend Clifford Rickard had been Curate at Kenilworth, and left to become Chaplain at Fulham Penitentiary. In July 1873, he married the daughter of William Carter of Abbey Hill.

The practice ground at Abbey Hill was retained for the next season and it was arranged to play matches *"behind Dr Wynter's"* house on Abbey Hill, possibly the same ground. Many of the matches played in 1873 were not against organised clubs. There was a series of North v South Kenilworth and Married v Singles games, as well as a match against Kenilworth Vicarage.

Amongst the exceptions, the team had two extreme performances just days apart in September. After scoring 239 against Stoneleigh, (A Black scored 54 before he was *"thrown out"*) they bowled out the opposition, which included the Hon F D and G H C Leigh, twice for just 86. In their next match, the club conceded 106 runs against Coventry only to be bowled out twice for only 63. *"Why the play of Kenilworth should be so utterly abortive...is difficult to say. The reason must be attributed to the wretched state of the weather. Immediately before our local team took to the wickets the rain came down heavily, rendering the ground almost like a mud pit."*

The AGM at the end of the 1873 season was held at the Institute. Expenses for the year had exceeded income from subscriptions by almost £3, but playing members were down to just 13. *"Although a fair number of working men had made use of the club, comparatively few had made themselves members."* Playing members had to find 5s and *"active members"* 2s 6d. There was some discussion about a new practice ground being found. The prospect of starting a football team was debated, but no agreement could be reached as to which rules, association or rugby, to adopt and so both rule books were obtained to help the decision at a future meeting. By early December, association rules, first written down just ten years previously, had been chosen and the season's first practice was at 3.00 p.m. on the following Wednesday afternoon, provided a field could be found. The site chosen was the Bowling Green Piece, a field south of the footpath behind the inn, and possibly where earlier cricket matches were played *"...behind Dr Wynter's house..."*. The first practice match was an eight-a-side game between teams chosen by Dr Wynter and William Pennington, Wynter's winning 3-0.

A match proper was played there in early February 1874 against Sutton Coldfield but it resulted in a two nil defeat. This seems to have prompted a trilogy of North v South practice games. The South won the first and the North the second by four goals, (after a postponement due to bad weather) which set up the "conquering game" in early March. *"The weather was beautifully fine and the number of competitors very good. Some capital play was shown on both sides and in the course of two hours hard contest, two goals were won by the South and four by the North."* But it seems that this initial interest soon ended.

At the first meeting of the 1874 season, it was decided to encourage youngsters in cricketing skills and each member was allowed to nominate one boy between the ages of 11 and 15 as a junior member. The youngsters were to be allowed only one practice a week, starting on the first Monday of June, and this was on the condition that the club Secretary or a committee member was present. Thirteen junior members enrolled. The club also secured a permanent ground, not surprisingly the Bowling Green Piece.

The club did not have a particularly good season, eventually winning seven of their sixteen matches, but there was one notable victory, having scored 246 runs against Whitnash, the opposition was bowled out for just 9.

As Charles Adams was now a leading club batsman, matches were regularly reported in his *Kenilworth Advertiser* in flowing terms, and the season also brought some memorable performances from umpires: *"We do not for one moment question the integrity of the umpire in deciding in favour of the batsman caught at slip for 4, but the said batsman returned to the wicket and, unluckily for Kenilworth, increased his number to 35. On Saturday too, a batsman who ran up a large score escaped in consequence of the wickets being pitched slightly too wide, in fact wide enough to allow the third ball to pass through without knocking off the bails."*

In scoring 155 all out to gain an innings victory over St.John's Wood, the team gave Adams another chance to extol the fortunes of the club: *"With all due deference to those holding opposite opinions, (we) affirm that the several defeats Kenilworth has suffered have resulted more from ill-luck than from any inability on the part of those who have contested the various games."* His own contribution to the victory was a duck.

By the time the finances were audited in late 1874, there were 32 honorary members paying 10s each, 15 active members paying 5s and six working members paying 2s 6d., but overall membership was down by nine. The total receipts for the year were a little over £28, but there was now a debt of £2. The club was again attempting to arrange a football team for the winter with subscriptions set at 2s 6d, and 1s for working men. Practices were arranged on the Bowling Green Piece in January 1875, this time on Saturday afternoons, but by the beginning of March *"scanty turnouts"* followed by

bad weather led to complete suspension of the practices. Despite this, a match proper was arranged against Whitnash for 20th March, but the opposition, perhaps mindful of the cricket match between the two clubs, failed to turn up.

There was a small deficit in the cricket club funds but despite an increase in the rent, it was decided to keep the same ground for the 1875 season, as it was conveniently near the centre of the town, and not to increase the subscriptions. The juvenile club was retained. The season started with a good run of victories and amongst the new players was seventeen year-old Charles Boutlbee, son of Henry Boultbee, the High Sheriff of Warwickshire. A victory over Bedworth, in which Pennington top scored with 28 and J L Smith added 15 in a total of 88, brought the observation: *"If the members would meet more regularly for practise, we feel sure much good would result from it, especially if style and finish were aimed at in the place of loose batting and careless fielding."* In July 1875, the club were invited to play a Mr Tonks XI, also referred to as Warwick CC, at the County Ground in Warwick. It ended in a draw.

After a run of poor results during the 1876 season, William Pennington resigned as Club Secretary in July due to the *"...difficulty he has experienced in carrying the club...consequent upon the apathy shown by many of the members."* He was replaced by C Dawes. This may have had a positive effect as a run of victories followed, although a defeat by Milverton was not *"...particularly creditable to the local players."* The team that day included the Hon Dudley Leigh and a still-playing William Pennington, although he failed to score in either innings.

The same week saw a Dr Wynter XI play against a Dudley Leigh team at Stoneleigh; Wynter himself did not play but the team included a young local man Charles Robbins. Top scorer in both matches was C Dawes, the son of William Dawes of Kenilworth Hall.

There was a *"deficiency in the accounts"* at the end of 1876 and a meeting was held at Charles Adams' office in May 1877 to discuss the position of the club. William Pennington occupied the chair and the others present were Dr T S Bourne, Brittain, Adams, Pagett and Smith. It was agreed that £30 should be available before the club could be proceeded with and the meeting was adjourned for a week to give the six a chance to raise funds. By the end of June, the finances had reached an acceptable level and practices began on the Bowling Green Piece. Eventually the first match was arranged against Milverton as late as August, and the club lost 95-55 with only H Smith reaching double figures. The following week saw a creditable performance at home to Mr Tonks XI who were restricted to 64 and 25 runs in their innings, to which Kenilworth replied with 47 and 11 for no wicket at the close. A few weeks later Coventry Victorias were beaten at home 78-52 with C Robbins and J Smith both scoring 20, followed by the beating of Whitnash, 51-35 with P Muddiman top scoring with 15. The last match of the season saw Coventry Victorias beaten again, 46-35 with the unusual statistic of six bowlers, Robbins, Lynes, Hornidge, Dawes, Adams and Lowe, all taking wickets; it was usual for only two, or perhaps three, bowlers to be used.

Despite the late start, twelve matches were played of which eight were won, and the season ended with the usual dinner at the Bowling Green chaired by Dr T S Bourne with Charles Adams alongside.

The perilous state of the club continued into the next year. Adams did his best, as editor of the Kenilworth Advertiser, to whip up interest in readiness for the new season, but when came the time for the first meeting in May 1878 it had to be postponed due to so few being interested. Eventually a meeting was held with just Dr Bourne, H Carter and J Davies joining Adams at his office. With a debt of £5 and so little interest, it is not surprising that the four decided that *"...it is unadvisable to take any steps towards the formation of the club for the present year."*

*　　*　　*

Upon the death of Edward Boddington, sometime between 1854 and 1861, his son John took over the Engine Inn. On 13th September 1867, John Boddington bought from Samuel Burbery land known as Albion Gardens, and on one corner of it, that opposite the police station, built for himself a new public house. The licence of the Engine Inn was taken on by one of John's two sons, Alfred (24).

John Boddington's other son, John Clarke Boddington, took a completely different course in life. At the age of fourteen in 1852, he had entered into an machining apprenticeship in Birmingham and by the age of 21 had acquired enough skills to call himself an engineer. He travelled the country working and in 1864, decided to emigrate to the United States. Once there, he changed employers rapidly, working at railway locomotive workshops at the New York Central, Jersey City and others before finding work at the Kansas Pacific Railroad (KPR). In 1867, just as his father was building his new pub in Kenilworth, John settled in Wyandotte County and it was his new home that gave his father the name for his new inn, The Wyandotte. The KPR became involved in the railway race to join the USA's coasts and amalgamated with the Union Pacific. John was made foreman in 1870.

The Wyandotte Inn, named after licensee John Boddington's son's new home, Wyandotte County.

On John Boddington's land alongside The Wyandotte, Mr Wheatley built Pyon Villas, two houses including a 24ft by 8ft workshop, and a nearby shop in Stoneleigh Road, but Wheatley soon left the country, and was to be followed by many more. In April 1872, 40 or 50 farm labourers left South Warwickshire to work building a new railway in New Zealand. They were engaged for two years at a rate of 5s a day. That October, another party left on the same promise of work for two years and these included 20 from Kenilworth.

Albion Street resident and railway labourer John Fulford (52) had a large family. His eldest son Thomas (28), a fellmonger's labourer, had left home and started his own family but there were still five offspring at home including John (25) an agricultural labourer, Louisa (16) a gimp-maker, and James another fellmonger's labourer. James, just eighteen years-old, decided to try his luck elsewhere and in 1872, he emigrated to New Zealand, ending up in Dunedin. He had a variety of jobs; driving teams of horses, butchering and washing wool on a large sheep run. He was making £2 a week and had no board to pay - no-one there was on less than 25s a week. Fulford had ideas of earning more: some railway navvies could earn 1s an hour and those trying their luck at gold-digging could make £500 a year but work for only six months of it. Fulford's letters back to Kenilworth reported that there were no poor people and that there was plenty to eat and drink. However, he identified one great drawback - a great scarcity of women and he suggested one or two he thought may like to join him! In a probable comparison to his life in Kenilworth James declared there was *"...no scraping or pinching, an abundance of everything. You never have to work on an empty belly."* How envious many of his friends back home must have been. Across Warwickshire, there was disquiet amongst the agricultural ranks due to low wages and harsh living conditions, and this led to an uprising against landowners.

The uprising first showed itself in Kenilworth on Tuesday 20th February 1872 with a well-attended meeting at the Institute chaired by non-agriculturist Mr Dencer. Very quickly, a list of grievances was aired. Mr T Arnold suggested that the working hours should be cut to 6.00 a.m. to 5.30 p.m., with a 4.00 p.m. finish on Saturday, and that wages should be increased to 2s 6d for each day. Mr Lake at length described the lot of the plough-boys, often working from 5.00 a.m. to 7.00 p.m. for a wage between 3s and 6s a week. He compared them to apprentices who in better conditions and of comparable skills would earn 20-30s a week. However, Mr Fulford said that the labourers should stick together and the problems of the plough-boys should be sorted by their parents. All were urged to discuss matters with their masters; the problem had arisen largely because farms were handed through generations of the same family and each generation continued the same ways as their father, so little changed. The meeting was adjourned for a week after it was agreed to arrange discussions with the masters. The main speaker at the second meeting was Mr Taunton from Coventry and he quickly established that the average rent paid by farm workers was 2s a week, which left barely enough to buy meat and bread for a family of five. Only nine of the fifty-nine present could afford to keep pigs *"...an agricultural animal most essential to comfort in the winter season."* Demands were increasing; it was now thought that daily finishing time should be 5.00 p.m., and wages 16s a week *"without beer."* A committee of J Freeman, Needle, Clarke, Pettifor, Tandy, Barber and Rollason was appointed and they began the steps necessary to form a union.

In March, Joseph Arch held a meeting at Wellesbourne that led to the amalgamation of several separate agricultural unions, and on 26th March the third Kenilworth meeting was held at the Rose and Crown, by which time the movement was gathering momentum - other meetings had been held at Leamington and Stoneleigh the night before. Some masters had agreed to an amicable settlement but had also stopped employing many of those advocating a union. Rollason was one treated as such and his motion that a union be formed that night was carried unanimously. The clergy believed that the farm workers ought to be comfortable with what they had, but it transpired that they had only spoken to those on Lord Leigh's estate where he charged only a shilling for rent, included an acre of land, and paid wages of 15s a week, very different to those in Kenilworth. The meeting was firmly against strike action, and the union was formed on that basis with William Taylor as chairman, Mr Spicer treasurer and J Freeman as secretary.

On Tuesday 7th May, a meeting was called at Castle Green and, with the promise that Joseph Arch himself was to appear, it is of no surprise that a very large crowd gathered. His rousing speech was often interrupted with thunderous cheering and at its conclusion, the Kenilworth Drum and Fife band struck up "The Warwickshire Lads". Continuing cheers were given for Arch as the throng, headed by the band, made its way to the Rose and Crown. A further eighteen members were enrolled in the union, bringing Kenilworth's membership to 119. The National Agricultural Labourers Union was officially established on 29th May. In early June another meeting at the Rose and Crown saw a further 44 members added, bringing the total to 175.

The last Friday of July 1872 saw another evening gathering on Castle Green, and the undoubted main attraction was the opening speech by Kenilworth-born George Potter, who had become a leading trade unionist.

George Potter...

...was born in Kenilworth in 1832 and lived in Albion Row. His parents Edmund and Anne were from Bloxham, Oxfordshire, and his father was then employed as a carpenter for 3s a week. George began his education at one of the five "Dame schools" then in the Parish, and ended it as one of sixty pupils then present at the Arlidge Charity School on Abbey Hill. Due to the poor circumstances of his family, he was taken out of the school at an early age to work first as a plough-boy, and then, to earn his keep at home until he was sixteen, as an errand boy being paid 6d a day. He then walked to Coventry and was lucky to be given a four-year apprenticeship with a master cabinetmaker, working for free in his first year but progressing to 6s a week for his last. Working as a journeyman he first found work in Rugby and then with George Taylor, building villas in Coventry's suburbs.

In 1853, aged 21, he took off to London and within two weeks found work with George Myers of Belvedere for whom he worked for four years, and for his next employer found himself working at the new Elliott and Watney brewery and at the Houses of Parliament. The year he moved to London, he joined the Progressive Society of Carpenters and Joiners, rising rapidly through its ranks to become Secretary, then Chairman. Becoming active in wider trade union circles, in 1859 Potter effectively combined the builders' unions of London into one and became nationally known for campaigning for a nine-hour day. In 1861 he founded a weekly trade union newspaper, the *Beehive*. In 1866 he formed the London Working Men's Association and in 1871 was elected President of the Trades Union Congress and became Chairman of its Parliamentary Committee.

As can be imagined, his speech, delivered from the back of a wagon, was well received. *"The question of the condition of the agricultural labourer is one of the most important that had ever occupied public attention."* *"How can a man in the wretched condition in which the agricultural labourers are, battle successfully with the farmers and landlords whose position is so powerful and strong."* He claimed £500,000,000 annually went to 2,700,000 people, amounting to £290 a year, whilst the other 11,000,000 averaged only 11s a week. Another speech, which caused some laughter and cheers, was by George Mitchener who once had earned only 4s a week working on a farm, and Kenilworth's own William Taylor and William Denman also made contributions. The final speech, from T Connolly, extolled the virtues of emigration, particularly to the fertile soils of Canada, and he *"...advised all who could to scrape enough money to go over there."* A London agent charged just £4 5s for an Atlantic crossing.

Despite, or perhaps because of, its popularity amongst certain groups of workers, such as the newly formed farm labourers' union, the Rose and Crown was known as an unruly place. On 7th August 1872, its licensee Edwin Spicer was convicted for allowing drunkenness and was fined 20s. A constable had also witnessed a man leave the establishment and assault a stranger in the street. There was also a system of illegal secret gambling going on. Not surprisingly, Spicer's license was not renewed at this time, but the public house was open again, still with Spicer, by the new year.

Probably due to this, the meeting of the agricultural union in February 1873 was held at the assembly room at the Kings Arms. There was an unusually large gathering in expectation of it being addressed by Joseph Arch but he was indisposed and so the Chairman of the Kenilworth branch, William Taylor, made the major speech. He described how the Government had been behaving like a builder, who built a large building for the middle and upper classes but had neglected the foundations, the agricultural workers, and had it not been for Arch attending to the foundations the building was sure to collapse.

Attendances at the public meetings began to fall and that in December, back at the Rose and Crown, was described as "*meagre*" but the public house continued to be a focal point for those not happy with their lot; in early 1873 it was the venue for a talk on the benefits of emigration, this time Brazil was the suggested destination, and the following year a similar talk by an emigration agent from Liverpool suggested Canada.

Under the will of William Hopkins, the Rose and Crown came up for sale by auction on 3rd June 1874, along with the adjoining house, shop-front and workshop occupied by William Buswell. The public house included a 31ft long clubroom, brewhouse, coalhouse, granary, stabling, piggery, coach-house and a walled garden, totalling an area of 720 sq yds. The rent was £42 a year. There was also a pump and well which was used by the adjacent eight dwelling houses. Also up for sale under the same will were twelve houses, in two lots of six, in Spring Lane.

In early 1873, Edward Boddington of Fieldgate Lodge, placed an advert for "*Two able bodied young men, good labourers and accustomed to ploughing, to go out next month with Mr E Boddington to America, passage paid. Apply at Fieldgate Lodge before 10 a.m. any morning.*" In October 1877, all the contents of Fieldgate Lodge, including baths, beds, sideboards, carpets, etc., were put up for sale by Boddington as he was "*removing*". A year later, a notice revealed that E F Boddington had a partnership dissolved: "*Robbins and Boddington, Beaufort, South Carolina, and at Kenilworth, merchants and timber dealers.*"

The system of co-operation between working men had existed since the early 1840s and was particularly strong in the northern industrial towns. Nearer to Kenilworth, the Emscote Co-operative Society had quickly grown to close on a thousand members by the early 1870s and was soon to open a new shop at Barford, its sixth. In the Spring of 1873, moves were made to establish a co-operative in Kenilworth, probably inspired by the success of the agricultural workers forming their union branch, and not surprisingly the same premises, the Rose and Crown, was chosen as their initial meeting point. Several members of the Emscote society were present at this first meeting, one took the chair and a Mr Robinson spoke long and clearly of the benefits to Kenilworth in having its own Society. He explained how his Society had started "*...with twelve members and just as many pounds...*" and took only 30s in its first week, but now took £160 a week. He advocated initial restraint and paying low dividends, to build up a reserve fund that would allow the scheme to expand. At the end of the meeting, Mr Taylor of the Emscote Society proposed that Kenilworth should start its own co-operative and this motion was duly carried. A second meeting was held three weeks later on 21st May at which a committee was formed and as many as 30 members enrolled. As the year progressed, the movement gathered momentum and it seems that the final arrangements were made at a meeting at Thomas Rice's premises on 21st September. The advertisement gives his address as Abbey Hill; Rice was a boot and shoemaker and grocer, and later also a lodging housekeeper and on all other occasions is recorded as being on Rosemary Hill. Rice actually lived a couple of houses to the east of the Bowling Green Inn, a stretch of road referred to as both Rosemary Hill and Abbey Hill. Within a week or two of the meeting, the Society was in business. Its initial capital was just £20 and its saleroom was the "*...front room of a small cottage on Rosemary Hill...*", likely to be that of Thomas Rice, now its manager. William Henry Walmsley (21) was the Secretary and Henry Street the Treasurer.

In its first quarter, sales amounted to just over £218 giving a bonus of 2s in the £1 for members purchases, but despite the advice suggesting the speedy build up of a reserve fund, just £1 3s 4d was paid into it. The first general meeting announcing these figures was held at The Stores, again likely to have been Thomas Rice's premises. In August 1874, the balance sheet contrasted favourably with the previous two and a dividend of 1s 10d was paid.

The society made rapid progress. At the meeting in January 1875, with Thomas Morris in the chair, sales for the quarter had reached £383, and a 2s dividend paid. By April, quarterly sales by the Society, now referring to itself by its full title "The Kenilworth Co-operative Industrial and Provident Society", had reached £455, up £209 on the previous year and £71 on the previous quarter. Membership was now up to 107 and dividends remained a few pence either side of 2s. The capital stood at a healthy £164 and the years sales amounted to £1,559 17s 1d giving a clear profit of £212 12s. The increase in sales had allowed the steady build up of the reserve fund. Doubtless pleased with their own success, eighty members had a tea by way of a small celebration. Costing 9d a ticket, it was held at the Institute.

By the final meeting of that year, at the Institute with over a hundred of its 123 members present, discussions about the society building its own premises to facilitate further expansion were at an advanced stage. An agreement had been reached on favourable terms with John Boddington for some land at the rear of his Wyandotte Inn, which was large enough for a stores and the already proposed later extensions of a bakery, butchers and drapers at some point in the future. In just two years, the society had amassed over £400 working capital. Sales for this last quarter had passed the £550 mark, almost 50% up on the previous year. The confirmation of the land purchase was given at the AGM in January 1876. Sales had now reached £531 for the quarter, and there were 129 members.

The new premises fronting onto Park Road were a splendid affair, three storeys high and with a degree of ornamental brickwork. Incorporated in the building were ground floor areas used as the shop, and other areas for storage. The first floor was almost entirely an open space to be used as a meeting hall.

At the time of the 15th quarterly meeting in mid-July 1877, held at the new Co-operative Hall, the society was in a very healthy state with sales of over £2,389 for the year, and a very large sum had been expended in land, building and fixtures. Within two months the Society were advertising for tenders to build a bake-house on the site. The plans could be seen at the Park Road premises or at the architect's office, Thomas Hind of Leicester. The tenders came from T and C Balcombe and Edward Smith, both of Kenilworth, and the

The Co-operative's new premises of 1876.

successful bid from W G Richards of Leicester. The building had to be completed by 12th November. The bake-house was nearing completion as the next quarterly meeting was held. Sales for the year had shown an increase of over £687 compared to the previous one, and as well as the planned sale of their own bread, the society had now added buckets, bowls and fire shovels. A year later, at a general meeting where few of the 210 members were present, it was decided to join the Central Co-operative Board.

The bake-house of the Kenilworth Co-operative and Industrial Provident Society. The white paint on the end of the building is the location of the privvy.

The Rose and Crown remained open with a new licensee, Andrew Sumner of Coventry, but in April 1875 he was he was charged with selling drinks after hours. PC Hawkes had found two men in the bar with drinks fifty minutes after closing time. The manageress, Sarah Waite, claimed they were friends, one of whom had intentions towards her daughter, but a fine of £2 was imposed. This is the last mention of the public house.

The Rose and Crown did not remain empty for long. Within months it was occupied by Thomas Dickenson (31), who employed six in his painting, glazing and plumbing business. By early the following year he was advertising that he was in the *"more commodious premises."* Dickenson had begun in business by taking on the concern of Charles Gibbs (then aged 73) in 1871. Gibbs had also been a pump maker and well-sinker.

William Riley was born in Coventry in 1846, the son of the licensee of the Antelope Inn. He was apprenticed with Allwood the grocers in Broadgate but came to Kenilworth to work for George Church. He started on his own in Castle End in about 1869. An advert from that year, says Riley (23), had a "Tea, Grocery and Provision Warehouse" and had for sale black or mixed tea from 2s to 4s. He was married to Hannah and they employed one boy. By 1874 he was selling petroleum at 1s 6d gallon and was licensed to hold up to 20 gallons.

The Rose and Crown is the large building in the centre. William Riley's premises has two dormer windows.

In 1875, William Riley *"...removed to more commodious premises, recently occupied by T Dickenson..."* and described himself as a grocer and provision merchant. In 1878, he advertised 50 American cheeses for sale and later that same year Kenilworth Castle Packet Tea. He also sold *"China, tea and breakfast services, nickel silver spoons, knives & forks, vases, plates, dishes, tea pots, glassware or almost any article of domestic use."* He was in the St.Nicholas Church choir and became a sidesman.

*   *   *

John Lenton was a letter carrier in Kenilworth. In 1847, he was in trouble for demanding excess postage of 2d on a letter, it appeared the stamp had been re-used. He was suspended but a petition was organised to have him reinstated and it was signed by most of the influential inhabitants.

By 1859 the mail, coming by rail, was received at the Post Office at 3.00 a.m., as opposed to 5.15 by mail cart. New arrangements gave an extra fifteen minutes to catch despatches to London and the north. Letter bags went by rail northwards twice a day.

The location of the Post Office was far from ideal,

particularly for those living in Castle End where there were a large number of businesses, and so a Post receiving house was established there by the early 1850s. This was at the premises of Overseer, churchwarden and grocer Thomas Fraser who was also trusted with the sale of stamps. Thomas Fraser died in May 1855 and the grocery and postal arrangements were continued by his widow Ann.

At some unknown date, but by 1861, the main Post Office moved from the Coventry Cross into its own premises in New Street. Postmistress Elizabeth Manton (57) had married ironmonger James Rae (55), and it is he who is recorded as the Postmaster. By now, services had increased to include the paying and granting of money orders.

The Post Office and Rae's ironmongery, New Street.

During May 1863, the postal arrangements were again improved with letterboxes appearing in town for the first time, and the closure of Ann Fraser's receiving office: *"During the past week letter-boxes have been placed in several parts of the town, which will prove a great boon to those resident at some distance from the central office. One of them has been placed contiguous to the lower window of the "library" where every accommodation will be given as at the head office in New Street, with the exception of registering letters. Another box has been placed near to Mr Blackwell's on Castle Green which will be a very great advantage to the widespread tenants of "The Chase". The free delivery will be extended to Parkfield, Whitemoor, and Windy Arbour. By closing the Receiving Office, the expenses attendant upon this accommodation will be about equalised."* Other new collecting boxes were likely to have been at the junction of the roads to Leamington and Warwick, and in Albion Street.

Despite the re-arrangements, many in the southern half of the town found it a great inconvenience having to get to the Post Office in time to catch the 7.30 a.m. despatch and in September 1867, a memorial was sent to the Postmaster General asking for the first

despatch to be delayed until 9.00 and for a branch office to be re-established, the suggested site being the railway station. Charles Bliss, William Clarke and J Brown collected the signatures.

Elizabeth Rae died aged 62 in 1868 leaving James Rae, himself in his 60s, to run the main Post Office on his own. In early 1870, it was connected to the ever-growing telegraph system. This came as a surprise to many as there had been no apparent forewarning or discussion. It was seen as an opportunity missed to move the Post Office to a more central location, perhaps near the railway station. The *Kenilworth Advertiser* suggested that the scheme was effected *"...cheaply and hastily. Is it too late to make matters better? Is everybody as deaf and blind as those graceless telegraph poles looking so unnecessary and stuck up amongst us?"* One immediate benefit was that Greenwich time was telegraphed to the office daily, and the parish clock was set by it. The telegraph was available the entire time the Post Office was open, from 7 a.m. to 8.25 p.m., the unusual closing time being dictated by the time of the last despatch of letters *"to all parts"*. Letters posted at the main office during the next 30 minutes were also despatched if an additional 1d stamp was attached. Of the other post boxes, those at St.John's and Castle Green were emptied once a day, including Sundays, at either 7.15 or 7.45 p.m., and that at The Library in Castle End at 6.00 a.m., 9.00 a.m., 10.55 a.m. and 8.00 p.m. Town deliveries began at 7.00 a.m. and 12.50 p.m. The New Street office was now advertised as the "Post Office Savings Bank and Government Annuity and Insurance Office."

Elizabeth Rae was buried with her first husband, John Manton.

Post Office Messengers were paid 14s for a seven-day week, working from 3 a.m. until three or 4 p.m. with breaks for breakfast and dinner. One class of messenger known as "rural proper" only received 8s to 10s a week. All were deducted 2s a day if absent through sickness.

In 1876, the building containing the Post Office came up for sale. This may mean that James Rae had died, certainly he was not mentioned in Kenilworth after this date. *"The house contains a large Front shop (now divided into two, the one lately occupied by an ironmonger, and the other used as the Post Office), Parlour, Kitchens, with Store Room over, 6 Sleeping Apartments, W.C., and other Conveniences, with capital Cellaring."* In November the following year, the building was advertised for sale again, but with an amended description. The two shops, one occupied by a dressmaker, the other "...*has for many years past been, and now is, the Post Office...*" had bay windows, the first floor had a parlour and two bedrooms with two more bedrooms on the second floor. There was a walled, paved yard, and a side entrance leading from New Street. For the first time, the new Postmaster is mentioned; viewing was by an appointment with Thomas S Morris. The freehold was bought by Mr Hardware for £480.

*   *   *

It was inevitable that on occasions, horses would be startled, and one quite extraordinary incident happened on the evening of 30th November 1876 on the railway bridge at St. John's. The 10th Warwickshire Volunteer Rifle Corps, led by Captain William Rigby Magrath of Leamington, was heading towards Leamington with its 14-man band at its head. There were a large number of onlookers, cheering and shouting. Approaching in the opposite direction was master baker, David Fancott, with his wife and serving lad Harris, returning from a delivery at Mr Willis's house. Fancott's horse became startled and ploughed into the band, knocking a number over, breaking several limbs and damaging instruments. The incident led to a court case with Fancott being sued for £7 7s 6d, the cost of the damaged instruments, on the grounds of his "...*wilful careless, or neglectful driving.*" Fancott claimed that his horse took fright "...*at the strains of the band, and the accompanying noise of the attendant rabble...*" and denied any blame. The judge decided against Fancott, believing that a startled horse would not head towards its cause, and therefore that he could not have controlled it properly. However, the judge also stated that volunteers must also face up to the consequences if "*making an unusual commotion*" caused an accident, but this was of little consolation to Fancott as he paid his damages with costs. More was to come; two weeks later Fancott was back in court, this time for evading a toll at Cubbington. He was fined 26s.

A new nuisance arrived in town in 1875 with bicycles being ridden along the footpaths at the side of the main roads. Despite the best efforts of the police, no riders had been apprehended until September when one out of a group of seven or eight offenders was caught. The riders, all youths, had been paid by cycle manufacturers in Coventry to show off their machines; the one unfortunate enough to be in court was fined a guinea with a warning that next time it would be the full 40s. It is not recorded which type of bicycle was involved, but it is most likely to have been the "ordinary" or penny-farthing type. The reason they were being ridden so regularly on the footpaths was simply because of the poor condition of the roads.

The first cycle club had been formed in 1870 in London, but just seven years later, on 23rd February 1877, a meeting was held at 8.00 p.m. at the Globe Inn that resulted in the setting up of Kenilworth's own cycle club. The Globe had been selected as the headquarters of the cycle club due to it having excellent accommodation "...*for both man and horse...*" and a central location. About a dozen joined at this first meeting, paying 2s 6d each, and Mr W Hosier was elected Captain and A Young

of Castle End secretary to whom all communication was sent. The club bought a small bicycle to encourage non-riders to practise. It was intended to hold regular races, and eyes were already firmly set upon attending a large cycle gathering in Leamington on Whit Monday.

In March, Dr Wynter accepted the post of President, doubtless keen to promote the health aspect of cycling, and Charles Adams the position of Vice President. The club had organised runs on Tuesday and Thursday evenings, and mid-March saw particularly favourable road conditions aided by a notably bright moon. Runs were normally at about 8.00 p.m. and riders had to wear the club uniform to participate.

When Whit Monday arrived, thirteen club members met in uniform in The Square at 11.00 a.m., and, with a small crowd seeing them off, left thirty minutes later for the cyclists' gathering in Leamington. The riders congregated in Holly Walk with members from clubs in Leamington, Coventry, Surrey, Banbury, Redditch, Leicester, Bradford and Halifax amongst others. Just before 1 o'clock, all 200 riders set off in single file in a grand procession to Warwick and back to Leamington where a meal had been laid on for those who had pre-paid. "*The great attraction was undoubtedly a tricycle ridden by a lady.*" This new product of the Ariel works (with one large wheel on one side and two smaller ones on the other side of a centrally positioned padded seat) was advertised, complete with an illustration, in the *Kenilworth Advertiser* and other local papers in the following weeks. It is probable that virtually all the other machines were Ordinarys, as the safety cycle with two similarly-sized wheels was a new invention and yet to become fashionable. It was suggested that the next meeting should be held in Coventry, the home of so many cycle manufacturers, but this motion was defeated by a large majority. The event closed with a firework display.

As 1877 progressed, bike racing became a regular event and A Riley of the Kenilworth club won a race at Brinklow in July. Sometimes races were held as part of another event; a fête at The Spring, held by the Coventry Philanthropic Society on August bank holiday Monday, included a selection of one and two-mile races; and four of the seven prizes were carried off by Kenilworth club members F Allen and T Robbins, now the club vice-captain. However, the excitement of the spectators caused problems; a number of riders were unseated by people going on to the course, and one was actually pulled from his machine whilst going at full speed. The route reported, although it is not clear if this was for a parade or the racing, was New Street Corner - Albion Row - Abbey Hill - Castle End - Kings Arms - Station Road - Southbank Road - Rosemary Hill - New Street.

The regular night-time runs were rescheduled for 5.30 p.m. due to the darkness of the nights. The last race of the year was held one late September evening, the four-mile course from the outskirts of Coventry was covered in 16½ minutes by the winner Edward Stokes. Interestingly, the sixth and last competitor home was a disabled rider, Mr W King. At a previous handicap race, King had come second to T Robbins. The club captain, Hosier, came only 5th and resigned his position soon after due to increasing business engagements. Edward

Stokes was elected in his place and his appointment was confirmed at the next AGM. Stokes was an enthusiastic cyclist, just a few months earlier he had been fined 18s 6d for riding on a pathway.

Although The Globe was the club's base, the first annual dinner was held at the Kings Arms on 13th November, just nine months after its formation, and this was to become the club's new home. There were now 34 members on the books of which 16 were active and 18 honorary. The second AGM in January 1878, was chaired by vice-president Charles Adams. A Young, the secretary, produced a favourable report announcing that the club had £1 11s 7d in hand. Several applicants were accepted as new members. T Robbins was again chosen as sub-captain, and retiring captain Hosier presented the club with a cycle that was to be placed at the disposal of honorary members who wished to learn the art of cycling. The Easter run that year was to Stratford. However, in the summer of 1878 changes were made, apparently due to several key members leaving. As already arranged, Hosier was replaced as captain by Stokes and S Newton was sub-captain, and Henry T Dean became treasurer and secretary.

Destinations for runs and potential new members were discussed at monthly meetings. There were club runs "...every Tuesday night, when fine." Perhaps the reason for the club's change in meeting venue was that in June 1878, Samuel Harding left The Globe and the town, and put up for sale some of his possessions including brewing equipment such as "...iron and copper furnaces, 16 bushel mash tub...".

Upon the death of Sarah Bury in July 1877, her many properties in New Street came up for sale, including Henry Arnold's grocers shop and the three cottages alongside, occupied by comb-maker William Spiers, wheelwright Richard Holmes and tanner Joseph Ball. Richard Holmes' son, William, later recorded that these three cottages were once an inn by the name of the White Lion. A piece of land at the rear was to be sold as a separate lot. Nearby, a group of five cottages and shops, between the Royal Oak and Coventry Cross, occupied by grocer and gardener Richard Trunkfield, cattle dealer Joseph Lenton, baker George Bennett, hairdresser William Beesley and dressmaker Jane Flanders, formed Lot 2. But the most eye-catching was Lot 3 - the Royal Oak Inn. On the ground floor were the bar, kitchen, parlour and brewhouse, and above were a large sitting room, two bedrooms and an attic. There was an excellent supply of water and extensive gardens at the rear. Included in the sale was the adjoining cottage occupied by Mrs McCarthy. The inn was sold to Evershed's for £755, the group of four cottages to B Laxon of Coventry for £430, and the group of five to John Judd for £565. Evershed's retained Thomas Brown who had been licensee since 1856, and he stayed for at least another seventeen years. Brown was also a fruiterer and market gardener.

Sarah Bury had also been the landlord of the Engine Inn; it came up for sale in December 1877. It was held on a twenty-one year lease from 29th September 1870 and the current holder was Alfred Boddington. It had a front bar, scullery, parlour, taproom, kitchen, offices and three bedrooms. Alfred Boddington bought it for £505.

Henry Clark had become licensee of the Green Man in the early 1860s and was also in a building partnership with William Ball. Ball had experience not just as a builder but also as a house-letting agent. In the early 1870s, Henry had suffered very badly from a neuralgic fever and more recently his memory had begun to fail. Ball said that his partner had difficulty in making calculations. In March 1876, Clark invited his daughter and son-in-law James Goldey to take over the inn with Goldey finally taking on the business permanently on 2nd August. There was no difficulty between the two but Clark later admitted that he had given up the wrong business. Comfortably off financially, Clark moved into a nearby cottage. At midnight on 17th August, he went outside to see to his pigs but did not return. People became concerned as he had not been his usual self for a while, and two days later his body was found floating in the river near Chesford Bridge. The inquest recorded a verdict of suicide whilst of unsound mind. His widow sold his building business to Thomas Lees of Leamington, William Ball continued on his own. James Goldey's stay at the Green Man was short; almost exactly a year after taking over, he was charged with allowing drunkenness and lost his licence. The Green Man was taken on by William Davis.

In 1871, Harriett Page was a 44 year-old widower and licensee of the Coventry Cross. It is likely that she took over the inn after the death of its previous licensee William Freeman in April 1868 at the age of 67. In 1872, having previously had the granting of her licence postponed due to the "indifferent manner" in which her premises were run, she had her licence granted as the result of obvious improvements.

William White, who had been licensee of The White Lion for only a year, was "admonished" in 1872 for allowing drunkenness that had led to complaints from neighbours.

Grocer George Church applied for a licence to sell beer and porter to be drunk off his premises, in addition to that for selling wines and spirits which he already held, but this was refused.

In 1874, Joshua Blackwell of the Queen and Castle, was found guilty of allowing after-hours drinking, it was his first problem in 20 years as the licensee. In January 1879, the Blackwell family were "picking wool" in front of a fire in a large room. When stopping to take some refreshment, a spark set the wool on fire but, with the alarm quickly raised, the flames were out before the brigade arrived. Damage was limited, but two oil paintings were burned. The summer of 1880 saw the visiting season get off to a slow start, but a party of 40 from the USA stayed at the Queen and Castle. In June, a party of 200 arrived at the station from Leicester and made their way to the Queen and Castle led by a band, and in August a party of 1,300 from West Bromwich were catered for at the same place. In October 1884, Joshua Blackwell gave up the Queen and Castle and the licence was transferred to Augustine Styles.

George Tarry's stay at the Earl Clarendon Inn in Warwick Road was short, but long enough to hold a marrow show, and by 1875 under John Davis the premises were known as The Clarendon Hotel. In July 1878, John Davis left to take over at The Globe; Joseph

Keene became the Earl Clarendon's sixth licensee in a little over eight years, and in 1880, James Barr became the seventh in ten.

* * *

Early one morning, just before Christmas 1868, a pack of crinolines fell off a freight train near the station, derailing two trucks. The train continued with the trucks bouncing along until one buried itself in the ballast up to its axles. The engine was uncoupled and ran on to Rugby to pick up the breakdown train. The line was closed for about six hours.

An accident on an 1874 summer's evening was caused by points being incorrectly set. A train leaving for Coventry ran into the siding where a row of coal wagons had just been shunted. Several trucks were pushed off the rails and the carriages of the passenger train were also lifted off. A buffer on the engine was broken off. There was a delay of only about an hour. *"Beyond a case or two of fainting and an unpleasant shake, none of the passengers were injured. Mr J Clarke was in attendance and did all that was necessary."*

In 1878 there was another accident, this time to a schoolboy. A ten year-old travelling with his school party from Leicester managed to get into one of the yards at the station as shunting was taking place, and was crushed between a wagon and buffer-stop. Dr Clarke was again in attendance and the lad was removed to the White Lion where he stayed for some weeks to recover.

The gravestone of station master Charles Nicholson.

Charles Nicholson had been Stationmaster for only two years when on 31st August 1869 he arose early to be promptly about his duties. Just as he was putting on his hat, he felt faint and after sitting down, shortly died. *"His gentle and conciliatory manner made him especially fitting for the post he held."* He had been in delicate health for some time and left a widow but no children. His replacement was Elijah Williams, transferred from similar duties at Marton. In 1879, the railway company wanted to remove him from his position but a petition was got up and was signed by many, including the local gentry. The Local Board of Health sent a letter praising his "...attention to duties and uniform civility and propriety of conduct which has been much appreciated by all classes." The desired effect was achieved and Williams stayed. However, his reprieve was short-lived and towards the end of 1879 he retired due to ill health. A collection was arranged for him at both the *Kenilworth Advertiser* office and by Thomas Morris at the bank. The following year his daughter Ada died, aged just eight.

The same week as the attempted removal, the L&NWR issued a new ruling that no employee should indulge in alcohol whilst on duty.

* * *

In the spring of 1876, following a conversation with the housekeeper Emma Perkins, gardener Stephen Hewins searched the back closet at the premises where they were both employed, the Reverend Twiselton's abode 'The Woodlands'. He looked down, lit a match, and saw lying in the earth the body of a baby girl. He alerted the rest of the servants and coachman John Allen fetched a pair of tongs from the kitchen and managed to pick up the baby and lay it on the floor. Tied around its neck was what appeared to be the hem of a skirt, and its mouth was stuffed full of dead leaves and dirt; there were bruises on its face and thighs. The Police were informed and Sergeant Ingram took possession of the body.

Missing from the house was 26 year-old Martha Busby who had worked for the Twiseltons for about six years. According to cook Mary Heden, Martha had recently been behaving oddly, complaining of neuralgia and "...*was not right in her head...did strange things and seemed bewildered."* Severe head pains had previously been treated with mustard plasters. In the previous couple of days, she had left the house with some belongings and headed for the station to make her way back to her mother's home in Culworth. It was here that Superintendent Lapworth arrested her for murder and took her into custody. She was committed for trial but was released on bail due to her poor health both physically and mentally.

The trial revolved around whether the child had lived a separate existence from its mother and was subsequently murdered, or had died before separation. The evidence of the three surgeons, Thomas Bourne, Daniel Wynter and John Clarke could only agree that the baby had lived but not at which point it died. It could not be substantiated that she was still alive when the skirt hem was tied around its neck. Martha was found guilty only of Concealment of Birth for which she was sentenced to 20 months hard labour. The circumstances of her pregnancy were never mentioned.

William Henry Dawes...

...moved from Moseley Hall in Birmingham to take up residence at Kenilworth Hall in 1871, following the death of its previous owner, Lady Cave-Brown-Cave. He was a much-respected iron master, owning the Bromford ironworks at Oldbury and the Withymoor Furnaces near Dudley. He was very influential amongst Staffordshire's iron men and was also a J.P. He was *"...uniformly genial and courteous towards all with whom he met."* Already in his late 60s, he did not become involved in local affairs when he moved to his new home town. His daughter Amelia died at Kenilworth Hall in 1874 aged 27. Due to failing health, his son took over the running of his affairs and William died in April 1878, aged 74. His funeral was a very notable event. The hearse left Kenilworth Hall in the morning of 15th April and travelled via the Bullring in Birmingham to Christ Church in West Bromwich. The streets of West Bromwich were lined with mourners and hundreds of his employees joined the cortege.

Kenilworth Hall, home of William Henry Dawes, a leading Staffordshire iron man.

As Christmas 1875 drew near, two young sons of Joseph Gardener, an Albion Street shopkeeper, were attacked by a dog near the Bowling Green Inn and sustained serious injuries. A Mr Waring was passing at the time and he managed to beat the dog off, and Mr Dencer the postman also helped rescue the *"...little ones from the savage beast."* A young man, employed by Mr Hine the butcher, took the two lads home on his horse. As he was getting back on his horse, it bolted and dragged him along by one leg until his boot came off and freed him. Mr Liggins caught up with the horse but it turned on him and kicked him in the jaw. By the time the story appeared in print, all the victims of the extraordinary sequence of events were described as doing *"as well as could be expected."* A month later, a young Trunkfield lad was bitten by Mr Dawes' dog a little way down the road at Townpool.

By 1872, the statute fair was well into decline. Despite drawing the same number of visitors as the previous year, the absence of any show or entertainment sent many home disappointed. *"Year after year the*

holiday becomes less noticed and will soon no doubt become a thing of the past." In 1875, it drew *"...a motley collection of pleasure seekers...a very poor semblance of what has been. From being a meeting for the hiring of servants, the fair seems to have become an excuse for a days rollicking fun and tippling. We think we share the wish of most of the townspeople if we say the sooner the statute ceases to exist the better."*

The *Kenilworth Advertiser* continued to be unimpressed by the proceedings and in 1877 reported, *"The annual gathering took place Tuesday last, and was the occasion for the usual debaucheries of so-called enjoyment. Fossett's circus was the centre of attraction to the town folks, and was fairly patronised. Shooting galleries, peep shows, and kindred attractions were well represented. The day has however once more passed away and we expect Kenilworth people would be glad if it was not likely to recur."*

In September 1878, possibly during the Statute celebrations, a young lad, James Sheldon, slipped as he climbed on to a swing-boat at the White Lion and his hand caught between the boat and an upright post, almost severing his fingers. That year, a large club and meeting room was added to the inn, and for hire were gigs, carriages and saddled horses. Milk and cream was supplied daily. It was not until November 1879 that there was a gathering to mark the official opening of the clubroom.

By 1871, Mary Elizabeth Taylor had set up a school in Morland House in Castle End, but by 1874 the same address was given for former brickmaker, and for the previous ten years coal merchant, Henry Hicks. Hicks supplied coal from Derbyshire, Leicestershire, Staffordshire and Warwickshire at the station at *"...the shortest notice and on most reasonable terms."* In 1876, the business was taken over by Hall and Baylis at a new address, but soon Edward Hall was dealing on his own. In early 1880, his son Thomas Hardy Hall was aboard the training frigate, HMS Atalanta, on its passage from Bermuda to England when it disappeared. It was the ninth Royal Navy ship to be lost without trace in forty years.

The address Morland House was replaced in late 1877 with the newly-built Moorlands. Set back from the road, and having a frontage of 269 yds, it was the largest building on the main thoroughfare and boasted a breakfast room, a 23ft by 16ft dining and a 27ft by 18ft drawing room, nine bedrooms, bathroom, kitchen, offices and cellaring, and had a conservatory attached. The extensive eight acres of grounds were tastefully laid out. *"The passages of the house are heated with hot water, and the sewerage from the house is arranged for distribution over the garden."* There was also stabling, a coach-house and a cottage at the front suitable for a gardener or coachman, this may have been the earlier Morland House. Initially for sale by private treaty, the property was eventually sold by auction in February 1878. Its first known occupant was Walter Watson, soon to find notoriety by poisoning dogs that strayed onto his land.

William Holmes was born in High Street on 29th June 1844, *"...in one of three cottages...which had been converted out of a public house with the sign of The White Horse...*" alongside Prospect House. "*There was also a White Lion in New Street...which was turned into three cottages and (his) parents removed into the centre cottage...*" where they were to stay for forty years. During his young days, William remembered laundry blue being made in Kenilworth.

William was a pupil at the free school in Borrowell Lane. Upon leaving school he began to learn combmaking, but became apprenticed to a Leamington wheelwright and made spokes for boneshaker bicycles. In 1870 he set up his own business as a wheelwright in a barn at the rear of the Kings Arms. William married Ann Lane of Stratford and they had six children.

In 1871 the family was living at 14 Odibourne Terrace (numbered from the Park Road end), and in 1877 they moved to live at Springfield in Crackley Lane and ran a dairy, originally Crackley Dairy and then Springfield Dairy. When he later moved to Station Road, he also named his house there Springfield.

William Holmes' new carriage and wheelwright works. The smith's with its forge was to the right of the entrance and had the shoeing house behind; the wheelwright's shop was to the left.

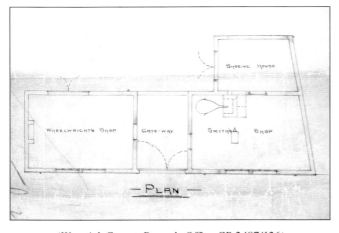

(Warwick County Records Office CR 2487/126)

In 1879 Holmes was placing large advertisements in the local press. His "Central shoeing forge" undertook shoeing at just 2s 6d a set due to the reduction in the price of iron. At the wheelwright's he produced light traps suitable for bakers, butchers, etc., from £14 and upwards, and light one-horse carts for builders and farmers from £15. His dairy delivered milk and cream to all parts of the town from 7 until 9 o'clock in the morning and from 4 until 5 o'clock in the afternoon. In about 1884, he built new large premises for his business in Station Road.

*   *   *

At its General Meeting late in October 1875, the Reverend Gordon suggested that the Institute could be of more use to the town, and that it could be the nucleus for a Working Men's Club. He envisaged its members could meet and read newspapers over a cup of tea or coffee, smoke and play any games that could be provided. The management of the club could even be left in the members' own hands. A great deal of conversation had taken place on the subject and two options were suggested; it could either be part of the Institute or entirely separate and on its own premises. A committee consisting of the Reverends Pennefather, Gordon and Button, and Alexander Carter, Luke Heynes, H E Barton and Joseph Roberts were appointed to consider the idea. By mid-November, the committee had met only once and "*...whether they will meet again we cannot say...*", but one of its members was about to take matters into his own hands: that man was Coventry Magistrate, Alexander Carter.

Alexander's father, Samuel Carter, had made his money in the Coventry textile industry and lived at The Spring. Such was his standing in Kenilworth that when he was elected MP in Coventry in 1868, the church bells of St.Nicholas were rung in celebration. He re-aligned the route of Love Lane to run in more or less a straight line, whereas it had originally run around a group of cottages. In 1870, Alexander built for himself a new house, The Spring.

Alexander Carter's home, The Spring.

When asked, he always made its grounds available for the recreation and amusement of the working classes. "*He was foremost in carrying out any good work in his quiet unassuming gentlemanly manner and especially in all matters tending to the welfare of the working classes.*" He took it upon himself to fund the leasing of a house in Castle End, and the considerable alterations and furnishings it needed, to turn it into a Working Men's Club. His swift arrangements enabled an opening date of 20th December to be announced. The club had a reading room on each of its two floors, a games room including the ubiquitous bagatelle board and other games, and a refreshment room that was served by a commodious kitchen that included an American cooking stove. There was also accommodation for the family of the person in charge, coal merchant John Riley and his wife.

At a public meeting held on 11th December, forty six members were enrolled, indicating the scheme's appeal. Membership fees were 2d a week, 7d a month or 1s 9d a quarter and were available to anyone over the age of eighteen, or younger via a vote by the committee. The founder, Alexander Carter, was unanimously installed as President, Joseph Smith as secretary and tannery manager William Clarke as treasurer. A provisional committee of nine was inaugurated - three were chosen by the President and the other six by a membership election.

On weekdays, the refreshment room was open for the general public, from 5.30 a.m. until 9.00 a.m., that was claimed it would *"...prove a great boon to those who cannot conveniently break their fast at home and who may prefer a cup of tea or coffee to the beer of a public house..."* but the lower reading room was open at these hours for members only. All rooms were open from 6.00 p.m. until 10.00 p.m. weekdays, from 2.00 p.m. on Saturdays and 2.30 p.m. on Sundays. Beer was available to members, in the evening only, and was limited to just two glasses per person.

Lord Leigh donated a *"...handsome present of books..."* and later Lady Leigh presented a watercolour to decorate one of the walls. The ground floor reading room was described as comfortable, and about ten weekly and four daily, (two Conservative and two Liberal) newspapers were taken of which at least one was donated. Within months, a second bagatelle and games room was opened.

Quite probably, but not certainly, this is the Working Men's Club.

The club was financially solvent from the start. The first six months saw a clear profit of £2 15s from an income of just over £35 collected from membership fees, refreshments, bagatelle and sale of newspapers. There were now seventy four members and they had voted for a new committee, consisting of William Clarke, G P Gregory, R Rees, W Arnold, A Woodford, J Cooke, H Webb, T Dickenson and J Brown jnr who took the position of secretary.

During its first year, the club received a number of notable donations. Dr Wynter gave a handsomely bound two-volume work *Pictorial Gallery of Arts and Industry of all Nations* and Lord Leigh *The life and letters of Lord MacCaulay*. Lady Leigh presented two more watercolours from her own hand, and the death of Mrs Frederick Russell of Clarendon Villa led to the donation of her large collection of watercolours and no fewer than 155 books. In addition, the club was in a position to borrow 60 volumes on a regular basis from the Working Men's Club and Institute in London to which it was affiliated. It is clear, from these donations at least, that the local gentry saw the club as an Institute for the working man and not just a place for playing games and socialising.

In July 1877, Alexander Carter presided over the regular six-monthly meeting. He had been out of the country for nine months and presented the club with some of Stanford's maps of Europe. Mr and Mrs Riley provided a supper at just 1s 6d per head which included roast beef and boiled mutton, an ample supply of vegetables, many of which were grown in the club's garden, and bread and cheese. Beer was available at additional cost. There were now thirteen newspapers and journals taken. There had been a small re-arrangement of the facilities in that there was now just the one reading room, on the ground floor with the refreshment room and kitchen. The two upstairs rooms were for games, each having a bagatelle table as well as draughts, backgammon, dominoes, etc.

By the time of its second AGM, in January 1878, membership had grown to 75, an increase of 11 in the year, and the meeting had to be held at the tannery as the club itself had no room large enough.

Although the club was very healthy its founder and President Alexander Carter was not and for some time he had not been up to his task of County Magistrate. It caused perhaps little surprise, but much sadness, when he died at his home, The Spring, on 24th November 1878, aged forty three. He was buried at St.Nicholas Church five days later.

Within two years of Alexander Carter's death, his gravestone, centre, was flanked by those of two of his father's sisters.

A little over a month later, on 28th December, the sixth general half-yearly meeting was well attended. It transpired that one of Alexander's last wishes was for his widow to give the club £50 to ensure it could continue as a "...*source of comfort and pleasure to the working men of this town...*" and with it was sent his best wishes for its continued prosperity. The average number of attendants at the club had slowly diminished during the year despite its fees being only 7d a month and there being such good facilities. The new President was William Clarke, continuing the close links with the tannery.

In an attempt to increase visitors, the club started coffee-and-bun evenings on Saturdays of which many members "*availed themselves*", thirty being present at the second such event. By March, the evenings were being successfully repeated on Wednesdays, and in June tea and coffee became available for non-members. Membership showed signs of slowly increasing.

By 1876, it was clear that improvements had to be made if the Institute was to be of any real benefit to the town, but the chance of involving the working class to a far greater degree had passed with the opening of their own club. The members generally refused to accept decline was inevitable and decided at the AGM in October to form a committee to investigate transforming the lower room into a reading room and redecorating the upper room, and this comprised the Reverend Somerset Pennefather, Joseph H Burbery, Luke Heynes and Henry Street. Estimates were presented by local tradesmen Smith, Ball, Dickenson and Nixon and a report was circulated amongst members. The improvements were estimated to cost about £110 of which just £20 would come from existing funds and the rest from donations. Work was not to begin until at least £40 was donated but this was quickly forthcoming and contracts were agreed on 28th November with Mr Ball to remodel the lower room for £67, and Mr Nixon to redecorate the upper for £3 13s 6d. New furniture cost about £30 and a new bagatelle table for the upper room cost £6 18s. The new rooms were opened on 18th May 1877.

This seems to have made little difference, income from subscriptions in 1878 came to just £21. The only wages paid, £10 annually to Richard Skutt the librarian, and the purchase of newspapers alone came to more than the income from members and it was clear that hiring out the upper room, bringing in £15, was all that was keeping the Institute financially afloat. Skutt had re-organised and classified the library and was in the process of re-numbering and cataloguing its contents. The Kenilworth Magazine Society donated a collection of *Frasers Magazine* and *All The Year Round*. Despite the Institute clearly not having the widespread appeal intended at the outset, it continued to "...*move in the even tenor of its way.*" In 1879, apart from the death of Charles Draper who had the honour of being number one on the original list of subscribers, "...*no stirring events have transpired to raise the spirits of the committee above the ordinary level, no unfortunate misfortune has occurred to mar their happiness.*"

Richard Skutt, then 34, had come to Kenilworth from Southampton in 1866 to take over as schoolmaster at Abbey Hill under the Reverend Alfred Jonathan Binnie who carried the honorary title of Headmaster. During his time the school flourished and whilst there, Skutt was also superintendent of the Sunday School and was "...*closely identified with all that has taken place at Abbey Hill.*" In 1874 he lived in High Street and also ran a lodging house. In 1876 he was approached by the parish and accepted the job of rate collector and vestry clerk. He was a very considerate collector, never hurrying the ratepayers, and at times was known to pay out of his own pocket to save ratepayers from facing summonses.

By the end of 1878, the *Kenilworth Advertiser* had once more changed hands. The Charles Adams businesses at The Library had been taken over by Miss H Richards, although she rarely advertised the "Miss". She became nothing more than an agent for the newspaper, its publisher and "*sole proprietor*" was James Edward Mugliston in Coventry.

Although the previous few years takings' were nearly £3,000 annually, Mrs Dempster put the Kings Arms up for sale in the autumn of 1879. At this time there were 15 bedrooms, the large first floor room was now described as a ballroom, and there were separate smoking, billiards, commercial, and coffee rooms, a private bar and three private sitting rooms. The detached building fronting onto Station Road, formerly the wine vaults, was now a public bar and refreshment saloon, and the large room above was used for entertainment. The stabling was sufficient for only twenty horses, (it was previously 40, suggesting that the new facilities fronting Station Road were originally stabling) and there were coach-houses, gardens and the bowling green. A flourishing horse and coach business was included, as well as the existing contract with the London and North Western Railway for coaches and parcels service to and from the station. The purchaser would also have to take the furniture and stock at an estimated value of £1,500. The new owner was William Clarke, the manager at the tannery and the town's elected Conservative candidate, who paid £2,700. Miss Richards was installed as manageress.

* * *

Vaccinating children against smallpox was compulsory, but market gardener Joseph Campion, of Spring Cottage, Spring Gardens, Spring Lane, objected to treatment for his daughter and was prosecuted by the vaccination officer Mr Thornett. His first appearance in court resulted in a £1 fine in the summer of 1876, and by the following March he was back in court for the fourth time. He was on this occasion represented by Amos Booth of Leicester "...*and between whom and the bench an altercation took place bordering on a scene.*" Campion had to pay the hearing costs and was again given 14 days to have his daughter vaccinated.

By May, he had paid over £8 in fines and costs, was still refusing to carry out the Court Order, and began to claim victimisation. Others, he stated, were only fined 2s and added that Thornett was not legally entitled to claim costs. His "*darling child*" was in perfect health and did not "*require vaccination for improvement.*" He also claimed that most of the 600 people in Birmingham who died of smallpox had been vaccinated, as had every child in a Bristol orphanage where 293 cases resulted in 19 deaths, but Thornett was unrelenting in his prosecutions. It seems that Campion's seventh court appearance in July 1877, and another £1 fine, was his last; he moved to Birmingham and within two years was declared bankrupt with debts of over £400.

* * *

The condition and misuse of Tainters Hill Common was causing concern in 1876. The enclosure award had made it lawful for gravel pits there to be used for "...necessary usages and repairs..." of the proprietors and their tenants, but now it seems that the gravel was exhausted and the area had become a rubbish dump, and was an "...eyesore to the lovers of the picturesque...to all persons entering the village by the approach of the Coventry Road." At a meeting of the overseers and occupiers at the Kings Arms, it was unanimously decided to remove the present, and prevent future, deposits. William Poole was quick to point out that it was not a health hazard in the manner of the stagnant lake on the approach from Warwick, but this nuisance was not being dealt with. A committee consisting of Dr Wynter, Joseph H Burbery, Charles Draper, Charles Nelson and Samuel Carter was formed to carry out the wishes of the meeting.

A further extension of the churchyard at St.Nicholas became necessary in 1866. There were two options; one was a 270 sq yds area to the south, the other a 180 sq yds plot to the west. Clarendon suggested the westwards extension, which was more private, but this would prove difficult for the carrying of coffins, as it had no road access from the church. In addition, in the past this area had been found to contain bones from the Monastery. The proposed southern area had better access and walling it in would also stop cattle straying into the yard, but Lady Cave objected to this as she had land alongside. Put to the vote, the southern area was the preferred choice.

Unfortunately, Clarendon refused to allow the preferred extension and he insisted upon the westward alternative, and additionally stipulated that the ruinous Priory wall and gateway in the area were not included and that the Parish must forever maintain the existing roadway at 15ft wide. He also made it clear that this would be the last time he would allow the churchyard to be extended. Reverend William Bickmore remarked that as in twenty-five years another extension would be needed, that perhaps it would be advantageous to look for a site for a new cemetery instead. By the end of 1867, a wall of scabbard stone was being built around the new westward extension.

In 1872, a visitor described the churchyard as being in "...a disgraceful and neglected state..." and things did not improve as the general condition of the yard caused a report to be made to a Parish Meeting in 1876. The volume of nettles was put down to the "...low rent paid for herbage..." and were to be cleared. There was also much untidiness due to graves not being properly made up; the surplus earth was now to be sifted to provide stones for the roads and the earth used "...to fill up the low parts." The path across the latest extension was to be altered to go closer to the new west wall, and the path across Clarendon's property was extended to the iron bridge. The path on the southeast side was altered to go "...on the other side of the wall."

Graves were dug very shallow in this most recent extension, and in December 1879, one had even been dug on a path. The path was not conveniently placed as it left an un-usable four feet gap to a wall and so it was suggested that the path could be moved a few feet allowing a little more space to be used for burials. Because of the rules governing the Churchyard, this apparently simple solution could only be carried out if it could be proved that the new path would shorten the distance to the church, and this it did. Later some graves were dug to a depth of up to 9ft to allow for multiple burials.

By the 1870s, this small area was very well-established as the town centre. It was the point at which the road from the south, for Leamington and Warwick, met the roads from the north, for Coventry and Birmingham. The much-used road to the railway station, Clarendon Street, was between the town's largest employer, the Tannery, and major hostelry, the Kings Arms that also housed the Assembly Rooms. Three more inns, the Rose and Crown, The Globe and the White Lion, were supplemented by the Working Men's Club.

A doctor's surgery, bank and Post Office provided vital services, and businesses included an ironmonger, chemist, grocer, draper, wine merchant, and a hirer of horses and carriages. It was also home to Charles Adams' Library and Kenilworth Advertiser office.

The Firs, Waterloo House (below "Lane") and The Poplars (opposite the Kings Arms) were major residences.

The arrow points to the entrance which led to Turner, Pace and Webb's comb factory.

The empty rectangle, just to the left of "273", was the reservoir that provided the tannery's water needs.

Part Two

"The Kenilworth that is to be..."

"What a delicious neighbourhood, What an attractive place of resort for hard worked people to spend their little leisure in. What a pleasant retreat for smoke-dried visitors from Birmingham, from narrow streeted Coventry. How cheering for the people of torpid Warwick. How refreshing for the sweltering denizens of grilling, glaring, stuccoed Leamington. This is a bright picture truly, but alas! It has another and darker side. With all its delights, Kenilworth is a place of smells - odours of the most overpowering description - odours not of Eden nor yet of Araby the blest, but ill smells, vile odours, the result of emanations from filthy pigstyes, reeking sewers, and stagnant cesspools...which convert Kenilworth from what it ought to be, a delectable abode, into a stench stricken wilderness. The number of deaths last winter was alarmingly great. This reputation is of no slight value to the place in bringing visitors and residents. The loss would be a blow to the trade of the town. The more people, the more trade the more prosperity and wealth."

In 1865, concerns were raised about the main sewerage ditch in Castle End and the "nuisance" it caused, and in 1867 another vestry discussion reached the conclusion that the time was approaching when something had to be done for the town as a whole. By 1871, the condition of the water in Finham Brook had deteriorated so much that litigation was threatened, and letters written by William Bromley-Davenport MP instigated a public meeting at the Kings Arms on 31st July. Such was the importance of the meeting that Lord Leigh presided. The water was so filthy that the fish had died, cattle were becoming ill and so were residents, a fact confirmed by Dr Wynter. It was claimed that Henry Street's skin-works were the major cause, which Street denied, whilst another blamed the tan-yard. William Clarke, representing the tan-yard, denied the works created any nuisance, as could be seen from an inspection of the outfall from the tan-yard pits. Street claimed the *"...mischief arose from the sewerage of the town emptying itself so largely into the brook."* A committee was formed to look into the matter, and of course, Clarke and Street were on it.

The *Kenilworth Advertiser* editorial recalled the days when boys could swim in the brook *"...without risking being flayed..."* and that a public baths fed by the brook ought to be provided for them. Baths had often been talked about and once the water was cleansed, it was certain that the scheme would be forthcoming. *"A greater boon to the town could not be provided."*

However, it was not until Warwick Sanitary Authority Medical Inspector Dr Wilson made his annual report in March 1874 that the extent of the problems Kenilworth was facing was fully realised and it became clear that major action was necessary. Wilson reported that out of about 800 houses, 38 were now unoccupied, 59 had only one bedroom, 50 were dirty and out of repair and many others dilapidated, but against this, there were also new and good class houses found throughout the town. The water supply was almost entirely from wells, but these were insufficient in a number of places, including Castle Green and the lower part of Castle End. In School Lane, 16 houses had only Finham Brook as a water supply and this was polluted from further upstream. The only supply for many houses at the lower ends of New Street and Albion Row was the spring on the Common.

The spring on the Common was the only water source for many living in Albion Row and New Street.

The efficient disposal of human waste was paramount. Many of the better houses had water closets that drained into cesspools, but 31 discharged into drains. Most houses had a privy and ashpit, (a privy was a shed with a wooden seat over a cesspit) but many were filthy, uncovered, and in wet weather filled and seeped into the surrounding soil. A serious nuisance was being caused by the daytime emptying of ashpits and privies; it was unlawful to empty these by day, so nightmen or scavengers were employed and often the contents of their carts leaked onto the roads. Walter Lockhart complained that the scavengers were *"...carting away the night soil after the proper hours."* Dung was also piled up and collected by the local authority's scavengers. The privies at 14 houses next to the Clarendon Arms near the castle drained through a common pipe into a sewer, the stench from which was extremely foul. Some sewerage came up through the grills of *"old rubble drains"* which were built purely to drain surface water. Other outlets were into ditches. Roads had to be watered due to various deposits left on them, and when dry to keep the dust down.

However, the source of many complaints was still Finham Brook; not only did it carry sewerage from the town but also, it was still claimed, untreated waste from both the tan-yard and skin-works, and until recently also gas-liquor from the gas works. Some of those out of town and downstream were again threatening legal action.

Following Dr Wilson's report, the Rural Sanitary Authority approved a Parochial Committee consisting of the Earl of Clarendon, Joseph H Burbery, William Pennington, Richard Robbins, Charles Nelson, Richard Hodges, Charles Draper, Luke Heynes and J Shearer, who were given power to consider the best way of overcoming the problems. It was known that it would be both expensive and entirely funded by Kenilworth rates. One way forward was the formation of a Local Board to give the town greater powers and to this end, a meeting of ratepayers was called at the Institute on 21st May 1874. The Reverend William Bickmore presided. It was soon revealed that the Parochial Committee already had powers to *"...call in the assistance of the surveyor and engineer to consult and advise, and propose plans and designs as to be the best course to be adopted to carry out such a works as may be required to place the parish in a satisfactory sanitary state..."* and so those assembled believed that the formation of a Local Board was not actually necessary to solve the sewerage problems. It was also generally believed that an application to form such a Board was likely to be turned down, as the Local Government Board had objections to small parishes having such powers. The Chairman had compiled a list of burials in the Parish Churchyard for the last fourteen years, which showed death rates per 1,000 people were actually falling in the last two years, and Dr Clarke admitted he had not had a single epidemic case to report. It was agreed that there were general nuisances that needed to be mitigated, but at the same time the general health of the town was good, and this led the Chairman to ask if it was right that ratepayers should incur the massive expense of a complete sewerage system? Cries of *"No, no..."* indicated the mood of the meeting. After Street and Clarke, whose skin-works and tan-yard caused much of the initial concern, had agreed to do all that they could to alleviate their problems, Henry Street himself proposed to the meeting that it was not necessary for Kenilworth to apply to have a Local Board, and this was duly carried.

As if to highlight the problems during these discussions and developments, a possibly slightly embarrassed Henry Street was in constant trouble for not providing proper sanitary arrangements at property he owned in Albion Row. Many times he had said that he would put the houses in order, but he took no action until being issued with an order to abate the nuisance in May 1875. At the same time, and in the same road, six cottages owned by John Swain shared only one convenience and the cesspool was in a shocking condition. Swain too had had several warnings and claimed to have started work, but this turned out to be the purchase of a barrow-full of bricks, and a doorframe so that he could put a door on the privy. The cesspool was about five feet deep.

The first step the Parochial Sanitary Committee actually took, in August 1874, was to appoint an engineer to undertake a survey and produce a map of the whole town from which a drainage scheme could be devised. Tenders were invited by advertisements in the local press and the committee must have been somewhat taken aback by the range of possible costs put in front of them, varying from just £55 up to £900. It was decided to accept that from Dean and Moore of Southam for £115. By May the following year, the survey had been completed but not drawn up and delivered. The surveyors had already had a time extension and were now working under penalties. Dr Wilson's report in May 1875 contained little good news; in the last year all that had been done, apart from the authorising of the survey, was the sinking of a single well for the inhabitants of School Lane. In a diplomatic understatement, Wilson said *"...at this rate of progress it is difficult to say when the drainage will be in a satisfactory state."*

Dr Wilson's report was sent to the Local Government Board in Whitehall, which in turn contacted the Warwick Rural Sanitary Authority to ask what steps were actually being taken over the removal of refuse, drainage, emptying of ashpits, scavenging, etc. If action was not taken quickly, it was quite likely that Whitehall would have to implement its own scheme at considerable cost to the town. At the Warwick Authority's direction, and in the presence of its Mr Passman, the Kenilworth Committee held a meeting at the Institute in October 1875 to discuss the situation. Passman stated that it would not be sufficient to tell Whitehall that the town was waiting for the survey, as this did not cover many of the outstanding problems. He concluded by saying that to organise scavenging properly the only course open to them was to obtain Urban Sanitary powers, which they had not attempted. Richard Robbins immediately proposed such an application and this caused *"a word storm"* but with no real alternative, the motion was carried. There was to be a sanitary meeting at Warwick just a few days later at which the application was made, and it was thought that the overdue survey would arrive the same day.

In late 1875, Whitehall contacted the Warwick Union to see if Kenilworth still wanted to obtain the new powers. The Kenilworth Parochial Sanitary Committee met at the Bowling Green Inn in December and agreed that powers should be applied for under sections 42, 44, 157 and 158 of the 1875 Public Health Act. These powers included the removal of house refuse, cleaning ashpits and cesspools, and for the proper cleaning and watering of streets. Also included were powers to govern the width and drainage of new streets. New buildings were covered with respect to construction to avoid the dangers of fire, the free flow of air around them and of course, the construction of water closets, ashpits and cesspools. All new plans had to be subjected to approval, with the authority being allowed to pull down any new building that did not conform. These powers came into effect on January 29th 1876, and Kenilworth had become an Urban Sanitary Authority.

In the summer of 1875, Anthony Morgan had been approached to start work on designing a sewerage scheme based on Dean and Moore's map, to which he was given access while it was still in preparation. Morgan had made improvements to the River Leam and designed a sewerage system for Leamington, before leaving in 1865 to carry out a similar scheme in Wolverhampton. He seemed well suited to the task and by early 1876, he was contacted about his progress.

Dr Wilson's 1876 annual report was made just a few months later and, as must have been expected, it again stressed Kenilworth's problems. *"Zymotic diseases of different kinds have been more or less prevalent during each of the four quarters and this (is) attributed in a great manner to the insanitary condition of the town."* In the two years since his first report *"...there has been but little zeal or enthusiasm shown in the way of an improvement."* However, armed with its new powers, the Kenilworth Urban Sanitary Authority was now trying to press Dean and Morgan to bring their work to a speedy conclusion.

Morgan's proposed drainage system was to collect all foul matter from water closets, all foul water from houses and manufactories, liquid refuse from cow houses and slaughterhouses, and rainfall from roofs and pavements associated with such buildings. What it would not collect was surface water draining from roads; as already mentioned some of this was already collected by old existing drains. The sewers, sufficient to carry upwards of a million gallons of water per twenty-four hours, which had been calculated to be eight times the output from all houses, were to be of 9 to 18 inches in diameter and would be of either glazed stoneware of fireclay socket pipes. These would be laid low enough to drain the lowest cellars except for those of two cottages on the west side of the Engine Inn. Eight hundred houses on eight miles of road were covered by the scheme. The outfall was planned for seven acres of fields just 180 yards past the gas works along Stoneleigh Road and after intermittent downward filtration and irrigation, the effluent could safely be discharged into Finham Brook. Part of the system required the artificial raising of effluent to a height of ten feet and this was to be done by means of a turbine, capable of providing at least twice the required power, driven by the flowing brook itself. The main sewer entered from the road and into settling pits. The sewage would then flow through a gravel strainer into a carrier to be dispersed into the fields, which were to be deeply drained and thus act as a natural filter. Crops could therefore be grown in the fields. Storm outlets, inspection and flushing chambers and ventilation grids completed the scheme which *"would not exceed £8,000"* and one man could operate it with annual running costs set at about £100.

An application had to be made to the Local Government Board for permission to borrow the £8,000, and the inquiry for this was arranged for Friday 26th January 1877. However, following a petition submitted by ratepayers, it was decided to hold a parish meeting the day before at the Institute to discuss the town's position. Henry Street was at the forefront of the meeting, and from the outset made it clear that he was against the proposal by questioning not only the necessity, but also the cost, which was due to be met by a sanitary rate for the whole parish. He was certain from his knowledge of other schemes that it was likely that it would in any event cost perhaps three times as much as the original estimate, and in addition queried whether as healthy a town as Kenilworth even needed such a scheme. If improvements were required, he suggested they could be done more cheaply. At this point, an alternative scheme, assembled by a Mr Mellis, was put forward. His suggestion was simply a streamlining of the existing system; efficient scavenging, current cesspools and middens to be filled in and new ones dug out, a proper ashpit for every house, all wells to be periodically inspected, all solid house refuse to be removed from premises, and the contents of earth closets, when not required for the householders' gardens, *"...to be moved once a week to a depot in a proper cart and mixed with earth and sold as manure to farmers."* The existing sewers would be used for surface water only. Not only was it claimed *"...that this system will lead to an improved sanitary system of the town than the proposed sewerage and water closets..."* but *"...for many years, if not altogether, will be found sufficient for the requirements of the place."* Although this perhaps was along the lines of what Henry Street and others had in mind, it was produced with no costings attached and Mr Mellis could not be present to discuss his ideas. How necessary a system was in the eyes of those at the meeting seems to have hinged on the outputs of the tannery and skin-works. Street said that he was bound by law to purify the effluent from his works at his own expense before it entered Finham Brook. Joseph H Burbery contested that the tan-yard *"...caused no unhealthy nuisance in the town, it simply polluted the water and...only killed the fishes."* However, Mr Boddington claimed it was worse than that, as his cattle refused to drink from it. Mr Heynes remarked that some of the town's sewerage ran into the same drain as that from the tan-yard and that if this was removed the tan-yard would then be bound to purify its output the same as Street was at his skinworks.

After much discussion, it was decided to form a sub-committee to represent the town at the Government inquiry the following day, and Henry Street, Luke Heynes, Gregory, William Mander and Alfred Boddington were appointed. Mr Mellis was invited to promote his own scheme, but he failed to appear.

John Thornhill Harrisson CE held the inquiry, the Rural Sanitary Authority was represented by Mr Passman, and Mr Broom was there on behalf of Mr Morgan who could not attend due to ill health. Mr Passman opened the meeting by explaining that its purpose was to consider the application to borrow £8,000 for Kenilworth's sewerage system, which he then read through in great detail. The Inspector then asked if there was any opposition to the scheme and it was Henry Street who explained the town's position in that all agreed that something must be done but the great concern was the cost - could it be guaranteed to be no more than £8,000? He also explained that as the Government paper was issued only a week before, not many had had the chance to study it in depth. Mr Broom then went into detail as to the costs of laying the required 6,085 yards of pipes. This came to £4,576. On top of this would be six storm overflows costing £286, and seven acres of land in Dalehouse Lane for the works themselves. This land then became the subject of discussion. Its owners were Lord Leigh and the Earl of Clarendon and without their agreement to sell, the scheme could not be sanctioned. Mr Harris, who occupied part of the land, claimed that it regularly flooded, and others remarked that the soil was very stony. Upon hearing this, the Inspector told Mr Broom that this part of the scheme would have to be carefully reconsidered, particularly as he also disapproved of the proposed emptying of the tanks by hand.

It was established that the tan-yard refuse would flow into the drains, but their capacity for this was questioned by Street who said his own works used 20,000 gallons of water an hour and believed the tan-yard used more. However Street's figure appears to have been a guess, as Mr Adams said the tan-yard used only 5,000 gallons in any twenty-four hour period.

Street, once opposed to the idea, then asked the Inspector if he thought that Kenilworth was competent enough to have its own Local Board of Health as many of the inhabitants would be glad of it and thought that they could better mange their own affairs. The Inspector replied that there was no reason at all why Kenilworth could not, and that the first step was to pass a resolution at a public meeting. He pointed out that the rateable value of property in town was £18,579 and that if it had a Local Board it could borrow up to double that amount. It was decided at this point to call such a meeting at the earliest opportunity and due to this, Mr Harrisson adjourned the inquiry until the 21st February.

To call the public meeting, ratepayers had first to petition the churchwardens and Charles Nelson and Phillip Newman consequently published the petition, signed by 34 ratepayers, and arranged the meeting in the upper room at the Institute for 10.00 a.m. Thursday 8th February (1877). Nelson took the chair. No one had anything but admiration for the way in which the churchwardens handled the town's affairs, but with such large sums of money and a large project to be handled, all thought it should become the responsibility of elected ratepayers. In addition, the Kenilworth Sanitary Committee and Authority had achieved little since its formation due largely, it was believed, to the Warwick Board of Guardians having the real power. Henry Street and Charles Draper were at the forefront of promoting the idea, and William Mander was one of the main dissenting voices. When put to the vote, there was an overwhelming number in favour of the town having its own Board, with just six votes against. Mander initially demanded a poll of the whole town, but subsequently withdrew the request. A committee was formed to present the case at the forthcoming inquiry, and this consisted of the Reverend Somerset Pennefather, William Clarke, Mr Harris, Charles Draper, Thomas Emery, Mr Gregory, Luke Heynes, William Poole, William Pennington, Henry Street, John Webb, John Judd and Mr Hodges.

The inquiry did not take place until early April at the Kings Arms. The outcome was perhaps by now inevitable, and it fell to Charles Draper to outline the reasoning behind the application. The town itself, with a population in excess of 4,000, 700 houses, 8 miles of roads, numerous responsible inhabitants, many visitors, 24 trains a day, a variety of schools, its own gas supply, the Institute and a rateable value of over £19,000, was enough reason as to why there should be a more direct way of governing. Nevertheless, it was the need for a drainage system and direct control over it that was the main concern. Already many were willing to take on the responsibility of being a Board member. With a suggestion from Harrisson that the Board, if permitted, should have nine elected members, the inquiry closed.

Within a couple of weeks, with the outcome of the inquiry eagerly awaited, all concerned must have been saddened to hear of the death of Anthony Morgan, the Leamington surveyor who had devised the drainage scheme for Kenilworth. He had suffered with cancer of the tongue for two years and had had two operations, but succumbed on 22nd April, aged 50.

It was early in July when the news was received that the application was successful, but the official order was dated 22nd August, and Kenilworth was constituted a District from the 30th of that month. It had now been agreed that the Board of Health should number twelve persons and as there were eighteen nominated candidates an election needed to be arranged. Only ratepayers were entitled to vote; for properties rated at £50 or below one vote was allocated, up to £100 two votes, up to £150 three votes etc., up to those exceeding £250 who were allocated six votes. Voting papers were issued by the returning officer Phillip Newman on 6th October and collected on 11th October for counting on 12th October. The result was as follows:

Joseph Holland Burbery	*831*
Henry Street	*827*
Richard Robbins	*773*
William Savage Poole	*763*
Luke Heynes	*749*
Alexander Carter	*730*
Reverend Somerset Pennefather	*710*
Charles Draper	*673*
Richard Samuel Hodges	*652*
William A Pennington	*588*
William Mander	*545*
Samuel Forrest	*533*
John Judd	523
Richard Smith	317
George Marshall Turner	303
John Webb	297
Joseph Stone Burbery	275
Reverend John Gordon	182

(Those in italics were duly elected.)

One man who had been involved in promoting the Local Board, Charles Nelson, did not live to see it come to fruition. He died at Crackley Hall in August 1877, aged 43, after an illness of several weeks. Nelson, a manufacturer at the Nelson Mills in Warwick, had lived in Kenilworth "*some time*". For his funeral, businesses were closed and blinds drawn. He left a widow, Emily, and a large young family including Frank (b.1870), Alfred (b.1872) and John (b.1876), and six daughters, who continued to live at Crackley Hall.

The first meeting of the Local Board was held

on 22nd October 1877 and Richard Robbins took the chair. The first decision made was to allow members of the press in to the meetings, and the second was to appoint a Chairman for the year and the choice was Joseph Holland Burbery. The design of the Board's Common Seal was also an important early decision, and the design incorporating Kenilworth Castle with the words "Kenilworth Local Board of Health" submitted by a Mr Waterlow was chosen. A screw seal press was also ordered. This first meeting was held at the Institute and an agreement was reached for the use of a room there for all monthly meetings for £5 a year, inclusive of fire and gaslight.

The key role of Town Clerk was advertised. The successful applicant would receive £50 a year, but had to have legal qualifications, provide his own office and live in Kenilworth. There was only one applicant and Board member William Savage Poole was appointed. However, he was not allowed to hold both positions and so he became the first person to resign from the Board. This left the Board one member short and so a replacement had to be found and this was discussed at the first meeting in 1878. It was the Board members themselves who had to appoint a replacement, and the obvious choice was John Judd who had the highest number of votes, 523, of the unselected candidates at the election. However, the residents of St.John's sent in a petition claiming that they were under represented on the Board as they had only one member representing a quarter of the population, and asked that Richard Smith could be appointed instead. Put to a vote, Smith was elected by six votes to three, despite him polling more than 200 votes less than Judd at the election.

On 5th December 1877, the Board received a letter from Mr Heath, solicitor of Warwick, again claiming Finham Brook was being polluted by both the town sewerage and refuse from the tan-yard. Communications were exchanged with Phillip Newman who stated that the tan-yard effluent was innocuous, but the Board decided to take samples and send them to Birmingham for analysis. Newman then complained at the way the samples were taken. Other samples were taken from below the filtering beds of Henry Street's works at Mill End.

Another cause of problems was a ditch running from St.John's, past the railway station and into Spring Lane due to "inproper matters" that were thrown into it. It was expected that the new sewerage system would end this sort of problem.

All the initial urgency with regards the sewerage scheme seems to have dissipated when the Local Board was formed. It was not until the middle of June 1878 that the Board discussed the subject at length when it was decided that a visit to inspect the new works at Bromsgrove would be beneficial. Another sticking point was the delay in receiving the town plans from Dean and Moore, and all agreed that nothing could be done until they were available. By August the Warwick Union Sanitary Authority were beginning to ask questions and Burbery, Pennington and Robbins had to attend their next meeting. Astonishingly, it became apparent that the plans had gone missing. Dean, on behalf of the WUSA, had executed them, but had then incurred penalties by

overrunning his time limit. Morgan had borrowed them to take off information but returned them to Dean to finish them. Due to the formation of the Kenilworth Board, responsibility had subsequently passed to them. This also created complications as to who was to pay for them; the cost was £115 and £80 had been paid. The plans finally surfaced in October 1878 when Dean handed them to Passmore of the Warwick Union.

By September 1878, a committee including Charles Draper, Alexander Carter and Henry Street had investigated the areas of town that would prove difficult to drain. The only notable area was that known as California, (Castle Green and Castle Grove) where the drain would need to be 16ft deep or require a pump.

Then, towards the end of the year, the Board were stunned by the deaths of two of its members just a month apart, Charles Draper and Alexander Carter. This time there was no disagreement as to whom the replacements should be, the next two on the election result list; George Marshall Turner (45, who owned two large drapery emporiums in Birmingham and had just moved into Montpelier House on Abbey Hill), and John Judd. Judd however declined the invitation on the grounds that he believed that a public election should be held and so Thomas Hawley took his place. The self-appointment of Board members was being much criticised, and a further complication arose by the departure from town of Richard Smith, leaving another vacancy.

At this moment of apparent disarray, the Board was due, by its constitution, to hold its next public election at which four Board members had to retire and be pitted against any new candidates, but four were reduced to three due to Smith's absence. The retiring members were drawn by ballot but by an astonishing coincidence, those drawn were those that received the lowest votes of successful candidates at the original election. All three, Pennington, Forrest and Mander, were returned and the fourth spot went to the popular man of principle John Judd. Unsuccessful candidates included Dr Bourne and tannery and Kings Arms proprietor William Clarke.

Having held the post since the Board was formed, Joseph H Burbery resigned his position as Board Chairman in April 1879, and mill owner Richard Robbins was unanimously elected in his place.

Thomas Hawley...
...the new Board member, was a Coventry silk dyer, in business since the early 1850s. By about 1871, he had moved into rented accommodation at The Poplars, opposite the Kings Arms. He regularly treated his workforce to a visit to Kenilworth; in 1873 fifty-five of them sat down to a meal, and afterwards played sports, at the Queen and Castle Hotel to celebrate his nephew passing his apprenticeship and being given a share of the company.

An advertisement had been prepared inviting tenders to build the sewer system as soon as the plans were available and when the deadline for submissions passed in mid-February 1879, twenty plans had been received, all under pseudonyms. Burbery, Street,

Pennefather, Pennington and Robbins formed a committee to examine the plans and eventually a special meeting was held to make the final decision. That chosen was submitted under the name *"Bis dat qui cito dat"* which had been submitted by George Lundie of Cardiff, who was immediately appointed engineer for the project with the instructions to complete the works as promptly as possible.

Lundie had chosen a new outfall site, where the sewerage works themselves were to be, 700 yards east of Harpersford (Common Lane), of which seven acres was owned by Clarendon and three acres by Lord Leigh. For reasons that were never explained, Clarendon was totally opposed to selling land for the works and the Board began proceedings to invoke compulsory purchase, but continued negotiations with the hope of a solution. Due to Clarendon's obstinacy, it was suggested that one of the other schemes could be adopted in place of Lundie's. Mr Hawley highlighted a couple of cases where other schemes failed under similar circumstances, but the Board generally agreed that the chosen outfall site was of perfect geological construction and thus ideal for the scheme. Additionally, it was by at least £1,500 the cheapest.

Harrisson now had to arrange another inquiry, in March 1880, to authorise the compulsory purchase of Lord Clarendon's land for the outfall site. Clarendon had no representation at the meeting but sent a letter stating a change of mind and agreeing to sell the land for £200 an acre. As this was the first time the Board members had heard of the offer, a Board meeting had to be held to discuss it before the inquiry could continue. Harrisson said that the Local Government Board was inclined toward granting the order and that he would do all he could to help. The Board took just a few days to accept Clarendon's offer.

In contrast, Lord Leigh was always in favour of the scheme and once various technical points had been discussed, agreed to the £700 sale of an area of his land. Mr Boucher, the tenant farmer on the land, was paid £75 in compensation.

There were a couple of difficult areas in the system. One was the low-lying area at the Engine Inn for which Lundie devised a system with a pump so sewerage could be removed once a week *"...or oftener if required."* The other difficulty was at Castle Brook and this was to be resolved by the use of cast iron pipes across the stream.

The next stage was an inquiry into the loan of the £8,000 required to complete the scheme. This was held again by Harrisson at the Board's office at the Institute in December 1880, but due to lack of space the meeting was reconvened at the Kings Arms. Dr Wilson explained that the powers being applied for came under the Public Health Water Act that assumed the district had a public water supply. Kenilworth had not; most houses were supplied by pump-wells, on average 40ft deep, but some relied upon the brook, which was contaminated by sewerage entering it near the Castle. There were regular, small, scattered outbreaks of typhoid due to this. Kenilworth did not have the power to enforce the act, and so the inquiry was being held to follow the procedures required for the request for the loan of £8,000.

The previous request had not included the cost of land and other expenses involved with the outfall site. The meeting concluded with the impression that Harrisson would report to the commission favourably, and the result was eagerly awaited.

The nature of the tannery inevitably produced a variety of stenches and these were sometimes brought to the notice of the Local Board. In the summer of 1879, Mr White of Beech Villa, Station Road, called attention to a particularly bad odour coming from the most offensive part of the tanning process, steepening and softening the hides, which was being carried out in an outbuilding adjoining Station Road. The liquid refuse was not being pumped out sufficiently often. However, Mr Wilson had already carried out an inspection at the request of the tannery themselves, and his lengthy report was now available. Its recommendations included moving the process to a covered building near the chimney so its smells could be vented through it, that liquid refuse should be limed or disinfected before passing into the drains and that horns and fleshings should be removed during the early morning scavenging hours. In addition, the premises generally had to be kept cleaner, the lime pits emptied and cleaned more often, and no waste material allowed to accumulate. It appears William Clarke acted quickly in the matter, as these particular odour nuisances were already abating.

Pollution of the local water, however, remained. Phillip Newman had claimed that he could solve the problems but he took no action and in early 1880 legal proceedings were taken against him. Organic matter in the brook had been found at 38.3 grains per gallon and acids found proved their origin. The trout in the stream were poisoned and dying in great numbers and one farmer had fenced off the brook to stop his cattle drinking from it. There were no such problems above the tan-yard outlet.

During the following summer, the tannery erected a new settling tank *"...in a field opposite the tanyard..."* into which was pumped condensed steam and wastewater with the intention of irrigating the field, but a lack of cleansing had quickly resulted in the build up of offensive material and again the local inhabitants complained. Once more, William Clarke ensured it was dealt with it quickly and the complaints stopped, but it was always the health of persons living in the neighbourhood of the works which was the concern, the lot of the tannery workers was never mentioned.

One of the first tasks undertaken by the new Board, in August 1878, was the drawing up of bye-laws. These were to deal with: 1) the cleaning of footways, roads, house refuse, closets and privies etc., 2) the regulation of lodging houses, 3) new streets and buildings, 4) slaughter houses, 5) licensing of Hackney carriages, and 6) velocipedes, bicycles and tricycles. It was that concerning bicycles, currently classed as *"nuisances"* that caused the most discussion. Bicycles now had to carry a *"...properly trimmed lamp..."* and bell to alert pedestrians of their approach and they could not be *"driven"* through the streets in a manner likely to be a danger to the public. This prompted a response in both the editorial comment, and a letter from Kenilworth Cycle Club Captain Edward Stokes, in the *Kenilworth Advertiser*. Stokes made the point that the dangers were in fact the other way round, the public were a danger to cyclists, regularly throwing objects such as caps and hats at the wheels, attempting to cause accidents. He also made the obvious observation that riders tried to avoid accidents at all times as they would invariably come off worse.

Cycle Club members continued to be successful at local events. At a Coventry meeting T Allen won first prize in two races with J Smith coming second in one of them. Smith had been a first prize-winner at an earlier meeting. The weekly club runs, mostly in the evenings, continued to destinations such as Stoneleigh, Coventry, Leamington and Mere End. In early November 1878, the club held its second AGM at the Kings Arms at which Mrs Dempster produced a feast worthy of consumption by those interested in their health. This included cod with oyster sauce, sole, boiled fowls with celery sauce, roast fowls with tongue, goose, roast beef, sucking pig, German and Eva puddings, apple charlotte, jellies, blancmange, tartlets, apple tarts, cheese and celery. There was plenty for all, especially as there was a smaller than expected attendance. The vice-president of the club, Charles Adams, spoke of the success and standing of the club in glowing terms, and remarked upon the prestige it had due to the efforts of members such as Allen, Smith and Robbins. In response, Captain Edward Stokes remarked how surprised everyone was that the club had survived at all. After all the usual toasts were drunk, songs were performed by several members, accompanied on the piano by Mr Porter of Coventry. There were now thirty-two members. The event dispersed at midnight.

* * *

At the fire brigade AGM in May 1877 held at the engine-house, Captain Soars announced his resignation from a position he had held for barely a year, as he was leaving the town. He had made no mention of this just the previous month at the annual dinner. H Webb was unanimously elected in his place. Captain Webb presided over a large number of members at the annual dinner at the Bowling Green the following year.

In 1878, the brigade made a request to the Board for more hose. Henry Street spoke as to its poor condition: *"If there were a fire, the consequences could be disastrous."* Hatchets and a saw were also requested. Following a big fire in Birmingham where there were fatalities due to people being trapped on the upper floors of a building, the Kenilworth brigade decided to hold another series of public demonstrations of the use of jumping sheets. The first of these was successfully carried out with brigade members jumping from the top floor of the Working Men's Club, but another demonstration at Mr Holland's house did not quite go according to plan; the sheet tore in the centre and fireman H Holmes fell through it, but was uninjured. After this, at a meeting between members of the brigade and the Highway Committee, it was decided to purchase six lengths of hose, several axes, and two new jumping sheets.

At a typical monthly drill, the brigade members mustered at the engine-house at around 6.00 p.m. and took the engine to the Abbey Fields, near to the iron bridge, for drills and exercises lasting about an hour and a half. At the March 1879 drill, the new lengths of hose were attached to the old for the first time, but this still left a shortfall of 100 yards from the brook to the high town. The lack of access to a good water supply, particularly south of the Abbey Fields, was a major problem. The tannery reservoir could prove useful should there be a fire near to it, but elsewhere the water pumps provided "scanty driblets." It was suggested in December 1879 that the old pound in the vicinity of the Castle End/ Borrowell Lane junction could be converted into a reservoir and filled by the brigade in a practice session by connecting a hose to the Barrow Well, or perhaps rainfall could be collected. The town had been fortunate in not having had a major fire since the brigade was formed but it was suggested it was ill advisable to *"...lock the door when the steed is gone."*

The condition of the engine-house deteriorated through neglect. It was believed that Sarah Ryley, who owned the house and received £3 a year rent, was paid sufficient for her to keep it in good repair. Dr John Clarke now lived in Hill House, alongside the engine-house, and he allowed the brigade to use his grounds for drying their hoses.

The year 1880 saw a number of fires attended by the brigade and perhaps inevitably the first, in February, was at the luckless William Mander's Oaks Farm. Mander and his wife were in Coventry on a February afternoon when the fire was first spotted in the rick-yard. Mr Mander jnr sent a messenger to Captain Webb and a Mr Brown made for the tannery from where a number of men were sent. Before the brigade arrived the fire was kept under control by using buckets, Charles Trepplin and his son Ernest, living at Green Hayes in Leek Wootton, were amongst those assisting. Half an hour after the alarm was raised the brigade arrived just as an adjacent barn began smouldering, but the damage was restricted to a pea straw-rick and a hay-rick. *"Kenilworth ought to be proud of its brigade and the admirable way in which they responded to the call of duty. The creditable manner in which the brigade got to work, and the short space of time that elapsed before the brigade arrived on the scene..."* were amongst the published praises. The Stoneleigh brigade arrived just as the fire was extinguished.

Several months later, a hay-rick estimated at upwards of eleven tons, the property of Abbey Hill contractor and builder William Ball, was set on fire by children playing with matches. The fire brigade was soon on the spot, but almost immediately the pump became blocked and the volunteers, assisted by willing members of the public, had to resort to using buckets. A small fire in a hovel was also spotted and quickly dealt with. Within 24 hours, the engine was working again and the following day a practice with it was witnessed by some of the Board members who left thoroughly impressed by what they had seen. The importance of the speedy repair could not be under-estimated, for within a week children playing with matches was again the cause of another fire, this one in a hovel at Mill End in a field belonging to Alfred Boddington of the Engine Inn. Little damage was done due to the efficiency of both brigade and engine.

Although outwardly the brigade had the admiration of all, internally there were difficulties. In early 1881 differences between various members resulted in the resignation of Captain Webb, Deputy Captain Poole and others. In their places were elected E Davies as Captain and C Robbins as deputy captain, but within a month the "...difficulties were settled..." and all returned to their former posts. However, just two months later at the AGM, Captain Webb was ousted and Ernest Trepplin, now living in Kenilworth, was elected Captain, with E Davies as his deputy, and R Holmes, W Walton, J Liggins and J Brewer as Lieutenants. T Hughes was secretary and C Robbins treasurer. As Trepplin had lived in town just a matter of months, to be given such a prestigious position so readily he must have been well-known to townsfolk during his time at Leek Wootton.

In November 1881, Captain Trepplin wrote to the Board asking that the "...cold hose and cistern..." be replaced as they were only suitable for practise, and that gas be laid to the engine-house - two jets would assist in keeping the engine in working order.

In late September 1882, there was a fire at builder Edward Smith's premises in School Lane. It was discovered in an outbuilding alongside his wood yard and carpentry shop, but the brigade, housed just a few hundred yards away, arrived in less than eight minutes and managed to stop the flames from spreading. Despite their efforts, the damage done was valued at £170. Smith subsequently made a donation to brigade funds of £5 10s and this boosted their income to a record £45 12s for the year. Subscriptions were at their highest, £32 2s from 127 subscribers, bettering even the year that Brigade members acted as canvassers. From this was paid the cost of the annual dinner, other refreshments, etc., and the repayment of a £13 6s 8d loan from Trepplin for the brigade tunics and caps. There were now 26 members and only three of them, H White, W Bishop and T Hughes attended the twelve ordinary and five special drills, but more than half managed fifteen in total or more. Three members, two called Holmes and the other Davis, only managed one appearance between them. One of the Holmes's was a Lieutenant and the election of the four Lieutenants "...caused a somewhat exciting competition and occupied a considerable part of the meeting." It took three ballots and the settling of a disputed nomination before Dr Myles Atkinson, W Walton, Thomas Plumbe and J Liggins were appointed; Aitken and Plumbe replaced Heatley and Holmes.

Captain Ernest Trepplin was not at this meeting as he was abroad; Deputy Captain C Robbins took the chair and with no opposition Trepplin was re-elected to his post. One of the Holmes's had written in to resign his membership and Edgar Lockhart, Prime, Oakley and Glenn had been nominated as replacements but no ballot took place.

Several members took exception to the way in which attendances were recorded, as some turned up late and others left early, and this was clarified by the ruling that a satisfactory reason had to be given for arrival after roll call, and anyone leaving early would be fined 6d and lose his attendance.

In the captain's absence, Dr Atkinson raised a point that at a recent practise three men "...exhibited little agility in getting up the walls of the Castle..." and thought they needed additional work as agility was vital in escape work. Amid laughter, someone remarked that one of the three was tall enough to be used as an escape in any case!

* * *

In early 1881 the Board received the news that the application for the loan to build the sewers had been successful, and tenders for the construction of the works were subsequently advertised in *The Engineer, Builder* and *Building News* at a total cost of £2 8s 6d. Two contracts were to be had, one for the sewerage system and one for sewerage works. There were twelve tenders for laying the pipes and the successful applicant was John Fell of Leamington for £3,935 11s 11d. Fell was also the successful of the three applicants to build the outfall site with his bid of £1,471 17s 8d although this was later reduced by £77 due to errors in the plans.

By mid-April 1881, work had commenced. Although a Mr Ingram was initially appointed, in August upon Lundie's recommendation, Alexander Kyd was appointed Clerk of Works at a rate of £3 a week.

Oddly, when came the time in early June to send the mortgage to the Public Works Loan Committee, it was realised that the Board had not formally adopted a name for itself and in January 1881 "The Kenilworth Local Board" was decided upon. The seal had to be recut omitting the words "of Health".

By early July, all the deeds and contracts for the workings had been signed and £5,000 of the agreed £7,963 loan had been paid into the bank. This had to be paid back in 60 half-yearly instalments - the final payment of £149 6s 2d being due on 30th June 1911.

Contract number one, for the sewers, was progressing well in September. The main 18ins outfall sewer was complete, as were all the 15ins pipes and those from Mill End to Odibourne Terrace and along School Lane, Odibourne Terrace to Ladies Hill, and Mill End to Albion Row. There was some delay in obtaining 8ins and 10ins pipes. The first £1,000 due to John Fell was paid.

Contract number two, for the sewerage works themselves, was almost complete with the exception of the tanks and fencing, and "carriers" which were awaiting special fittings. The straining tanks at the sewerage farm were almost complete by the end of November and at about this time, Clarendon was paid £1,191 7s 1d on account of purchase money, interest and costs for the sewerage works land.

Frederick Slade, who was the spokesperson for the drainage committee, reported in October that in many places trenches had been dug for the sewers but delivery of the pipes was still awaited, causing much complaint. He was instructed to tell Fell not to dig up the roads in future until the pipes were delivered. Later that month, the gas company were asked to keep two or three lights lit until dawn at the places where the sewer scheme caused obstructions. The town drain leading from Clifton

Terrace to Washbrook, where it crossed the main road, had to be lowered to pass under the main sewer, and the original town drain running north from Townpool Bridge was taken up and laid at a lower level with a 15ins pipe to allow the new sewers to be connected to it.

There had been a great deal of dissatisfaction at the state the contractor was leaving the roads in, many were practically impassable. It was difficult to see where any of the work had been satisfactorily completed, and in some places it was left in a dangerous state, particularly at the bottom of Park Road. It was decided to withhold some payments until the problems were rectified. The "navvies" employed on the works were given a treat at the Mission Hall near the end of October, but of the 89 who sat down only about 20 were from Kenilworth, the rest were from Leamington and Warwick.

Early the following month, the laying of pipes was almost complete but the condition of the roads was again causing great concern. *"Once remarkably smooth..."* they were now *"...utterly impassable."* Station Road came in for particular criticism as mud went over the tops of shoes and boots.

On 14th November 1881, the flushing tank at the upper end of Albion Row was the first to be successfully tested with water carried by carts from the brook at Mill End. *"The action of Field's patent annular syphon has proven satisfactory, discharging the water from the tank into the sewer at the rate of 60 gallons a minute."* Similar tests were carried out elsewhere as sections became completed. The existing sewer in Southbank Road was finally deemed as belonging to the Board and so it could be connected to the new scheme. The *"...embanked sewer across the meadow leading to Castle Grove (was) abandoned..."* and a new sewer built. This began at a junction with the Castle Green sewer in the Abbey Meadow, crossed the brook near the iron bridge, and went in a straight line to the Borrow-well Lane bridge where it crossed the brook again and then to the houses at the back of Castle Grove. As the sewer work progressed in the Abbey Fields in November, worked stone with carved flowers was found at a depth of just 3ft. Also found were un-worked stone, glazed pottery and other relics. Beyond the 6ft depth of the works was found *"...a subterranean passage, supposedly to Warwick."* Part of the stonework collapsed on a Kenilworth labourer called Heath, injuring his legs.

One necessity of the scheme was to straighten the run of the brook through the Common to the sewerage works and the building of a bridge at Harpersford (Common Lane). This was to be carried out by the Board's own employees, separate to the contracts for the sewerage scheme, and the cost of the bridge was raised by donations. The Earl of Clarendon gave £150, Henry Street and Richard Robbins £25 with a promise of another £15 each if required, and others contributed lesser amounts. The main discussion point was whether the bridge was to be temporary, wooden with iron girders or an iron bridge. A 20ft wide bridge with iron girders and wooden soleing would cost £181 and carry 10 tons, an iron bridge with brick arches would cost beyond £200. £235 was already collected and, when taking into

account the stream re-alignment, the deficiency to be met by the Board, would amount to about £187. With additional donations expected, it was decided that the more expensive option was preferable. By the next meeting, Lord Leigh had donated £20 and a sizable amount from Charles Adams was expected - he promised £20, rising to £35 if the more expensive option was taken up. The final decision was made in favour of the expensive option in August 1881; stone parapets, blue brick arches and iron girders, would cost £230, and the brook diversion £245. £305 was the final total of donations leaving the Board to pay £170. By this time, the new brook course had been dug and on 16th August Mr Evans was directed to fill in the old course, a task that he completed within a month.

By mid-September, the abutments of the bridge were complete and ready to receive the girders that were arriving in the next few days. Evans, the road surveyor, started raising the road level on the northern side of the bridge with *"...soil and gravel from the road on the southeast side of the Common."* The southern approach was raised by Fell using material obtained from widening the Stoneleigh road opposite the entrance to the sewerage works. By mid-November the girders were in place, the brick arches were ready for concrete, and at the December 1881 Board meeting it was announced that the new bridge was complete and that the roadways to it were proceeding satisfactorily.

Further donations towards the *"...stream diversion and Common improvements..."* were received early the following year and included £40 from Mr Robbins, £10 from Mr Burbery and £5 from Mr Nelson. Henry Street contributed his extra £15 as promised.

By February 1882, it was thought that all the sewer works would be completed within ten days and it was decided to advertise for a tenant at the sewerage farm on a lease of seven years. In April the following year, the Board agreed to have Charles Trepplin as tenant of the sewerage farm for eight years, with the first rent-free, the next two at £2 an acre and the remainder at £5 an acre, to reflect the uncertainty of yields. In addition, it was decided to contact the managers of the tan-yard and fellmongers to see what steps they were taking to purify the effluent from their works. Once more, the condition of Station Road was causing concern; a leak had been suspected in the system and so the road was dug up again while the problem was sorted and the excavation re-filled. Unfortunately, the repair had not been inspected and so the road was dug up a third time and left several days before the inspection was carried out. Piles of earth were left along the road. Nearby, it was also realised that the sewer pipe was not long enough to reach the tannery and so had to be extended. A man in Station Road breaking up stone for the roads was considered a danger and a wooden screen was erected around him to protect passers by.

By mid-April 1882, Fell's original contract for the sewerage works and drainage were complete, but an amount of additional work was being undertaken in Parkhill Road and Station Road. Mr Kyd, who had been Clerk of the Works during construction, was now employed at the same salary to oversee the connection of private drains to the new system.

Whilst all this was going on, the Board itself was once more in turmoil due to members leaving. The Reverend Somerset Pennefather had announced his intention to leave Kenilworth for Lincolnshire and resigned in February 1880, but within a month he had reversed both decisions. However, by the end of 1881 his future had been assured in the Parish of Jesmond and so for a second time he resigned from the Board. At the same meeting, John Judd, now 70, resigned for personal reasons, his wife Rebecca died at their home in Ladies Hill a few weeks later.

This created two vacancies on the Board and at the January 1882 meeting, there were heated exchanges during the nominations for their replacements. It began with Dr Wynter trying to propose two names as replacements, before being told he could only nominate one; his choice was hotelier and tannery manager William Clarke, 56, who had been in town 20 years. There were objections to him on the basis that he was an hotelier, but Wynter pointed out that board Chairman Richard Robbins was a principal shareholder in Coventry's Queens Hotel. In addition, it was claimed his position as tannery manager would conflict with the sewerage problems, but against this Henry Street had managed well enough. Clarke had also spent six years as Clerk to the Warwick Board, which made him eminently suitable. Joseph H Burbery then nominated Luke Heynes, in business as a horn dealer, as he was such a well-respected member of the community. Henry Street proposed Ernest Trepplin in preference to Clarke with his credentials being a large ratepayer, the way in which he captained the fire brigade and taken a keen interest in the Institute, but Trepplin had lived in the parish for just 18 months and was *"...only just fresh from college."*

It was then that Wynter interceded and said that as Street's nomination of Trepplin was in effect an amendment of his own proposition, he had a right to reply, to which Henry Street objected. Wynter again rounded on Street claiming inconsistency in his arguments and an altercation took place. Once order was restored, it had to be decided how to proceed with three nominations for two seats. When put to the vote, Heynes was elected without opposition, and Trepplin appointed in preference to Clarke by five votes to three. However, within two months there was an election when once more, retiring members by rotation were up for re-appointment along with the new members, Heynes and Trepplin, and other nominations, William Clarke and William Evans of The Spring. Trepplin was ousted, just two months after being elected, and the popular William Clarke successful, along with William Evans.

At the meeting which welcomed the new members in April 1882, Richard Robbins announced his decision to retire as Board Chairman, a position he had held since 1879, due to *"...troubles at home and business."* The cause of his domestic problems became apparent ten weeks later with the death of his wife, Mabel, 55, at their home The Hollies in New Street. Robbins recommended Frederick Slade as his successor who, as a Civil Engineer, knew the practicalities of both the sewerage and water systems better than anyone else on the Board. Henry Street remarked how fortunate they

were to have such a man at this time, and so a very surprised Slade who had been in town less than two years, and on the board for one, became Chairman despite his very honest observation that he knew so little about Parish affairs.

The Hollies, the New Street home of mill owner and Board Chairman, Richard Robbins.

In November 1881, there was an outbreak of scarlet fever amongst schoolchildren and of the first twenty five cases, five were removed to the sanatorium at Warwick. The closure of schools was considered but the blame was initially put upon parents who were *"...going to other peoples houses while the disease existed in their own."* Dr Wilson was certain that the disease was not of the fatal kind, yet within weeks two deaths, in High Street and New Road, had occurred and eventually 43 cases were reported. A quarter of these were removed to the sanatorium, as they could not be isolated at home.

Sending a child to the sanatorium cost the town 7s 2d a week and the bill for 1881 was £31, £11 more than that for Leamington. Patients, or their families, only paid the fees if they went of their own accord. It was suggested that if the families could afford to pay for themselves when sent by a medical officer, they should. The Board claimed they only sent cases *"...to prevent disease spreading...for public safety..."* and patients were thus mostly poor people.

As the sewer works were nearing completion, Dr Wilson had stressed the need to connect houses to it without delay and recommended that as connections to houses were made all drains should be thoroughly inspected to ensure they complied with the latest bye-laws. Just three months later, there was an outbreak of typhoid at Whitemoor at two cottages alongside the brickworks. The source was a well used by the Constable and Moseley families and several children from each family went down with the disease. Annie Constable, aged 11, died on 10th May. There was another case at Little Virginia attributed to using the same polluted well as young Annie. The infected well was *"...opened, examined and cleaned out and the drains cleansed, relaid, trapped and the yards repaired."* Later in the month, there was another typhoid death, this time in Albion Street, of which "...the cause was doubtful." At the same time, there was another scarlet fever outbreak, a dozen cases mostly in the Albion Street and Mill End areas. One child, Elias Steed's 4 year-old, died. In these later cases, only one was removed to the sanatorium; perhaps the discussion about the cost had had an effect. 1881 had also seen 9 cases of overcrowding, 17 houses fumigated and lime-whitened, 3 houses unfit for habitation and pulled down or closed, and 37 "...cesspools and ashpits cleansed and manure or pigs removed." Perhaps surprisingly, Dr Wilson declared, "In other respects, the health of the district continues to be satisfactory."

The overcrowding cases of large families were of great concern. John Needle had seven people sharing one bedroom and was ordered to send three into lodgings or move house. George Littleton had his family of ten in two bedrooms including one that was just 6ft square, whilst Henry Bayliss had nine in one bedroom a little over 12ft square. He was told to send four into lodgings or move to a house with two bedrooms.

Another bad case was at the house of Thomas Perkins (44), a former Cross Row coal dealer and now general labourer of Albion Street. He, his wife, sons aged 22 and 15, and daughters aged 13, 10, 8 and 5 shared two bedrooms, one was 12ft by 10ft by 7ft, the other was a 6ft cube. He was ordered to move or send away just three of his children. Two years previously, he had been warned to remove two of his children.

Some attempted to supplement a meagre or non-existent income by taking in lodgers, but this also caused problems: James Harris was in trouble for having 13 people in just three bedrooms but as four of these were lodgers, he was told to make them leave. In late 1882, there was a shortage of accommodation in town due to the influx of navvies involved in the improvements to the railway but the worst case of overcrowding did not involve lodgers. An unnamed family had a husband and wife sharing a bed with three of their children, and a further four children sharing a mattress on the floor of the same solitary bedroom.

* * *

The exploits of Captain Webb, in particular his crossing of the English Channel in 1875, brought the sport of swimming to the attention of the public on a previously unseen scale. Bathing in cold water was believed to be a cure-all medical treatment, as experienced, for example, by visitors to Leamington Spa, but the benefits of swimming as an exercise and sport were beginning to be appreciated for the first time. In the spring of 1876, a writer to the Kenilworth Advertiser, signing himself as "Kenilworth Dust", was certain "...plenty will be willing to assist...in forming and keeping in repair an open bathing place, similar to what are provided in Leicester...with the recollection of the noble feat of Captain Webb fresh in our minds, surely Englishmen generally will be proud to learn to swim." A second letter the following week, by "Aquatic", said the subject had often been talked about and he was certain there would be no difficulty in raising the

necessary donations and funds if a site could be found. However, "Piscis", writing in the first week of June, explained that some time since, progress had been made as far as the preparation of plans and specifications, but that the scheme had fallen through due to the lack of a suitable site. With this, the subject fell temporarily from the newspaper's pages.

In 1878, another committee was appointed to raise funds for a proper and safe bathing place, specifically aimed at the boys and young men of the town. It suggested the formation of a public company and the issue of shares, but again the scheme fell through as Lord Clarendon refused to enter into discussions about the use of land.

The public baths in Coventry were well situated but ran at a dead loss; one day a week for example was set aside for ladies, but so far only six had attended. The most numerous visitors were "street arabs" to the outdoor pool taking the opportunity to get clean once a week. But early in 1879, letters once again started to appear in the Kenilworth Advertiser. The first suggested that a section of the brook through the Abbey Fields could be fenced off for Kenilworth youths, as at the moment they "ran the risk of being summonsed" or walking all the way to the river at Chesford. Another letter claimed that every boy should learn to swim and "...every man should have a cold dip every morning for health's sake only." An editorial showed that the newspaper itself was in favour: "As a recreation swimming is one of the few amusements that invigorate while at the same time they refresh the muscle energies. We are not talking of prolonged exertion, but of the ordinary "header" followed by its attendant swim. Anyone who knows what a luxury it is to enjoy a matutinal plunge in the hot days of July will endorse what we say. Then again, we come to our strongest point of all. Every boy as our correspondent points out, should learn to swim - and we would add every girl too - and where can a lad learn the art better than in a public swimming bath." It further suggested that the Local Board should discuss the matter, but at the same time conceded that it was probably too occupied with the sewerage system to be concerned. The Reverend Somerset Pennefather did raise the matter at the next Board meeting and claimed "...the scenes in the Abbey Fields are not particularly decent..." but the matter was, as predicted, dropped with no action taken. Further letters appeared signed by schoolboys, although it was later claimed they were written by an adult. One said "...it is a very shocking sight to see a few boys enjoying themselves in the water..." whilst another highlighted other problems: "...the water in the Abbey Fields barely reaches the pockets of your breeches..." and when swimming from Chesford towards Blackdown bathers soon got stuck in mud.

The relevance of learning to swim was highlighted by an incident which occurred at the time these letters were appearing. A young girl, Lizzie Bastock, was walking home from school when she fell into the millstream opposite Odibourne Terrace. Mrs Barlow, who lived in the terrace, jumped in and saved her. It was a favourite area for children to play, but there was no fencing of any kind so it was an accident waiting to happen, and all admired the pluck of a woman carrying out the rescue. It was perhaps no surprise that the Local Board announced it would be discussing the subject again, but one wit was not too hopeful: *"How are we to expect to have any baths, when we want quiet waters and our Board Clerk is a Savage Pool?"* Poole had been called upon several times by Joseph Stone Burbery, the son of Joseph Holland Burbery, but he regularly told him that the Board was too busy with the sewerage system and suggested he contacted the Reverend Somerset Pennefather, and Pennefather again raised the matter at a monthly meeting. This led to the same lack of action as before and so Pennefather called a public meeting at the Mission Hall on Friday, 20th June 1879.

He was voted to the chair, and was quick to say that he would be glad to see the establishment of a swimming baths, and that Dr Wynter had written to him expressing their value. After some discussions as to the likely cost and possible sites, it was decided to form a thirteen-man committee to investigate further. Three days later the committee met where it was understood that the preferred site was in Borrowell Lane alongside *"...the pumping station..."*, presumably the water pump used by the water-carts. It was decided to write to the Earl of Clarendon to see if he could assist, as he was the landowner. At a meeting on 4th July, the Earl's reply was read, unfortunately its contents pass unrecorded, but it seems that it was none too helpful as once again nothing came of the proposals. Amongst those present at these meetings was committeeman William Holmes, (who later reminisced that as a small boy he was once chased home to New Street from a swim in the Abbey Fields *"...in my original birthday suit..."*), and John Swain a School Lane builder, whose son was soon to be the victim in Kenilworth's most tragic swimming accident.

It became clear that a new proposal was required that relied upon voluntary contributions, and Joseph Stone Burbery became active in acquiring promises of help, but the summer of 1880 saw the tragedy that was perhaps responsible for giving the scheme a new degree of urgency. William Ernest Swain, 13, son of John Swain, had gone to bathe in Finham Brook at the Common near to Harpersford with a number of other boys. Although not a swimmer, he tried to cross the brook at its most popular bathing spot, known as the whirlpool, where the water was seven or eight feet deep, and he was soon sucked under. An eleven-year-old boy called Rice made a valiant attempt to reach him but was not strong enough. Other boys called for help from men working in nearby fields and Charles Cockles was the first to reach the scene just as another boy, called Plumbe, attempted a rescue. Cockles dived in and managed to grab young Swain and pull him out, but he was already dead. PC Thomas Wakeley went to fetch Dr Clarke, who was attending his garden, but astonishingly he refused to attend the scene unless payment could be guaranteed beforehand. On reporting this back at the police station, Wakeley was sent instead to Dr Wynter, and the pair arrived just as the deceased was retrieved. At the inquest at The Wyandotte, a verdict of accidental death was recorded. William Swain was one of over 3,000 annual deaths by inland drowning. He was a choirboy at the St.Nicholas

and of the previous 245 practices and services, he had missed just one, and that was with permission. The entire choir attended the grave during his funeral, as did Mr Davis, head of Abbey Hill School, and twenty of his boys. The following year, this part of the brook was filled in as part of the sewer scheme.

Within two months, a meeting had been arranged to promote the establishment of a safe swimming baths in Kenilworth, and this was held in the Mission Hall. An editorial in the *Kenilworth Advertiser* stated the newspaper's support for a safe place *"...in which boys may learn to swim without much trouble..."* and the establishment of a private baths for individuals because *"...the command to wash and clean is much more easily obeyed when the means are at hand."* Perhaps a little optimistically it suggested an analysis should be made of the water *"...which we have always thought to be as efficacious as that at Buxton, Leamington or anywhere else - without being so nasty. Once the baths are established, cures will be sure to be effected, and the development of Kenilworth into a goodly city will only be a matter of time."*

The first to address the meeting was Joseph Stone Burbery who announced that the fund already stood at £55 with donations of £10 each from Joseph Burbery, Richard Robbins, Mr Trepplin and Samuel Forrest, and £5 each from George Turner, Colonel Woodcock and himself. He then detailed three selected sites, all of which were alongside the Finham Brook but avoiding Clarendon's land. The first was opposite Odibourne Terrace in School Lane where a bath could be constructed very cheaply in the meadow and fed from the mill-dam. There was a major problem in that this would interfere with the water supply to the mill at Mill End for which Mr Robbins would claim compensation, and conversely, there could be little water in the dam when it was needed for the bath, particularly in the mornings and evenings which was both when the mill was in use and the most popular time for bathing. The second suggested site was "in the backwater" by the mill, with the possibility that it could be steam-heated by the mill itself. The major objections here were that the pool would be narrow and that the necessity of damming the stream raised the possibility that heavy rain might cause the pool to overflow and flood the lower parts of Mill End. The third site was at the foot of the Common where the bath could be fed by the spring. The advantage was the abundant supply of water, but it was so cold that heating it all year round, again from the mill, would be a necessity. In all three cases, proper accommodation for bathers would be provided along with screening for privacy.

Henry Street was particularly in favour of the third scheme and was so sure that a pool of 30 yards by 14 yards could be built for £130, that he offered to pay every pound it cost over that amount, but after Charles Adams suggested this offer should be accepted, and the method of heating was discussed, Street began to back down. As always, it was decided to form a committee to investigate the three sites and J S Burbery (secretary), Ernest Trepplin, Henry Street, Samuel Forrest, J Hughes, Richard Robbins, George Turner, P Norman and Mr Jeacock were appointed to report at the next meeting two weeks later. All three sites were subsequently rejected due to the problems outlined and additionally the two at Mill End were declared too far from the town centre. A fourth site was however suggested, this being in Clarendon's Abbey Fields halfway between the iron bridge in the centre and Townpool Bridge. Mr Adams had worked out that a bath of 25yds by 10yds, increasing in depth from 3ft 6ins to 6ft 6ins, surrounded by a hoarding 10ft high, would cost between £250 and £300. It would be possible to fill it from the stream but there would be difficulty in draining the pool back into the stream when necessary. It was decided to send out a circular around the town detailing the plans and asking for support.

The site opposite Odibourne Terrace, where Lizzie Bastock nearly drowned in the mill-race, was one of the suggested sites for a swimming bath.

However, as the town's sewerage system was by now close to becoming a reality, thoughts were turning to providing the town with a water supply, the provision of which would obviously be a great advantage to the swimming baths, and so the scheme was held in abeyance. In August the following year (1881), Joseph S Burbery resigned his position as secretary to the Kenilworth Bathing Place Committee due to ill health, and at this time £21 12s 6d had been collected of the £111 15s 6d promised.

*　　*　　*

At the July 1881 meeting of the Board, it was mentioned that George Lundie had stated that the sewerage scheme could not be considered as complete unless there was a complementary water supply. The roughly estimated cost of one was £5,000. The first to object was Dr Wynter who claimed that his 18 years experience in town had shown him that the current supply was satisfactory. He questioned whether the town could actually afford a scheme, and then declared that it was "...*totally unnecessary, and if it were adopted it would mainly be used as a means of luxury by the wealthier inhabitants...*" and that not one-tenth of the population would use it. There was, however, no scheme to consider and the chairman, Richard Robbins, disclaimed any intention of adding another burden to the town. Henry Street announced that private speculators had found a good supply of water and questioned whether the town may later regret a water supply being in private hands. The general discussion produced no firm outcome.

Dr Wynter's claim that the town's water supply was satisfactory was challenged. The only water supply over which the Board had direct control was the Borrow-well spring. From this sole supply, the two 300-gallon water-carts had to flush the sewers and water the roads. The spring, and tank that it supplied, were on private property and it was quite likely that at some point the land would be built upon and the supply cut off. Personal consumption was estimated at 25 gallons a day; many had to carry their water 30 or 40 yards, some were as much as 300 or 400 yards from their source. There were "...*many places in Kenilworth where the water supply is deficient.*"

Then in the autumn, the Board received a formal application on behalf of a company to supply the town with water. Nothing was known about them except for the names of their solicitors, Elborough and Deans, and the company engineer, George Lundie. The Board Chairman, Richard Robbins, was in favour of the town and not a company being in control of the water supply and claimed that if only half the houses in town took it, just 2d on the rates would show a profit. It was decided to meet representatives of the company and get terms as advantageous as possible to the town. Wynter, Slade and Edward Mander met with Lundie and Elborough to discuss it, but Wynter wanted to meet members of the company itself and was about to leave the room when his colleagues changed his mind. Lundie and Elborough said they represented a company of London gentlemen. In the proposals was an arrangement whereby the Board could buy the works for a sum fixed by arbitration.

At the end of October, the company published the proposals that were to be taken to Parliament. The water-pumping house was to be on Kenilworth Common, with a water tower to be installed in the steam mill at Tainters Hill in what was by then a disused windmill tower, owned by Board Chairman Richard Robbins. A service reservoir was to be constructed alongside the water tower on land owned by William James, a market gardener.

It became clear that the flushing of the sewers had not been properly discussed at the time the sewerage works were being planned. There were at least twenty flushing tanks in the scheme, each holding 340 gallons, and three flushings a week would total 20,000 gallons. Using the existing horse-drawn water-carts being filled at the Borrow-well, this would cost £350 a year, and of course, there was always the risk that at the time flushing was needed the most, in hot summers, there was likely to be a shortage of water. At the same time, the streets would need additional watering, stretching resources still further.

As the time approached in November 1881 for Parliamentary deposition, the water company's solicitors approached the Board with the proposition that if the Board did not oppose their plans they would supply all the Board's needs for 1s per 1,000 gallons, coming to just £52 a year for flushing, a huge saving. Wynter was still adamant that the current drinking water supply to the town was not a problem, despite claims that almost all of the occupants of houses in Albion Row and Spring Lane had to carry their water in buckets from springs if they wanted any water fit to drink. Those living in Odibourne Terrace were in the same position. Often water was collected in the evening ready for the morning and left overnight before being drunk.

The Board was split between those in favour of the scheme but wanting to see exactly what was proposed (such as Slade, Street and Burbery), and those against, but wishing to have a public meeting confident in the belief there would be widespread opposition (Wynter, William Mander, Edward Mander, Forrest and Judd). The Chairman, Richard Robbins, and Turner did not vote, and consequently a public meeting was arranged for Friday 2nd December at the Institute.

The *Kenilworth Advertiser* was most put out that the Institute meeting was held on a Friday, at the same time the newspaper was being printed, and not earlier in the week to allow a more prompt publication of the details. As expected there was a large turn out at the Institute including almost all the members of the Local Board; one notable absentee was its Chairman, Richard Robbins. There was much discussion as to the legal status of the meeting and whether any resolution passed was binding upon the Board, but it was established that the Board just wished to discover the feelings of the town so that it could represent them better. Dr Wynter detailed the story thus far, recounting the planning stages of the sewerage scheme and the fact that all then accepted that there was an adequate water supply to fill the system's 25 flushing tanks. However, in the summer of 1881, before the question arose, surveyors had been boring holes on the Common and testing the springs. The question of water supply was subsequently informally mooted by the Board Chairman, Richard Robbins. Formal proposals being made led to this meeting. Initially he, Wynter, was against the project, but he revealed that having discussed the matter in detail with the engineer Lundie, he was now in favour, provided the company supplied the Board with water at a nominal rate and that a clause was inserted so that the company could be bought by the Board in the future. The Board could simply not afford to pay for the works themselves, largely due to the debt incurred by the sewerage works.

Frederick Slade was second to speak and enlarged upon the problems that would be encountered if the sewers were not properly flushed. Additional tanks and water-carts would be needed and would cost up to £200 a year, representing an additional 4d on the district rate, whereas the company could supply water direct for £30 or £40. He also wished to see every house supplied with "...*good clear spring water (so as) not to fetch it from the Common in buckets.*"

William Poole observed, "*Would we wait ten years for the most inestimable boon in pure water then pay for it by a rate, or allow a company to bring that boon to our front doors without the cost of a farthing?*" Mr Bagshaw said that they may have been better off not having the sewerage scheme but now that it was there, it had to be looked after in the cheapest way possible. Henry Street stated how useful hydrants would be in the case of fire and thought the scheme would be a great boon, and remarked upon the high esteem in which the engineer was held. Others pointed out likely upcoming expenses to the town such as a new cemetery being

required within two years, and even the possibility of the town having to establish its own school board.

A resolution was finally put to the meeting and passed with 50 votes in favour to 18 against. It read, "That this meeting is not disposed to oppose the formation of a water company, but expresses the hope that the Local Board will try to get the best possible terms from the proposed company, and if they should not obtain terms which they find satisfactory, this meeting pledges itself to assist the Board to oppose the provisional order."

It was decided to hold a special Board meeting the following Thursday to discuss the resolution passed at the Institute and it began quite farcically as Board members tried without success to recall the resolution that had been passed; it was left to a news reporter to quote it from his notes! There were interesting discussions as to whether the Board should pay for water by a lump sum or by volume; there was also the fear that sinking boreholes on the Common could interfere with the supply to the nearby extensively used spring and a guarantee should be obtained that in this event a pipe should be installed to replace it. A motion was carried to write to the water company asking for the lowest terms upon which they intended to supply water to the town. Again, at this hastily arranged meeting, Richard Robbins was absent.

It was in January 1882 that the Board's water committee met with Elborough and Lundie to discuss charges. The company had suggested 1¾ million gallons be supplied for £30 with an additional charge of 6d for each extra 1,000 gallons. A million gallons was more than sufficient for flushing the sewers and the remainder for watering the roads was twice the normal consumption. In addition, 25 hydrants were agreed, including six in positions to be determined for watering the roads, to replace the continual trips to Mill End and the Borrow-well. Supplies to houses were suggested at a sliding scale with the cheapest being 2d a week for houses rented at up to £5. All these costs were considered maximums, they could become lower.

On 11th January 1882, the Board received confirmation that the Kenilworth Water Order, which included amendments, had received the consent of the Board of Trade.

The next question to be raised was about the site of the pumping station alongside the brook on the Common. James Whittendale, representing the water company, attended the February 1882 Board meeting to press the point that if the contracts for the sale of land could not be sent to the Board of Trade within the next few days, it would not be possible to obtain a provisional order this year. Lord Clarendon, the owner of the Common, was not going to object to the sale of ¼ acre, provided the Board stated that it was for the good of Kenilworth, and so such a resolution was immediately made and sent to Humbert, Clarendon's agent.

On 18th March 1882, an entire page of the *Kenilworth Advertiser* was given over to the Provisional Order authorising the construction of the works. There was now no opposition to the scheme particularly as it would save the town money, but it was considered unlikely that the Act would be passed before June.

The week before the water Bill's pre-amble passed unopposed before Mr Lyon Playfair, Chairman of the Ways and Means Committee, in early May 1882, the Board received a letter from James Whittendale, on behalf of the water works promoters, saying that the water company was "...willing to entertain an offer...to transfer their powers to the local authority." Dr Wynter was appalled that the Company was now trying to release itself from its obligations and called a meeting at the Kings Arms, promoted by handbills, to consider "...the question of maintaining the contract entered into between the Local Board of Kenilworth and the promoters of the water company." The meeting in the long room had a "...tolerably large attendance..." or "...deplorably small..." according to witnesses. Despite suffering a cold, Wynter immediately made out his case declaring the scheme was one that ought to be laid before ratepayers prior to the Board making a decision. He then explained the situation: The Board had received a letter from the company secretary Whittendale on 8th May 1882 stating that as the orders had been passed by the Board of Trade, the promoters were willing to entertain an offer for the company before commencing the works - and Whittendale verbally suggested that it would be at a small profit. The whole of the company, it now appeared, consisted of just Lundie and his friend Thomas Floyd, a fellow engineer. The purpose of this meeting was to compel the original agreement to be carried out as the company appeared to be behaving less than honestly with the parish. In a rousing speech that several times drew cheers and applause, Wynter then began to recite figures; the sewerage works had cost the ratepayers £9,000, a new cemetery would cost £3,000, and the water works £5,000, the total of £17,000 to be split between a population of just 4,150 men, women and children in the parish. He suggested the meeting put a resolution to the Board asking that the company be compelled to stick to the original agreement. Wynter was sure the Board would be bound to follow the resolution of the meeting, as they were their representatives. The resolution was put to the meeting and carried unanimously. The general opinion was that there was no real company at all and that the money to build the scheme simply did not exist and they believed that Lundie, having got past the standing orders, was trying to sell the scheme at a profit.

This led to a lively debate at the next Board meeting. The new Chairman, civil engineer Frederick Slade, immediately condemned Wynter for calling a ratepayers' meeting in preference to a special Board meeting, or even a properly-constituted Parish meeting, and for Wynter to think that "...the few who responded to that summons should have any influence on the Board seemed perfectly ridiculous." In addition, he stated there was no contract between the Board and water company, just some agreed figures that were included in the Provisional Order upon which basis the Board would not oppose the scheme. Due to the terms of the Provisional Order, the water company were not in a position to start so it was not possible to compel them to complete it.

Wynter responded by saying that ratepayers would take note of Slade's "...sneering, sarcastic and slighting speech..." and that it would "...redound to his discredit in the future." Wynter went on to say that he hoped that someone else would take Slade's place on the board the next time he was up for election in two years. Henry Street was very much behind Slade and several times interrupted Wynter's onslaught, and said that he had "...shown a great want of respect to the Board". Wynter, on this occasion, was clearly in the wrong. William Poole explained that for an agreement to be legally binding it had to have the Board's seal and no such document existed: "The Board cannot enforce that which is not in existence." Poole continued to explain that the promoters did not have any powers until the act was passed and that there was in any case no way in which the Board could enforce an Act of Parliament to be carried out. Despite the altercation, the Board were all agreed to send a letter to Whittendale declining the offer, which would have been the outcome anyway, without the arguments.

The Act was passed in July 1882 and it gave the Company one year to commence construction. The water company was registered on 22nd December 1882 with a capital of £10,000 in £5 shares. A list of seven subscribers was published, all were from London including the two solicitors Elborough and Deans, Thomas Floyd and a builder. They took one share each and were to act ad interim until the first general meeting at which directors would be elected. A minimum of 20 shares were required to become a director.

But nothing happened. In late May 1883, Elborough and Deans on behalf of the company made an application for an extra year in which to start the scheme and wrote to the Kenilworth Board urging their consent, but they decided to make no decision. The extension application was, however, successful.

*   *   *

The Board was beginning to find that the Institute was unsuitable as a permanent home for its proceedings and so, in the summer of 1882, began a search for more appropriate premises. The property that was first investigated was the former Edwards Charity School in Borrowell Lane, which had closed in mid-1880. Richard Robbins viewed the property and reported to the Board, who then approached Mr Heath, the solicitor dealing with the charity's affairs, about a potential 21 year lease at £25 a year. It was proposed that the school site could also be used for stabling the Board's horses, but some modifications were needed and, of course, it would have to be furnished. Some of the Board members were uncertain of the financial commitment required and so the Clerk wrote to the Local Government Board asking if a loan could be sanctioned. As the subject was not discussed again, it is safe to assume that expenditure on a leased building was declared undesirable. They also declined an offer from William Dawes for property alongside Townpool Bridge for £1,000; this was likely to be the old tannery.

Three months later, the Board had decided to buy a property on Rosemary Hill for £800. There were two cottages on the site and, fronting onto Savage Lane, John Savage's former builders yard that included a workshop. This had been occupied for some years by the Heatley family, John Heatley had been a builder and carpenter and his widow was now a lodging-house keeper. The other cottage was unoccupied. Earlier, the buildings had been used for basket-making and as a Dame School. The owner appeared to be a Mr Campbell (this was later refuted). With the purchase agreed, the Board invited tenders for the construction of stables on the site, designed by architect Edward J Purnell of Station Road, and the successful tender to build them was submitted by Lawrence. The Board needed £800 for the purchase of the two cottages, £100 for converting them into offices, £70 for furniture, £230 for the stabling and £50 for legal and other fees.

Again, the Board had to apply for a loan of £1,200, which also included an amount to cover a shortfall in the expenses for the sewerage works. £250 was required to finish the sewerage works to double the size of the silting tanks, and to install a sludge tank and chain pump. Also, the main sewer was to cross Lord Clarendon's land but "...as that nobleman thought it would be somewhat injurious to him, the Board were obliged to divert it at a cost of £48 11s. 10d." There were additional smaller sums for fencing and connections to the flushing tanks. Everything else was more or less finished. There had to be the usual formal inquiry to apply for the loan, and this was held once more by Harrisson at the Institute in February 1883.

Just four days after the inquiry, and before the result was known, the Board changed their plans and decided to demolish the uninhabited cottage and to put up purpose-built offices. Eventually, the site for the offices, stabling and stone-yard was bought for £800, and an additional £650 was allocated for the building work. In May the loan for this was agreed.

In June it was agreed that a cart shed was required to keep the Board's water-carts out of the weather and Lawrence won with his tender, for £46 11s, to build the shed out of wood with a corrugated iron roof. The same month, the plans for the new offices, designed by Kyd who had been retained by the Board on a contract as a surveyor, were passed and it was decided to go ahead as soon as possible with the building work. On 25th August, the Board advertised inviting tenders to construct the offices, and the applications had to be in by 5th September.

In September, £850 was raised by a mortgage with the Prudential Insurance Company to be repaid in fifty annual instalments of £39 11s 4d but the purchase of the site was still not complete due to delays at the solicitors. There was also a design problem with the proposed new building; a suggested extra two feet on the frontage would have involved altering the gable end of the adjoining building and it was decided to avoid this if possible.

The tender for the construction of the offices was won by Edward Smith for £398 19s, but this caused a row at the next, October, Board meeting. William Lawrence's tender was originally lower than Smith's and he had been told unofficially by Henry Street that it was likely to be accepted. When the small alterations were added Smith came out victorious, but Wynter claimed that Street had no right to have spoken to Lawrence, an accusation Street denied and counter claimed that Wynter should not have brought up the reasons for accepting tenders in front of reporters.

With the purchase finally completed, the old building was demolished by the Board's own men and building work, which was expected to last ten weeks, started that same month. By the second week of November, the walls were up and the floors and roof timbers were being erected - completion was expected to be just five weeks away but the rapid progress on the building came to a halt in mid-December due to the weather being considered too wet and cold to plaster the wall. This was overcome in the new year when fires were lit in the building to help the drying process.

With the building finished, there was now no more work for Kyd, and the Board, not in a position to renew his contract as his salary could not be justified on a permanent basis, very reluctantly let him go with a glowing testimonial. In the new year, Thomas Hillier was appointed "engineer" to the Board for £20 per annum.

As they were built by Edward Smith, the Board's new offices on (Upper) Rosemary Hill are likely to incorporate bricks from his works at Crackley, and stone from his Love Lane quarry.

It had originally been decided to purchase a fireproof safe for documents to be kept in, but in early 1884 it was decided instead to have a strong room and the contract for the door and lock went to Edward Smith for £9. In late 1885, it was agreed to have mains water supplied to the offices and heating was provided with firewood from Walter Stickley. Mrs Trunkfield was paid 2s a week, rising to 3s in 1886, for keeping the offices clean. The offices were still a little Spartan so in early 1886 floor covering was discussed and the original suggestion of *"kamptulicon"* was second choice to linoleum. Then *"...the interior walls and ceilings (were) coloured and washed as necessary."* Mrs Heatley continued to live in the adjoining property, as the Board's first tenant.

*   *   *

As the number of trustees had fallen, by death, from seven to three, by its own rules the Institute had to fill the four vacancies and at the 1881 AGM, William Pennington, Dr Daniel Wynter, Samuel Forrest and Jonathon Prime were duly elected. The library had completed its period of closure and was now completely re-arranged, being in *"...better working order than it had been before..."* and was open for book exchanging at Monday and Thursday lunchtimes, and Wednesday and Saturday evenings, a total of six hours a week. The Reverend Somerset Pennefather, Dr Atkinson and Mr Nixon were entrusted with making arrangements for the sale of tea, coffee, and cocoa in the society's rooms.

The circular announcing its 1883 AGM stated that it was *"...of much importance for the welfare of the Institute that the meeting should be a large one as it is hoped that every member will endeavour to attend..."* yet fewer than twenty of its hundred and nine members appeared. There had been an income reduction of over £19 during the previous year despite an increase in subscriptions of £6 10s. This was largely due to a large decrease in income from concerts, and a notable drop in donations and St.John's Ambulance meetings. During the last two years tea, coffee, bread and butter had been made available to members during evenings and the income from this, £6 10s in two years, paid for alterations to the gas fittings. The provision of refreshments was not seen as profit-making but to *"...render the Institute attractive and beneficial to a particular class, and by this means counteract evil influences at work in this town."*

William Evans of The Spring donated a billiard table, *"...one of the most useful presents which could have been made..."*, for the downstairs ante-room which had previously been virtually unused and this required the removal of a partition and the building of a fireplace and chimney. The table was to *"...induce members of a certain class to join the society..."* but by making a small charge it *"...placed an obstacle in the way of it becoming harmful to junior members by inducing them to idle their time."* The table produced an income of 6s in just three weeks. Mr Hodges had donated a bagatelle board, which was used every evening. The downturn in income from lectures and concerts was put down to a town meeting which formed a Recreation Committee to organise events with surplus monies going to the Institute rather than the Institute organising them for themselves; only two such events had been organised and it was obviously hoped that the situation would change.

Four paintings from the will of Kenilworth resident Phillip Carmouls now hung on the walls, as did three watercolours by Miss Dockray, daughter of James Dockray the railway engineer then living in town. *"Pictures by a local artist have very much improved the appearance of the rooms."* Donations to the library included several bound volumes of the *Illustrated London News, Transactions of the British Association, Everyday Life in School* and *Military Heroes of England,* but the library had lent out only 150 books in an entire year, less than three a week. It was suggested that unsuitable and imperfect books, and a large accumulation of magazines, should be disposed of and that a choice selection of fiction and poetry be obtained. Additionally,

the ineffectiveness of the library could be overcome by making it more presentable and it was proposed that the internal staircase should be removed and a porch built to make the library room more accommodating. Edward Smith had provided a rough estimate of £70 for the work. With the expected large increase in residents due to the general improvements to the town, all agreed that the Institute should *"...be in a form for the Kenilworth that is to be."*

At the end of the meeting, the election of the committee took place. Those present were allowed to vote, but proxy votes were allowed only by absent ladies. It was claimed that it was unfair that gentlemen could not vote in this way but it was then pointed out that the reason the rule was made was that *"...before, we could scarcely get anyone to come to the meetings."* Only three ladies sent in votes, and the thirteen-man committee was duly elected.

In an attempt to make the Institute more attractive to young men, in late 1883 a room was set aside for billiards; it was carpeted and the walls hung with *"...parti-coloured matting."* The Committee, led by Dr Atkinson, was praised for its efforts to increase the membership.

*   *   *

Somewhat alarmingly, in early 1884, it was found that Dr Wynter, who had at one time deemed fresh water to houses unnecessary, had a defective privy too near his home at Hyde House, Station Road, and his water, obtained from a well, was not fit to drink. Within a month, a new well had been dug and a w.c. connected to the sewer system. Wynter blamed the work being carried out for the sewer system.

During the extra year that the water company had obtained, negotiations took place with Lundie and his London-based associates, and the company came into the hands of local people after all. It appears that Richard Robbins led the takeover, becoming the Company Chairman, and Henry Street too was heavily involved. A new engineer had to be found and Mr Pritchard re-assessed the plans - the reservoir alongside the water tower was deemed unnecessary and was dropped.

The contract for building the water works was won by Edward Smith and by mid-1884, work was well under way. To lay the pipe to the water tower he had to apply for permission to dig up the road to Coventry across the Common and this he did in July. The ditch had to be properly fenced and lighted at each end, and a watchman had to be in place all night as a safety precaution. By October, mains were being laid and the pumps were in place. At the beginning of December, the company advised the Board that they were in a position to start flushing the chambers.

The works consisted of two 12hp Clarke gas engines built by L Sterne and Co in Birmingham; two complete sets of throw pumps allowed either or both of the engines to operate the pumping system manufactured by Piercy and Co of Broad Street, Birmingham. The water was raised from a well just 20ft deep; a great quantity of dynamite had been used to cut through the ragstone to form a water receiver. After passing through cast-iron air vessels and a Kennedy positive meter, it travelled at a rate of 16,000 gallons an hour, 667 yards along a 7-inch main to the water tower on Tainter's Hill. The original tower top had been taken down and new brickwork supported a 26,000-gallon tank, which had additional support from the three cast iron pipes that carried the water. The tank was made from five-eighths iron plate by the Glenfield Iron Company of Kilmarnock. The maximum lift from the well to the water level in the tank was 136 feet, 302 feet above sea level. The water was distributed by 5$\frac{1}{2}$ miles of six 3ins and 4ins mains to all parts of the town where in most parts it was predicted a jet could be thrown 60ft into the air. The piping contractors were G and S Roberts of West Bromwich and the hydraulic fittings were by Glenfield of Kilmarnock. All the general pipe-laying, and building work of the water tower and pumping station was carried out by Kenilworth's own Edward Smith.

It is not surprising that the task of opening the works, on 1st January 1885, fell to Richard Robbins. After a brief tour, and an even briefer speech, Robbins turned on the gas and set the works in motion. At this time, all 1,500 of the 2,000 £5 shares taken up were by local gentlemen.

The water works pump-house built by Edward Smith.

A six-man party of the fire brigade, led by Deputy Captain Robbins, Lieutenant Atkinson and engineer Plumbe, carried out some spectacular demonstrations of the water pressure. The standpipe near to the Kenilworth Advertiser office in The Square was the first tested and a considerable amount of water was thrown up and down the street to the delight of the large crowd, especially the throngs of youngsters. Another trial was held further down Castle End.

In the evening, a large celebration dinner was held at the Kings Arms. It was perhaps ironic, or apt, that the toast to the success of the Kenilworth Water Company was made by Dr Wynter. He said how pleased he was that the Local Board had reached an agreement with the company and that there was no ill feeling between them. Chairman Richard Robbins stressed the importance of the scheme being in the hands of local people, as the Board could not afford it. The Board could now have no excuse for dusty roads or foul-smelling sewers, and at the same time could save about £200 a year of ratepayers' money. He stressed that the company was born out of necessity and not to seek a profit, and hoped that the town would support them. Pritchard eulogised the water's quality and quantity, it was hard but not permanently so and about 50% of the hardness could be removed by boiling. It was "...*amply sufficient to supply the wants of future generations.*" The dinner ended in sufficient time for the visitors from Coventry to catch the 9.15 train.

The following month, the fire brigade made more tests of the water pressure at the newly-installed hydrants. The two places chosen were at the highest point in town and therefore with the lowest pressure, just outside Montague House and conveniently close to the fire engine-house, and just around the corner near the Albion Chapel. All were impressed as the water would easily go to the tops of the highest buildings in town.

Not everything went smoothly. Some of the hydrants were above ground level for the benefit of the water-carts but the continual use of these, and mischievous boys turning the taps on, had a detrimental effect on the road surface by washing the gravel away and leaving holes. Nobody had thought to put drains in and it was down to the water company, and the patrolling policemen, to resolve the problem. Even now with the

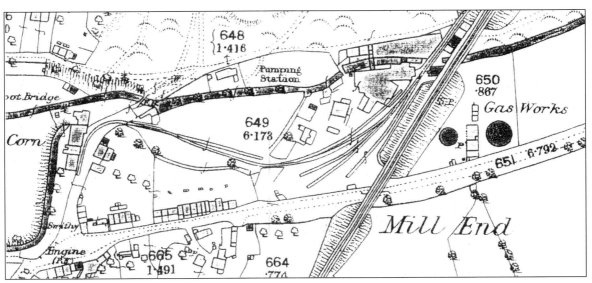

Mill End had become vital to the town's well-being. It provided the town's gas and water needs, and vital employment at Richard Robbins' flour-mill (left) and Henry Street's fellmongery (centre). The railway siding was also used by coal-merchants. A saw-mill was built alongside the gas-works in the 1890s.

waterworks in full operation, there were still complaints that the sewers smelt, and more regular flushing was advised.

So cheap and easy was it now to water the roads that the Board decided to order an extra van; it held 350 gallons and cost £37 and was ordered from Glover & Sons of Warwick. As an additional extra, a brake was fitted for £3. By the end of 1885, 82 houses had been connected to the mains water.

The water supply gave the Board a new weapon to use against "nuisance" households and the conversion of privies to w.c's in eight houses at Washbrook was the first to be discussed. Not all householders thought the new supply was essential: Henry Street had been ordered to lay on water to his properties at Mill End, but his tenants petitioned the Board and asked for water not to be connected. The order was allowed to lapse.

The Water Company sought, and obtained, permission to use the Local Board office for five or six meetings a year for its seven Directors, the November 1886 meeting being the first. A fee of a guinea was charged. In the summer of 1887, Charles Trepplin took advantage of the water supply to provide a trough on the Coventry Road. His wife, Elizabeth Trepplin, paid £12 to provide a tap and bowl inside the Castle grounds and a trough outside for animals, and added a bowl and tap to the Coventry Road trough.

The water company struggled to make a profit. By 1887, the dividend was down to just 1% and with a called up capital of £9,350 it made a profit of just £376. *"We can be thankful that with the perseverance of Dr Wynter and other gentlemen, the capital did not come out of the ratepayers pockets."* At least part of the reason was the agreement to supply the town so cheaply, in fact at a dead loss to the company. The Board members were to a degree sympathetic, as whilst they wanted their water cheaply they *"...did not expect (the company) to loose by the agreement..."* and were willing to listen to the company's suggestions. By now Henry Street was the company chairman.

* * *

In July 1883 the Board was struck another blow with the unexpected announcement that Frederick Slade was to resign not only as chairman, but as a Board member, as he was moving to Gloucestershire. Despite the obvious disappointment, and calls for him to rethink his decision, there was no chance of Slade staying and so another chairman was needed. All were agreed that the then absent William Evans of The Spring would be an ideal choice but Henry Street stated that Evans had already decided he did not want to be chairman, and so attention turned to 34 year-old farmer Samuel Forrest. Forrest said that he *"...would very much rather someone else was appointed..."* but he was unanimously voted to the position, giving the Board its third Chairman in 18 months. *"I am very sorry you could not have found someone more suited to the post. You must bear with my shortcomings and with your help doubtless I shall succeed..."* was hardly an acceptance speech to inspire confidence. The vacancy on the Board created by Slade's departure was taken by George Turner who had lost his seat by just five votes at the most recent election.

The system of four members retiring and standing against other candidates was repeated by law each spring, but was still often subject to ridicule. One such occasion was April 1884 when the retiring members were Turner, Street, Burbery and Wynter with the new potential coming from J Clarke and Walter Lockhart. Before the election took place, Clarke and Burbery withdrew, leaving only four contenders and so an election was not necessary. Walter Lockhart thus became a Board member without ever receiving a single vote. It was soon suggested that the Board had become a closed shop: *"When this Board was first constituted it was a nice little amusement for a certain "clique" to elect their own particular friends and allies. But we live in hope that as every succeeding year passes and an election for the Board comes on, this "clique" will find themselves gradually being reduced and "improved" off the Board."* This year saw William Evans finally accept being elected as Chairman.

* * *

The regular use of stones as weapons appeared again at the end of 1877 when Kenilworth labourer William Hubbard was fined £1 with 11s 6d cost for firing one with a catapult at Mr Willis's gamekeeper on Newbold Common, but just a few months later a far more serious incident occurred at the house of Thomas Fletcher in Clinton Lane. Some larking about by a boy named Barber with the cap of 6-year-old Silvister Newey, led to Fanny Newey throwing a stone at her brother, hitting him on the right temple. The Newey's parents, Phoebe and Henry (having moved from New Row to Clinton Lane after an earlier incident), did not notice Silvister's injury until the following Saturday when his mother noticed his eye was swollen. He explained how his injury was caused and that his sister had been dressing it whilst going to school. He was now kept off school and a week later Dr Clarke was called, but nine days later, Silvister died, almost three weeks after the incident. The inquest verdict was accident and much sympathy was extended towards Fanny and the group of friends.

This was the first of a sequence of unusual deaths involving Kenilworth residents. William Poole held an inquest at the Earl Clarendon Hotel into the death of already widowed Ann Arch, just 26 years old, who fell down the stairs at 6, Clarendon Terrace. Dr Bourne tried to revive her by throwing cold water upon her. She regained consciousness but died the following morning from a *"...haemorrhage of the upper spine."* Henry Hammond, a well-liked Kenilworth tailor, died on a business trip to Coventry; he choked on a large growth in his throat that had suddenly become inflamed. He left a large family of young children. Worse was to come for the Hammond family the following May; Henry's sister Mary, aged 24, was looking after their father at Castle Green; as a break from some ironing, she went in to see her father but felt unwell herself, she lay down on his bed and very soon died. Her father died just a few hours later.

Fifty five year-old James Phillips was employed *"getting clay"* at Lockhart's brickworks in mid-July when he collapsed, and died the following day from sunstroke. Perhaps the most curious of all was the death of G Webb, a traveller in the leather trade - he trod on a needle at the fire brigade fête at the Castle and died from its infection.

1879 saw another birth concealment case involving a young serving girl. The house at which it happened was that of William Potter, auctioneer, at Lady's Hill. The body of a baby boy was found in privy, some short distance away from the house. Servant and cook, 26 year-old Julia Mills, had no hesitation in admitting that she was the mother and claimed the birth was unexpected and that she had intended to leave the house and go to the Coventry Workhouse. She had another child to look after as well. When apprehended by Inspector Hinde she declared, *"I don't care for myself but I hope my poor father will not hear of this. I don't care what I suffer myself if the scamp who got me into this trouble was going to suffer too."* The "scamp" was not named and Julia was charged with concealing the birth. Dr Clarke admitted there were no injuries and that it was not possible to say the child had led a separate existence. It was found wrapped in a pair of drawers in a place in daylight where it was bound to be found. Julia's box was searched at the house where it was found that she had started to make new clothing for the child with material to make more. With nothing malicious nor evasive found against her, Julia Mills was acquitted.

Another quite awful death, this one by accident, occurred in April 1879 at Bridge House on the corner of Bridge Street and New Street, the home of Edward Draper, solicitor. Richard Moss, 45, and James Ward were employed by decorator Ernest Nixon to paint the outside of the house and on the day in question both started work at 6.00 a.m. To reach the top of the front of the house, two ladders were spliced together to make one of 52 rungs. Both men had used the ladder during the morning, then at about midday Moss, who was 5ft 10¹/₂ins tall and weighed 15 stone but described as active and nimble, climbed the ladder to finish painting the last few stones at the top of the house. When he was just a few rungs from the top, the ladder snapped, neither the rungs nor splice gave way, but the side supports, and Moss fell. He was *"...impaled on the iron pallasading in front of the house...stabbed in three places and groaned very much."* Ward tried to lift his colleague off the railings but needed the help of William Freeman and the two carried him to Henry Barton's chemist shop directly opposite, where he was attended to by Dr Wynter. From here, he was taken to Warneford Hospital and on the way Moss remarkably claimed that he was in no pain. One of the spikes had entered his thigh from behind, the second his abdomen and the third had broken a rib, punctured a lung and pierced his liver. He died on Monday 28th, six days after the accident. Surprisingly, by the time of the inquest, no one except Nixon had examined the broken ladder and he did not even bother to take the pieces. No blame was attached to Nixon, the ladders were four years old and in good condition and Ward had been up them just before the accident. It was decided that the cause was a combination of Moss's weight and the foot of the ladder being not close enough to the building - had it been closer the sidepieces would

have supported the weight better. A verdict of accident was returned. Moss was a Sunday-school teacher at the Independent Chapel and some of its members acted as pallbearers at his funeral. Most of the shopkeepers closed their blinds as a mark of respect. A collection for his widow was quickly organised with collections made by Dr Wynter, the Reverend Smith, at the Working Men's Club and by Miss Richards at the *Kenilworth Advertiser* office. Hundreds of donations were listed, totalling almost £100. Just a few weeks before he witnessed the accident, James Ward had had his waistcoat and overcoat stolen by fellow worker Thomas Cook whilst he was working. Cook absconded and was finally caught in St.Neots in December, wearing the waistcoat.

Just before Christmas 1881, the stepson of builder William Ball, Charles Robbins, was out shooting birds in a field leased by his stepfather. After taking a short break, he picked the gun up but noticed some water upon the barrels. As he was wiping it off with the sleeve of his coat, he accidentally touched the trigger and blew away his elbow joint. He bravely attempted to reach home but collapsed. He was discovered by a man named Brassington who immediately bound a handkerchief tightly above the wound to stop the bleeding. He then raised the alarm; Dr Wynter was soon in attendance, and he tied a wooden splint to the arm to support it. The following morning the arm was amputated and despite fears for the worst, Robbins recovered.

*   *   *

The late 1870s saw the start of a number of successive hard winters; perhaps the first sign of what was to come was the frost on mid-summer's day in 1877. As 1878 drew to a close it was reported that the number of paupers in town had fallen from 290 to 246, but the oncoming winter was to prove the hardest since 1860 and many more were to struggle. By mid-December, there was already a hard frost and several inches of snow, the soup kitchen had again been set up twice-weekly for all religious denominations in the Mission Hall. This was soon being abused as those less hard-up were taking advantage and so the poor and needy were visited to be issued tickets. By Christmas everywhere was frozen, the streets were just sheets of ice, many men had been *"thrown out of work"* and business in general was almost impossible to attend to. But on Christmas Day a thaw set in, followed by sleet and rain turning the roads into a quagmire, and still impassable. The cold weather soon returned. The charitable distribution of bread to the needy was particularly welcomed this time and about £15 of bread was handed out. A 4lb loaf cost about 5¹/₂d, making the gift equivalent to about 600 loaves of this size.

Not surprisingly, there were a number of accidents. A man called Colling was carrying a young boy called Webster across a frozen Castle End pit when he slipped, falling upon the lad and breaking his thigh. Elderly and respected businessman Mr Liggins slipped and broke his ankle, and William Poole had a narrow escape being brushed aside by a difficult-to-control horse and trap. As the fifth week of frost started, there was another snowfall of four or five inches and many had to dig their way out of their houses.

There was also a lot of fun to be had. Richard Robbins flooded one of his Abbey Fields, to provide a "safe skate" at just 3d for the day, the takings being donated to the soup kitchen. The last Thursday of January saw 250 skating by torchlight which "...made a very pretty effect..." when viewed from Abbey Hill. The following day saw the numbers increase by a hundred and on the Saturday, an astonishing peak of 503 was recorded. However, inevitably there were to be casualties. Mr H Harrisson of Castle End left the coffee stall carrying a basket and slipped, falling backwards, as soon as he touched the ice "...rendering him insensible for some time." The coffee stall was obviously a dangerous area as the same evening Miss F Bishop, daughter of Abbey Hill shoemaker George, put her foot in a hole as she headed for the seating near it. Her leg doubled underneath her, breaking her ankle and causing several ladies to faint. Several gentlemen lifted a gate off its hinges, covered it with straw and carried Miss Bishop to Dr Clarke's Hyde House in Station Road, a praiseworthy effort considering the conditions! It cast a cloud over the whole evening and by 9.00 p.m., the ice was almost deserted. Needless to say the girl's parents were most grateful to all concerned, and George had more reason to be grateful to the doctor just a few weeks later when he fell on the way home and broke his shoulder - a quite disastrous accident for a shoemaker. In early March, both father and daughter were recovering from their ordeals.

The poor weather continued. Easter weekend saw another three or four inches of snowfall and already the farmers and market gardeners were concerned for the year's crops. In the fields there was little green fodder for the cattle, strawberries "...for which Kenilworth is famous..." were in poor condition although some fruit, plums and pears for example, looked promising. The cold winter became a wet summer; 5th July saw the first strawberries despatched from Mr Whateley's Spring Gardens and Mr James in New Street, and 18th July was declared "...the first summer's day we've had...", but then the rain fell for another week. This was of course having a noteworthy effect on employment at farms as well as trade for shopkeepers, tourist numbers were comparatively low, affecting the business notably of innkeepers and publicans. By mid-August, there was hope of a good but late crop, but there was now disease amongst the potatoes. As harvesting gathered momentum in late September it became clear that oats and barley were well below average and wheat was just a third of what was expected. Potatoes were going bad. Plums turned out to be successful but apple yields were poor. By the end of November, skating had returned upon the frozen marl pits, and in December, skating by torchlight on the flooded field "...alongside the church..." again provided funds for the needy: "Some learning, some teaching, others skimming over the glassy surface with a fair partner, presenting a very pretty scene."

Wet weather though did have its advantages as excessive rain "...washed away a good deal of the filth that would otherwise lie about in ditches..." and this had the effect of notably reducing the death rate.

A deluge on Tuesday 5th October 1880 saw the start of another difficult period of weather. The Castle Bridge and ford were impassable, the Castle Meadows were a vast lake, and the Abbey Meadows one immense sheet of water. At Mill End, houses were flooded, work was impossible on the lower floors of the fellmongers and from Harpers Ford to Worsley Bridge nothing but the tops of hedges was visible. This was possibly the largest flood since 1834. More rain followed, but at the end of the month there was snow and ice on the ground. As a distraction, the Northern Lights were clearly visible.

Three weeks later, there was a heavy snowfall for six hours before heavy rain brought a quick thaw and more swollen brooks. The end of December saw a repeat of heavy snow followed by rain and again it was Mill End that got the worst of it with several acres under water near the gas works and railway viaducts.

At the end of January, a freeze set in. Two miles of the river was frozen at Stoneleigh and Richard Robbins again allowed skating on his Abbey Field, the proceeds being donated to the soup kitchen. During the following days, 70 unemployed men, organised and assisted by the vicar, started to clear the roads of snow. Donations for payment were invited and those received included one of £2 from the Co-operative Society. Pennefather gave a special sermon, and wrote a letter on the workmen's behalf thanking all for the donations and contributions towards his fund. There was of course little or no agricultural work available. At the end of February, with the roads still "...in a very sloppy state...", a supper at the Mission Hall was arranged by the vicar for those who had helped to clear the snow and for "...members of the men's meeting." Over 200 attended and tables had to be laid in the adjoining coach house to accommodate them all. Eleven stewards selected from the Bible Class served the food whilst the carvers included Dr Atkinson, Walter Lockhart, Frederick Slade, George Turner, William Clarke, Robbins, E Hodges, William Evans and Reverend Alfred Binnie. It had all been arranged and provided by Reverend Somerset Pennefather, his wife and a few friends, and none of the expenses came from the relief fund.

As he was soon to leave the district, in April 1882 the Reverend Somerset Pennefather decided to place in the Board's hands £35 left over from the snow-clearing fund. He wished it to be kept by the Board for some similar purpose and it was placed in an account in the names of Burbery, Turner and Evans. It was jovially insinuated that members of the Board would like to get their hands on so useful a sum for other projects and the clerk, William Savage Poole, advised Pennefather "If I were the vicar I should stay clear of the Board altogether." Pennefather's reply, perhaps a veiled reference to Poole's past, brought a round of laughter; "If you were the vicar, you would have acted very differently to me in many things."

*　　*　　*

A travelling waxworks arrived in town in the summer of 1879, and was set up in a field. The travelling show had to pay a £2 deposit to the field's owner for security against damage to the field. Several locals, including carpenter Matthew Arnold, were watching Thomas Mullett setting the show up when he asked his spectators to keep off the grass. They refused and a fight ensued; Mullett was fined 10s 6d.

For the first time in twelve years, The Royal Windsor Travelling Menagerie (late Wombwell's, now Edmonds) visited the town on the 25th May 1880. The huge cavalcade of caravans arrived from Solihull, its previous place of display, at about midday, with the camels, elephants and other animals walking, and children taking great delight in feeding the elephants biscuits etc. It is not known where *"the World's Great Show"* set up, but 1s was charged for adults to enter, and children 6d. *"We might add that at great expense they have secured the services of the great lion hunter Ledger Delmonico. An important feature was (his) feats with the lions, tigers and hyenas, the latter of which he makes jump through burning hoops."* Delmonico was often referred to as the greatest lion tamer in the world. There were several well-patronised performances during the day, spectators included the local gentry. Estimates of the number of specimens on display varied between 500 and 600 and included *"...the only blue and red faced gorilla in Europe...an assemblage of dasyures...bearded argali...the great vlacke vark or emgella...artic sea monsters..."* as well as tapirs, gnus, pumas, families of baby lions and a *"...vast collection of interesting novelties too numerous to detail."* This impressive collection, recognised as the best travelling, moved on to spend the next two days in Leamington.

* * *

With a number of different concerns using the coalyard at the station, it is not surprising that occasionally there were incidents between them. One such occurrence happened in June 1880 which resulted in Richard Caldecott, an employee of William Jacks, being charged with assaulting Edgar Lockhart, an incident witnessed by William Turner, an under-foreman at Lockhart's. Caldecott apparently backed his cart up against Lockhart's who warned him about the possibility of causing damage. Caldecott threatened him with his fists, trying to goad him into a fight, but Lockhart declined. Caldecott was fined 16s 6d.

A new boiler was delivered to Lockhart's brickworks on 13th January 1881. The contractor was Thomas Brassing of West Bromwich. The boiler was lifted off the railway wagon by use of an hydraulic jack, and Edward Sharp of Oldbury was in charge of a plank of wood supporting the boiler dome. Without warning, the plank broke and the boiler rolled over onto Sharp, killing him instantly. At the inquest held the following day at the White Lion, it was suggested that a chain should have been used to secure the boiler rather than a plank. In his defence, Brassing said he had moved many boilers the same way without so much as pinching a finger, and a Mr Swain who was assisting at the time said he had moved forty boilers and rarely used a chain. No one in the jury believed the absence of a chain amounted to negligence, and indeed even Sharp's widow attached blame to no one and considered Brassing a *"kind and careful master."* A verdict of accidental death was recorded.

The boiler was twenty five feet long and supplied steam to a variety of equipment including the steam press and other brick-making equipment. The steam fed a 16hp horizontal engine with a 9ins wide, 8ft diameter driving wheel that had a water-pump attached to feed the boiler. There was also a "central fugal steam pump" from which ran 81ft of 4ins pipes. An iron tank held 3,000 gallons of water. The engine drove at least a dozen pulleys and over 200ft of belting, and a 30ft long elevator strap with 30 tins attached. Another group of equipment, four clay wagons, 3 iron turn tables, 3 iron rolls and pulleys for chain to run on, and 50yds of chain, suggests a small tramway for moving the clay. The boiler house had a 60ft high chimneystack, a machine and engine-house and what was called a blacksmiths shop but was more likely used for general maintenance and repair work.

For making the bricks themselves there were 50 brick moulds of various descriptions. A "Steam brick machine complete and 1 steam press" made the bricks. In the kilns were 58 iron frames with 696 iron bars. There was also a scattering of old and new tramway rails, and a railway carriage which was part used as an office and part *"...for men and boys to have their meals in."*

Amongst those working at the yard at this time were brickburner Joseph Constable and widower John Moseley (55), who was the "engine driver", and several teenagers. In July 1881, the temperature reached the upper 90s fahrenheit, which led to a spate of absenteeism. First Samuel Tolley and Edward Smith were fined 12s each for *"absenting themselves"* from work, and the following week William Adkins was summonsed for the same reason, and he was absent from court as well.

* * *

In 1882, there were complaints to the Board about the unsafe state of the gravel pits on the Common, but it was decided that this was a matter between Clarendon and his tenant, Joseph Roberts. Monumental masons Mellor and Dyer of High Street had a stone quarry on the Common and successfully appealed to have their rates for it reduced in 1881.

Thomas Hancox...

...was born in Kenilworth c1845. The son of a railway labourer of Whites Row, Thomas spent much of his working life on the railways, notably in the Clapham Junction area. But late in the 1870s he emigrated to New Zealand, a place where neither he nor his wife had any relations, and worked at the Victoria Sawmills felling trees. On 14th January 1882, he was inexplicably struck by the branch of a falling tree, crushing part of his skull. *"It appears more mysterious every time one looks at the scene...if he had stepped one pace either way he would have been clear."* When his funeral procession passed the Police Camp, the Oddfellows in full mourning regalia fell in in front of the hearse, and the coffin was carried to the grave by past Grand Masters. Thomas left a wife and five children.

As 1881 came to a close, a public meeting was held at the Castle gatehouse for establishing classes in connection with the Leamington branch of the St.John's Ambulance Association, which nationally had over 200,000 members. Due to the late arrival of the intended chairman, Lord Leigh, the Reverend Somerset Pennefather outlined the benefits of *"...being better acquainted with relieving suffering from accidents, restoring the drowned or accidentally poisoned..."* before proper medical assistance could be found. The intention was to hold a series of lectures, for 5s, with ladies and gentlemen in separate classes and the participants having to provide themselves with a triangular and roller bandage. A third class was proposed for *"...working men, the police force, fire brigade and railway officials."* A committee was formed, consisting of the Reverend Somerset Pennefather, doctors Thomas Bourne, John Clarke, Daniel Wynter and Myles Christopherson Atkinson, and William Evans, William Clarke and William Ball. Dr Atkinson was proposed as Honorary Secretary and he accepted the position. It was suggested by Bourne that a class should be arranged for servants and the wives of working men and that a ladies committee should be formed to arrange the women's classes, and so Mrs Pennefather, Mrs Trepplin, Mrs Jones, Mrs Mary Nelson, Miss Woodcock and Miss Pennington were chosen. Lord Leigh, when he finally arrived, said that he would invite the Deputy Chairman of the St.John's Ambulance Central Executive Committee, Major Francis Duncan, Royal Artillery, to visit the town and give a lecture. Meantime, Atkinson was to take the names of interested parties, provide bandages and give news of arrangements from his practice at Abbey Hill.

Major Duncan's military duties restricted his availability, which resulted in the lecture being arranged for Saturday 31st January, at 3.00 p.m. The meeting at the Institute was also for the formal formation of a Kenilworth branch of the St.John's Ambulance, and in attendance was Lord Leigh, President of the Birmingham branch, and the Marquis of Hertford, President of the Leamington branch to which Kenilworth was to be affiliated. Major Duncan made the important speech explaining the benefits of knowledge on *"...how to treat cases of drowning, scalds, wounds &c., and how the police are taught to give the benefit of the doubt in cases of intoxication."* He concluded his speech by giving a demonstration of some of the 39 ways he said a simple pocket-handkerchief could be applied as an emergency bandage. Dr Atkinson then read the committee minutes and the meeting ended with the Marquis of Hertford wishing all a Happy New Year.

The advertisement for the classes stated they were to *"...probably commence on or about the 10th January."* Ladies' classes were on Tuesdays at 3.00 p.m. and taken by Dr Bourne, men's were later the same day at 7.30 p.m. and taken by Dr Wynter, with the women's lectures on Wednesday at 3.00 p.m. taken by Dr Atkinson. It is interesting to note that "ladies" and "women" were taught separately, but "men" were all in one class. The 5s annual subscription enabled attendance to the lectures and membership of the St.John's Ambulance Association but free tickets were available for *"...working men, their wives and domestic servants."*

In December 1882, the Marquis of Hertford chaired another meeting at the Institute as a precursor to another series of lectures. This time the classes were on Fridays, 3.30 p.m. for women and 7.30 p.m. for men.

In September the following year, the success of the training proved useful to one unlucky lad when the difficulty in keeping a smooth top surface to the roads was the cause of a serious mishap on Rosemary Hill. An eleven year-old lad named Hinks, son of a well-known Birmingham lamp manufacturer who lived at Milverton, was one of three boys riding down the hill on their bicycles. They had just reached the bottom at speed when Hinks hit a large stone and was thrown violently over the handlebars and landed on his head. He was badly cut and bruised about his head and broke both his arms. Mrs Payne, who lived in a cottage nearby, was the first on the scene, followed by Mrs Jepson, the Misses Bourne and Clarke, and also railway porter Francis Haggar - all five of them being members of the St. Johns Ambulance class. Dr Bourne arrived soon after and with the help of Dr Atkinson, set both arms (using splints donated to the Ambulance Society by the Marquis of Hertford) and treated the other injuries. The boy was then put on a stretcher taken from the fire engine-house and carried to Dr Clarke's house. He was later able to walk to a fly borrowed from the Bowling Green Inn and was taken back home.

*   *   *

By the end of 1878, total sales of the Co-operative Society had topped £12,000 and the dividend was up to 2s 4d for the 221 members - the quarterly sales were now up to £1,123, an increase of £337 on the previous year. The new stores were having a marked effect. There was too great a workload for William Walmsley to be both secretary and treasurer, and so Mr Vincent took over the latter. Walmsley still did well enough to be given a £2 a year pay rise. The un-named storekeeper and baker were being praised for their efforts, and they appear to have been the only paid employees. It was decided to start a penny bank.

May 1879 saw another milestone passed, sales of over £4,000 in one year. However, for unexplained reasons, a dividend of just 1s 4d was paid, but the following quarter it was exactly double this, the highest ever. It was decided for the time being to fix the price of selling a loaf of bread to the same price as in Coventry, and now stock-taking was to be done once a year. By the first meeting of 1880, the membership stood at 254, 45 had joined in the year and 22 withdrawn. Total annual sales had now reached £17,252 and a total dividend of almost £1,400 paid. The clear profit of £1,540 now allowed the society to look at further investment. In February 1880, a special meeting, which over a hundred attended, was called and after lengthy discussions it was agreed that reserve funds could be invested in building cottages alongside the stores. The great majority were in favour, and the building of six cottages facing onto Park Road was approved by the Local Board at its meeting in March 1880. Tenders were invited and those received included Ball (£999), Berry (£1,075), Balcombe (£1,116) and Vincent (£840) all from Kenilworth and

John Fell from Leamington who was in town building the sewer system. However, the successful bidder was neighbour and former landowner John Boddington whose tender for £660 was accepted. As the cottages were going up, letters were sent to the Kenilworth Advertiser suggesting that they were of an inferior quality but this was refuted and an apology published. At the 27th quarterly meeting, the good quality of John Boddington's work was re-iterated. The society sales of £1,222 were up £227 on the corresponding 1879 quarter.

In October 1880, William Henry Walmsley resigned his position as secretary, a position he had held since the society's formation. John Brown jnr was elected in his place, but due to the number of people then out of work it was decided not to immediately open a subscription list for Walmsley; he had to wait until the following summer to be presented with a handsome silver cruet stand.

The depressed state of trade in town began to show in the society's accounts. In July 1881, the annual sales of £4,507 were down £91 on the previous year and membership had fallen to 254, but this was a temporary trend. The depositors in the penny bank numbered 142. E Swann and W Watson were elected stock-takers.

By the end of 1883, the Co-operative had a new manager, Walter James Robertson. One notable member to leave was baker George Bennett who terminated his association with the Co-operative and returned to his own business in School Lane.

The Co-operative building and three of its cottages.

*   *   *

Woodcock Family
Edward H Woodcock had married Charlotte Brodie whilst serving in India. She was the daughter of another serving officer.

Charlotte and Edward had six known children, Ann, Maria, John, Jane, Isabella and Edward. Edward snr died in 1870, by which time the family were living in Kenilworth at The Firs. Ann continued to live there with her three daughters, Maria married but returned as a young widow. Edward moved to Wigan where he became registrar at the County Court, but John followed in his father's footsteps, joining the Army

and serving in India. He joined the Madras Fusiliers in 1847 and fought in the Second Burmese War of 1852, receiving the Medal and Clasp for Pegu. He later served with the Central India force in the India Mutiny campaign of 1857 gaining the Medal and Clasp for Central India. In 1863 he married Joanne Tweedie, daughter of Major-General Tweedie of the Madras Staff Corps. He retired in 1874, having attained the rank of Colonel, and was making money by trading in tea. He moved to the town of his family, living at Crackley Gables. When Charlotte died in 1884, Colonel John was the chief mourner.

George Peyton Gregory began his business as a cabinetmaker and upholsterer in High Street in 1864, aged about 27. In 1870, he moved to nearby larger premises which had previously been The School of Industry. In 1871, Gregory was employing a man and two apprentices, but in 1877, he decided to give up the furniture manufacturing side of the business to James Jackson, and early the following year he sold up completely as he was *"...removing to a distance."* In early February 1878 the whole of the premises' contents were put up for auction, from his antique writing desk to the local photographs he had collected. Also for sale was his 6ft carpenter's bench, wood, horse-hair, gimp, handles etc., associated with his business.

The building itself was purchased by Miss Jane Woodcock (46), sister of Colonel Woodcock, of The Firs, with the sole intention of making it available to become a convalescent home. Hospital patients were often discharged into poor habitation and the Reverend Mr Fitzgerald of Leamington worked particularly hard in setting up the home to work hand-in-hand with Warneford and other hospitals, but it was the contribution of Reverend Somerset Pennefather and Mr Pennington of Thickthorn that initiated Kenilworth's involvement, it being regarded as more salubrious than Leamington. By the time of the opening in June 1878, twelve beds had been fitted for the reception of patients paying 5s a week, and one room set apart for use of a private female patient at a cost of a guinea a week. There were separate dining rooms for men and women, and a matron's room. Donations had flowed in from the ladies and gentlemen of the district, well beyond the expectations of the promoters and these amounted to over £200, £50 more than required to furnish the Home. Doctors Wynter, Clarke and Thomas Bourne, all of Kenilworth, were the institution's medical officers. The view from the rear of the building across to the Castle was used as a promotional point; the equally clear view of the graveyard was not. The patients were not completely confined to the Home; in 1880 Mrs Booth of Clarendon Villa in Fieldgate Lane, entertained those who could get there, accompanied by the matron.

Despite the promising start, the Home soon began to hit financial problems. In early 1881, it was lamented that the initial level of donations was not being maintained and it was predicted that within a year, the Home would be in debt and so it was decided to hold a concert at the Mission Hall in aid of funds. Held in April, this was a stylish event with a string quartet playing Haydn, Mozart and Mendelssohn *"...compositions seldom heard in a country town."* Also performed was Nicolai's Merry Wives of Windsor which brought *"...four hands on the pianoforte, two violins, viola and two violoncellos."* Another fund-raising performance involved Colonel Hughes-Hallett, reciting passages from Shakespeare and other authors, at St.John's schoolroom in February 1883. There was a good attendance and 15 guineas was raised. These concerts raised the profile of the Home and the giving of donations improved.

George Gregory's furniture warehouse was reconstructed as a Convalescent Home.

The fifth annual meeting, in February 1883, of the friends and subscribers to the Home saw a disappointing turnout of fewer than twenty, and additionally one of its most influential members, Henry Wise of Woodcote, had just died and his widow, also a committee member, was unable to attend and had decided to leave the county. Financially the Home was now in a sounder state. Donations were actually higher than in the early days, but the Chairman, W Willes, thought they should be greater; Leamington donated well but Coventry little, despite it being the only such home in the area. Subscriptions had risen from £118 to £193 in the last year, and church collections were up to £44. Concerts held in Leamington and Kenilworth raised £35, and Miss Percy donated all the required coal. The major expenses were salaries £95, rent £50, butcher £95, grocer £56, baker £39, washing £25, and ale, wine and spirits £22 which was almost twice that of medicines, £12. There was a balance of just £2 16s 3d, but a carry-over debt from the previous year of £1 17s 6d reduced this. There had been a generous legacy from the late Mrs Pratt of £300 and this was invested on the Home's behalf in Great Western Railway Consolidated Guaranteed Stock. The number of patients had increased year by year, from 63 in the first year to 191 in the last. These were not just local but had come from as far afield as Hampshire, Worcestershire, Oxfordshire and London. The Matron, Miss Keates, was singled out for praise. It was now decided to abandon the private room available for £1 1s a week as it was so little occupied and could be used for other purposes.

Entertainments to raise funds became regular events. Between April 1884 and February 1885, three were held in town; at St.John's school, the National School and the Assembly Rooms. Events were also held elsewhere, Mrs Mary Nelson for example arranged one at the Nelson Mill at Emscote.

St.John's school was becoming very overcrowded. By mid-1879, there were 159 pupils, including 27 under-fives. "The crowded state of the rooms is a great drawback to the efficiency of the school." By October, plans were drawn up for an extension, and advertisements were placed in the local press by the architects, George and Isaac Steane, inviting tenders for construction. By mid-December, the foundations were being dug and in May 1880 the pupils were given a half-day holiday whilst doors were fitted between the old and new parts of the school. The new room was 18ft 6ins wide and 21ft long. On 29th October 1881, the same architects were advertising again for further additions to the school, possibly for a new room over 40ft long that was built at this time. Two months later, somewhat belatedly, the architects submitted their plans to the Local Board; as the work was now close to completion, the initial reaction of laughter was soon replaced by the realisation of a great lack of respect for the Board and its rules.

Part of the early 1880's extension used by the infants of St.John's school.

New desks and other equipment were bought and, combined with at least twice as much space and an additional teacher, the Inspectors soon reported the investment had produced an all round improvement in the children's education. The school fees at this time were *"Middle-class department, 9d a week; mixed department standard 6 and 5, 3d a week; standards 4, 3 and 2, 2d a week, standard 1, 1d a week. Infants department, 1d a week."*

*   *   *

By 1880, the reputation of Kenilworth fruit growers was established: "*Kenilworth strawberries, the most highly flavoured in all the land, will be seen on the Lady's Hills and other parts of the town in abundance and high flavour. The decree of the gardeners of Covent Garden has gone forth, no fruit can surpass the delicious flavoured strawberries of Kenilworth.*" Early signs in June 1881 were for a good strawberry season and in July berries "*...large in size and plentiful...*" were being despatched by rail to Leamington, Coventry, and Birmingham, ready-packed in baskets, for prices between 6d and 1s a pound, and large consignments went to Covent Garden. The later crop was affected by drought. In 1883 up to two tons a day were sent to London alone. The following year the berries retailed for 4d to 8d a pound but Kenilworth Castle visitors could get a basket full for just 6d.

By early 1881, Castle Farm had a new tenant. Ernest Charles Trepplin was brought up by his parents, Charles and Elizabeth, at Green Hayes in Leek Wootton. In 1876, Ernest, then 19, entered Brasenose College at Oxford and left in 1880 with an MA and BA. He also achieved fame as a sprinter, winning the Varsity 100 yards in three successive years. He moved into the Castle Gatehouse and was farming over 1,500 acres and employing 7 men, 24 boys and 11 women.

In 1881, William Mander had Oaks Farm valued ready for its transfer to Charles Trepplin the following February. There was no mention of its brick-yard, but of interest are a brew-house, and an engine-house, which was home to a 7hp portable engine and a steam engine by Clayton. There were also hay-making machines and dairy equipment. In early 1882 William Mander took on the spirit licence of his brother Edward, who had been living at Camden House at St.John's but now moved to Wellesbourne.

In 1882, Charles Trepplin sold Green Hayes and took up residence at Pleasance Farm. Between them, the Trepplins now had leases on eight farms and over 3,000 acres. In the summer of 1882, the Trepplins blocked a number of paths across their land, claiming an intrusion on their property. At California, a swing gate was blocked off and at Villiers Hill, a style was blocked with a railing. Three men removed it and one of the Trepplins had them taken to court where the case was dismissed. Over 100 people, 70 of whom were ratepayers, attended a meeting to protest at his actions. Ernest Trepplin claimed a misunderstanding had arisen over the blockage at California; he had built a new roadway from there, past New Buildings, and across Oaks Farm to Roundshill Lane for his own benefit and said a notice board he had put up was only to stop people using the new road and not the right of way. He was ordered to put up a less misleading sign.

In November 1882, Ernest Trepplin arranged a shoot in Chase Wood. Between 9.00 a.m. and dusk, 42 pheasant, 17 hares and 561 rabbits were shot. Lunch was taken in a marquee erected in the wood; the beaters were rewarded with wine and cheese.

Frank Stevens started working for the Trepplins as a boy of 13 in 1882. In common with other farm boys, he was given charge of a team of horses and often, particularly at harvest time, the boys were left on their own with their charges moving wagons around the farms. At 2 p.m. one September 1883 day, farm bailiff Robert Neil saw an unattended team of horses making their way back to the farm across Bulkington Meadows. Suspecting something was wrong, he went in the direction from which they had come, and found young Frank lying unconscious and bleeding from his head. He summoned Dr Atkinson, a door was procured to use as a stretcher, and Frank was carried to his home by five workmen. He died just four hours after he was found. Remarkably, at the inquest at the Green Man, no medical evidence was called for. Coroner William Poole thought it a waste of time because "*...as there were three medical men in attendance I could not call one without the others...*" and so it was left to another witness to state that he overheard one of the doctors say that the boy had suffered a fractured skull. It was assumed that Frank had fallen and been kicked by a horse.

In early 1881 there had been another outbreak of foot and mouth disease in Warwickshire, but even when Warwick and Solihull were affected, Kenilworth somehow remained free. However, from late 1882 onwards, there was another outbreak and farms around Coventry, Leamington and Coleshill were soon affected, and it was inevitable that eventually this time Kenilworth would become involved. The first farm so to be was in Roundshill Lane in May 1883 with cattle infected at Mr Branstons, who had been fined for not reporting the previous Kenilworth outbreak, and within weeks 80 cattle were infected at one of the Trepplin farms. Charles Trepplin was in trouble a few weeks later for not reporting an outbreak at his Villiers Hill farm: Mr Stanley, the cattle inspector for the district, found Trepplin's sub-bailiff "*...dressing two beasts with salt and water...*" and it was clear that these and three other animals had been suffering for several days. Trepplin was described as one of the largest tenant farmers in England, occupying twelve farms, his defence that he was not aware of the rules was simply not believed, and he was fined £2 for each beast. Not long after, Charles Trepplin was again in trouble for allowing pigs to wander onto the highway, an apparently regular occurrence.

In August 1883 farmer Richard Hodges of Camp Farm was fined £1 3s 6d for moving six cattle from his farm through an infected area, the first of two such fines. The same week Joseph Hoddell, son of butcher Mark Hoddell, committed a similar offence when moving two of his father's sheep from Dial House farm to St.John's for slaughter. He was fined 15s 6d. There were now 98 cases in Kenilworth.

By September the whole district around Kenilworth, Ashow, Milverton, Leek Wootton, Honiley and Stoneleigh, was infected and yet an agricultural show was held in Coventry with Kenilworth's Samuel Forrest amongst the prize-winners. Unsurprisingly, cattle entries though were described as disappointing. Their were now 185 infected cattle in Kenilworth, only 6 in Warwick and 7 in Solihull, but by mid-January the area was clear of foot and mouth, and there was just one case of sheep scab. It was not until May that it once more became permissible to move cattle without a licence.

A particularly good year for strawberries was 1885 with up to two tons daily leaving the station. Their wholesale price was as little as 3d to 6d a pound and retail 4d to 8d. Amongst the chief growers was Charles Trepplin at Crew Gardens where Joseph Murdoch, his gardener from Green Hayes, was manager. Others were Joseph Burbery, R and Thomas Brown, (Thomas was also licensee of the Royal Oak), Henry James (who grew his fruit at the Strawberry Gardens on the Ladies Hills and was a grocer and fruiterer in New Street), William James, Henry Arnold (also a grocer and fruiterer in New Street), Henry Clarke (of the Cherry Orchard in Spring Lane), R Wakelin and H Sturge. 1886 was a good year for plums, 1s buying 72lbs: *"How many families are there in Kenilworth that haven't made plum jam?"*

Despite a drought giving strawberries a bad season, over five tons were sent from the station in one July 1887 day. William James of Ivy Cottage gardens, Coventry Road, had the honour of supplying strawberries to Queen Victoria for her summer trip to Balmoral. Obviously a success, James supplied her again the following year. The London dealers with which James worked were Browning and Wesley of Paddington.

Due to his health, William Poole relinquished his position as Clerk to the Board in late 1883. As a token of gratitude he was given a gift of £50. He moved away from Kenilworth and died on 3rd April 1885 at his home in High Street, Leamington. His funeral was a quiet affair, just two wreaths accompanied the coffin on its journey to St.Nicholas, there were no mourning coaches and the mourners were conveyed in just two carriages.

The tomb of one time County Coroner, Town Clerk, Solicitor and bankrupt, William Savage Poole, is covered by what appears to be a sepulchral slab unearthed from the Abbey remains.

The position of Coroner for the central district of Warwickshire was quickly filled, Dr Daniel Wynter being appointed the following month. Elmdene was transferred to Poole's wife Kathleen in 1886, and in September that same year it was bought by William Henry Mitchell, who was already in residence. In October, Mitchell obtained permission to build piggeries; pigs appear to have been a passion of his as he won prizes with them at shows.

*   *   *

The Statute Fair maintained its place in the calendar. In 1878, The Square was full of roundabouts, swing-boats and shooting galleries. The town and its hostelries filled during the day, and the Coventry watchmakers apprentices were there *"...in all his glory, chaffing, larking and smoking bad cigars all day long."* The Bowling Green with its own swings was particularly popular and in the evening The Square *"...presented a very animated appearance, flags flying, drums beating, trumpets squeaking and Shah scent flying."* This continued until 9.30 p.m. when the crowd began to *"clear off"* and the town *"resumed its quietude."*

Other Statute attractions were listed in 1879. *"Bowling for cocoa nuts..."* was set up by gypsies in a field owned by Mrs Arnold, close to the lawn tennis courts; stalls with toys for sale reached down to the Kings Arms and just beyond was a photographer who undertook to supply a print in just ten minutes. Kenilworth's Mr Harrison had a sweet stall, and pears were on sale for 1d a pound. Although set for the Tuesday, much of the fair was in operation by the Monday evening and the *"...most objectionable feature..."* of the event were small tin syringes filled with water that were *"...discharged...much to the annoyance of the receiver."* Signor Bosco again drew large audiences in a field near the Bear Inn. There was generally a poor attendance due to the wet weather and many of the roads were in a deplorable condition.

As the fair approached in 1880, William White of the White Lion made his own preparations in a field opposite his inn, which he advertised as being the closest to the station. White arranged for a band to play for dancing, a whole pig-roasting and a variety of sports including *"...Aunt Sally, sack racing, stone racing and climbing the greasy pole for a new hat."* The rest of the town saw the usual swing-boats, stalls, and other attractions, and *"...towards evening most of the townspeople turned out."* The attractions proved to be too great a temptation for six men in particular; Samuel and James Gloucester, Giles Stephens, Joseph Miller, William Newman and James Mousley, as they attended the fair in preference to being at their workplace, Walter Lockhart's brickworks. All six were charged with being absent from work as *"...in consequence other men were delayed."* Each was fined 5s 6d except for the last two named who, due to their non-appearance at court, were fined an extra 5s each.

In 1883, the fair was set up in The Square on a Monday, ran until Tuesday evening, and was well attended. There was now little or no hiring of servants but the watchmakers of Coventry still regarded the day as a holiday, and large numbers came from Leamington, Warwick and Birmingham.

*   *   *

On 2nd September 1880, the last luggage van of a train derailed near Milverton station disrupting services into the night. Amongst those helping to repair the damage was a ganger called Jonathon Hancox, and a permanent way foreman George Sewell, both of Kenilworth, and when the repairs had been completed, they started walking home along the track. Not long before, Sewell had been in trouble as cattle had strayed onto the track at a point where he was responsible for the fences. He subsequently received a letter saying that he was to be "removed". Believing he was to loose his job, he had become very depressed and despondent and as he walked home that night with Hancox he took out a knife and started to cut his own throat. Hancox grabbed his arms but Sewell broke free and continued to saw at his neck. Hancox struggled with him for ten minutes before the commotion attracted assistance. Sewell was by now exhausted and lost consciousness for several hours. Weeks later, Sewell found himself in front of Kenilworth Petty Sessions charged with attempted suicide. It was revealed that he was under a misapprehension - had he read and understood the letter fully he would have known that he was only to be removed to a "...place where there would be less work and not so much responsibility." His mental condition was assessed, the bench admonished him and he was discharged.

In 1880, the London and North Western Railway made plans to double the railway line from Leamington to Kenilworth and build a new railway from Kenilworth Common to Berkswell. Included in the scheme was an entirely new station building at Kenilworth. Henry Street raised the matter at a Board meeting as he thought the scheme "...might not be generally known..." and much discussion took place as to whether the railway company could be induced to build a new road to the station, on its eastern side, as part of the improvements. Initial ideas were for a road southwards, but it was then suggested that a northern approach would be better with a road from the level crossing at the station's northern end, alongside Lockhart's brickworks, to connect with Whitemoor Road, and possibly continue it parallel to the railway up to Park Hill. The railway company could not be persuaded to pay for the road, and as they intended to spend about £10,000 on the new station, the Board could not really complain.

In July 1881 work was underway on rebuilding the line at the Coventry end, the new line to Berkswell was started in June 1882. As work progressed, the Board wrote several letters to the contractors, Holme and King, who had set up a depot in Castle End. One was concerning a temporary bridge over the railway in Spring Lane, and another was to grant permission for the contractors to build a temporary tramway across the road near Crackley in conjunction with building the new bridge over the Coventry Road. Two months later another letter was sent: "Clerk to call the attention of Holme and King asking the railway contractors as to the repairs of the road from their quarry near Crackley to the railway bridge near the gas works to which they were hauling stone."

The building of the new railway line provided a spectacle. As Dr Wynter was returning from seeing a patient in Berkswell in November 1882, he stopped his carriage alongside the railway workings in Burton Green and walked a short distance to watch a steam digger in action. The doctor's servant was left in charge of the horse and carriage and he walked it back and forth along the road. As he crossed "...the rails which run across the road, a steam sawing machine was suddenly started into work." The horse took fright and turned sharply, throwing the groom and turning the carriage over and breaking it in two. The horse tried to jump a hedge but the remains of the carriage became caught and the horse fell just yards from the top of the cutting. Neither the horse nor groom was injured. A year later, there was an outbreak of smallpox amongst the navvies based at Burton Green.

In early 1883, work started on the new Kenilworth station building. It was built slightly to the north of the existing one, so that passenger facilities were maintained during construction. It was a very grand affair, obviously in keeping with the projected future of the town. Another improvement was the replacing of the level crossing at the northern end of the station with a footbridge. When construction of the new station was complete, the old one was dismantled. The re-building of the bridge carrying Park Hill was particularly slow. In January 1884, it was still under construction and only one parapet, the northern side, was up but it was finally completed in March. "The roadway is finished with stone sets." However, the actual road surface had not been finished and it was still closed.

William Clarke decided to improve the existing Kings Arms Assembly Room that fronted onto Station Road. Although of a useful size, access to it was via an objectionable approach through the hotel yard. New plans were put before the Kenilworth Board in October and passed. When complete, entry was to be through a new vestibule fronting onto Station Road, off which were retiring rooms and the refurbished refreshment rooms and public bar, and an exit to the bowling green at the rear. A broad staircase led to the assembly room which was capable of seating five hundred persons, and at the far end of which was a raised platform capable of seating a further sixty. It was lit with mediaeval style gas-brackets down both sides. The most interesting aspect of the reconstruction was the acquisition of the original sandstone railway station building and its re-erection as the new façade of the building. "No visitor again coming to Kenilworth from its new and magnificent station cannot be other than pleased to notice the red sandstone building, being the old railway station, be erected there intact, and forming the new refreshment rooms to the Kings Arms Hotel."

In June 1884, the new railway works were complete and the line to Berkswell opened for passenger traffic. The locals were certain that the new line would lead to an influx of new Birmingham wealth to the town and that in a short space of time Kenilworth would become a serious rival to Leamington. W H Smith had intimated that they intended to open a bookstall at the station, and William Clarke planned to provide refreshments; neither plan came to fruition.

The railway provided a distraction for children and it was inevitable that some would get into trouble. Two Albion Row boys, David Smith (9) and William Chaplin (10), were caught throwing stones at a train as it passed under a bridge in July 1883. The brakeman of a luggage train said a lot of stones came down on his van and these were produced in court, but as it was a luggage train, it was decided that the offence was more thoughtless than malicious mischief. Station Master Taylor said that stone throwing at trains was becoming very frequent and that the boys deserved *"a good whipping."* Ordered to receive six strokes of the birch-rod each, the boys were led from the court *"roaring."*

The original railway station stonework formed a new frontage for the Kings Arms refreshment room and bar.

*　*　*

At the Board meeting in December 1881, Mr Hodges sought permission to plant lime trees in High Street as far as Thomas Emery's establishment - the whole of the work being done voluntarily. Permission was granted, and Henry Street amusingly suggested that that they could also do Albion Row while they are at it!

James Clarke of Albert House in Spring Lane, describing himself as a herbalist, applied in the autumn of 1882 to sell wine, cider and beer both on and off his premises. He claimed that he lived in a fast developing area of the town and that there was no public house *"...within several hundred yards..."* but not surprisingly opposition from the Bowling Green Inn and Albion Tavern saw the application refused. It would have been an interesting combination of professions as Clarke's advertisement read, *"Herbalist, leeches etc"*.

The area being developed to which he referred was south of Albion Street, which was soon to be called Henry Street, but the Board had caused themselves a problem here by passing plans for houses already under construction before the road itself, existing in some form for twenty years, had been properly built. There had recently been litigation on just this point in Hillfields in Coventry and the Board now realised that they were putting themselves in a difficult position. The first two houses were at the eastern end and set well back from the provisional road-line. It was Board member Henry Street who had sold the land for building and he claimed that the new owner had not intended to build upon it for many years and there was no intention of making it into a proper road, and in any case it *"...was really only the back of Albion Row."* It was agreed that the Board should be able to compel owners to build new roads in these cases.

As 1883 progressed, William Lawrence received permission to build several groups of houses along the road, six in January, three in June and five in December, as did another builder, Edward Hall, who received an occupation certificate for three houses in October. Henry Webb, a tailor, was listed as the first business in the road.

The Board, however, still had the problem as to the making of the road itself. Having decided to compel the owners to make it, they then decided to allow building on one side only. At a special Board meeting in June it was again decided to enforce the construction of the road, but Henry Street said that it was invidious as there were other incomplete roads in the Parish, but as the resolution was on the books it could not be overturned. Street gave notice of his intention to have the decision rescinded. It seems he failed.

The first houses built in Henry Street were set well back; then the problems started...

In early 1884, the Board received a letter from the occupiers of the road, now numbering about 150. The road was in a deplorable state, only ten feet wide in places and in wet weather was a *"...bed of mud from end to end..."* except where householders spread ashes. *"To walk along Henry-street by day takes considerable courage, to do so by night, enveloped as it is then by an almost Egyptian darkness, is simply out of the question."* It was also surprisingly signed by the land- and house-owners, Lawrence, Hall and Edward Martin, the reason for this became clear at the next Board meeting.

It was Dr Wynter who raised the matter; he had that very morning been given a covenant, signed at the time the land was sold, that gave an undertaking by Henry Street to make the road - this was why nothing had happened in a year and why the residents were so annoyed. Street counter-claimed that he was to make it but the new owners were to pay for it, and they had not sent him a single penny. He also claimed that he sold the land for agricultural use so the road he made did not have to be of any great quality, and he had improved its access by enhancing the road to it (Herberts Lane) from Albion Street. He further claimed that, after his first two houses, Lawrence had not stuck to the agreed building line, again making the full width of the road difficult to implement. This led to another sharp exchange of words between Wynter and Street, with Wynter at one point pushing the covenant across the table to his adversary, only for Street to say, *"I can't read that thing!"* William Evans had to rise to restore order, only for Wynter to say, *"I think it is scandalous that a member of the Board should know this and allow it to go on so long."* Street started his reply "warmly", *"I think it is scandalous that a member of the Board should......"* only to be interrupted by cries of "shame" and "order" and Evans had to step in again to point out that the debate was becoming personal. The resolution that the work should be carried out was referred to the Highways Committee, and upon Street's suggestion, due to their condition Lower Ladies' Hill and White's-row were added to it.

"We may now hope that this street, so long a disgrace to civilisation, will shortly become worthy of our beautiful village. Our spirited and enterprising builder, Mr Lawrence, will soon be able to carry on his laudable work of erecting cheap and comfortable cottages for the poor with greater speed and less difficulty."

However, if anyone thought the matter was now settled they were much mistaken. The following week William Lawrence wrote a letter condemning Street's statements at the Board meeting; he denied ignoring the building line, declared Street had not attempted to improve the road and further stated Street *"...said that if I should not press the matter in a certain quarter he would see to it being made."* An anonymous reply, purporting to be from five owners along the road, claimed Street had put hundreds of loads onto the road and that Lawrence's building work had damaged it, only for Lawrence to counter-claim the letter was a forgery.

Lawrence agreed to do his share of building the road as long as the others were compelled to do theirs. It was now that another name enters the story; William Stickley had bought the area of land, 5872 sq yds, part of plot of 12,000 sq yds, on the northern side of Henry Street at the Spring Lane end on 17th August 1882, and he was soon in dispute with Lawrence about the road construction. In this case, the difficulties were quickly overcome and after discussion with Henry Street and Mr Bagshaw, Stickley agreed to start his work in September. When construction began, however, it soon became clear that the whole road was being built far too narrow, 21ft instead of the 36ft stipulated in the bye-laws. When it was completed, and the Board were asked to take it over, disagreements started again. Lawrence had been told in writing that the full width must be made otherwise the Board would not take it up, but Henry Street pointed out that the road would not be much used and had been made well and if the Board took it, it would not cost them a penny for years. Remarkably, Dr Wynter agreed with Street and said the Board should accept the road due to the *"extraordinary circumstances."* Bagshaw thought the Board should not accept it as they had given out all the proper instructions for it to be made the full width. Street pointed out that the road was close on twenty years old and was close to 30ft wide towards *"Spring-hill."* The matter was referred to the surveyor and Clerk who were asked for their recommendations, and the Board agreed to take the road despite its shortcomings.

The duties of the road surveyor William Evans had greatly increased as were his wages, from 28s to 30s a week.

* * *

At the end of 1880, Joseph Stone Burbery of Castle Grove wrote to the Board suggesting a *"...public recreation or playground for the young working men and boys of Kenilworth..."* was needed. He thought a central location was preferable but the flat area on the Common, suitable for hockey and football but less so for cricket, could be improved by *"...voluntary and other labour."* The Board agreed that such a facility was desirable but could not entertain it due to other commitments.

In February 1881, Dr Wynter wrote a letter to the *Kenilworth Advertiser* complaining of the lack of respect the churchyard had: *"It must be most distressing to see the desecration of the graves by sheep-grazing and by wanton mischief done to the monuments and railings which surround them by the children who are allowed to make it a public playground."* Flowers were also torn up by the roots and Wynter suggested that perhaps a subscription should be raised to pay for the churchyard's upkeep.

Despite Reverend W Bickmore's prediction in 1866 that it would take 25 years, by November 1881, the churchyard was nearly full and it was becoming a matter of some urgency. It was quite clear from Clarendon's earlier statements that there was no possibility of the yard being extended again, and the problem was undoubtedly the Board's and not the Vicar or Churchwarden's. A committee was formed, including several parishioners, to find out just how long it would be before the burial ground was full and to take provisional steps to a solution.

At the first meeting of the Cemetery Committee on 19th November 1881, a report was produced stating the probability that the existing churchyard would be full within eighteen months. Two options were suggested; either the provision of a new burial ground, which it was unlikely the Board could afford, or an extension of the existing one. The best way to extend was still to the southeast, continuing the existing south wall to meet a wall built up to the end of the Abbey chancel. This however was likely to involve a Local Board Inspector and currently the prejudice was against extending churchyards. The sewerage scheme debt was also likely to be a problem. There was also, of course, the certainty of Clarendon refusing to sell any land; he had already refused to for the proposed swimming baths. No decision was made by the Board and the committee disbanded.

More than a year later, in January 1883, the necessity of an extension was again discussed and another committee was formed. The reason for Clarendon's reluctance to sell a couple of acres of the Abbey Fields for the extension became clear when it was revealed that he intended to sell the entire Abbey Fields estate for building purposes, and clearly an extension of the cemetery would have a detrimental effect. It was feared that the selling of the Abbey Fields, if bought by a private speculator, *"...would spoil Kenilworth possibly by the running up of factories and small houses."* The Cemetery Committee came up with a solution - if the Board bought the entire estate for recreational purposes, the churchyard extension could be accommodated. On 18th January 1883 it was agreed at a Board meeting to offer Clarendon £16,000, plus an estimated maximum of £1,000 for the value of timber, for the entire Abbey Fields estate, which included Sion

House and a number of cottages. Within a month, the offer had been accepted, subject to certain stipulations and a proper contract being drawn up, and to this, the Board agreed. The agreement was of course, subject to the Board being able to borrow enough money. The major voice of dissent, not surprisingly, was Dr Wynter who opposed the borrowing of such large sums on top of the debt the town already had.

The same week that the inquiry was held regarding the loan for new offices, Dr Wynter wrote a letter to the *Advertiser* continuing his stand against the majority of the Board, totally opposed to the idea that the town should fund the purchase of the Abbey Fields for £17,000, and the subsequent increase in rates, without consulting the ratepayers. He suggested the churchwardens should call a Parish meeting at which he was sure the majority would be against the move and this was duly called at the Assembly Room at the Kings Arms in early March, just four days before the public inquiry into the possible loan was to be held. Wynter placed an advertisement in the *Kenilworth Advertiser* explaining the reason for the meeting and listed a number of those who opposed the scheme including Bagshaw, Hawley, Lockhart, and Judd.

At the meeting, Wynter was adamant that no necessity existed for recreational grounds, and that there were plenty of lanes for walking. On the question of money, the amount required would take the total Board borrowing to £6,000 more than the whole rateable value of the town. The suggestion that this could be retrieved by selling off some as building land Wynter described as "*speculative*" and that the Board was not elected to speculate with public money. Practically the only notable voice against Wynter was Edward Mander who hoped the Board could "*...save this aspect of the town being marred...*" and that the cemetery could be extensively enlarged. However, Wynter won the vote by a considerable majority and those on his side included Thomas Hawley, John Judd, Walter Lockhart, John Bagshaw, T Davis and G Page who formed a committee to oppose the scheme.

The public inquiry was held at the Institute by J Thornhill Harrisson on Friday 9th March. William Evans outlined the progress so far. An agreement had been signed with Clarendon for the purchase of 78 acres of land bounded by the roads, Sion House, 19 cottages and a smithy, provided the Local Government Board sanctioned the required loan within two months. The deal was set to be completed on 29th September. The Board's intentions were twofold, to provide a public park, and to offset the cost of a new cemetery by selling two acres to the churchwardens for £400, the amount refused by Clarendon. The total rateable value of the town was a little over £20,000 and the current debt due to the sewerage scheme and the requested loan for new offices for the Board was over £9,000. For this reason the possible loan for the Abbey Fields was now limited to £12,000 but the Board hoped to recoup the difference by selling off portions of the estate for building purposes. There was much in favour of purchasing the fields for walks and sports-fields, and it was agreed that if this opportunity was missed it might never return; Clarendon had already had other enquiries. With the evidence so

well put, Mr Wilks a Coventry solicitor representing Wynter and the other opponents, abandoned his arguments, and it was left to Harrisson to present his report to the Local Government Board.

On the 18th April 1883 the Board received the news it had hoped for; the £850 loan to buy the site for new offices, stabling and stone-yard; £650 for building the offices, stabling and furniture; and the £12,000 for the purchase of the Abbey Fields estate had all been approved. Unfortunately, it had been overlooked that the intention to raise the shortfall by the sale of plots was illegal. The Public Health Act of 1875 "...required that the proceeds of sales of land not required to be retained should be applied in repayment of the monies borrowed on the security of the rates..." - the sale of plots could only go to pay off the loan and not to Clarendon for the sale.

In December 1883 Clarendon asked for the purchase of the estate to be deferred until 25th May 1884; then at the 2nd April 1884 Board meeting, the first held in the new offices, it was formally resolved to cancel the provisional agreement with Clarendon for the whole estate and that a memorandum was attached to it releasing him from it. It was then unanimously agreed to purchase only the centre portion of the fields, amounting to 40 acres 2 roods 30 perches, for £6,000, the said sum to be borrowed from the Prudential Assurance Company at 4%, repayable over 60 years. This figure had been carefully calculated to ensure the annual repayments for the loan were covered by the rent raised from leasing the fields, effectively the town would acquire the central parts of the fields without it costing a single penny on the rates. The negative aspect was that the fields could not then be opened to the public as they would remain in private hands. The area bought by the Board was not marked by field boundaries, but was an irregular shape including two places that reached the surrounding roads to provide access.

The remaining land was split into four areas and was bought by Board members on behalf of the Board, on the understanding that as individuals they would make no gain from the deals - the intention was that they could retrieve their outlay by selling building plots around the extremities and convey the rest to the Board. In this way, the restrictions of the Act of Parliament were avoided. However, the area of just over thirteen acres bounded by Abbey Hill, Rosemary Hill and Bridge Street, thought of as the most picturesque, was the subject of an appeal fund set up at the Leamington Priors Bank in the name of "Mr Samuel Forrest and Mr William Evans re the Abbey Fields Estate" to ensure that it was kept out of the hands of developers. The first donations received were from Mr Badley, Mrs Dawes, Henry Street and George Turner who each gave £500, Mrs Porter £200, Mr Brittain, George Church, Edward Draper, Thomas Emery, Mrs Morris, William Evans and Edward Smith £100 each, and J C Carter, Joseph H Burbery, Samuel Forrest, Richard Robbins and Charles Trepplin £50 each, and finally a £20 donation from the Reverend Alfred Binnie. On 12th May 1884 the purchase of this area was completed for £3,500 in the names of Street and Turner.

On the same day, the three remaining plots, covering the area from Abbey End to New Row totalling just over 24 acres, were bought for £6,200 by a syndicate of Board members Joseph H Burbery, Luke Heynes, William Evans and Samuel Forrest. The three separate sales ensured that the whole of the estate could come under the jurisdiction of the Board.

To enable the syndicate to recoup their outlay, on 9th June 1884, the first of the plots around the extremities were auctioned by James Whittendale. The area alongside High Street and part of New Row had been split into twelve plots, numbered 2 to 13, each with an area of 2,000 to 3,000 sq yds, and as they commanded the best views were obviously aimed at the upper end of the market. Alongside Barrow Well-lane were ten plots with a frontage of 22ft 6ins and "suitable for small villa residencies"; and next to this in Millbrook Lane were five larger plots with frontages of 40ft. On the sale plans for this area were drawn dotted building lines - these were to ensure that the view of the Castle from the Reverend Thomas Jeffcoatt's house on Abbey Hill was not interrupted.

Lot 1 was Sion House, and was bought by grocer George Church, and plots 14 to 28, on the corner of Barrow-well Lane and Millbrook Lane were also bought by Church, with Burbery and James Whittendale buying others. Included in the sales information was a plan showing the intention to build a road around the back of these premises with more building plots alongside it.

A covenant for the central area bought by the Board had been drawn up to protect its future. The fields were "...for the purpose of being for ever used as public walks or pleasure grounds under the control of the said Board." The area alongside Abbey Hill and Rosemary Hill was conveyed on the 28th November 1884 to William Evans and Joseph Roberts, in their capacity as Churchwardens, as Trustees for public grounds, and included the same restriction as for the central area, with the additional phrase that they "...should for ever remain unbuilt upon." Several exceptions were added, including the building of necessary roadways, fences and gates, or the widening of adjacent roadways. The total area now vested in the board was 52a 1r 18p which produced an annual rent of £150.

Most people had a grasp as to the status of the central part of the Abbey Fields bought by the Board, and the area of the south-eastern corner paid for by donations, but confusion surrounded the other areas and a special meeting was convened in May 1885 to clarify the situation. The rest of the estate had been purchased by the syndicate of Joseph H Burbery, William Evans, Samuel Forrest and Luke Heynes for £10,781 16s 1d, (a sum contradicting an earlier figure). Since June 1884, the syndicate had sold Sion House, lots 17-28 alongside Barrow Well Lane, and plots 6, 7, and 8 (three plots alongside the highest point in High Street), bringing their deficit down to £5,560 7s 4d. This left them in possession of the remaining building plots and large areas of the fields behind them, of which the *"...value far exceeds the amount of the balance." "Their sole desire has been and still is to benefit the town..."* and were now willing to sell to the Board for the outstanding balance. This would, of course, involve another enquiry which the Board members were sure would fail due to restrictions in the Public Health Act. Thus the Board resolved *"...that*

having regard to all the circumstances of the case, the committee regret that they cannot advise the Local Board to take a conveyance of the property, and they must therefore leave Mr Burbery and his co-proprietors to deal with it as they think best in their own interests."

The syndicate also gave up some land to allow the churchyard to be extended, saving the Board another expense. Unfortunately, as it was necessary to lease the fields to have an income to repay the loan, it meant that the fields still could not be opened to the public.

With the preferred site now in the hands of the Local Board, the great obstacle against providing swimming baths, the Earl of Clarendon refusing land or permission to build, was removed. Edward Stokes doubtless spoke for many when claiming the purchase of the fields for recreational purposes was in itself favourable towards building the baths, and suggested they were more necessary than the grounds themselves. Joseph S Burbery had by now left town, and the money he had earlier collected was in a Post Office savings account in the names of Reverend Somerset Pennefather and Richard Robbins.

Despite the absence of a pool, by 1880 a swimming club existed. In 1881 it was reported that they had recommenced their operations, a spot at Chesford had became popular with the small group of gentlemen. In 1884 they met every morning 500 yards below Chesford Bridge for *"...indulging in undisturbed evolutions in the tepid and tranquil water."* Hidden in the undergrowth they kept the necessary equipment for making coffee, a cup of which they had before returning to town for their day's business. The group had the intention to ask Lord Leigh, the landowner, for permission to build an iron dressing-room, at a cost of about £30, which in turn they hoped would increase their numbers. So content were they with their own arrangements that they were not too concerned whether proper facilities were provided in town or not, but it was mentioned that ladies needed facilities as well. It was then suggested that ladies should have a shady nook of their own, perhaps 100 yards further along the river, but there would of course be no objection to the two groups meeting up for a coffee afterwards. It was suggested that perhaps Lord Leigh would allow a second changing room, to encourage the fairer sex. The outcome was that by July that year, the men had obtained permission and built their changing hut. It was positioned just inside Wootton Spinney on the footpath from Chesford to Hill Wootton. It was a wooden structure covered in corrugated iron and carried the legend "La Lenoile" (*sic*, Leonile?) in gold letters on a board over the door. Inside was a seat running around three sides with an oak-stained back, and hooks for towels etc. On a wall was a poster from the Humane Society describing action to be taken in the case of cramp or "apparent drowning", and safety equipment included a belt attached to a roller, and a life buoy. A bucket, brush and mop were kept to ensure cleanliness. Planks stretched out from the hut several yards into the river acting as a diving board. It was all enclosed by a privet hedge, this and other shrubs dotted about were donated by Lord Leigh. The swimmers, and there were many, indulged in their healthy and invigorating recreation between 5 and 6 each morning.

In late July 1884, the Swain family suffered another fatality. Edward (23), who still lived with his parents in Adibourne Terrace, went fishing in the Abbey Fields at a popular spot not far from Townpool Bridge. Edward had become prone to fits and had just given up work as a page. When he failed to come home that evening his father went in search and early next morning he found his son face down in the stream, drowned. It was probable that Edward had had a fit and fallen in; the inquest at The Wyandotte returned a verdict of simply *"found drowned."*

In addition to the swimming club, others made use of the water at Chesford. On 30th August 1886, Kenilworth Post Office clerk Bernard Reynolds, a stout youth six feet in height, went swimming there with two brothers from Henry Street, 17-year-old Austin Penney and the younger Joseph Penny who could barely swim. Austin Penney and Bernard Reynolds decided to have a race, and soon Penney was comfortably in the lead. He looked back for his opponent, only to see him struggling in the water, which at that point was 12 ft deep. Without hesitation, Penney swam towards his friend who grabbed his arm in desperation. With Reynolds being much the stronger, he soon had his would-be rescuer in trouble as well, and there was a real danger he too would be dragged under, but Penney managed to free himself. With astonishing presence of mind, instead of going for help he stayed in the water close by until his friend had twice sunk beneath the surface and become exhausted; now he could safely grab him and pull him to the bank. The ordeal was not yet over as there were no footholds, but the non-swimming Joseph Penney, who had been watching the drama from the bank, grabbed hold of a tree branch and flung himself over the water to grab his brother's hand. With a great deal of difficulty, the brothers managed to get Reynolds out of the water. After about fifteen minutes rest, the two had dressed and recovered sufficiently for the group to walk home.

In addition to the well-deserved praise from all quarters, Reynolds' employer, Banker and Postmaster-General Thomas Morris, contacted the Royal Humane Society and after the writing of many letters and the filling in of numerous forms, the society was convinced that Austin Penney should receive an award. The Parish room was provided for the award's presentation, and after a well-received speech by the Vicar explaining the circumstances, it fell to Thomas Morris to read and present the testimonial written on vellum and enclosed in a richly gilt frame. After a modest speech by young Penney, there was great applause. Penney's father was obviously proud of his son, but could not let the event pass without saying that he *"...hoped that the Kenilworth Local Board would not allow another meeting like the present one to take place. The erection of a swimming baths would prevent it."*

The Abbey Fields remained the popular place for youths to bathe. In September 1887, Frank Watson was charged with damaging a fence belonging to David Fancott to get to the brook. He had been warned of this on several occasions, but he claimed that he just climbed over the already broken fence where he and others went

bathing regularly. The gap also seemed to be used by ladies who were fishing nearby at the time.

It was not just young men who enjoyed refreshing themselves in local waters; in September 1888 two ladies were seen at 4.30 one morning at the stream near the Castle: *"First came off some dainty shoes, then silken hose. Jumping up, both raising their garments around their waists, they paddled fearlessly along the stream."*

In August 1884, Thomas Hawley proposed a new road between Abbey End and Borrowell Lane along the edge of the Abbey Fields and plans were drawn up and deposited with the Board in January 1885. The land required for it was part of the Abbey Fields Estate owned by Joseph Burbery, Luke Heynes, William Evans and Samuel Forrest and it was they who were to pay for the road but the Board's employees who were to do the work. The intention was to provide a carriage drive around the whole of the fields and as it was to be a continuation of Abbey Hill, it was un-surprisingly decided the new road should be called Abbey Hill Road. The plan was approved perhaps partly because it replaced *"...one of the ugliest, dirtiest and most dangerous bye-paths that could be imagined."*

Due to the difficulty of the terrain, permission was sought and obtained from the Board to raise the level of Borrowell Lane *"...from the spring to the Borrow arch..."* to ease the gradient of the new road, particularly at the junction with the new lane. At the other end of the new road, Abbey Hill had to be widened about eight feet on the Abbey Fields side and re-aligned to form the junction. This work cost an additional £108, and involved the acquisition of 34 perches of land from the area of the Abbey Fields bought in the name of Street and Turner.

There was a good deal of excavation work involved to keep the gradient to a minimum. A surface drain was included in the plans and this ran into the brook in the Abbey Fields. During its construction *"...rounded stones, suggestive of huge stone bullets..."* thought to be relics of the great siege were found. Not everyone was convinced the road was necessary; *"No-one has yet expressed satisfaction at it. Had it been brought into Borrow-well Lane at the spring it would have made a better job of it."* As work on the road progressed, all were saddened to hear of the death of one of the four owners, Samuel Forrest, who died of gout and apoplexy at his home, Fern Bank, on 4th May aged just 36. He was described as an advanced agriculturist and was particularly known for his long-horned cattle at Chase Farm, which were frequent prize-winners. When the work was finished in early November, it was announced that the new road was to be called Forrest Road in his honour. It seems that none of the land adjacent to the road was ever put up for auction as building plots.

The stimulus for the purchase of the fields, the extension of the churchyard, could now go ahead and a meeting of the parishioners was held in the Parish room just before Christmas 1884. The earlier possibility of providing a completely new cemetery at a cost of a 6d rate for 60 years was briefly mentioned as it was in the minutes but was not discussed; the extension of the present churchyard was estimated as a 4d rate for 3 years.

Samuel Forrest, who contributed much towards the purchase of the Abbey Fields, was buried in a picturesque spot.

There were two plans proposed, one of which had been drawn up by Job Satchwell, and that which was not taken up suggested enclosing the entire church with consecrated ground. The accepted scheme extended the yard "South West by East" from the present yard and included a dwarf wall with iron pallisading to enclose the whole yard for the first time. The cost of purchasing the land from its new owners was put at £300 with a further £300 required for the alterations. This was to be raised by a voluntary rate of 4d and a subscription list was also opened with John Judd £10, Edward Mander, Joseph Roberts and Mr Barton, £5 each, contributing to the £60 raised at the meeting. By February 1885, the 2 acres had been acquired and work started. There had been a favourable response to the voluntary rate, but there were concerns that too much cost had been incurred by the *"elaborateness"* of the wall and the unsightly "zig-zag" of the path, and this was eventually blamed for the ultimate shortfall in the rate collection.

The design of the new path and wall was deemed responsible for the shortfall in voluntary funding.

After the Board meeting in April 1885, Luke Heynes was found dead in one of the offices. He had spent much of his 72 years involved with comb manufacturing and was still a horn dealer or merchant in his final years. Such was his responsible attitude to his duties, he had been the only member of the Board to attend all 15 meetings of his final year in office. Two of the four who had bought much of the Abbey Fields on behalf of the Board had now died, and so a new conveyance was drawn up in the names of Evans and

Burbery, the two survivors, and George Turner and John Bagshaw. This was signed on 23rd May 1885.

Luke Heynes is buried in an area of the churchyard alongside the visible Abbey remains.

The new churchyard extension was consecrated on 28th May 1885 and by comparison, the earlier western extension looked *"...like a cattle pound..."* but it was not the ceremony itself which became the headline news due to the coincidental swimming in the brook near the iron bridge by a group of 9 to 15 year-old boys: *"In addition to the indecency of youths bathing at a point where there are persons passing at all times, the language of the bathers was filthy in the extreme."* There were hopes that *"...steps will be taken to prevent a repetition of this reprehensible practise of bathing at midday in such a public place."* This again started the debate about the provision of public baths; some advocated the simple screening of this part of the brook and as there were many unemployed men in the town, there would have been no difficulty in arranging cheap labour. The earlier fund in the name of Joseph S Burbery was still available. The lack of action by the Board was now becoming the butt of jokes by the Kenilworth Amateur Minstrels. William Clarke and Dr Wynter reminded the Board that the ideal location for both the swimming baths and a cricket field was the Abbey Fields which had been purchased for recreational purposes, but again there was no real development.

Events in the Abbey Fields continued to prompt claims that the baths were required out of common decency: *"Let our (Board) members walk by the iron bridge any afternoon or evening with their lady friends and the matter will be promptly dealt with."*

"Modesty: first prize medal awarded to the lady

who stood one evening in the last week gazing admiringly upon several young men (of ages ranging from seventeen) near the Iron-bridge, in their costume of nature. The young men having divested themselves of such garments as Adam scorned, were enjoying unadorned the freedom of nature, when some horrid frolicsome fellow seized upon their garments and was making off with them. They rushed from their bath - the river - to give chase to their would be robber, when the lady, stood face to face, without the semblance of a blush, gazing upon their watery and dripping forms, thoroughly enjoying these poor fellows embarrassment."

*   *   *

In its five years, by July 1880 the Working Men's Club had gained an envious reputation, if only in the *Kenilworth Advertiser*. The paper claimed it was one of the oldest and best-run clubs in the county, and that the recent growth of coffee houses in large towns was merely following the lead of the club, which had provided these facilities from its beginning. Membership still cost less than a farthing a day, and its rooms were "...*well warmed and lighted.*" Notices in all rooms enforced the complete ban on gambling, and there was a well-stocked lending library. Alexander Carter's widow continued to support the club, and Kings Arms proprietor William Clarke was a popular president.

But by early 1882 the club was in financial difficulties and had a debt to clear and it was decided to hold an entertainment at the Kings Arms Assembly Rooms. William Clarke allowed the room to be used free of charge and Dr Wynter presided. In an evening mostly of song, some comic and some performed by Kenilworth residents such as Miss Holmes, the Kenilworth String Band and its conductor H J Stone were singled out for praise and "...*showed a great improvement on their last performance.*" They opened proceedings with a selection from HMS Pinafore. The audience numbered about 400. In early December 1882 another concert was held to raise funds; again around 400 attended what was the first performance in the *"long room"* at the Kings Arms.

Just a few weeks later, another was held in honour of Rupert Leigh. Lord Leigh had taken an interest in the club from the beginning and the career of his son, the Hon Rupert Leigh, in the 19th Hussars would have been closely followed. He had four campaigns in six years: Afghanistan twice, Transvaal and Egypt. He had recently returned home from Egypt and eagerly accepted an invitation to "Chair" the concert. A reception fit for the war hero was arranged. A huge throng gathered at St.John's bridge and the route to the Kings Arms. Just before 7 p.m., the small detachment of Kenilworth Volunteers led by Private T Robbins marched into place, as did the Fire Brigade in full uniform led by Deputy Captain C Robbins. The darkness was dispelled by about twenty torches and right on time the carriage was seen approaching. The crowd surged around it, risking injury under the wheels and hooves, as cheer after cheer filled the air. The carriage windows were lowered and its occupants, Rupert, and his brother and sister, Dudley and Agnes Leigh acknowledged the cheers. The

Volunteers and torches were formed around the carriage and the procession, headed by the Gospel Temperance Union Drum and Fife Band playing "See the Conquering Hero Comes", made its way to the Kings Arms Concert Room with "...*Castle End echoing to the combined strains of the band and cheering.*" They were received at the Kings Arms by Dr Wynter who escorted them into the concert room to "God Bless the Prince of Wales" performed by a brass band. There was a tremendous rush for seats and the room was filled "...*almost to suffocation.*" Windows had to be opened, and one person sat on the mantle piece for the entire evening. Over the principal entrance was "Welcome Gallant Leigh". *"The stage had been covered with red cloth and decked with flowers and plants, and overhead was hung the triple device, Afghanistan-Egypt-Transvaal, the names of the three campaigns in which the Hon. Rupert Leigh had engaged. Trophies of arms were prettily arranged while the whole of the walls were hung with wreaths."* A portrait of Lord Leigh was hanging near the stage. After a welcoming speech by Dr Wynter, Rupert Leigh briefly responded amidst loud cheers. The concert itself perhaps took on the appearance of a sideshow but was well received, and at its conclusion the party was escorted back to the edge of town in the same manner as its arrival.

In February 1885 another concert at the Assembly Rooms in Station Road was arranged to raise funds for the club. Dr Wynter again presided and there was a large attendance, including many who travelled from Warwick and Leamington. C S Birch, the organist at Emscote church, played the piano, as did Kenilworth's Hannah Riley. Songs were sung by Mr Hollis, Francis Trepass, J Boddington, Mr Whittendale and others.

*   *   *

In late spring 1883, there began a move to give shop assistants a few hours recreation on Thursday afternoons by closing early. On 14th June, six traders shut at 4.00 p.m. "...*to give their assistants and themselves an opportunity of breathing a little fresh air and enjoying needful recreation.*"

Those who closed were milliner Rebecca Smith at Rosemary Hill, the wife of builder Edward Smith; Edward Stokes, draper, and Helen Coe, milliner at adjacent premises in Castle End; Mr Davis, draper; John Richards, saddler at Abbey End, and Mr Glenn, tailor. The following week they were joined by four ironmongers, Shard, Riley, Sumner and White, and another draper, A Dawes.

*   *   *

In 1883, Ernest Trepplin began experimenting in silage. First he dug a trench 80yds by 20yds "...*on an eminence opposite the Castle...*" in the little wood called Park Hollow, for the storage of crops, clover and grass. He then carried out an experiment that avoided the construction of a new silo; he converted a very large old barn, ensuring it was waterproof by boarding up the bays and filling the interstices, and stored in it about 1,000 tons of green grass. So confident had he been of success that he turned over 1,000 acres, about a third of the

Trepplins entire land, to grass for ensilage. In the winter, *"The food appeared very appetising for cattle. They eat it readily, choosing it in preference to meadow grass, while horses will actually leave oats for this novel diet."* The experimentation did not impress his neighbours: the following winter the stench rising from one of his silos caused complaints to be made by Castle Grove residents.

By now the Trepplins were in possession of over 3,000 acres of farmland around Kenilworth; "North Chase, Goodrest, the Oaks, Roundshill, Villiers hill, Crewe, the Gate House, East Chase, the Pleasance, Warrior Lodge, the Castle, and Fernhill farms are held by Charles Frederick Trepplin and Ernest Charles Trepplin esqrs." They were not, of course, immune to the usual difficulties; in October 1887 over 200 head of their cattle strayed through a damaged fence onto neighbouring Honiley Grove Farm. Charles Trepplin paid £35 in damages.

The successful livestock farming was however having an adverse affect on local employment. In October 1887, a hundred or so workers were disposed of by the *"large employer of agricultural labourers"* due to there being no work. Trepplin had no labour-intensive cereal crops.

* * *

A branch of the Leamington Priors and Warwickshire Bank existed in town in 1841. Charles Bliss was its agent/manager. In 1868 partners in the Bank included Dathan Brown, Thomas Finnemore and others from Kenilworth. Charles Bliss died in November 1868 and it was probably then that Walter Lockhart took his place. In 1878, Postmaster Thomas Morris became the Kenilworth agent for the bank as a replacement for Walter Lockhart who had resigned. Morris conducted the bank business in new premises adjoining the Post Office in New Street.

In 1879, the Coventry and Warwickshire bank merged with the Lloyd, Barnett and Bosanquet Bank and five years later, a branch was opened in Castle End with George Gaydon as manager.

The summer of 1879 heralded a change in the financial possibilities for the whole community, but in particular the working classes. The people of Kenilworth had requested a representative of the Coventry Building Society to hold a meeting at the Kenilworth Institute to explain its workings and benefits, and this was arranged for 26th June. The society advanced between £100 and £400 to be paid back over 1½ to 12 years interest free. The way it worked was simple; the value of a share was £100 and any member could apply for more than one upon the payment of 6d a week subscription. When the Society decided enough funds were available, a ballot was held and the member that was drawn out received his loan against his share, and repayments could be made weekly, monthly, or quarterly. The downside was obviously that members could not know when, or even if, they would get their loan. It was intended to arrange for payments to be made in Kenilworth.

No doubt prompted by this, Kenilworth members of the Warwick and Warwickshire Benefit Building Society (established in 1854), thought it was an opportunity to establish a branch of their Society in the town. Just two days after the Institute meeting of its competitors, a large advertisement appeared in the *Kenilworth Advertiser* stating the attributes of the WWBSS, and announcing that its dealings would be carried out at the Kenilworth Working Men's Club. This Society was fundamentally different to the Coventry in that it paid interest to investors as well receiving interest for loans. For each £50 borrowed, specifically for buying houses, land or building premises, 3s 4d had to be paid fortnightly over a period of fifteen years to pay off the loan with interest. It could additionally be used as a bank for savings upon which interest was paid, one month's notice being required to withdraw an investment. On 9th July the Society Chairman, Secretary and Committee were all present at the Working Men's Club between 7.00 p.m. and 8.00 p.m. and in that time twenty nine £50 shares were taken up. This was clearly a popular move and brought the possibility of owning property to a far greater number of people, but at least one person thought Kenilworth should have its own Society. Signing himself as "Kenilworth for Ever" he wrote, *"Why in the name of all that is good do we allow ourselves to be placed in the hands of neighbouring towns?"*

In 1883, John Bagshaw of White Thorn, Clarendon Terrace, organised a petition amongst inhabitants in the vicinity of St.John's requesting improved Postal accommodation in that area. This was received favourably by the General Post Office, who promised an office at which money-orders and savings business could be transacted. However, its own telegraph service was out of the question.

The new office was at the premises of greengrocer William Riley and came into effect from 1st November 1883; it was closer to St.John's than the main office but still some distance away, being between the Kings Arms and Globe Hotel but on the opposite side of the road. William and Hannah continued to expand their business interests and in April 1885 became the Publishing Office for the *Kenilworth Advertiser*, taking it on from Miss H Richards. In 1886, Hannah Riley advertised herself as having a school for *"young ladies and little boys"* and promised a *"good, sound education"*. She also gave music lessons, being particularly proficient on the piano.

In September 1883, the High Street family residence, The Priory, was auctioned at the Kings Arms. It included three reception rooms, a library, nine chambers, three dressing rooms, four attics, offices, garden, coach-house and stabling. At the time, it was let to a Miss S Gibbs. The small number of bidders slowly raised the bids from £1,000 to £1,200, and when a bid of £1,300 was thrown in, it was accepted. It was not until early the following year that it became generally known that the successful bidder was the Leamington Priors and Warwickshire Bank. Plans were deposited with the Local Board to convert the building into a bank; initially these were unacceptable but were finally passed in May 1884, the same month that the Lloyd's Bank branch opened for business.

Conversion of The Priory into a bank needed a good deal of interior reconstruction, but for it to have the status a bank merited, a complete rebuilding of the frontage was necessary. The designs were by a Mr Cundall, and the contract was awarded to Kenilworth builder William Ball for £2,000.

In November 1884, the building work was *"...being pushed forward with considerable vigour. The open space near the shop of T.B.Emery & Son is alive with workmen sawing stone and fixing it."* The new Leamington Priors and Warwickshire bank was opened on Wednesday 8th May 1885.

The Post Office General Secretary, George Blackwood, wrote to the Board in January 1885 stating that as he was in the process of arranging to move the Post Office into the new bank building, he wanted their consent to erect two new telegraph poles with two wires to extend the lines. One was to be by the river bridge and the other in the Abbey Fields "by the wall". In March, Mr Lumley of the National Telegraph Company was asked by the Board for his plans, as they thought it *"...highly undesirable any poles or wires should be erected or fixed on the main road."*

Soon after the bank opened, the Post Office moved from New Street to share the premises. Thomas Morris moved into the house alongside the new bank; it was his *"energy and exertion"* which were credited with the successful outcome of the scheme. Morris's talents also saw him become the Board's Treasurer. Despite the alterations, there was still room in The Priory for a resident and Major Lewis Maltby Boileau moved in with his wife.

The opening of the new building brought back memories; just thirty years before, customers had to stand out in the rain at the Coventry Cross to get money orders and stamps *"through a hole in its window."*

The reconstruction of The Priory into a bank and post office, was carried out by Kenilworth's William Ball. Stone for the façade was sawn in the space, to the right, between it and Mr Emery's shop.

The vacated building, 1 & 3 New Street, was not empty for long. Directly opposite was Jeffs' shoemakers, established in 1845. There, Thomas Jeffs and his son John, in 1882 had a sale of 8,000 pairs of shoes and boots, at least some of which, perhaps many, were made on their two-floored workshop at the rear. They also had a shop in Leamington. John took over his father's business, sold the premises including a small house on either side, and moved into the double fronted number 3. He did not stay there for long, moving to Leamington in 1889, but mindful of his old customers, gave a free delivery service to Kenilworth. The New Street premises were then taken on by draper John Knight.

*   *   *

With the opening of the nearby Mission Room at the bottom of Park Hill in 1884, the services that had been held at the Co-operative Hall since about 1880 ceased and the hall was advertised to let. In 1887, the newly-formed Kenilworth branch of the Salvation Army made the hall their barracks, its two founders being Miss Ward and Miss Card.

In December that year, after dropping in to a service out of curiosity, "Disgusted" was prompted to write the following letter: *"I occupied a seat at the back and had not been there a quarter of an hour when the Captain, to my great astonishment, ordered those at the back to leave the building, who were trifling. As I paid great attention to what was going on, I was greatly surprised to learn that she meant me for one. Another victim was a most respectable woman, the wife of a gardener of this town, whose only offence appeared to be that she smiled at someone. I cannot understand how people, especially elderly people, can allow themselves to be influenced by the doctrines of these two young girls."* The Co-operative Society also came in for criticism: *"I hope those responsible for letting the room...rectify the great blunder they have made in letting the room for such gatherings."* Probably unknown to the writer, the *"two young girls"* had already decided to leave and they were replaced by two women, Captain Watson and Lieutenant Craven. The meetings continued and congregations numbered around 120.

In May 1888, Arthur Beck, a Kenilworth youth, was summonsed for disturbing a Salvation Army Service at the Co-operative Hall. Beck had already been spoken to once and when he called out *"take your coat off"* to speaker William Emmett; he was then threatened with removal. To avoid this, Beck decided to leave but *"...stamped down two flights of stairs very noisily."* As proceedings against him progressed, the prosecutor was asked to produce the certificate that allowed religious services to be held on the premises, but that produced had not been sealed and thus called into question the legality of the services. The court case was held-over for a week, and upon resumption the correctly sealed documents were produced. It was all for nothing as, after hearing that young Beck would have to face a full trial, the prosecutor withdrew the charge.

August 1888 saw the first anniversary celebrations of the branch; 120 sat down to a tea and heard addresses from Captain Limester, J E Jackson, T

Holmes, T Bastock, W Cox and C Dutton. The juniors sung *"some very telling solos"* and the event closed with the swearing-in of officers. The 1891 fourth anniversary was marked with a procession headed by a band, open air services and *"a public tea, which was largely attended."*

A regular Sunday evening procession was disrupted by a group of visitors: *"A disgraceful row was caused by a trap load of Coventry excursionists who were all, more or less, under the influence of drink. At the junction of New-street with Bridge Street the Salvation Army were marching to their barracks, and a deliberate attempt was made to drive through the ranks and break up the procession. The conduct was accompanied by disgraceful language. After the "Army" had passed, one of the excursionists stood up in the trap and offered to fight the best man present. This offer was promptly accepted, and in a few seconds the whole of the excursionists were in the street ready for a row. For a few minutes the greatest uproar prevailed. Blood flowed freely and in the end the excursionists were obliged to beat a hasty retreat. The police have the matter in hand."*

Just a few weeks later, another march through town marked a special Whitsuntide event with tea at the barracks. *"In the evening, a demonstration and procession took place to the Castle Green, and open-air services were held."* A number of Wesleyan friends were at the meeting, which was conducted by Captain Thompson and Lieutenant Wheatley.

*　　*　　*

Two years after the meeting in Charles Adams office at which it was decided to let the cricket club lapse, a letter, signed by "Erasmus Holiday", appeared in the *Kenilworth Advertiser* in April 1880 asking why a cricket club did not exist and questioned several reasons as to why the old club failed. The first reason given was that cycling had taken over as the young mans sporting pursuit, but he pointed out that cyclists *"in the flower of youth"* could play cricket as well, and that youth was not necessarily required to play the game. He continued with his second argument contradicting the claim *"...that there are comparatively no young men in the place, I venture to say that at least a hundred might be beaten up and induced to join a club. The third is a more serious argument, that cricket here has hitherto been demoralized by the public-house influence. This difficulty might be obviated by a wise choice of field and stringent rules."* This was clearly a criticism of the choice of the Bowling Green Field as the cricket club's home. The letter was replied to with the suggestion that Erasmus himself should call a meeting to discuss the subject; whether it was he or not is unclear, but a meeting was arranged for mid-June at the Mission Hall.

The meeting was a success and officers were elected with Reverend Somerset Pennefather as President; William Pennington, treasurer; Ernest Trepplin, secretary; and a committee consisting of Charles Adams, T Davis, E Hodges, G Jenneway, C Robbins, J Smith and N Smith. Despite the words of warning from Erasmus Holiday, the old ground behind

the Bowling Green was used for a "pick-up" match at the end of June. The club was arranged very much as before; Honorary Members' subscriptions were 10s 6d and they had the privilege of nominating a working man at 2s 6d a year, and playing members paid 5s. Those wishing to become members by election had to give their name to committeeman N H Smith of Castle End. Practises were held on Mondays, Wednesdays and Saturdays.

The 1880 season proved to be not the best for the club, even managing to loose to the newly-formed tannery team after bowling them out for just 16 runs, but there was an influx of new players including Mr Baulcombe and F H Lynes, the headmaster of Abbey Hill School. By the end of season dinner there were already concerns that the club would fail like its predecessors, but its members re-assembled at Ernest Trepplin's Castle Gatehouse in April 1881 in good spirits. Ernest Trepplin was voted to the captaincy. Another new member was H J Stone who had become headmaster of the National School in the summer of 1880, having been the successful of eighty five candidates. He was an active man, becoming organist at St.Nicholas church and starting a thirty-strong Musical Society that produced an 11-piece string band. For the 1881 season, Lynes and Stone were the undoubted stars of the team; in the now annual match against the Tannery for example, between them they scored 30 of the clubs 40 runs and took 9 wickets as the opposition were bowled out for 13, the other being a run out. Following on, the Tannery scored 25, their leading player being J W Haughton who managed double figures batting, and also took four wickets and a catch.

An end of season summary was provided by Secretary H J Stone. Seventeen matches had been played of which nine were won, and the batting performances, for those playing more than three innings or more, were as follows;

	Inns	runs	highest score	not out	average
H Lynes	16	213	41	3	13.3
W Robbins	18	191	38	2	10.6
H J Stone	18	181	31	1	10
H Balcombe	6	48	18	1	8
E C Trepplin	4	30	7	7(sic)	7.5
T Robbins	5	31	20	1	6.2
J Boucher	19	111	22	0	5.8
C Robbins	16	87	18	1	5.4
F C Worcester	8	31	9	0	3.8
W Davis	5	18	10	1	3.6
J Heatley	3	8	7	1	2.6

Lynes was presented with a bat for being the club's highest run scorer. A regular bowling analysis had not been kept but *"...as in the batting, the chief honours go to Mr Lynes."* *"It is a source of regret that the matches have not been honoured by the presence of many spectators. The cricket has often been really good. Allow me to express the hope that during the next season the club may have the pleasure of seeing many more of the inhabitants of Kenilworth present to witness and encourage the game, which for nobility and manliness is without rival."*

Other clubs were being formed. In June 1882 the Abbey Hill Cricket Club was created amongst old boys of the Abbey Hill School. At least 30 enrolled as members and H Lynes was elected captain, J Davis deputy captain and W Jeffcott Secretary. Practices were held twice a week on Tuesday evenings and Saturday afternoons. Lynes continued to play for the Kenilworth Cricket Club.

It was a memorable season for bowling achievements. In a match for the Kenilworth club against Warwick School, Stone produced the rare feat of taking four wickets in successive balls, and just a few weeks later Keatley, playing for Priory against Abbey Hill, almost repeated it, taking four in five.

Club secretary Stone continued to produce a detailed analysis of the Kenilworth team's performance. Of its 1882 *"bona fide club arrangements"* the club won 9, lost 5 and drew 3. Lynes topped the batting averages with 9.1, Stone was second with 8.7. Complete analysis of the bowling had again not been kept but Lynes was the leading wicket taker with 80 in 14 matches. The season saw the re-emergence of Charles Robbins, playing with one arm after his gun accident, who took a remarkable 54 wickets in 12 matches.

On 2nd February 1883, the cricket club organised a concert to raise funds which was performed by a local talent and very well received. However, the venue, St.Nicholas Church School in School Lane, came in for criticism; *"Perhaps it would not be amiss to suggest that some means be taken to do away with the excessive draughtiness of the school-room, and with that increased enjoyment would the audience listen, if they felt free from the carking cares attendant upon a possible attack of influenza, not to mention bronchial catarrh."* These were the same conditions, of course, in which pupils were taught.

The number of members of the town club continued to increase, amongst those new for the 1884 season was James Dockray, the engineer responsible for the new railway works. Thomas Bourne was President, Ernest Trepplin still Captain, Dr Atkinson Treasurer, Charles Robbins deputy captain, H J Stone Secretary, and they, along with Lynes and Edmonds, formed the Committee. The club remained at the same ground for the year but already knew that they would have to find a new pitch for the following season; it was hoped that the Board would find somewhere suitable, with the Abbey Fields being the popular suggestion.

*   *   *

A new cinder track had opened at the Bicycle and Athletic Ground in Warwick Road, Coventry and a large cycle racing event was held there at Whitsun 1878. Members from the Kenilworth Club who took part were Allen, Smith, Rouse, Newton, Pittaway and T H Robbins who came second in the one-mile race and won the five mile.

At the monthly meeting in March 1879, it was decided that the first run of the new season was to be to Stratford on Good Friday. It was also decided to award a medal to the member who completed most runs in the season, the next being to Warwick and Leamington. Although these regular runs were well attended, they were not very challenging and so club members continued to enter events in other towns; Club founder member F A Allen was the leading prize-winner, winning two races at an event in Redditch in October 1879, for example. Twelve prizes were won in the year by club members.

At the 1880 AGM, W J Robinson, J Brown, T Robbins, W Arnold and Johnson were elected as Committee members; W Hosier remained as Captain, J Brown Jnr as sub-captain and Henry T Dean was secretary. The first run was to be Stratford on Good Friday.

Cycling was hazardous for pedestrians even when cyclists stayed on the road; Miss Twigg of Abbey Hill suffered *"a severe shaking"* when crossing the road outside the Kings Arms when a cyclist *"...ran violently against her..."* turning the corner from Station Road in July 1881.

Despite its success, the club's best days were behind it and no more is heard of cycling clubs in Kenilworth until May 1882 when a meeting was held at the Mission Hall in an attempt to form a Bicycle and Tricycle Club. The first run, with about a dozen members, was the following month to Warwick and Leamington. By the end of June, there were over twenty members and separate captains for two- and three-wheeled riders; Mr Smith with Mr Gardiner as his deputy was for the two-wheelers and William Riley and deputy Mr Bushell for the three, but Edward Stokes was overall Captain. Walter Lockhart was the treasurer and Dr Wynter consented to be the club's President. It was now known as "The Kenilworth Cyclists Club" and they used the Kings Arms for meetings. More than 30 were present for the January 1884 annual dinner, but by now, yet another club had been formed.

In late May 1883, a meeting was held at the Kings Arms to set up a club, not for Kenilworth but for the district, under the name "The Wheelmen of Warwickshire". Lord Clarendon became president and the Captain was C Wincote of the Leamington Cycle Club, the bugler was C Oakley and the secretary C O Clarke of the tannery. The committee was formed of four Kenilworth men, Austin Joseph Emery, who called the meeting, Bryce, William Mander and H J Stone. A uniform of a grey Norfolk coat and knickerbockers, straw hat with a broad brown ribbon and badge, and brown hose was chosen.

Their first run took place on Friday 25th May when ten members, including four women, set off from the Kings Arms with several members from the Leamington club adding to the numbers. A few more Leamington members joined the party at the Chesford bridge and headed to the Bath Hotel in Leamington. An excellent supper was provided and this was followed by songs performed by members Beck, Cunnew, Emery and Oakley, and the evening was completed with dancing. After a short delay caused by lighting the cycle lamps, the Wheelmen set out for Kenilworth at 11.20 p.m., arriving on the stroke of midnight.

Within a couple of weeks, the club held a garden party at the Kings Arms. It was intended to use the immaculate bowling green for dancing, and lamps and coloured fires were arranged in preparation, but rain caused the plans to be amended and the event was held in the *"long room"* - the Assembly Room. The members were in uniform, ladies also wore the hat and badge and several had a small badge on the front of their dress. Late in the evening the rain stopped and the bowling green was lit up to provide a pleasant promenade.

The Wheelmen held an annual dinner at the Kings Arms in 1884 just a week after the Kenilworth Cyclists held theirs.

* * *

The annual Fire Brigade dinner was by now preceded by a drill competition. In 1883, this took place on the cricket field in front of a large audience including the town's leading clergy, Board members, and deputations from the Coventry, Leamington and Warwick volunteer brigades. There were three competitions: the one-man drill, including the operation of the hose, which was won by James Heatley in 47 seconds; the four-man drill, consisting of getting the engine in working order, running out two lengths of hose and carrying the nozzle up a ladder and across a scaffold 25ft above the ground, achieved in 53 seconds by the winning team led by Lt Liggins; and the final race, designed for amusement, involving carrying a bucket across the field, over a fence and back again, and the joint winners of this were F and James Heatley. Afterwards, William Clarke provided a meal for all, including the visiting brigade members, in the ballroom at the Kings Arms.

As a mark of respect, in October 1883 the brigade presented to a very surprised Captain Trepplin, two photographs of *"the efficient little corps"*. The members were greatly appreciative of the way in which Trepplin treated them, and of the occasions he had given assistance from his own purse. Trepplin *"evinced considerable emotion"* in thanking the brigade. He took the opportunity to praise their discipline, and the hope that it would not be too long before *"...their present engine would have as a companion one to work by steam."*

Just weeks later, on 9th December 1883, the brigade's landlord, Sarah Ryley, died aged 86, and a month later the Board received a letter from her solicitors telling them that the brigade had to leave her (Upper) Rosemary Hill premises by 25th March. This in turn led to Ernest Trepplin writing to the Board asking them where they intended to keep the engine and equipment, and subsequently the town surveyor was instructed to investigate altering the former Savage and Heatley carpentry workshop fronting onto Savage Lane at the rear of the Board's premises. His report was positive, and Edward Smith won the tender for the work which included "Converting the old workshop into fire engine shed £21, erection of a tool shed £9 10s, footway and north west boundary wall at back of premises, £13." The deadline to move had already passed but Mr Draper considerately extended it until the end of June, although it was not until mid-July that the fixtures and fittings of the old engine-house were moved into the new. Several months later, a gas-supply was installed by way of a T-junction with the supply to the Board's stables.

John Bagshaw had suggested that building a entirely new engine-house, with provision for meetings

and drills, should have been considered and thought that the proposed arrangements would be *"useless at some future time"*, but Captain Trepplin was perfectly happy with the re-organisation.

The new fire station fronted onto Savage Lane, about 60 yards from (Upper) Rosemary Hill.

The annual event in September 1884, began with a full inspection of uniforms for a prize at the new engine-house. Dr Atkinson withdrew, after admitting that he did not clean his own uniform, leaving fireman Webb as the prize-winner. Engineer Plumbe came in for special praise for the condition of the engine. Afterwards, they all marched down Savage Lane to the nearby cricket field for a competition witnessed by few spectators because of the heavy rain showers - virtually no one witnessed the final event, the six-man drill. The entire brigade attended the subsequent meal at the Kings Arms that was chaired by William Evans. By now, many hydrants were in place and it was claimed at the meal that just two lengths of hose from any one of them could reach any potential fire.

The installation of mains water was obviously of great use to the brigade, but it necessitated the purchase of additional equipment to enable hoses to be connected to the hydrants. Although Trepplin had placed an order for two stand pipes, *"...as they could not feed the engine without one on either side..."*, costing £7 12s, in January 1885 Deputy Captain Robbins had to write a letter to the Board hoping to push the matter along. This led to a deputation from the brigade, Captain Trepplin, sub-captain C Robbins and Lieutenant Dr Atkinson, attending a Board meeting in January 1885 to expand on the brigade's complete requirements. The initial discussions raised the suggestion that some fire-fighting equipment could be stored at Castle End; valuable time could be lost in sending a messenger to muster the force at the opposite end of town, and although it was agreed that this was desirable, Trepplin said he did not wish to *"...weaken the central station."* The party then adjourned to a field at the rear of the Board's offices where a large crowd had gathered to witness a demonstration of the *"...Anchor Compressed Air Portable Fire Engine (Vinnings patent) introduced by Martineau and Smith of Birmingham"*. A large bonfire was lit and an employee of the manufacturers strapped the "fire engine" to his back and, running around the fire, extinguished it in a few seconds. The demonstration was successfully repeated with larger fires. Upon returning to the Board

Room, Trepplin said that the "engine" would be admirable for use in house fires, but wished to keep the brigade's equipment as simple as possible, and instead recommended the purchase of a Metropolitan hand-pump with fittings. He also wished to purchase other necessary equipment including a cistern for £2, two hand pumps for £3, hose for the hand pump for £1 10s, a handcart for £4, drying lift and hose for £2, and new hose pipes costing £20. A resolution was passed to authorise Trepplin to purchase the equipment of his choice up to a total of £42, and Dr Wynter was appointed to oversee the expenditure. The following month, the aforementioned water pressure tests outside Montague House took place.

By chance, a situation to highlight the potential difficulty of getting the brigade quickly to a fire at Castle End as discussed at the Board meeting, arose just seven weeks after the discussions when a fire broke out at Thickthorn Lodge. The brigade arrived within fifteen minutes of the alarm being raised and the only damage sustained was to the thatched roof, which was pulled off.

The night before the Annual General Meeting in May 1885, Ernest Trepplin tendered his resignation as Captain which he thought *"...would be for the well-being of the brigade, as he thought a change would have a tendency to do a great amount of good."* A unanimously signed petition persuaded Trepplin to remain as captain for another year, which he did upon agreed unrecorded conditions.

*   *   *

In March 1880, a former White Lion servant, Henry Garratt, was charged with stealing 15s from a box kept with the pint pots in a glass-fronted cupboard in the inn's bar. A live-in servant, Sarah Jenkins, claimed that Garratt broke into her bedroom around midnight, the window only being held by a piece of string, grabbed her by the neck and threatened to kill her. He then went downstairs into the bar, she heard cups rattling, and next morning she found Garratt in the coach-house; he said that he had spent the night in the skittle-alley. However, under cross-examination at his trial, Sarah told a very different story. When Garratt worked at the White Lion, the two lived together and she admitted *"impropriety"* with him on the night in question. Early the next morning she took him a glass of rum and milk in the coach-house. All this failed to prove the charge of theft and the case was dismissed.

In early October 1884, the license of the White Lion was transferred from Thomas Skelcher (Skelsey?) to John Matthews, formerly of the White Horse at Balsall Common. Early the following year Matthews was granted a license for operating three carriages; a Hansom carriage for three persons, a 4-wheeled landau for five persons and a 4-wheeled wagonette to carry six. After a fight with Bowling Green licensee Thomas Cooper in 1885, Matthews left the White Lion and concentrated on his horse and carriage hiring, becoming based at the rear of the Kings Arms.

John Davis of The Globe was a popular tradesman. In 1880, he was the only working man to put himself forward for election to the Local Board, and although he failed to be elected he received more votes than either Walter Lockhart or Dr T S Bourne. In 1885, Davis extended The Globe by building more stabling and a new clubroom for the use of visitors.

After her father, Cottage Inn licensee William Green, had died in 1875, Emma Green, who had the appearance of a middle-aged matronly woman, turned to drink. In 1876, she was found so drunk she could hardly stand up. This was not the first time and her brother had often complained about her conduct.

William snr's widow Sarah died on 13th August 1879 aged 66 apparently leaving Emma with neither parent, but the complicated family history was to be revealed the following year. Emma's drinking habit continued and in the summer of 1880 she was charged with being drunk in Clifton Terrace; her brother, William jnr, appeared in court on her behalf as she was *"...utterly unable to appear. She was addicted to drink which could not be kept from her, she obtained in surreptitiously. She was now in a most pitiable condition."* It became known that William was actually her half-brother and that her natural mother was still alive, but in a lunatic asylum. Emma was in a worse state than ever and William said he could no longer be responsible for her conduct. She had been fined five or six times and it was he that paid them. On this occasion a fine of 23s 6d was imposed but William refused to pay, and it was hoped that Emma's jail term of one month could prove beneficial. William said that when she came out this time, she must go elsewhere as he could no longer cope with her.

Soon after her release, doubtless annoyed that William had refused to pay her fine and had her jailed, she was back outside The Cottage, causing a commotion and attracting a great crowd, and just six weeks after her previous court appearance she was locked up again for a month. Once more, upon her release she confronted William at The Cottage and directed at him a *"...variety of threats, couched in very coarse language."* William was afraid that she was likely to cause him serious injury and Emma, now 45, promised that she would now stay away and not threaten him again.

In October 1881, William Green and his wife Mary had a son, also named William, but he lived just twenty days. Another tragedy struck the family on 2nd July 1885. Mary had become ill with consumption of the bowels in February and despite treatment from Dr Clarke had become very low and weak. At about 11.30 p.m., after the pub had closed that particular night, William, Mary and William's sister Ellen began to prepare supper. William went to the cellar to fetch his wife her usual soda water whilst Mary and Ellen prepared food in the kitchen. Mary left the kitchen carrying two mugs; Ellen heard a crash and found Mary outside on the gravel at the bottom of the steps, two of which were quite high. William picked her up and put her in a chair but she never spoke again. Dr Clarke was summoned and he found her lying on a sofa in the front parlour and pronounced her dead. At the inquest at The Engine Inn, the jury returned a verdict of accident to the Coroner, Dr Wynter, concluding that in a state of weakness she lost her balance, fell down the steps and died from a severe head wound. William was now 56 and had bought the Cottage Inn in 1883 for £400.

William Tustin was a brickmaker. In July 1883, he went for a drink with a group of friends at The Globe where at the other end of the same room were a group of navvies employed on the new railway works. They all became the worse for drink. *"They had a dance, and the navvies were annoyed because the Kenilworth men beat them at stepping."* One of the navvies, Thomas Bester whom Tustin had known for eight or nine weeks, called Tustin *"an epithet"* then hit him. There was a scrimmage and the landlord turned them all out onto the street. The fight continued and Bester bit off a part of Tustin's nose; he appeared in court with his face covered in bandages. According to the surgeon who treated the wound *"...the right wing of the nose is completely gone...it has the appearance of being completely torn off."* Bester was jailed for six weeks, it would have been more but for the drunken circumstances.

Tustin lived in Henry Street; the new houses in a new street would not have been the cheapest in town. Living with him was a girl called Brotherton who had children of her own. On 18th February 1885, Tustin's stepson Robert Brotherton, 17, was charged *"...as a rogue and vagabond with loitering about with intent to commit a felony."* He had previously been in trouble for stealing carrots from a policeman's garden in Deddington and as a result was sent to an Industrial School in Gem Street, Birmingham. On this occasion in Kenilworth, he had tried to obtain money from a child heading for a music lesson, and then approached a servant, Selina Atkins. First, he asked for her brooches and earrings, and then put his hand in her pocket to take money. Selina explained to the court that she grabbed hold of his collars and shook him, bringing laughter from those present. The Bench remanded the case for a week in the hope that he might be induced to emigrate. His mother appeared at the court the following week to say Robert had been badly influenced by his stepfather Tustin, but Robert was jailed for three weeks and it was still hoped that efforts could be made to get him sent to one of the colonies.

Still in town, just five months later Robert and his sister, thirteen year-old Mary Jane Brotherton, were charged with stealing a towel from the drying line of William Wells Ridley. It had been found in their possession when they were arrested for vagrancy having been found in a hovel by Sergeant Price. In May the previous year, the pair had been seen in a Kenilworth lane *"...committing an act of immorality..."* but after this latest arrest, Mary Jane claimed that she had been the victim of a criminal assault by James Tuckey, at his place of employment - the signal-box controlling the railway junction at the Common - and she had a shilling from him as proof. Tuckey was arrested and in his version of events he was *"...attracted out of the signal box by a whistle from the bridge. On looking up, he saw Robert who made an indecent proposal to him with respect to his sister. He then asked them to come round to his box so that he could speak to them. The girl told him she was 15. Her brother said she had been intimate with*

several men before and she added that it was her brother who had first seduced her. He then gave her a shilling to buy some food and they left. There was no undue familiarity between them." Mary Jane was described as precocious, extremely intelligent and having a great deal of low cunning, but she was scared to go back to her home in Coventry in case she *"got thrown in the water"* and could not go to the Tustin's house in Henry Street as stepfather William would not allow Robert in the house. She described William's girlfriend as her sister, not her mother as stated at other times. Seemingly at a loss without each other, Robert and Mary had spent the night before the incident sleeping on the Common.

Tuckey was released on bail and eventually cleared; for the theft of the towel, thirteen year-old Mary Jane was jailed for fourteen days and sent to a reformatory for five years and Robert to ten days jail, but he was also then charged with assaulting his sister and was committed for trial at the assizes. He was found guilty and sentenced to 9 months. There appeared a degree of sympathy for him; he was *"...probably led into the atrocious act by the circumstances in which he had been placed."*

Thomas Fulford was, in 1871, a fellmongers labourer and by 1876 a carpenter living in Mill End. Later that year he was a bricklayer and was involved in a fight at Mill End with John Brewer and John Rainbow, but he failed to appear in court and a warrant was issued for his arrest. Later that year he was charged with damaging a fence. In 1878 he was fined for being drunk and disorderly.

In the summer of 1879, he was charged with threatening his wife Hannah; he struck her three times, knocked her down and *"...threatened to kick her to death, kick her brains out."* She ran away and did not return home until he had been arrested, but she was still frightened as he had behaved in this way many times before. Upon finding two sureties of £10, and a further £20 of his own, Fulford was released and ordered to keep the peace for six months. The Fulfords' house soon came to the attention of the Inspector of Nuisances as it had a foul privy and broken windows.

Four years later, Fulford was back in court for shooting a carrier pigeon, but within months he was again charged with threatening Hannah. The Fulfords had taken in a lodger named Rolfe and this had caused some *"unpleasantness"* between the couple. On one occasion when Fulford became abusive towards Rolfe, Hannah stepped in between them and as Rolfe left the house Fulford struck his wife in the face and then picked up a gun and threatened to shoot her, but he claimed in court the gun was not loaded. In default of finding sureties to keep the peace he was this time jailed for six months.

In the summer of 1884, it was Fulford's dog that was causing problems. First, it tried to bite Walter Freeman, a blacksmith, and then Police Sergeant Price. Then, whilst a group of young children were watching the first train using the new line to Birmingham, it attacked and bit Alice Shelswell twice on the arm, an incident witnessed by Lizzie Brewer. Fulford was fined 10s 6d.

In October 1885, Thomas Fulford was back in

court again, only this time as a victim. By now, he was teetotal but still socialised at the Engine Inn, which was just across the road from his house. John Sabin (groom), Owen Sheepkin (plumber), and William Pace (carter), began making *"obscene expressions"* about Fulford and his drinking habits and so he left, only to be followed home by the three and, in Sheepkin's case, into his house. Fulford threw him out and claimed that a stone was then thrown which broke one of his windows. The three were in court charged with assault and damaging Fulford's property, but upon the evidence of two of his neighbours, the charges were dismissed.

Born in Devonport in 1848, by the time he was Thirteen Joseph Young was earning a living as a brickmakers boy and was living in St.John's Street with his mother Mary, having lost his father. At some point, he joined the Coldstream Guards but was dismissed as *"an habitual drunkard"* and later from the 15th Hussars as *"worthless"*.

Becoming a well-known local character and vagabond, Joseph found himself in court on a charge of poaching in December 1874. William Barber had found three snares on his master's land and had kept watch, seeing Young whom he had known for twenty years, remove a rabbit from one. As he approached him, Young threatened *"...to knock* (the rabbit) *about his head."* Young was fined 40s or upon default one months hard labour. The following December, Young was charged with being drunk and fighting - this time the penalty was a guinea or three weeks in jail. The following September he was drunk and disorderly again, this time it was a 2 guinea fine, and in February 1877 he was found trespassing in search of game, (with his dog for company, he was beating a spinney on Richard Robbins' land) and fined 40s with an additional 18s costs.

After an apparent lull of six years in his criminal activities, he was caught in December 1883 by Trepplin's gamekeeper, Daniel Kibbler, armed with a powerful catapult, which he had used against roosting pheasants. On this occasion he did not pay his £2 fine and was sent to jail for a month with hard labour. His next crime could be described as being out of character; he stole a brush from Mellor Hetherington at The Firs and was jailed for two months in September 1885. He was now 37 years old.

Through all this time, it seems Young remained single and lived with his mother, but, obviously, their relationship was likely to be fraught at times. At 11 o'clock on 30th October 1886, PC Sloss came across a disturbance in St.John's Street. He dispersed the crowd that had gathered outside the Youngs' house but as he walked away, he heard screams of "murder!" and "Police!". Joseph Young had turned his 71 year-old mother out of the house and locked the door. PC Sloss ordered Young out of the house and found him so drunk that he could hardly stand. Almost everything in the house had been broken. In court, Young claimed that Sloss gave evidence with lies in and that he did not expect justice as he had been in court before. He assured the bench that he had only drunk two pints of beer and that his mother was *"...an old Irishwoman and had a very hasty temper."* Unimpressed, the Bench fined him £1 with 13s 6d costs.

Henry Heritage, carpenter, pumpmaker, Fire Brigade engineer and one-time dairyman at Thickthorn, had suffered from heart disease for many years. One August 1881 day, he went for a drive with his daughter and son-in-law, Mark Hoddle, and whilst lying on the grass was seized with syncope. His companions got him home and summoned Dr Wynter, but he died soon after. He was a much-respected man and held in great esteem. His wife Ann continued the business.

After a tip-off one winter's day in early 1883, Mark Hoddle, whose butcher shop was opposite St.John's church, was visited by David Jones, an officer from the Prevention of Cruelty to Animals. There he found a whole sheep carcass with a large mass of bruises on its back and a hindquarter of another carcass covered in cuts and bruises. Mrs Hoddle showed Jones another joint from which pieces had to be cut due to bruising. When the sheep had arrived at Kenilworth, Hoddle had noticed how they were *"...knocked up...one was blind in one eye."* Regularly employed by Hoddle was Henry Hollins, a Coventry drover, who had driven six sheep from Coventry for Hoddle the previous week, and he was charged with unlawfully and cruelly beating three of them. Two Kenilworth lads, John Trunkwell and Henry Foster (10), were called as witnesses, as they saw Hollins beating the sheep as he drove them up Rosemary Hill; he was thrashing them for nearly a quarter of an hour. John Beresford (14) who helped Hollins, was called as a defence witness but even he admitted the sheep were struck twenty or thirty times and that he had not seen a beating like it. Hollins was fined £2 and given fourteen days in which to pay.

After the death of her husband, Elizabeth Richards married Mr Hambridge in October 1874, she had property and he had a grocers shop. Elizabeth soon began to complain of her second husband's drunkenness and in 1881, he left her for nearly a year but returned. In 1884, he became violent and tried to throw Elizabeth out, but on 4th April that year he left again. Elizabeth was given information as to his whereabouts and with two friends went to an address in Coventry where she found her husband with his mistress. *"You've caught me at last..."* he exclaimed, *"Yes you bad man..."* she replied. She was granted a divorce, which had been legal for just a few years, in January 1885. The story caused a sensation in the local press and may well have influenced events just two weeks later involving Mark Hoddle, the St.John's butcher.

Hoddle *"...introduced a second lady into his household to share the joys of his home and the profits of his business."* The following day, customers were asked to *"...pay their accounts to the intruder..."* and several scuffles broke out between Hoddle and his wife over possession of the cash. That night, several hundred people gathered outside the shop and created a disturbance by banging trays and frying pans. Hoddle tried to remonstrate with the mob but, having been covered in whitewash, retreated inside only to have all his windows smashed. The police were by now present and they prevented further damage. The commotion continued until after midnight when an effigy was burnt in the church field opposite. On the Monday night, hostilities continued but with six police constables and a sergeant present, damage was prevented. Two effigies, illuminated by chinese lanterns, were paraded through town to The Square where they were dipped in tar and burnt. By now, the unnamed lady had returned to her home in Wolverhampton, and Mrs Hoddle had moved in with her mother, Ann Heritage. She applied to court for a protection order but this was deemed as unnecessary as her income from the business was guaranteed under the Married Woman's Property Protection Act.

* * *

There seems to have been a sense of camaraderie at the tannery, and this is perhaps due in part to the mutual respect between worker and employer. To herald the beginning of 1880, Phillip Newman treated his workforce to a supper at, not surprisingly, his works manager's establishment, the Kings Arms. A hundred and five sat down in the upper assembly room to a meal provided by the host, and Evans, Adams, Peake and Faxon, all tannery employees, assisted as carvers. Newman and Clarke took the Chair and Vice Chair. *"The usual loyal and other toasts were given, and the evening spent in a most enjoyable, harmonious manner."* Newman repeated the treat for his workforce between Christmas and the New Year in 1880. His amusing speech was well received by his seventy or so employees, and in turn a number of them sang songs.

In the summer of 1880 the workers had formed their own cricket team and about thirty enrolled as players. A field in Southbank Road was secured and the first practice match was on Saturday 10th July at 4.00 p.m. The club Captain was J Brown, G Freeman was vice-captain and W T Haughton the secretary. In 1881, a Second XI was established.

The Tannery initially played just other Kenilworth sides. In a defeat by The Priory club, the Tannery's second innings was notable for having all ten batsmen clean bowled. The leading batsmen for the first team were J W Haughton, and Charles (19) and Hubert (17) Clarke, the sons of William Clarke. In 1881, they played further afield. In a match away to Rotherham's, played at Whitley Common, the home side scored 109 runs before bowling out the Tannery for just 15. Many of the club's matches seemed to be one-sided affairs. In June 1862, they scored just 65 runs at home to Emscote Buffs, T Simpson scoring 24 of them, and then bowled out the opposition twice for just 43. The following week the Tannery Second XI bowled out the Kenilworth Priory for 23, were all out themselves for 17 but managed to win on the second innings by six wickets thanks largely to a stand of 32 by H Went and J Ward. W Aitken took 9 wickets in the match and H Pettifor 8.

The Second XI had another easy win in September against Abbey Hill. R Faxon scored 17, the same as achieved by "extras", in a total of 57; Abbey Hill managed 44 in two innings. Aitken took another nine wickets and, with Pettifor missing, Weston took nine of the others. A match between the First XI and the town club on Statute Fair day in 1882 looked likely to produce a Tannery victory as they bowled out the opposition for just 31, but the match had to be abandoned due to heavy rain. The same week saw another easy win

for the Second XI, scoring 99 against Abbey Hill's 32, a match completed in the dusk.

The 1883 season opened with the traditional Single v Married match, on this occasion it was thirteen players against fourteen. The Singles managed 50, including 12 extras, but this was more than enough to win as the Marrieds, nine of whom scored ducks, managed only 21. The annual match against the town club saw the Tannery beaten 138-31, but, *"The members of the Tannery Club expressed much surprise at the Captain of the Kenilworth Club bringing several gentlemen, non-residents, to compete with them to the exclusion of several of its regular playing resident members. They wish, should another match be played, to compete with their fellow townsmen."*

The tannery also had its own benefit association. For a payment of just 3d a week, sickness pay of 8s a week was ensured. Whatever was left in hand at Christmas was divided equally amongst members, the amount one year being 16s 6d each, actually 3s 6d more than they had paid in, and only 12s 6d, equivalent to about one and a half weeks, had been paid out as sick pay in the entire year.

Then, unexpectedly, in the summer of 1885 the tannery closed and all employees were thrown out of work. No one was quite sure what was going on, even in the summer of 1886 when it was reported that the tan-yard had *"...made a start, albeit a very small one...".* In October smoke was seen coming from the chimney, but the business remained closed.

* * *

At about 2.30 in the morning of 13th November 1886, William Clarke's daughter was awoken by the sound of breaking crockery in the kitchen of the Kings Arms. She alerted her father who, accompanied by *"...the ostler and boots..."* went into the yard, found the kitchen window wide open and saw a man *"...making free with the eatables and drinkables."* For fifteen minutes, they watched him; then after he checked the coins in his pocket he muttered to himself, *"One and fivepence, time to be off."* As he climbed upon a dresser to ease his escape through the window, the ostler grabbed him and as he fell, he hit his head and was easily overpowered and tied up. The ostler went for the police and Sergeant Allcott duly arrived.

The man who had been captured was Thomas Norbury, a former Coventry seaman who spent 30 years of his life in jail and who, just a few weeks previously, had been released from Dartmoor Prison after serving a lengthy sentence. He soon told Allcott to check a particular ditch in Leek Wootton where he had hidden 106 pieces of silver, taken from the Red Horse Hotel in Stratford a few nights before. Norbury was charged with, *"Burglariously breaking into the Kings Arms Hotel and stealing therefrom various articles..."* but it was agreed that the robbery at the Red Horse was the more serious offence and so he was transferred to Stratford.

* * *

With his business profits, Henry Street invested

in numerous properties and pieces of land including some in Whitemoor, Spring Lane and Albion Street, and Crew Farm in 1874. Then on 25th March 1884, he bought the hilly fields, south of the footpath behind the Bowling Green Inn and north of the railway line, including the Bowling Green Piece where the Kenilworth Cricket Club played, from Maria Porter, widow of Henry Porter and niece of Thomas Cotton, on the understanding that no building on the land would take place during her lifetime. Soon after this, Mrs Porter moved to Llandudno.

It was obvious that the route from the railway station to High Street could be shortened by a new road roughly northwards from the station to the vicinity of Upper Rosemary Hill across Street's newly acquired land, but access to Abbey Hill or Upper Rosemary Hill was restricted. There was a pathway, from the railway crossing at the station running up the boundary of Street's land to Savage Lane, a short road that Street also owned, which was unsuitable for horse-drawn vehicles and indeed parts of it were sometimes impassable by pedestrians. Henry Street suggested a road from the station to Savage Lane, but this ran into opposition, for unrecorded reasons, and was not pursued. In June 1884 it was announced that the Bowling Green Inn was being put up for sale the following month by its landlord, Lord Clarendon, but this auction did not happen.

At the western end of the inn was a gateway, giving access from Abbey Hill to the stables and coach-houses at the rear, and it was possible that with the demolition of buildings in the vicinity of the gateway, a new road could be built giving Street the access he needed. Something similar had happened in 1844 at the Kings Arms when Station Road was constructed, and that had notably improved the access to the inn by giving it a second frontage. Street and Clarendon commissioned Thomas Hillier CE FSA, to design a road to pass through the western end of the Bowling Green Inn, which would necessitate the demolition of a dining room, kitchen, two bedrooms, a billiard room and stables. With the new plans for the road passed by the Board in August 1884, Lord Clarendon quickly put the inn back on the market again. Licensee John Phillips decided to end his 26-year association with the inn and advertised for sale some of his property "...in consequence of extensive alterations..." and he sold the mahogany furniture from the rooms, a tea service, thirty iron garden seats and benches, and the four carriages he often advertised for hire - a landau, an open phaeton with folding seat, a six-seat wagonette and a barouche with pole. Two dismantled buildings were also for sale, the first was a two storey 50ft by 15ft building with a dining room upstairs and skittle alley below, and the second was another skittle alley, 40ft by 20ft. All skittles, skittle frames, twenty pairs of bowls etc., were included. At a separate sale organised by Clarendon's agent, Humbert and Son of Lincoln Inn Fields, the Bowling Green itself was put up for auction on 2nd October. It was described as "...a fully licensed posting, commercial and family hotel, with pleasure grounds and bowling green..." and included were four cottages alongside. Within days of the sales, the relevant parts of the Bowling Green were dismantled and carted away and the first cuts for the

new road were made near the station. It was being made by Board roadmen but at Henry Street's expense.

The new road was to be 36ft wide and upon its satisfactory completion by Street, the Board was to buy two strips 2ft wide running the whole length of it, presumably for walkways, for £72. There was also to be a short branch road from it to open up Albion Row passing through Clarendon's land to the east of the new road. However, at the next, September 1884, Board meeting, at which Henry Street was absent, Dr Wynter accused Hillier the Board's Architect and Surveyor of altering the plans between the date they were deposited, 6th August, and the day they were passed by the Board, 13th August. A long exchange of views, including those of Clarendon's agent Mr Oakley, confirmed the differences; Hillier admitted that he had in fact deposited plans concerning kerbing and channelling which were drawn by Mr Kyd the previous year and had destroyed those he had prepared himself. Not surprisingly, Hillier was immediately given three months' notice to leave and he instantly reacted by saying he was withdrawing the plans on Henry Street's instructions. The next Board meeting opened with Street saying that he gave Hillier no such authority, but Chairman Evans said that if he wished for the road to go ahead he would now have to redeposit the plans and start the process again. Street reacted angrily and said that in that case he would withdraw the plans and make a 36ft wide private road and not involve the Board at all.

A change of heart saw Street re-submit the plans after all, and the highways committee recommended that the original agreement with regard to the small additional strips should stand. Street's regular sparring partner, Dr Wynter, immediately objected as Street had previously stated he did not want any money from the Board, but Evans had met Street privately between meetings and agreed the payment, with Street happy to agree to the Board's wishes. However, William Clarke moved that Street should make the road the full 40ft width and on a vote, eight of the twelve present agreed. Street responded by saying he would make it 36ft wide and take the consequences.

With the road already under construction, the matter was settled at the December 1884 meeting with the reading of a letter from Street: "Having had general conversation with my friends with respect to the width of the road, they strongly advise me to make it 40ft wide without payment from the Board, to avoid being accused of receiving payment from the town. I have decided to make it 40ft wide although I had arranged with Messrs Humbert in my first agreement to make it 36ft wide. The making of the road at all is a serous loss to me, owing to so much of the land being under a restriction not to be built upon. Should I not be able to attend the Board meeting, please get the Board to approve the plan." This produced a round of applause from all those present.

Construction of the road had actually started in October 1884 near the station, and by the third week had reached "the second field" with drains being laid. Edward Purnell jnr had replaced Hillier as surveyor and engineer for the Kenilworth Board, and he quickly produced a new full set of plans. The Earl of Clarendon wrote a letter on 7th February 1885 giving his consent to the new road crossing his land where part of the Bowling Green Inn had been demolished. The blocking up of the footpaths that the new road was to replace was passed by JPs on 25th February 1885. By April the road was almost complete and in July, the old footpaths were finally closed. In August, kerbing was being laid. The name Abbey Road had been chosen.

But the problems were not over. The certificate stating Abbey Road was complete was signed by Purnell on 17th October 1885 only for him to withdraw it again when he discovered that the top surface was only of gravel when it had apparently been agreed it should be of hartshill stone. This meant that the Board could not yet take the road over, but Street, waving a copy of the erroneously completed certificate, said that as far as he was concerned, the road was finished, and if the Board were not to take it over, he would close it and pay not a penny towards the cost. Dr Wynter, never apparently needing too much of an invitation to take an opposing stand to Street, insisted that the Board should enforce strictly its own stipulations and as a result another stalemate ensued.

On the second Wednesday of February 1886, an extraordinary exchange of views took place at the Board meeting. Henry Street, whilst refusing to pay the Board £40 needed to finish the road as he already held the erroneous completion certificate, offered to pay £50 for the Board to spend on other roads if they would take Abbey Road over that day. Dr Wynter backed Street and advised the Board to accept the offer. Chairman Evans immediately stated that the road could not be taken over that quickly, and so Street immediately withdrew his offer and said that it would remain a private road. The Clerk agreed the road should not be taken as it stood, but suggested the acceptance of Street's offer. Bagshaw, too, backed Street, as did Lockhart. The sticking point was that the Board had no power to take it over unless it was in a completed state, but as it was not the surveyor could not sign a new certificate. Street withdrew his offer, and Wynter immediately withdrew his backing for Street and insisted that he finished the road as planned. With the clerk and surveyor both saying that the offer could not be accepted, Street ended the meeting by stating that during the next week he would put up gates at each end and the road would be locked up.

Common sense eventually prevailed and the Board completed the top surface, finally taking Abbey Road over and opening it in April 1886. Even then, the footpaths at the side were not complete, and they ran into another problem - a little extra land was needed to circumnavigate a prominent tree near the Bowling Green Inn - but this was solved with minimal fuss.

Three months after Abbey Road was opened, Board Chairman William Evans questioned its name, as it could cause confusion with Abbey Hill and Abbey End. He suggested a change to Priory Road and this was agreed. At the same meeting, he raised a similar point that Castle End was not near the Castle and perhaps a new name should be sought there as well. In October two enamel road signs were ordered, one for each end of Priory Road; another name change almost took place when it was inadvertently called Priory Street.

Two enamel road-signs, possibly the first the town had, were ordered for Priory Road in October 1886.

The new owner of the remaining part of the Bowling Green Inn was Thomas Bernard Cooper and within three months of buying it, he made his intentions clear. He deposited plans for two semi-detached villas on his "Bowling Green Estate" (which were passed upon the condition work was not commenced until the new road had been completed), and at the same time he submitted a plan for a new hotel to replace the Bowling Green Inn itself, but a decision on this was deferred until after a special meeting to discuss alterations to it.

Unfortunately, despite several warnings to do so, Cooper had overlooked the necessity of transferring the existing licence to himself from former licensee, John Phillips. He ended up being fined £5 in February 1885, and within two months, he was back in court again, this time as a victim. John Mathews, landlord of the White Lion, visited the Bowling Green to call in a bill but Cooper had just returned from a long journey and the two agreed that Mathews should return the following day. Later he came back and after an exchange of words struck Cooper, knocking him to the ground. He attacked him again and upset a table smashing the jugs and glasses that were on it. Mathews was then paid his debt by the barman and left, and a piece of iron immediately came through the window. He was fined £2 10s plus costs.

On 14th April 1885, the former licensee, John Phillips, died at the home of his son in Burton upon Trent. He was 86. He had resolutely refused to leave the Bowling Green until its partial demolition became inevitable. It had always been well patronised by visitors from his home city, Birmingham. *"The Bowling Green Hotel and host Phillips combined to form one of the leading features of Kenilworth."*

The architect of the new hotel was Mr Hartington and the builders were Horton and Redfern. In May 1885, the plans had still not been finally passed, there were difficulties with the building line, yet construction had started at the rear of the old building, fronting onto the new road. In September 1885, bricklayer John Mason, who in 1883 had been in court for fighting, was accused of damaging boards on the site, an incident witnessed by Thomas Cooper. Mason was subsequently accused of assaulting Richard Berden, an employee of Cooper, in the Bowling Green bar and not surprisingly the two ended up in court. Mason was fined 6d and Berden's case was dismissed.

On the same day, Thomas Cooper applied for a licence for his new premises for when they were completed. A Mr Field raised a legal point suggesting that since Cooper had already been found guilty of supplying beer without a licence he should not be entitled to a new one, but this was side-stepped when Cooper said he would transfer the licence to a new tenant within three months. Deputy Chief Constable Moth raised another legal question - could a licence be issued to new premises whilst the old one was still in use? It was finally agreed that a new licence could only be issued to Cooper on the condition that the old premises were demolished, which was of course Cooper's intention anyway.

Cooper's problems continued. In March 1886, he was fined £2 for allowing drunkenness at the Bowling Green, and also appeared at Warwick County Court on two summonses of owing money. One was for £49 1s 3d to Samuel Mason, "beer engine maker" of Birmingham, and the other to Kenilworth haulier John Betts for £16 2s 6d. There were already several other orders against Cooper and in these most recent cases commitment orders were held in the office for a fortnight. *"If he is bankrupt he could not be made to pay, but if he could pay (I do) not see why the present summons should be dismissed."* Cooper is not heard of again, and it seems that ownership was transferred to the builders, Horton and Redfern.

Building materials being scattered around was bound to prove a temptation to some and in early April 1886 Charles Garratt, a groom, was seen by a policeman carrying away 18 roof tiles, valued at 1s, under his arms. *"It's a lie! It's a lie!"* exclaimed Garratt in court; *"They were not under my arms but upon my head!"* Horton and Redfern dropped the prosecution upon payment of costs.

On 20th May 1886, the licence was transferred to a Mr Arkulus as the hotel's occupier, but when this came up for renewal in August that year a confusing situation was revealed. A Ms Phipson was now in occupation and she did not even know Arkulus. The excise officer sent a certificate stating that the spirits had been supplied to a man named Humphreys (sic. Humpage?) who was the owner that had engaged Phipson. Builder Mr Redfern of Birmingham subsequently applied for a temporary transfer of the license from Arkulus to Alfred Humpage who was described as the lessee, and this was granted upon the condition that a responsible tenant was soon found to conduct the business.

With the old buildings at last down, plans for the part of the hotel fronting onto Upper Rosemary Hill were passed, but it was later proved that the bay windows were 3ft 6ins over the building line; the error was the Board's by incorrectly approving wrongly drawn plans.

During the autumn of 1886, it was noted that the new Bowling Green was a long time in *"...getting into a complete state...",* but it finally opened in October and by November 1886 was *"in full swing."* Humpage was now clearly in charge and in his name, plans were deposited and passed for stabling at the rear. With its troubles sorted, Priory Road was now fully lit.

The new hotel was of red brick with Bath stone dressings and half-timbered gables. There were two large coffee rooms, a public and private bar, bar parlour, billiard room, smoking room, a 30ft by 20ft club room, large entrance hall and a staircase leading to two large sitting rooms on the first floor with commanding views over the Abbey Fields to the Castle. There were 18 bedrooms as well as all the usual kitchens etc. The height of the ceilings diminished on each floor, the ground floor

being 12ft, the upper being 10ft. A notable feature was the corner turret with a parapet 55ft from the ground, that gave spectacular views. The building line of the hotel was 4ft 6ins behind that of the old inn. It now belonged to William Horton Esq.

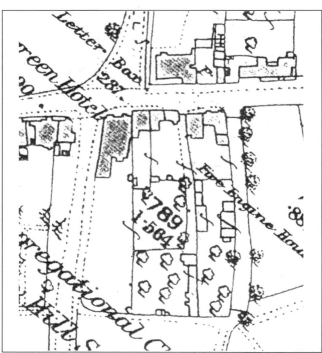

Initially, Priory Road (left) was to join with Savage Lane (right). Alongside the Bowling Green Hotel were three cottages - one of which was the first home of the Co-operative. The Board offices are alongside the narrow central trackway. The new fire station (below "Engine"), replaced the old which was between the two houses on the opposite side of (Upper) Rosemary Hill.

During the various legal transactions, old documents came to light that suggested the demolished Bowling Green had the oldest licence in Kenilworth. It had been one place supplied with wine and spirits by William H Mander, and his son, also William, was a frequent visitor. Working at the inn as a barmaid, since 1882, was Annie Steel, and soon she and William began courting, with her eventually accepting his proposal of marriage. All went well until January 1885 when John Phillips gave up the business and she lost her position and went to live with her parents who were at the time living in Kenilworth. One February evening whilst they were out walking, Mander *"...took advantage of his position and seduced her, promising to marry her in as short a time as possible."* During the spring and summer, Annie worked in the Swan Hotel in Warwick and Mander continued to promise that he would marry her and that all would be well. She worked at The Swan until her pregnant condition became apparent.

Annie's father had by now earned a position as Inspector on the Lancashire and Yorkshire Railway and had moved with his wife to Manchester, but Annie, upon returning to her parents, was forced by them to take lodgings. Mander promised to marry her in early August, but made his excuses; Annie visited Kenilworth on 17th August and Mander offered to put her in lodgings but she refused saying that if she were not to be his wife then she would not be his mistress. Mander had told her that he had £300 and was going to buy the Clarendon

Hotel and that in due course he would become a partner in his father's business, yet William snr claimed that his son knew that he was not in a position to marry. Mander jnr became extremely miserable, began drinking and did not *"feel fit for anything"* but continued to promise to do his best for Annie. In November, her sister wrote to tell him that Annie had given birth to a daughter and he replied saying that he was sorry at the result as he was hoping for a son. Action was taken at Shire Hall against Mander jnr for breach of promise, and Mr Fitzgerald, appearing for Annie, stated that the child *"...unfortunately, is still living."* Even Mr Overell described his client Mander as a *"...ne'er do well, whom the plaintiff was fortunate in having failed to marry."* The jury awarded Annie £180.

The next building to be given planning permission in the new road was in May 1885 for Ernest and Claud Flint's Coffee Tavern on the corner with Station Road. This was an attempt to win the custom of those using the railway station and must have come as a blow to William Clarke of the Kings Arms, as not only did he have the nearest refreshment facilities to the station but also had hoped to provide refreshments at the station itself. The Flints had arrived in Kenilworth from Cubbington in 1882, when Ernest was 23 and his brother just 17, and with £360 capital between them they began trading as coal dealers, renting siding space from Henry Street at Mill End and stables and other premises at Castle End. They added timber to their dealings, advertising the sale of firewood for 16s a ton, for example, then bought more horses, rented space at the station and briefly two fields in Windy Arbour, which they gave up for two in Priory Road. They borrowed all but £110 of the money needed to build the Coffee Tavern, which was opened on 1st December 1885 and was described as having *"...a clean room, cheerful fire and cheap coffee...success is certain."*

The tavern quickly became a popular venue for gatherings; in January 1886, twenty seven men who worked at the railway station and yards were charged a nominal sum for a meal, and just a few weeks later the Kenilworth Amateur Minstrels met there for their first annual dinner. The food was *"cooked to perfection"* by Miss Oakley and not surprisingly, the Minstrels sang songs during the evening, concluding with the national anthem. The Flints also supplied food off premises; in August 1886, they provided *"a capital collation"* to members of the swimming club at their shanty at Chesford. Amongst their coal customers was the Local Board.

Unfortunately, through all their dealings, the Flints kept no cashbook nor purchase ledger, and by the end of 1886 they were in a serious financial position. In March 1887 they were declared bankrupt with gross liabilities of over £1,800. Their Coffee Tavern was bought, not surprisingly, by William Clarke, who had given up in his bid to provide refreshments at the station, and he gave it the grand title of "The Railway Coffee Tavern and Refreshment Room."

Other buildings were now being put up nearby. On *"...the corner of Priory Road adjoining the railway station..."* Mr Whittendale had for sale the Railway Temperance Hotel and at auction the winning bid was by William Clarke acting on behalf of J Sarbet of Kenilworth. It had a refreshment bar, sitting room, clubroom and full accommodation for excursionists. (Note: this may have been the Coffee Tavern which had been given a grand name to improve its appeal.)

In August 1887, Clarke applied for a liquor licence at the tavern. It was easy for him to argue the case for providing refreshments for weary travellers awaiting a train and that the only potential loser was the Kings Arms - his own business - and he submitted an *"...influentially signed memorial in support."* There was a petition against the application, reportedly signed by only six people, in which someone had calculated that after deducting children and teetotallers there was already one licensed premises in Kenilworth for every fifty five people, and due to this the application failed.

* * *

With the building of Abbey (Priory) Road, the cricket club lost its ground for a second time due to a new road being built to the railway station. It was initially believed that an agreement could be reached with the Board for renting one of the Abbey Fields, but these hopes were soon dashed. This time a generous benefactor was on hand to provide a solution. Thomas Hawley granted the club a fourteen year-lease on a 6-acre field at Castle End. Secretary Dr Edmund Bourne, from his home Cumnor House on Abbey Hill, advertised for tenders to level a playing area, and the club spent a large sum of money on levelling 1,700 sq yds ready for the 1886 season, and intended to extend the area the following autumn. A carriageway to the ground was built and a pavilion was planned. The club itself had also been re-organised, chiefly due to the efforts of William Evans, its treasurer. Dr Thomas Bourne was its president, W Wells Ridley its captain and Ernest Trepplin vice captain. The Committee consisted of H J Stone, T Mitchener, H Edmonds, H Went and J Brown.

A concert was arranged at the Kings Arms to raise funds in February 1886. An extraordinary and classy affair started with a piano quartet by three Miss Nelsons, including Alice (23), and Miss Newman. Afterwards, a long line of dazzling lights from carriages gave an *"...illusionary idea that we had emerged from a hall in the capital instead of the Kings Arms Assembly Room."* The concert raised £18 6s. The Nelson family of Crackley Hall were deeply involved in the cricket club at this time; in one memorable match away to Harbourne that August, opening batsman F W Nelson scored the club's first recorded century, his opening partner was C M Nelson.

In the first match at the new ground, the "Married" beat the "Singles", but the first match proper, on Thursday 13th May starting at 11.00 a.m., was the newly-formed Second XI against Nuneaton. The new ground opened up possibilities for other events; on 28th - 30th June a tennis tournament was held. Perhaps practising for the event, players upset one local: *"I was sorry to see from the railway, on Sunday, some young gentlemen playing at lawn tennis, for it seems a pity that a questionable example should be set to youths who are ready to break the sabbath without any pretence of example whatever."* The genteel pastime of tennis was played amongst the more affluent inhabitants who could afford to provide their own facilities. Mr Farwig's Spring Cottage was advertised as having a *"tennis lawn"* in 1883, and in early 1888 William Pears gave winter employment to the poor by having tennis courts made at Kenilworth Hall. It was thought that the new cricket ground was big enough to house a tennis club. The local players held end of season suppers at The Queen and Castle; in 1889 *"...the tennis players with their friends from Leamington and Coventry made a party of forty."*

June provided two notable cricketing defeats, 131-18, and 112-52 at home to Nuneaton which was due to the weather: *"Mitchener prepared a capital wicket on the new ground. Considering the home club had to bowl nearly all the time in the rain with a wet ball, while it had cleared when the visitors were fielding, the result was not as unfavourable as would appear."* Thomas Mitchener was another budding star who, in a notable victory against Coventry and North Warwickshire, scored 80 out of 130, the opponents managed just 81. Mitchener, an *"inveterate smoker"*, became the permanent groundsman. He was a chimney-sweep by trade and rode *"...a tricycle on his chimney sweeping expeditions..."*. He was also an excellent skater. Circulars were handed out to encourage children as young as six to go to practices, but youngsters were already having an effect on the results as they continually distracted the scorers, and there were severe doubts as to the accuracy of their tallies! A pavilion of sorts existed, but a separate score hut was suggested. All agreed as to the merits of the new ground, but no-one had thought to put a sign up in Castle End announcing it, and so many visitors passed by the trackway leading to it without realising it was there.

By the season end, eleven matches were won against ten lost. The annual dinner had two interesting guests; it was chaired by Dr Thomas Bourne who played for Kenilworth as far back as 1848, and Stationmaster Taylor who used to play cricket at his previous appointment in Burton, until his weight reached 16 stone. The receipts for the 1886 season totalled just over £110, but expenditure was £119. Despite protestations, Ernest Trepplin resigned as Captain at the end of the season as he believed *"...a thorough cricketer..."* should hold the position and he proposed Percy Evans, son of William Evans of The Spring, as his replacement, to which all agreed. Trepplin was praised for his efforts in raising funds for the continuing programme of levelling the new pitch, and the total area was now to be raised to 3,186 sq yds. Mr Smith was to do the work which he regarded as *"...a labour of love."* The fund-raising concert had now become an annual affair.

The 1887 season was to see the Kenilworth Cricket Club play the most prestigious match in its history as it was invited to play Warwickshire at the County Ground at Edgbaston in May. The team, undoubtedly full of excitement, made its way to Birmingham for a mid-day start, in a coach drawn by four horses, but unfortunately the club had been practising for less than a week. The inevitable drubbing was not reported in the local paper: *"This match has*

already been commented on and reported by various papers so we will pass over our first appearance at the County ground in silence."

Accounts from elsewhere show why: *"It is doubtful if a more one sided, not to say farcical, match was ever played than the encounter which took place on Monday at the county ground between the Club and Ground and Kenilworth. For the sake of all who like to see tall scoring or a sensational downfall it is to be regretted that there was an attendance almost as meagre as the total runs made by the defeated team. The Club and Ground went in first and kept the wickets till 5 o'clock compiling 311, the largest score we believe, yet made on the ground. There was an hour remaining in which the visitors might hope to earn for themselves the negative satisfaction of a draw; but they were unequal even to that modest effort. They fell like nine-pins before the brilliant attack of A Bird and Leake, supported by the smartest of fielding, and compiled the apologetic total of 3 runs, one of which was an extra. A Bird took 7 wickets for one run, Leake three wickets for the other."*

The runs for Warwickshire were scored by Durban 44, Richards 126, Hill 6, Lester 38, Cox 5, Hill 39, Vince 13, A Bird 10, W Bird 12, Barwell not out 6, Leake 2, extras 10. Five Kenilworth bowlers succeeded in taking wickets: Robbins 2, Farthing 1, Mitchener 4, Stone 2, Nelson 1. The Kenilworth team, and the runs they scored, on this famous occasion was F Mitchener 0, W L Tyrer 0, E K Bourne 0, J Smith 0, G W Ridley 1, H J Stone 0, Reverend F Mitchell 0, W J Farthing 0, A L Nelson 0, H Pettifer 0, C Robbins not out 1, extras 1. When one of the younger players was asked why he failed to score a run, he replied *"The ball did not go far enough."*

From January 1887, there had been a new tenant at the Bowling Green, William Tyrer, and he gave a dinner for about 50 of his friends. During the evening, he announced that the hotel was to renamed the Abbey Hotel. Just a couple of months after the Warwickshire debacle, Tyrer challenged the one-armed Charles Robbins to a single wicket competition with no other fielders involved. In the first innings, Robbins ran out Tyrer for 2, and Tyrer bowled Robbins for 5. The second innings proved to be somewhat exhausting with Robbins eventually bowling Tyrer for 44. In reply, Robbins was on 18 when he hit the ball for what should have been 3 runs, but his opponent, doubtless worn out, made no attempt to get the ball and Robbins ran 25 runs for the one hit. *"Such a curious collapse was not expected by the on-lookers and gave rise to a great deal of merriment."* It was light-heartedly, and somewhat hopefully, suggested that since Charles Robbins was the not-out batsman against Warwickshire and could score 25 runs off one ball, he might at Edgbaston *"...have altered the fortunes of the day, and the Kenilworth Cricket Club might have returned victors."*

The Kenilworth ground continued to develop. A scoreboard was in place by July 1887 and Mr Baulcombe provided refreshments but *"...the pop and ginger beer shanty does not improve the look of the nicely painted Oxford and Cambridge house of the Kenilworth Cricket Club..."* which suggests it was painted two-tone blue. Perhaps due to the Warwickshire match, the club engaged a professional for a few months, T Newell, who was predominantly a bowler, but he left in August for Canada amid-complaints about team selection.

A description of the Abbey Hotel published in 1889 stated that it cost £7,000 to build and that another £2,000 was spent on furnishings. It had three bars and 38 well-ventilated rooms, which were lit by 50 or 60 gas lamps. The rooms were "...divided into suites for weddings, families, bachelors and commercial gentlemen." There were also tea, coffee, smoking, billiard and ballrooms, as well as bathrooms with both hot and cold water. There were four broad flights of stairs, which were richly carpeted and well lit. From the top of the turret could be seen Honiley Church, Edge Hill, Hatton, Coventry and Warwick. "The old Bowling Green Inn inherited the rural beauty of the past, the Abbey Hotel possesses the sterling loveliness of the present." But the hotel was not a great success. After conversing with Tyrer, a visitor wrote; "The manager informed me, whilst showing me the American Bowling Alley, that only in the summer months was anything doing, although from the number of glasses of cherry brandy served by the two pretty girls behind the bar, I should imagine that the consumption of that liquor alone must bring the manager a large revenue."

Tyrer did not last long. In early 1890, William Tyrer of Southsea, and described as a late hotel-keeper formerly of Kenilworth, was made bankrupt. The new proprietor, by April 1890, was J Sutcliffe, and that Easter he catered for over 1,500 visitors, but Sutcliffe lasted barely a year. The "responsibilities and control" of the Abbey Hotel passed to townsman Mr Kimberley in May 1891, although it was still owned by Humpage who was described as a "contractor and hotel proprietor." At one time in 1891, eight servants and only three guests were recorded. It was being described as one of the best-fitted hotels, particularly after recent enlargements and extensions, and the bowling green was "...one of the largest and best..." in the county, but Kimberley too lasted barely a year.

The new Bowling Green Hotel was re-named The Abbey Hotel by William Tyrer, one of three of its proprietors known to have become bankrupt in the first ten years of its existence.

*   *   *

The large area of land forming a rough triangle southwards from the tannery to the railway station and Castle End was in the main known as The Kendalls. The 12 acres were bought by William Clarke from Clarendon for £3,000 in February 1885, just months before the tannery closed. William had married into the Oakley family, and a Timothy Oakley set up The Kendalls Building Estate Office in the Working Men's Club. On 16th May 1885, Clarke had plans passed for two new roads on his land; one was to run roughly westwards from the station to Castle End and be known as Oakley Road (Waverley Road), and the other was a branch from it to abut the tannery land and was called Bertie Road. A provisional plan for a third road, from the end of Bertie Road and back to the station, was dropped.

By December 1885, construction of the new roads, by Leamington's John Fell, was well underway. He employed a number of Kenilworth workmen. By mid-July the following year, William Clarke announced that his two new roads were finished "...except for the corners." There was however a problem. At the station end, part of Oakley Road had to go onto a small plot owned by Mr Hedges and due to his illness, this last piece could not be completed. William Jacks' coal office stood on this piece of land. It was possible to put in an undesirable kink in the road to form the junction with Station Road but it was obviously preferable to keep it in line with Priory Road. The Board were refusing to take the road over unless it was completed. Otherwise finished, in August 1886 Oakley Road remained closed, was gated at both ends and had weeds growing upon it. Despite this, in the triangle between Bertie and Oakley Roads, John Fell began to build 16 houses.

Hopes of a solution to the Oakley Road problem were raised in November 1886 when the weeds were removed and the gates opened. It was soon described as the best made road in town, "I wish we had many more roads as well made as that one...", but early the following year the fences were back up and the road marked as "Private". The brief usage proved to make great benefits to and from the station, but the members of the Board who freely used it were also those objecting to the Board taking it over. By May, the fences were being damaged. During the brief period of usage, on 2nd December 1886, the rest of the building land was sold by William Clarke to Michael Lakin, of The Cliffe, Warwick, for £3,500. Much was soon sold on to architect Frederick Foster of Leamington.

By the end of 1886, a new company had been formed to restart the tannery. The Directors, all from out of town, included four boot and shoe manufacturers and two leather merchants, who, by owning a tannery would have immediate access to their raw material on agreeable terms, but the undoubted driving force behind the scheme was its former manager and Kings Arms owner William Clarke, being both Secretary and Managing Director. The Kenilworth branch of Lloyds, Barnett and Bosanquets were the bankers and the company solicitor, somewhat poetically, was a Mr Shoosmith.

On 24th November 1886, a contract was entered into with Phillip Newman for the sale of the business for £10,000 with the first £3,000 coming from fully paid up shares on 5th January 1887, the next £3,000 four months after this allotment date and the balance a further four months on. This bought the whole of the tannery premises, covering about five acres, and its plant and machinery. The stock and tanning material was to be taken upon valuation. Once again, disappointingly, it all came to nothing, but in August 1887, it seems the premises were put up for auction, with bidding starting at £2,000. It was sold to none other than William Clarke for a surprisingly low sum of £3,500, precisely the same amount he sold the Kendalls for just eight months earlier, but the tannery remained closed.

Then, just three weeks later, the bank Greenway, Smith and Greenway locked its doors and folded with debts of over £200,000. There was massive concern in Leamington and Warwick; the local authorities had accounts at the bank as did John Fell, over £30,000, but the real story of the fall was in Kenilworth where the bank did not even have a branch. For as long as 25 years, Greenways' Bank had been putting money into the tannery. Back in 1862, Henry Draper's debt had reduced the bank's capital to just £14,000, and it was already insolvent. By 1873, the debit on the tannery's account was £20,864, by 1877, it had risen to £48,222, and 1881 to £58,473. Phillip Newman, the one-time schoolteacher, had managed to convince Greenway, the banker who never actually examined the books, that he would be able to pay off the debt and as such, the tannery was treated as a good asset. Around 1880 it had been suggested that one of the Greenways should become a partner with Newman in an attempt to secure some profits towards the debt but this did not happen. In 1882, Greenway borrowed more money and put it into the tannery with Newman promising some would be paid back annually, but the following year the Greenways insisted that the business should be so managed as to produce a profit. This resulted in a considerable quantity of stock being sold off, but a loss was still sustained.

By 1885, the debt had risen to £85,000, and in addition, there was another account, untouched since 1870, which had an overdraft of £12,376. When it closed, the tannery and Phillip Newman were in debt to a total of £104,769. Newman held a mortgage of £8,500 on the premises from an unnamed London gentleman. From the time the tannery closed until the bank folded, the Greenways still paid Newman a wage, £6 a week.

During his public examination as a bankrupt, Kelynge Greenway honestly admitted that he knew the debt was desperate as early as 1879, but continued to show the business as an asset. He knew that it was not legitimate banking practice and that his conduct was "utterly unjustifiable." There was an oft-repeated phrase locally, that money had gone "down the Kenilworth chimney". John Fell, by then Mayor of Leamington and the contractor for the Magdeburg tramway, also had some choice words about the Greenways: "One was over-sanguine, the other fit for a lunatic asylum." The other partner in the bank, Smith, had died shortly before the bank's collapse.

The degree of William Clarke's involvement in the tannery's financial irregularities and closure is not clear, but in February 1888, he was in possession of £535, which was due to the Greenway estate and despite promises he failed to make payments and so a warrant was issued against him. He clearly had financial problems and in September 1888, Clarke sold the Coffee Tavern for £550 and four months later, the Warwick and Warwickshire Building Society applied to extend the premises, but this was turned down as the extension would have protruded beyond the building line of the houses in Station Road. The operation of the Tavern was recorded in the name of both J and T E Clarke, neither is thought to be related to William. It opened at 5.00 a.m. for working men and served tea, coffee and cocoa at 1d a cup.

The same month he sold the Coffee Tavern, William Clarke tried to sell the Kings Arms but it was withdrawn as it failed to reach £3,000, however a new tenant was in by the new year. In-between, the following notice was included in local newspapers: "Notice to creditors and debtors, re William Clarke, Kings Arms Hotel, Kenilworth. A dividend is intended to be declared in the above matter, all persons having claims to the estate are requested to forward particulars of same to the Trustee on or before Monday 24th December. All debts due to the estate must be paid to the trustee forthwith. Henry Suffolk, Trustee, West Orchard, Coventry." Despite this, although the tannery remained closed, it appears Clarke managed to retain ownership.

The Kings Arms new landlady, Mrs Sarah Adams (60), held a meal to mark the occasion of her tenancy. John Matthews left the White Lion in early 1889 and took over the transport operation at The Kings Arms Mews advertising "Post Horses, Broughams, Landaus, Four-in-hand and Unicorn teams, with careful drivers." He also had 20 loose-boxes, which he hoped would attract hunters, obtained a licence for running three hackney carriages and had a cab that met every train. His office was in the hotel.

*   *   *

By 1884, for a small monthly contribution the Kenilworth Friendly Insurance Society paid sickness benefit at the rate of 12s for the first week and 7s for each subsequent week, and £10 upon death. Funds amounted to almost £1,000, an average of £8 13s 6d for each of its 116 or so members. William Sutton suggested, and W Jeacock seconded, that the entrance fee should be reduced from 10s to 5s and this was adopted. The trustees were G Page, E Smith, H Thornett (who was also the treasurer) and W Turner; the secretary was H White.

However, by the time of the meeting on 19th March 1888 at the Institute, the situation had changed dramatically. Membership was now down to 101 and in the last year two members had died, two members' wives had died and four had left. During the previous eight years, only three new members had been admitted and owing to the large amount of sickness, the benefit fund was down to just £137. The total funds were down to £782 and that included some now lost in the collapse of the Greenways' Bank. The auditors recommended a prompt dissolution according to rule 57, and of the 46 present, 41 voted in favour. The final winding-up came towards the end of September 1889 and the members received payments dependant upon their contributions; these varied from £15 to 15s. The closure was particularly harsh on the older members who were too old to enter a similar society, but Dr Wynter offered to retain these on his medical list on the same cheap terms he received from the society.

The Kenilworth Cycle Club was in terminal decline. When the "club" left town for the annual Whit Monday gathering of cyclists in Leamington in 1886, the captain led a solitary rider. This was in contrast to 16 or 17 riders and a small crowd gathering to see them off in better days.

The following year saw a "Grand Cycling Concert" at the Assembly Rooms, but it was poorly patronised by Kenilworth people, the small audience being composed almost entirely of cyclists from Leamington and Coventry. The show included trick riding, but unfortunately, one of the two performers was absent due to a sprained wrist. The highlight of the evening was when "...Mr Baylis gave an exposition of trick-riding which pleased the audience...one difficult performance being mounting his bicycle which was placed on two chairs." Songs were sung including three by Miss Randall who had come from Shrewsbury for the event, "...her voice being sweet but not loud enough for so large a room...", and Mr Hollis with his ever-popular comic song "I did it".

* * *

From the AGM of 1886, the fire brigade had another new Captain; Trepplin stepped down as arranged and was replaced by the popular Lieutenant, Dr Myles Christopherson Atkinson, and he soon made a memorable impression. At the outbreak of a rick fire in William Clarke's field at the rear of the Kings Arms, Captain Atkinson commandeered a baker's cart, fully laden with bread, and drove it to the fire wearing his helmet. The fire was dealt with quickly; the brigade and its captain were often complimented for the speed and zeal displayed in attending fires.

After the death of Charles Bliss in 1868, his premises were taken over by Elizabeth Bushill who continued a similar drapery trade. Thomas Emery started his drapery business in High Street in 1846 and in the summer of 1878, his son Austin became a partner. In 1880, Austin bought out Elizabeth Bushill and advertised it as gentlemen's outfitters, but in 1882, he sold the business on to former Elizabeth Bushill manager, Edward Stokes. Edward Stokes was the son of the Reverend Edward Stokes, who also lived in Kenilworth, and he lived in the rented Ashleigh in Castle End.

Calling his business The Castle End Drapery Emporium, in 1883 Stokes advertised an array of goods including cloaks, trimmings, muffs and capes all in fur, and shirts, ties, braces and collars in his hosiery department. Ready-made suits were sold from 18s 6d and handmade suits run up in just three days. In the autumn of 1883, Stokes opened a new department for ladies and children's outfitting and underclothing; his advertisement stressed that this department was in the personal charge of Mrs Stokes.

The following year, Stokes added a new showroom to his business in additional premises in Castle End. Later the same year he bought the entire stock of "...the late Mr Haines of Leamington..." and advertised it for sale at very low prices, some items being only a quarter of the original price. Stokes and his wife travelled far in search of stock: "Mr and Mrs Stokes have just returned from London with an immense assortment of all the leading novelties in dresses, mantles, jackets and fancy goods of every description." Just before Christmas 1885, his father died, aged 72, at his home in Percy Terrace.

From 1878, a part of Elizabeth Bushill's premises was rented to Miss Helen Sarah Coe who made straw hats and bonnets and sold flowers. This arrangement continued with both Austin Emery and Edward Stokes. She had her own shop and workshop. Helen Coe sold the "...newest styles in black and white chip and straw hats and bonnets..." and also made up garments for ladies who provided their own materials. By 1886, she added felt and velvet hats, woollen wraps, boas, capes and trimmings, Macintoshes and umbrellas, gloves, collars, "ladies' underlinen", and ladies' caps, fronts, laces and frillings.

After returning home from church late one November Sunday evening in 1886, Edward Stokes decided to write a couple of letters in time to catch the late train. He now lived on his business premises, and after lighting a lamp to find paper and envelopes in his shop, he carelessly discarded the match without ensuring it was extinguished. Having finished the letters, he made his way to the railway station. Edward's son had gone to bed, but another boy staying with them smelt smoke and called out to Mrs Stokes - Edward's discarded match had started a fire. Mrs Stokes raised the alarm with neighbours; William Riley was the first to respond and assisted by Mr Gregory they entered the shop and tried to tackle the flames, but were beaten back. The fire brigade was quickly on the scene and was greatly helped by the water supply from a nearby hydrant. Two of William Clarke's men from the Kings Arms brought into use the inn's garden-engine and hose, and Clarke himself brought several "extinctors" but these proved inadequate, as the base of the fire could not be reached. As hundreds of people flocked to the scene, the whole of the front of the shop became gutted, as were the two floors above. Efforts were concentrated on stopping the fire spreading to Helen Coe's two rooms and workshop on the same property and this was largely successful. Mrs Garlick's property next-door was saved, preventing a possible disaster, as she had Mr Shard the ironmonger, who was licensed to sell gunpowder and had a store of petroleum and oil, as her neighbour. The containment of the fire was attributed to the fire brigade and the water hydrants; had the only supply been from water-carts there was little doubt the fire would have rapidly spread to other properties. The flames had been completely subdued by the time the Warwick engine arrived. "(Our) townsmen willing to leave a comfortable bed of their fireside, to risk life or limb, or at least a bad cold, in the exercise of their self-imposed duty for the benefit of their fellow townsmen is beyond praise."

Helen Coe's shop and workshop were

"*distinct*" from Stokes's but suffered much damage. Neighbours and friends helped her to rescue what they could and she put some items up for sale despite them being smoke-damaged. After the fire, Stokes continued his business at the nearby outfitters shop and advertised himself as "*...rising from the ashes.*" However, despite his efforts, his business never recovered and eighteen months after the fire, in the Spring of 1888, Edward Stokes sold out his entire stock and business to 29 year-old Charles J Carter.

The Edward Stokes Drapery Emporium, scene of the town centre's major fire.

Having had their first major town centre fire to deal with, within a few months the brigade wrote to the Board requesting additional equipment to make better use of the water hydrants, a stove for the engine-house and a gas lamp for the yard. Also required was an alarm to summon the men to either a drill or emergency. It was hoped that objections from the churchwardens for the use of a church bell could be overcome but in addition "*...a bell, bull or a horn...*" could be provided at the engine-house. The proposition was carried unanimously, and former captain Dr Wynter took the opportunity to praise the brigade's performance at Mr Stoke's fire. "*(I) have never seen men exert themselves more willingly and show greater energy and enthusiasm in their work than the brigade did on that occasion.*"

The attendances at drills had become much improved since the appointment of Atkinson as Captain and this in turn meant that at the fires attended, especially the Stokes conflagration, they could perform much more efficiently. Atkinson was aware of the brigade's shortcomings but was pleased with the way the brigade met the hardships in the right spirit. Three members had left in the year 1886-7, two had left town and the other due to poor health, and the stability too was likely to be a result of Atkinson's influence.

In August 1887 George Beard (69) invited the brigade to give a demonstration of its abilities at his house, Thickthorn, after which he provided a supper for them. When living in Solihull, Beard had had his house completely destroyed by a fire due to the fire engine valves being frozen. George Beard was London-born and had needle and pin manufactories in Birmingham, Redditch and London. Moving from Hillfield Hall, he bought Thickthorn from the Penningtons for £16,000 in April 1884. Three years later he bought the adjacent Woodlands Farm from Reverend Twistleton for £7,150,

into which his son Richard later moved. Mark Pettifer was the farm bailiff. Beard had over 300 chrysanthemum bushes of 100 different varieties at Thickthorn, and in 1891 a shooting party on his land bagged 155 pheasants. He was also a keen huntsman, a pursuit he eventually gave up at the age of 81.

In late January 1888, the popular former brigade captain, Ernest Trepplin, returned from a trip to America and was given a reception at Mr Prime's Virgin's Inn by the fire brigade, arranged by Captain Atkinson and Deputy Captain Hodges. Trepplin recounted his adventures during the evening and members of the company performed songs. Trepplin was awarded the position of Honorary Captain.

In June, "*A pair of pictures representing our gallant fire brigade in working order stationed in the ruins of the Castle, and photographed by Mr W.J.Kimberley, of Castle Grove, was presented on Wednesday night by the members of the Brigade to Deputy-captain Hodges on the occasion of his marriage.*" The photographs had been taken two weeks previously, by arrangement no doubt, with the Castle's occupant, Ernest Trepplin.

Having not had a fire to deal with in over eighteen months (except for two small ones that had been put out before the brigade arrived), the brigade were to tackle four in a week towards the end of the year. On the evening of 19th October 1888 a fire broke out in James Bostin's cottage in School Lane. The alarm gong at the engine-house was sounded and the fire bells rung and the brigade duly arrived on the scene - but unfortunately the engine itself was still at a large fire, attended by several engines, at Wainbody. At James Bostin's cottage, a wrought iron safety door had been cemented over, and a flue had become blocked with soot and ignited, but with a good supply of water and buckets to hand, the available brigade members soon had the fire under control.

Just three days later, street lamplighter Dale, on his way home after extinguishing the street lamps, was alarmed to see flames coming from the rear of the Board's offices. Somewhat embarrassingly, the fire brigades own hose-drying stack was on fire! Dale contacted the police and, as the alarm gong on the station tower was obviously inoperable, the church bells were rung for the third time in four days. The firemen who lived nearby were quickly on the scene and prevented the fire from spreading to the stables where the Board's horses were kept. Much of the stack was destroyed, as was the new gong apparatus, and much of the hose which was being dried. The cause was attributed to the overheating of the drying flue. Another small fire in a hovel rounded off the week.

"*Four fires in a week are enough to put any fireman out of temper, but a little more courtesy on the part of the Captain would not be amiss. Several complaints have been made of the manner in which non-members of the brigade have been ordered away after they had been doing all they could to put out a fire before the brigade arrived. I have no doubt it is want of thought on the part of the Captain. Perhaps this reminder will serve to make him remember that the least people expect is courtesy.*"

During 1888 there had been six fires with total damage of £811 5s, and in the summer of 1889 the brigade requested four scaling ladders at a total cost of £7 15s 6d.

*   *   *

The Kenilworth Homing Club, for pigeon fanciers, was amongst the town's smaller societies. Its activities were not too extensive and the races were kept local. For one race in 1884, the birds were *"...thrown up from the Great Western railway bridge..."* in Leamington. The winning bird took 8 minutes to find its way home to T Bennett. Other club members were E Greenstand, C Holland, J White, R & G Burden, G Perks, H Checkley and M Hubbard.

Some locals worked a potentially profitable swindle involving the local pigeon racers. In 1890, at several locations around the town, pigeon traps were set up on roofs and when a bird was near, stones were thrown at it hoping it would find safety in the trap. Once caught, its legal owner was charged for the safe return of his bird. It was not the profit-making, though, that was frowned upon, but the dangerous throwing of stones in areas of housing.

By 1890 a gun club had been established which included members from Leamington and Warwick. Shoots were held in Kenilworth and a handsome trophy was won outright by Dr Edmund Bourne in April 1890. The Gun Club had its own grounds: in 1896 a competition was held there between Mr Shovelton and Mr Blake, the former won by killing 34 pigeons to his opponents 32. One assumes none of the targets belonged to the Kenilworth Homing Club.

Under the Board, the town was certainly a different place, but not necessarily seen as for the better: *"Kenilworth has for the previous half century, lived in a subjected and lethargic condition as to progress - it can challenge the county for being the most stagnant town in it. A new era has been dawning, and let us hope that a change has come over the spirit of our dream." "The Gentry used to patronise the tradespeople and all seemed to have the good of the place at heart. Now it is called The Birmingham Bedroom."*

One of the pair of photographs, taken by Kimberley, presented to Deputy Captain Hodges as a wedding gift on 16th June 1888; it had been taken two weeks earlier. (see page 120)

As he is wearing a different uniform, it would seem likely that the gentleman standing bottom right is Captain Atkinson, however, he closely resembles a known image of former Captain, Ernest Trepplin, who at the time the photograph was taken, was an honorary Captain, and living at the Castle.

(Reproduced, courtesy of Kenilworth Fire Brigade)

Part Three

"What nature intended – the paradise of Warwickshire."

Despite the obvious optimism generated by some developments, trade in town was in a slump. The tannery closure alone left up to 100 out of work and there was *"...a scarcity of food and fire in many homes."* Mrs Dawes still sent the poor as much coal as when she was a resident, the soup kitchen was up and running again and was boosted by a donation of 5 guineas from a Kenilworth Amateur Minstrels concert, and others were supplying the needy with soup of their own. The income of some traders was down by a half. This was not helped by out-of-town shopping - a leg of mutton cost just 6d per pound in Leamington but 10d or 11d in Kenilworth, a particular type of medicine required during the winter months was 9½d a bottle in Leamington and 1s 1d in Kenilworth, and many took advantage of these prices. Due to the excessive demand for 4lb loaves amongst the unemployed in March 1886, in less than a week the price rose from 4d to 5d.

There was *"no room in town large enough"* to hold a meeting of those in difficulty and there was a fear of riotous scenes as seen in other towns. There was also the observation that there was now *"one large farmer in place of ten"* which further affected employment and trade. The town had become *"infested with hawkers and beggars"*, some were described as *"singing tramps"* and these were known to congregate outside the Parish church during services *"drawling out (their own) hymns."* *"Kenilworth has to thank itself for the swarms of tramps, beggars and peddlers that it is infested with..."* due to the way in which peddlers were licensed. One of the tramps, Ann Riley, died at the roadside in Castle End in June 1886, and her funeral was a pitiful sight as the small party made its way through town, with just one mourner.

With *"trade stagnant"* and *"enterprise dead"*, suggestions and comments soon began to appear in the *Kenilworth Advertiser.* Much was aimed at the purchase of the Abbey Fields. One of the fields, eight acres known as Horse Close fronting onto Barrowell Lane and Castle Grove, was rented from the Board for *"an inconsiderable sum"* by Trepplin - it was suggested that he did not really need it and that it could be turned into allotments for the growing of fruit and vegetables for the needy. It was also suggested that as there was so much spare cheap labour available a start could be made on the long delayed swimming baths.

With so much unemployment, it was of no surprise that in August 1886, just forty-two months after the extraordinary scenes at its benefit concert at the Kings Arms in the presence of Rupert Leigh, the Working Men's Club closed as it was no longer self-supporting. Claims were called in against it, William Clarke dealt with them, and the premises were let.

With the tannery closed, seasonal agricultural work became even more important, but the Trepplins were now only employing for dairy work - over 100 were displaced by lack of work on their 3,000 acres. They had scarcely any cereal crops on their extensive acreage. The comb-making industry had all but died out, 80 year-old Job Constable, 60 year-old Charles Newey and Town-Crier William Drury, in his mid-60s, being exceptions. In the 1830s there had been 150 comb-makers but machinery made it possible to make two combs from a piece of horn that would produce only one by traditional methods. Kenilworth comb-makers did not keep up with the times.

There was an almost complete lack of indoor industry and it was only a matter of time before the obvious comment was made: *"I wish some of the gentry of Kenilworth would put some of their capital and start an undertaking that would employ one or two hundred of the population wet or fine...a vast deal more good than planning and making new streets."* *"Scores of men are standing at street corners."* *"Not in the history of Kenilworth can anything be remembered by the oldest inhabitants at all to compare with the depression and inactivity in general throughout the town."*

There were many good empty houses to let and so building more was seen as a poor speculation. The expected influx of permanent wealthier residents, particularly from Birmingham via the new railway line, simply was not happening on the scale expected. Brief visitors were not going to make a difference; *"If our town is to become a bedroom and a Sunday out for Birmingham Tradesmen, the shopkeepers of Kenilworth may as well shut up and emigrate..."* and emigration was an option again taken by many. On 16th March 1887 over 100 people assembled at the station to bid farewell to a party bound for Canada, which had been organised by Anthony J McMillan jnr of South Hurst Farm. The individuals had raised the money by going around town with a subscription list. The number of people out of work was described as *"large"* and there was *"...certainly at present no chance of anyone doing themselves any good here."* The people of Stoneleigh had set up a Jubilee Emigration Fund to finance chosen villagers to a better life and two of them were on the 16th March trip. In the second week of April, a cablegram arrived from Winnipeg saying that all from Kenilworth and the neighbourhood had arrived safely at their new home.

Anthony J McMillan snr was born in Scotland in 1818. In 1849 he settled in Coventry in business as a clothier and draper but in 1868 went into farming, first in Berkswell and then at South Hurst Farm. He had two daughters and three sons; William who had moved to America at an early age, Anthony J who was the agent in England for the Manitoba Government, and Alfred J who managed the farm.

In January 1888 Mr McMillan of Brandon, Manitoba, was back in the district, giving talks upon the benefits of leaving to live in Canada, and one such talk was at the Assembly Rooms. Lord Leigh presided and there were a fair number of working-class persons present. The party that left the previous spring were all doing well and none wished to return, many had sent letters to Lord Leigh expressing their gratitude towards McMillan. The lecturer explained that all were in full employment, wages were above those in England whilst *"the cost of maintenance is less."* After giving guidance to intending emigrants he made a special plea for females whom he assured would find employment within 24 hours of arrival.

This lecture brought about a small but very influential meeting at the parish room on Monday 20th February 1888 to discuss the emigration question. Francis Stanger-Leathes of Parkfield House took the chair. There was already a list of 37 men and women, not including their children, who wished to emigrate, and it would cost something like £7 to send each of them to Canada, the chosen destination as *"...labourers are more plentiful than work in Australia."* Stanger-Leathes suggested the money could be raised as a loan to be returned as soon as the emigrants could send it and this would then finance another group. William Pears seconded the motion; Kenilworth was he said *"...overstocked, and there is not enough work to employ all who need it."* The Reverend Binnie agreed it was *"...much better to run out of England for foreign parts where there was work than here where there is a lack due to the agricultural crisis."* Henry Street questioned whether *"...it is of use to send out the best men, leaving behind the loafers. It would be better to mix them for we could very well spare the loafing gentlemen."* George Beard was sure there would be *"...a portion of men of idle and dissolute habits who would go out if only to see foreign lands."* A committee was formed to put the scheme into action and with William Pears at its head over £80 was subscribed to the fund that very evening, with Pears himself leading the way with £20.

The scale of the proposition soon became clear; *"Applications for passes are numerous, and the collectors have been actively engaged in canvassing the town, but at present the funds are wholly inadequate to meet the demand..."* and not surprisingly, it was soon questioned why such an effort could not be made in helping those not eligible for emigration who were desperate for work. It was suggested that as gravel was always in demand, Knowle Hill could be opened up further for sales out of town; men were willing to dig it out for just 1s 6d a day.

"The emigration scheme...the object of which was relieving the community of some of its surplus labour..." was effectively run by William Pears and Board Chairman William Evans, and just three months after McMillan's talk their work was rewarded when a party of 40, including wives and children, left from the station. They joined over a thousand others on the Beaver Line ship 'Lake Huron' at Liverpool, C Robinson being the shipping line's representative in Kenilworth. The following week another ship, 'Lake Ontario', had a smaller Kenilworth contingent aboard.

One of those who left in April 1887 was Samuel Lynes. Although knowing nothing of the work, he was engaged by a farmer and after twelve months, he was knowledgeable enough to start on his own and obtained a free Government grant of 160 acres. He also managed to obtain an adjacent 160 acres for a friend who intended to leave Kenilworth in April 1889 and the two planned to amalgamate and make one large farm. A nineteen year old girl, Nora Stevens, happily settled into service and was treated like one of the family and another girl, Elizabeth James, was earning £2 a month with board. Harry Diamond, who never had regular work in Kenilworth, and may have been one of Henry Street's "loafers", was working continually and saving £1 a week in addition; his ten year-old daughter was receiving 3s a week and board. Others doing well were brother and sister, Thomas and Sarah Perkins, Walter Collett and Phillip Swain who was working as a timber feller. John Stoney got work on the Central Pacific Railroad and William Garlick, despite rumours that he had changed his mind and refused to embark at the last minute, was supporting his family by working as a gardener. These Kenilworthians were just a few of the 2½ million people who left Britain in the space of twelve years.

Harry Diamond wrote a letter from Poplar Farm, Elm Creek, Manitoba on 20th March 1889. He had his own farm of 160 acres and hoped to get some cattle on it soon. He worked for a good wage in the summer and on his own farm in the winter. There was plenty of work and you *"...only had to ask and you can get it, and not get your nose snapped off like you do in England."*

Such tales must have added to the despair of some in Kenilworth. Twenty year-old Robert James of Albion Street had hardly worked for two years. This played greatly on his mind, often sitting still and not talking for hours at a time. The cold winter probably added to his depression. At 8.40 on the morning of 25th January 1887, he walked out of his house and up Park Hill where he clambered down next to the railway tracks. Using a lead pencil on a scrap of paper he wrote "Dear father, mother, brothers and sisters, I write these few lines to tell you not to put yourselves about. Remember me to my mates. Good bye", then stepped out in front of an oncoming train. Driver Pearson said he was just 12 yards away and had no chance, Robert James' mutilated body came to rest 27 yards further on. William Gardner, a platelayer on his way to Thomas Plumbe's blacksmiths shop at Mill End, was first on the scene and found the note - James was a friend of his. The body was removed to the police station in Albion Street where the inquest was carried out that afternoon. His father Frederick said that his son had been very excitable that morning but did not know of any trouble hanging over him. It was established that *"Beyond the fact that the deceased was out of work, his friends did not know of anything to cause him to destroy himself..."* and a verdict of "Suicide whilst in a state of temporary insanity" was returned by the jury to the Coroner, Dr Wynter.

Another casualty, though not fatal, was George Page jnr (his father, also George, was a tailor). In 1878, at the age of 26, Page set himself up as a coal dealer with a capital of £50. Sadly, within a year his wife Elizabeth died aged just 25. Soon after, Page also became a farmer of 280 acres for a few years and added corn and hay to his dealings. But largely through poor trading, and an intriguing "marriage settlement" before which he was solvent, his debts began to mount, he sold much of his property and even sub-let his premises, but could not avoid being declared bankrupt in February 1887.

To add to the difficulties, in early 1888 there was an outbreak of swine-fever, the whole town being affected, and dozens of pigs died. Most were owned by wokingmen on who *"the loss falls heavily."*

Despite the general slump in trade, one particular organisation was flourishing - the Kenilworth Co-operative Society. In May 1886 it applied for permission to build further extensions to its premises. Onto the rear of the main building was added a trap house and stable with a hay and straw store above it. This presumably means the society also now had its own transport. There was also an addition to the bakery.

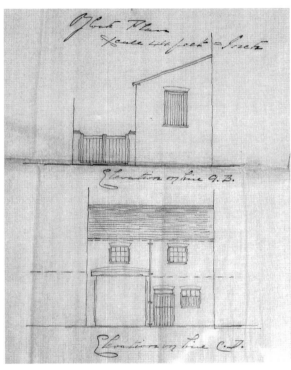

Plans for the Co-operative's trap-house. Straw and hay was kept on the upper floor, with access provided at the end. On the ground floor, the trap was kept in the left-hand bay and the horse in the stable behind the smaller door-way. A gate-way provided access to the yard. (Warwick County Records Office CR 2487/55)

By the time of the 57th quarterly meeting in February 1888 the society was in a very buoyant position. Total sales for the year were over £7,500, an increase of £1,400 on the previous year, and the last quarter alone saw sales of over £2,200, an increase of over 30% on the previous corresponding quarter. In July, annual sales passed the £8,000 mark for the first time. Much of this was put down to bread, with sales of over 1,500 loaves a week, and coal with 29 tons sold a week. The 417 members were paid a dividend of 2s 9d in the pound. The society's three-story building had extensive cellaring, shopping, an assembly room, bakery and stabling, and alongside six cottages fronting onto Park Road. Market gardener William James was now the secretary and Richard Knight the storekeeper.

At its 60th quarterly meeting, in October 1888, the Co-operative continued to show improved figures.

Sales for the quarter were £2,203, an increase of £314 over the previous year's corresponding quarter; sales for the year were £8,490 an increase of almost £1,500, and a dividend of 2s 7d was paid. In the quarter, ten new members were enrolled, nine left, but seven of them saw the error of their ways and re-joined, making the total 340.

By the third quarter of 1889, sales were up to £9,531 and membership to 454. The society made an expansion of their business by agreeing an arrangement with an un-named draper in the town whereby members would receive their usual dividends on purchases made at the shop. The year saw a clear £300 nett profit and dividends were now 2s 3d, later rising to 2s 10d.

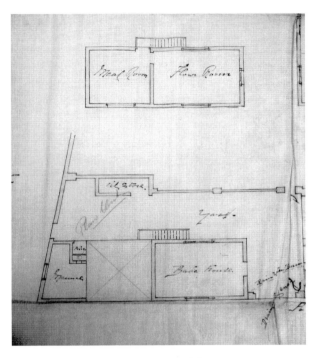

The bake-house had a meal-room and flour-room on its upper floor. At one end was a privvy and manure storage area, and across the yard was an oil store.
(Warwick County Records Office CR 2487/55)

Despite the generally depressed state of trade in town, a new shop, considered *"quite an acquisition"*, opened in The Square in the summer of 1887 and caused a stir. Blythe Brothers of Coventry and Nuneaton opened to sell fish, game and poultry. William Ball had rebuilt the shop front, which now had a one sheet of plate glass window with a ventilation grill at the top, and installed a marble slab to display the wares; *"A capital shop front."* There was a special bar for oysters when in season. The shop *"...will keep in stock everything that can be obtained at any first class shop in Leamington, Coventry or Birmingham. It is hoped that a first class shop like this will obviate the necessity of many of the upper ten of Kenilworth going out of town to make their purchases."*

Six weeks after opening, Blythe Brothers became the centre of attention by displaying a salmon, frozen in a 2cwt block of ice. All were apparently perplexed as to how it got in there until it was explained that the ice had been made by artificial means. In August they were advertising grouse for sale at 10s 6d a brace and partridge at 4s or 5s a brace.

*   *   *

At the January 1887 Board meeting, Dr Wynter raised the question as to what the town should do with regard to Queen Victoria's Golden Jubilee later that year. Kenilworth was not large enough to receive official notices from London for guidance, but Chairman William Evans was against the frittering away of public money and wished to see a meal provided for every man, woman and child in town. It was decided a committee should be formed to discuss possibilities.

The three suggestions it arrived at six weeks later were that the day should be public holiday, a meal and amusements should be provided, and that a start should be made on Abbey Fields becoming pleasure grounds by the building of a promenade opposite Abbey Hill. The promenade, being seen as only for the benefit of the wealthy that lived in Abbey Hill, was thought to be "*a ridiculous idea*", and far better suggestions for the Abbey Fields were provided. These included making a boating lake, "*...the pond exists, all we need is the water...*", which would even increase board revenue by the granting of licences, and properly-made pathways could be created along the stream from Townpool to the Castle, but of course the most popular suggestion was the building of swimming baths.

Despite the clamour, by mid-March all the suggestions of anything permanent being arranged by the Board had been discarded, but this did not stop individuals from their own attempts. Probably the most prestigious offer came from Edwin H Lingen Barker who was one of those totally against the idea of a promenade. As his and his father's "subscription" for the jubilee, he presented an impressive water-fountain design that, he suggested, should be erected in The Square. He no longer lived in Kenilworth but his business partner, Ernest Morris, lived at Waverley House in Southbank Road and it was he who would oversee construction. The massive structure was "*...for man and beast, with an illuminated fountain above and a reflecting lamp above that. No-one need be thirsty again.*" The design was described by Barker's friend, Sir Gilbert Scott, as "*Both elegant in form and original in conception.*" As Scott had died in 1878, it must have been an old design. It was claimed that there was nothing like it in the United Kingdom, nor probably in the world. The design was put in the window of Mr Dickenson's shop. The cost of the marble and stone alone was put at £300, but a smaller version would cost £250 all-inclusive, less still if the stone could be provided at cost from a local quarry. Barker claimed his idea was "*...the most reasonable and feasible project for commemorating the Jubilee year as yet presented to the Kenilworth public.*" In June, Clarendon agreed to donate all the necessary stonework for free and Morris pleaded for donations to be sent to either bank, but the scheme did not come to fruition.

A suggestion, which was actually executed, was the planting of three lime trees in The Square. Under the supervision of the road surveyor, this was carried out by William Sutton, William Anstey and William Mander, and soon became the subject of wisecracks. Due to its shape, The Square had already become known as "The Triangle" and the planting soon gave it the name "The Tree-angle", and it was also remarked that the trees were planted by "*three sweet Williams.*" One of the limes even "wrote" a letter to the newspaper on behalf of "*the tree-o.*" Despite the amusement, it was generally agreed that at least individuals had succeeded, where the Board had failed, in providing something permanent.

At the end of April, the now disregarded promenade idea was officially withdrawn, and plans were progressing for the provision of a meal. Clarendon had given permission for free use of the Castle grounds for one day. The town had been divided into six areas with two committee members responsible for each. They toured their zones to obtain donations for a public meal, and to ascertain the likely turnout. The income from the collection was almost £110, and the estimate for attendance was 750 adults; it had been decided to provide a tea for all schoolchildren, who also numbered about 750. Augustine Styles of the Queen and Castle Hotel calculated that he could provide a meal for 1s 4d per head without beer and 1s 6d with and it was decided to go with the cheaper option due to the teetotallers. Allocated for each child was 7d, which was for a tea and a commemorative medal, even though this was regarded as excessive by some, as most towns and cities were spending only 4d per child. It was decided that adults should apply for a meal ticket at a pre-arranged place in each of the districts and to help with this an additional committee member was allocated to each area, bringing those directly involved to 18. It was questioned how many of the working classes would wish to take up the offer as the "*...labourer or artisan will lose half a day's pay which is 1s 3d or 2s as the case may be.*" After a discussion, the Board's own employees were to be given the whole day off with pay, which cost the town almost £1.

The eventual number of meal applicants was 531 from St.Nicholas Parish and 193 from St.John's giving a total remarkably close to the estimate of 750. The number of schoolchildren was almost 800. The children's tea and medals, supplied by an unnamed town tradesman for 16s a gross, was not seen as having any problems, but providing the adult meal in a public place was. It was questioned whether Styles had the capability, as he was already committed to feeding the 400 Oddfellows, but no other hotelier in town was interested. It was alternatively suggested that perhaps food should be made available for each family to have a meal at home instead, but this went against the principle of the plans. Styles was very confident of his capabilities and agreed to provide, now for 1s 6d a head, a meal of boiled and roast beef, mutton, veal and ham, vegetables and plum pudding, the potatoes and pudding being hot. He would provide plates but the diners would have to bring their own knives and forks, and the committee would provide the tent. A seating plan was drawn up with about 20 sitting around each of the 34 tables with three waiters at each and about a dozen carvers. 22 of the committee volunteered as waiters, leaving a shortfall of about 80, and so each was asked to arrange the services of two ladies to help. On the day, the waiters and carvers were to wear red, white and blue rosettes.

A sub-committee had been formed to arrange sports events in an Abbey Field loaned by butcher Joseph

Roberts for the day. The 34 events were to include; *"A one-mile race, a half-mile race, races for old men over 60, egg-and-spoon races for women, skipping races for girls, jockey races, the novelty of which will be that for half the race the jockey will have to carry the horse, consolation races, pole-climbing, putting the stone, cricket-ball throwing and other athletic feats."* William Pears had been elected captain in charge of the sports, which were strictly for Kenilworth people over 14 years of age.

The two Oddfellows' lodges in town, The Dudley and the Elizabethan, had decided to mark the occasion by parading through town to a morning church service and Wynter suggested that the Board members and fire brigade should join them and this was agreed. There were reservations as to whether the two lodges, totalling over 400 people, and everybody else would fit into the church.

Styles had managed to procure the services of the band of the 2nd Battalion of Coventry Volunteers - ten of them would play at the Castle and ten at the Oddfellows' meal.

"Jubilee day, June 21st, was celebrated right loyally in Kenilworth. The day was beautifully fine and Kenilworth, always lovely, looked its very best. From an early hour people were astir putting finishing touches to the decorations." *"In most cases these amounted to flags; mottoes and evergreens being the exception."* *"...several of the houses looked very nice especially Mrs Smith's on Rosemary Hill. At the National school, the decorations were most elaborate and effective. The iron palisading was decorated with flags and several mottoes adorned the building including - The Royal Jubilee Cricket score - 50 not out."*

The parade assembled at St.John's at 9.00 a.m., and the Oddfellows and other societies, the Board members, fire brigade with their engine and other parishioners, were headed by the Coventry Volunteer band with Kenilworth's own drum and fife band in the middle of the procession. The route taken was through Castle End, Abbey Hill, Albion Street, Park Road and New Street to the church. *"The parade was quite a sensation, but why on earth was the fire engine included in it? If it was necessary to take it to church, why did not the Local Board men take their water-carts?"* They were all met by the Reverend Alfred Binnie and his choir, already in voice. *"An admirable and suitable sermon by our worthy vicar was attentively listened to."* The collection amounted to a little over £7 and was donated to the assistance of distressed clergymen.

Despite the misgivings, the most important aspect of the day, the meal served at 1.00 p.m., was a resounding success. *"The whole arrangements seemed perfect...gave universal satisfaction."* The female waiters came in for particular attention: *"To see the fair element bustling about and trying to outdo each other in their attention to the seated ones afforded a most pleasing charm."* Local photographer William Kimberley took two pictures of the scene inside the tent. Various societies had meals at different venues around town. The Oddfellows at the Queen and Castle also had their own sports.

The 400 children of the National School assembled at the front of the school building and sung the National Anthem under the leadership of Headmaster H J Stone, and, headed by the Drum and Fife band and a splendid banner, made their way to Mr Hodges' field behind the vicarage for their tea. At St.John's School, the 204 pupils assembled at 2.30 and marched to a field loaned by Edward Mander for games and races. Promptly at 4.00, they returned to their schoolroom for their tea, which had *"...in addition to the usual cake and bread and butter, veal and ham pies."*

Next came the sports in the Abbey Fields in front of a large number of spectators. The races were well-contested and caused great amusement, the most popular being the steeple-chase (the start of which was also photographed by Kimberley), obstacle race, blindfold race and *"...catching the bell man caused roars of laughter."* *"Joseph Young was quite a feature in the sports, causing more fun than anything else, running in most races, and winning one."* Refreshments in the fields were provided by Mr Baulcombe. At 10.00 p.m., an hour after the sports finished, the day was brought to a close by the lighting of a huge bonfire on Castle Green. There were attempts at illuminations: the vicarage displayed some Chinese lanterns, Lythe House had *"...some pretty lights..."*, and all the windows of the National School were lit from ten until twelve.

"Not a single unpleasant incident marred the pleasures of the day, and right loyally and successfully did Kenilworth celebrate the Queen's jubilee."

Despite his eye-catching performance at the sports, within a month Joseph Young was back in trouble; having been thrown out of the Bowling Green Hotel, (although it had been re-named the Abbey Hotel, the old name was still used), four times in a day, he was arrested for constantly ringing the doorbell of a private house. Having been described as the worst character in town, he was once more fined £1.

* * *

The effect of the tannery closure on the town was clear; with the capability to employ 100 men, who with their wives and families would involve about 400 people, or about one in ten of the whole community, the potential income of local shops was down about £100 a week. Even whilst closed, the deserted tannery remained in the news: in May 1887 it was used by the fire brigade in an exercise to practise their response to an imaginary fire, and potential alternative uses were discussed, including the suggestion that it would be a *"splendid institution for carrying out...cremations"* whilst such was the *"superabundance"* of fruit that William Sutton was surprised that no one had tried to make wine, and a jam factory was suggested as another possibility. There was also potential as a brewery, and someone even suggested that the smells from the sewer system could be diverted up the chimney. There had also been talk of the site being cleared. It was difficult for people to understand how the tannery could fail when Henry Street had made a fortune from his fellmonger's works and it was suggested that perhaps a railway siding would prove beneficial.

One explanation why the premises remained empty was provided in the *Kenilworth Advertiser*: *"The *company which Mr Clarke tried to float about 15 months ago, but was defeated by the apathy - if one said strong opposition of the upper classes - one would not be far wrong. The gentry thought it would spoil Kenilworth as a residential place but what good those who are now here do to the tradespeople and working men, I will leave them to say." "People in high quarters are averse to seeing the tanyard started again. (But) there are plenty of places out of reach and smell of the tan."*

Eventually in March 1888, almost three years after its closure, its future as a tannery was assured. It was announced that a new firm, Thomas Day and Company Limited, were to take the works on a seven year lease from William Clarke. *"The fine old landmark of the midlands...in a very short space of time will emit its smoke as in days gone by...old fashioned English bark-tanned leather is to be manufactured as in days of yore when Kenilworth held its own against any tannage in England."* On Thursday 22nd March at 11 a.m., the tannery bell was rung, not to call men to work, but in celebration of the news. Flags were flown in Castle End; tradesmen, particularly shop-keepers who had been struggling for so long, could look to a brighter future, and a celebration dinner was held at the Kings Arms of William Clarke who *"...has done all he could to get the tanyard into work." "May long life and a prosperous one be the lot of our new tannery...our most important hive of industry."*

Renovation work began on some parts of the buildings. Scaffolding and ladders were put around the chimney to make repairs and when finished it looked *"...quite gay with its red paint..."*, and a youth climbed the scaffolding, an act which *"...could have caused him injuries that would have spoilt his life."* Kimberley took several photographs of the workmen suitably posed. By now, the old hands were anxiously awaiting the re-opening.

Shortly before the tannery re-opened, a dinner was held in May 1888 at the Kings Arms to celebrate its now secure-looking future, but despite being seen as the beginning of a change in the whole town's fortunes, the meal was not as well attended as expected. There was only one tradesman from High Street and even Thomas Day did not attend, his excuse being that he had only arrived in town the previous day.

Dr Wynter took the chair and remarked how trade was so much better twenty five years ago when the tannery was flourishing and he wished for the same again. From his own experience working amongst them *"...the labouring classes had long and patiently borne their distress..."*, but it took no time for Wynter to start criticising the Local Board over the Abbey Fields affair.

In March 1886, the lease of the Whitemoor brickworks, in the hands of Walter Lockhart, was taken on by the Leamington and Lillington Brick Company and its chairman John Fell, the builder of Kenilworth's sewer system. The agreement with Lockhart included a £1,000 payment for much of the equipment he had installed on site.

Despite the owner himself being a builder, in April 1887 the company advertised for tenders to take down and rebuild its brick kilns, they had to be submitted by the 20th. It is probable that this was when seven small Skotch kilns were replaced by a Sercombe continuous kiln. The new kiln had fourteen chambers, which could hold up to a quarter of a million bricks. The kiln was 132ft long and 51ft across and the bricks were in here for fourteen days. At one end was a tapered square chimney, 115ft high, 12ft square at its base and 6ft 6ins square at the top. Into this, via four draught holes, was fed the smoke from the underground fires of the drying sheds; these had just been increased from 4,000 sq ft to 12,000 sq ft and were heated by exhaust steam. The bricks spent two days in there. The new kiln had been built alongside the railway siding, and another siding was built along the opposite side. A raised platform was built around the kiln to enable the loading of the bricks directly into railway wagons. Other facilities made possible the loading of carts for more local deliveries. The kiln and chimney were made from about ¾ million bricks and cost about £1,000. About 50 tons of coal were used in a week and this was fed into funnels from the top of the kiln through *"iron capped apertures."*

Just prior to Christmas 1888, John Reynolds was severely injured when buried by a landslip as he was digging out clay. Fellow workmen had great difficulty in extracting him.

Thomas Hawley's residence high on Park Hill overlooked the land between Whitemoor Road and the railway. For at least forty years it had been in use for fruit produce, primarily a cherry orchard for William Penn, and when Hawley bought the land in 1880 it was in the occupation of another market gardener, Henry Clarke (51). Clarke included strawberries in his produce and was helped by his son, also Henry (18). It was known as Spring Gardens, a name shared with nearby Richard Whateley's similar business.

In December 1881, Hawley successfully applied for permission to build brick kilns on part of the garden ground but, perhaps due to the state of trade, Hawley never took up the option. Then in 1888, he entered into a mortgage arrangement with a George Dall who took ownership of the site. Dall and his partner Mason quickly set about building kilns and sheds for a brickworks on the part of the site nearest to the bridge over the railway and also successfully applied to have a railway siding installed in June 1888 at a cost of £86. This suggests a large concern was intended from the outset, and a degree of experience on behalf of the company.

As work was nearing completion in September 1888, the Local Board enquired as to why no plan had been submitted for approval. In a most apologetic letter, Mason and Dall explained that they took over the earlier approved plans when they purchased the site and had been told that as permission had been granted already for a brickworks they believed there was no need to apply again, but they agreed to send a copy of their plans anyway. The Board were not sure if, or by how much, the bye-laws had been disregarded, but all members were sure of the sincerity of the brick-yard proprietors.

By January 1889, brickmaking was under way at *"the new hive of industry"* and there were hopes that soon additional workmen would be taken on. Bricks were made inscribed "Mason and Dall". The works did not occupy the whole site, and Henry Clarke remained in business.

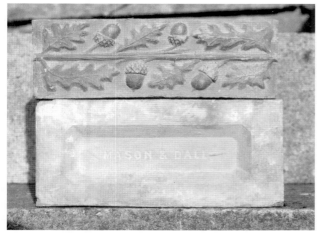

The short-lived operation under Mason and Dall produced the most attractively decorated of Kenilworth's bricks.

By the summer of 1889, Percy Richard Croydon was involved with the business and it became known as The Cherry Orchard Brick Company, with "and tile" sometimes added to the title.

In January 1889, with no reason given, the Whitemoor brickworks was closed throwing twenty people out of work. This was a blow, coming so soon after the start of the Cherry Orchard works and re-start of the tannery, but within months it reopened.

With a year still left to run, in April 1891, the Leamington and Lillington surrendered the lease of the Whitemoor works back to the Hawkes family, now Henry. This would appear to have been a hasty withdrawal as Hawkes had to pay £50 compensation for "...movable and other effects belonging to (The Leamington and Lillington Brick Co) at the brick-yard." Henry Hawkes himself now took on the yard, in partnership with Bolton Joberns; Joberns came from a Staffordshire brickmaking family and had brothers and his father manufacturing in Aldridge.

In the Spring of 1892, there was another accident due to a clayfall; a Mr Miller had his leg broken.

Richard Robbins died suddenly from heart disease at his home The Hollies, on 18th June 1887. Amongst his possessions were three carriages, a bay gelding, and in the cellar, 260 dozen bottles of wine. His partnership with John Powers was dissolved and once more Francis Robbins was in control of the mill,

but it was in decline. The rates, which in the 1860s were over £200, were now down to just £60. By August 1890, the mill had closed. *"The two flour mills are relics of the past, they used to work day and night but have closed."* The effect of the closure was devastating for one family as was revealed at an inquest at the Engine Inn in January 1891. Elderly William Humphries, with poor eyesight, failed to find work once the mill closed and he could only support himself and his wife Elizabeth on hand-outs. Parish relief gave him 2s 6d and two loaves a week and his son, who himself was not always in regular work and was struggling, gave 2s a week and from this they had to pay rent which had just been lowered to 1s a week. Two visits to the Warwick Board of Guardians towards the end of 1890 had seen their allowance increase by 6d. Miss May sent them 2cwt of coal and the vicar 3cwt to see them through the winter and in early January the curate Mr Bissett gave them a ticket for 1s 6d to spend at George Church's. This was the couple's entire income. Elizabeth became so weak that when her husband bought 6d worth of meat she did not have the strength to eat it and it had to be made into soup. Despite their neighbour Ann Harris sometimes providing breakfast and tea, Elizabeth became ill and died. Of those that knew of the Humphries' plight, the vicar claimed he did all that he could, the son was praised as he could do no more.

The mill however was not empty for long. By the autumn of 1891, it was let to John George Eagles (44), a Leamington oil-cake manufacturer. The lease was for £100 for seven years and in addition, Eagles took some garden ground and two seven-acre meadows. The materials of the mill were valued at about £500. Eagles moved to Kenilworth to live, in Eversfield in Southbank Road.

Coventry-born William Thompson Pears JP, then aged about fifty, had moved in to Kenilworth Hall probably c1885 when the widowed Mrs Dawes left. Pears too was widowed. His daughter Frances, born in Liverpool in 1875, came with him. Pears was related to the Woodcock family; he was the nephew of A H Pears and Edward Woodcock (brother of Jane and Colonel Woodcock) had married a daughter of the same man. In 1893, William Pears bought the mill at Mill End, and its associated land up to Townpool Bridge, from Richard Robbins' daughter Mabel, for £3,420.

Walter Lockhart's brother Edgar, living in Stoneleigh Road, started a coal club in 1883. Customers paid 1s a week for coal that cost between 10s and 15s a ton. Lockhart delivered to Kenilworth on Saturdays, and Stoneleigh, Ashow and Wootton fortnightly on a Monday. A L&NWR weight ticket accompanied each load. It is not known if he was still at the brickworks at this time. In 1885 he set himself up as a *"Commission agent, rents and debts collected"* but early the next year Walter placed an advert in the local press declaring Edgar was no longer collecting orders and debts for him; orders were put in the hands of Joseph Wilson and then Thomas Paxon. In September 1886, Edgar was advertising himself as sole agent for the district for "Lucas, Blackwell and Arkwright", the Leamington brewers, and selling beer for between 30s and 60s, a barrel. This was in direct competition with Walter, an agent for "Hunt and Edmunds" of Banbury. Edgar had by now moved to a more prestigious address, Robsart Villa in Station Road, but he was soon in financial trouble as his annual income of £125 was about half his outlay, a path that led him to the bankruptcy court in early 1889. His liabilities amounted to £331 and his assets were entered as nil. Even his household furniture was not his own as it had been left to his wife under her father's will. Edgar attributed his position to *"...sickness, expenses in excess of income, and loss of position..."*, the last may be a reference to his work at the brickworks. In September 1889, Edgar and Mrs Lockhart decided to leave town and their effects were advertised for sale at the Assembly Room, a second advertisement stressed that the effects were those of Mrs Lockhart.

On 9th February 1886, the Green Man had a new occupant, H A Jones, a former Kenilworth resident but lately of Coventry. To mark the occasion he held a supper for friends and neighbours. Jones declared it gave him great pleasure to be back amongst his friends and that his *"...sole object would be to conduct the house well and respectably and only sell articles of the best quality."* Beers were brewed on the premises. Jones was in a partnership with William Bird, a Coventry man who had been working for the London and North Western Railway and who put £40 into the venture. The arrangement was for Bird to *"...manage the business and to pay the balance of his share out of his proportion of the profits."* However, Jones repudiated this agreement. Bird, having left a good position, bought the business from him, the money being lent on the security of the lease. Having to trade on this borrowed capital during a period of depression, and having *"heavy family expenses"* Bird was soon in trouble and was declared bankrupt in spring 1889, with gross liabilities if £1,251, but with assets of only £591. Bird had managed to continue the Green Man's tradition of brewing its own beers. The new landlord was James Glenn.

*   *   *

The Cycle Club appears to have been responsible for the inauguration for what became a local entertainment phenomenon, the Kenilworth Amateur Minstrels. They made their debut in July 1885 at a concert to raise funds for the cyclists. The first part of the programme was made up of songs and glees performed mostly by Kenilworth people, Mr Overton, Miss Keatley, the Misses Robertson, as well as minstrel members. The second half of the event was given over to The Minstrels; Mr Kerfoot - tambourine, C Oakley - bones, W Anderton - banjo, E Gregory - guitar, W Heatley - piccolo, T Cotson - flute, William Riley - interlocutor, T Gardner - cello, M Riley - 2nd violin, Edward Stokes - 2nd violin, Mr Hollis - 1st violin, T Bushill - tambourine, C Hardin - bones, A W Stokes - bones, and they were accompanied on piano by William Riley's wife, Hannah.

In great anticipation, the crowd was unexpectedly large and as the *"coloured gentlemen"* took the stage their *"...appearance and get up awakened so much favourable comment."* The town had not seen a performance like it. They started with a mixture of English, Scottish and Irish airs strung together, but soon settled into the routine for which such troupes were popular, performing Camptown Races and Golden Slippers amongst others. There was a continual stream of witty puns and comments by the sidesmen but all too soon, the performance was over. The show was chaired by the cycle club's president, Dr Wynter, who expressed the hope that it would not be long before the minstrels performed a whole show of their own. He also brought laughter by admitting that the only time he had been on a bicycle he *"...got up one side, and very quickly came down on the other."* Cyclists continued to cause problems on the roads as they *"...whirled past pedestrians without the slightest notification of their presence."* It was expected that the bye-law regarding the ringing of bells was to be reinforced.

The Kenilworth Amateur Minstrels' reputation grew and they gave performances in Allesley, Ashow, Stoneleigh and Westwood Heath amongst other places. They were particularly popular for charitable performances and raised funds for the Convalescent Home and town cricket club. Their members included a number of swimmers and four members of the parish choir. They also played cricket matches, in costumes and character, notably against the fire brigade who were in their own uniforms, and the Town club.

But by early 1888, their appearances were beginning to become fewer. *"Have the Minstrels expired? This is the worst season for entertainments that Kenilworth has ever known."* They survived, but 1889 was to be a difficult year for the troupe. In April they learned of the death, after a brief illness, of Hannah Riley, aged just 41, the pianist wife of Minstrel William. Six of the Minstrel troupe, John and James Heatley, Gregory, Paxton, Baulcombe and Woods, acted as pallbearers. Hannah had endeared herself to all who came in contact with her due to her bright and happy temperament. Later the same year, founder member H Hollis emigrated and stalwart Thomas King left for Glasgow. E B Woods was another who left town, but with new members, rehearsals continued and the new season opened at the Assembly Rooms shortly before Christmas. It included a debut for P Piggott, a powerful tenor. Despite their losses during the year, the Minstrels produced *"...as mirth-creating a performance as any of preceding seasons."* Mr Hughes was now the general manager, being singer, actor, musician and orator, and was a favourite with the audience.

* * *

Fire brigade Captain, Dr Atkinson, was instrumental in arranging a grand Warwickshire fire brigade display at his friend Lord Leigh's Stoneleigh Abbey. On 27th August 1889 at 2.30 p.m., the participating brigades began to assemble outside the Virgins and Castle and thirty minutes later embarked upon their parade to Stoneleigh via "*The Bowling Green Hill...*", Castle End, and through Thickthorn to the Grecian Lodge. The procession was led by a 4-horse coach "Hero" with the Coventry Silver Band aboard, followed by ten men of the Coventry Brigade in their new uniforms copied from the Metropolitan Brigade, and their steamer. Behind were the Warwick and Hatton brigades with their steamers, followed by Leamington, Southam, Kenilworth (with the largest contingent, 20 men), and Stoneleigh with their manual engines. At the rear were representatives from the Nuneaton, Banbury and Harbury brigades without their engines.

After Lord Leigh's welcoming speech, the brigades were put through various drills as a demonstration, not competition. The steamers were impressive, getting 100lbs of pressure in a little over ten minutes; the Coventry engine used four hoses at once, and the jet from the Warwick engine reached a height of over 130ft. The steamers, with just three men operating, could throw 400 gallons of water a minute, and the manuals, one with up to thirty men operating it, could at best manage 100 gallons. A meal was provided at 6.30 in the riding school and after a few brief speeches and toasts, the evening concluded with dancing.

The Kenilworth brigade issued a circular explaining the expenses incurred in maintaining their standards and the financial support that they needed. It mentioned that their uniforms were now over ten years old.

Walter Lockhart lost his seat on The Board in 1887, at what proved to be the last election for four years, but members continued to come and go. Dr Wynter resigned due to lack of time: "*The whole community are indebted to Dr. Wynter for the zealous and indefatigable way in which he always discharged his duties, he always had the welfare of the town at heart.*" It was suggested that Lockhart should resume his position, but he was overlooked in preference to Dr Atkinson. However, Wynter put himself back up for re-election in 1889; to save the cost involved in an election Bagshaw resigned, allowing Wynter to return unopposed. Atkinson later resigned, allowing Edmund Kemp Bourne (30) to gain a seat as another unopposed, unelected candidate. The death of Augustine Styles in 1890 was to allow Bagshaw to regain his place, and so the election of 1891 with seven candidates provided a little excitement. Thomas Day had rapidly become very popular in his handling of the tannery business and was a successful candidate, along with William Evans who retained his position as Chairman, market gardener Richard Whateley, and Frederick Wyer, of the Pleasance, Ladies Hills, who had retired as a Civil Servant having served in India. The three who were not elected were Walter Lockhart, William Anstey and bank manager Harry Francis.

When Town Crier William Drury died aged 67 in September 1888, he was one of the last comb-makers in town. He was the son of comb-maker Joseph Drury, first of New Row then Albion Row, who had his own business back in the industry's heyday of the 1830s. Having been involved from his early years, William had taken it on at the age of 31 when his father died in 1852. William became town crier in the early 1880s and retained his position despite gaining several convictions for being drunk and disorderly.

William Jeacock, born 1831, was the son of Bull Hill blacksmith Thomas and he followed in his father's footsteps, continuing the family business after Thomas died in 1867. In the late 1870s, William took up bill-posting. The custom of the Town Crier wearing a uniform had died out, but with the appointment of Jeacock after the death of William Drury in 1888, the custom was revived. After discussing several possibilities, the Board opted for "*A handsome green frock coat bound with a profusion of gold lace and tall hat with gold lace band, dark trousers and vest.*" The right sleeve carried "*...the Kenilworth badge, the Clarendon Bear and Ragged Staff...*" in gold on a shield. This was a copy of the badge on the carved marble mantle-piece in the Castle gatehouse. His first public appearance in the outfit was in January 1889 when he announced the forthcoming distributions under the Duchess of Dudley charity.

The couple lived in Priory Cottage in High Street. The old family smithy at the top of Bull Hill was facing demolition in August 1889: few would regret "*...the downfall and disappearance of this dirty looking, placard covered, worn-out smithy.*" Unfortunately, it was discovered that it was largely responsible for holding up the cottage to which it was attached, still occupied by an old lady, and so supports had to be erected to stop it falling.

In 1892, William Jeacock fell down a flight of stairs and sustained a serious injury. He was attended to by Dr Wynter. He had another accident in the summer of 1897 whilst "posting a bill" up his ladder in the Abbey Fields. The ladder broke, he fell, and remained unconscious for four hours. At six the next morning, his wife was seen doing his billposting, and it was enquired as to whether she would also take the role of town crier! After this, the couple were regularly seen driving around in a pony and trap for William to make his proclamations.

* * *

The paths around the church were in a poor condition and in mid-1886 the decision was made to repair them using asphalt in the same manner to some recently laid at Emscote. Being Kenilworth's first attempt at such a surface, it is not surprising that a lack of experience showed. Instead of laying the path early in the week and fencing it off, the work was done late in the week and left unguarded. The result was that the Reverend Alfred Binnie diplomatically asked the Board not to "*experiment*" with his paths as "*...the mats, hassocks and floors of many pews are well covered in tar.*" "*A score of ladies have avowed vengeance (on the churchwardens) for spoiling their dresses.*" It was generally thought that not enough gravel had been added to the mix, but a month later, there were similar problems at a funeral; the paths were *"in a disgraceful state"* and tar was once again taken into the church on boots. There were other problems in the churchyard, in the following summer it was reported that sheep were eating the flowers left on the graves.

The path from Bridge Street to the church was the first in town to be asphalted.

In January 1886, Edward Smith obtained approval to build himself some new premises at the rear of his house and wife's milliners shop. It was a two storey building - the lower floor was used to house a trap, cart and coal supply, and stairs led to the upper which was split between an office and storeroom. Edward died just three months later on 2nd April 1886. He not only had a good reputation in Kenilworth but also in Coventry, notably in Stivichall, where he had built a number of houses. The business was carried on by his son, Joseph Lawrence Smith, but it retained the name of Edward Smith and Son. As Edward's grave was being dug alongside the gatehouse, more Abbey remains were found *"...consisting of a chamber, with a very fine groined roof with three passages leading out of it, one of them going to the old monks hole..."* but these were covered up before a local antiquary could make a full examination.

It was inevitable that as graves were dug in the latest churchyard extension, relics of the Abbey would be found. When the first grave of 1887 was dug, a skeleton was found *"...the position of which proved conclusively that it was not the remains of a priest."*

It was not just in the churchyard that interesting discoveries were being made. In August 1887, new licensee Charles Mealin (44) made some alterations to the Bear and Ragged Staff that it was claimed would

"...make quite a feature in that neighbourhood, altering the old-fashioned looking Bear into a smart inn." During excavations, at a depth of eight feet, the workmen came across pieces of wood and oak beams and parts of stag horns which led to the conclusion that the site was once a pond or lake. Mealin put the finds on display. In 1888 The Statute fair was held in the Bear Field and there were now a much smaller number of stalls. The *"...amusements were confined to rifle shooting and the improved merry-go-round."* There were also the *"wretched squibs"* and one young lady, after squirting a couple of young lads, was embarrassingly *"punished"* by being kissed by both of them, and their friends!

The gravestone of Edward Smith.

In the autumn of 1888, more discoveries were made whilst digging graves in the old part of the churchyard. Window jambs, mullions and tracery, stained glass rich in ruby, amber and other colours were found, and they were put in the gatehouse in the churchyard. When the foundations of a wall running at right angles to the monastery gateway were found, it was quickly suggested that a full excavation should be made. Here too were found stained and painted glass, as well as tiles, and these were added to the gatehouse collection.

The original grand scheme for the Abbey Fields was in disarray. A plan had been drawn up showing a lake with boats upon it and the park laid out with a cricket field; this reportedly cost £100 and was now hanging in the Board offices, but as rents were collected for the fields, members of the public still did not have access to them. The plots around the outside bought by the syndicate had so far had only one house built upon them, and yet the Board intended to borrow another £425 *"...for the purposes of public walks through their grounds."*

The Local Government Board had written to say that it would be necessary to hold a public inquiry into the Board's proposal.

The inquiry was held at the Board's offices on the last day of January 1889 by J T Harrisson. Although it had been claimed that the sum would also include a provision for laying out the fields as a park, it was in fact purely for the purchase of land, 3 acres 1 rood 2 perches surrounding St.Nicholas Church and yard, roughly the area covering the Abbey remains, that was in the hands of Joseph H Burbery, William Evans, George Turner and John Bagshaw. One particular attraction of this additional area was that it would enable the Board a make a 26ft wide road into the park from High Street, just outside the cemetery wall. If the Board did not buy the land, it was likely that a builder would, despite the fact that *"...many houses have been built since 1884, but a great number are unoccupied."*

Harrisson was somewhat taken aback when he realised that the fields already purchased were still rented out and had yet to be thrown open to the public, who did not even have the right to go across a field. The cost of the repayments minus the rent received now left a deficit of £125 per annum. He asked, *"Do I understand that the rates are burdened £125 a year for no good to the public?"* and was received with applause. It was pointed out that the Abbey Fields now cost 2½d in the £ but a new cemetery would have cost 6d in the £ and so it was in fact a saving, but Harrisson was not convinced. He did not see what benefit to the town the land was in its current state except for the pleasure of paying for it for future generations. *"If I were an inhabitant...I would like to enjoy it now."* He was also unsure as to whether the Board could legally exclude the public once the Board had made the purchase. These comments brought both applause and laughter from the spectators who were clearly against the Board.

Mr Bagshaw claimed that the total scheme that the Board had in mind, presumably the one hanging on the office wall, would cost a shilling rate and that was why the fields had not been turned into a park. It was stated that there was no real opposition to the new application but in fact, many thought that the money would be better spent on what the majority really wanted - the swimming baths. The Inspector concluded by saying he was considerably surprised that there was no park yet, but the Clerk assured him that a public meeting would soon be taking place on the subject.

The Local Government Board granted the Boards' application and the loan was arranged with the Prudential Insurance Company at a rate of 3¾% over 50 years, amounting to £18 18s 11d a year, and so another area of the Abbey Fields was conveyed to the Board, and the syndicate were now out of pocket by a little over £5,000.

Following Harrison's observation that the fields should be opened up to the public, the Board wrote to the Secretary of the Local Government Board in Whitehall, asking for clarification, and permission to let the fields *"...until such time as in the opinion of (the) Board, it will be advantageous to the inhabitants of Kenilworth and the public generally that such lands should be laid out as public walks or pleasure grounds."* The reply was quickly received: "Under section 177 of the Public Health Act, 1875, (they) hereby consent to the letting by the Kenilworth local board...of the lands recently acquired...for public walks and pleasure grounds." The Board thus had permission from Whitehall to keep the fields closed.

On Wednesday 10th April 1889, the priory boundary wall was uncovered *"...with a doorway leading to an underground passage, running apparently in the direction of the old monastery."* The doorway was 2ft wide and had an arched top formed of three stones. In the doorway were various pieces of tile, one of which was *"beautifully ornamented"*, and a clay jug which was unfortunately broken as it was moved. Carved stone, part of a window frame, was found with some large bones. There was much anticipation as to what might be found in the passageway, and during the following week it was dug out and the outer wall of the monastery exposed. One block of tiles, measuring 18ins by 6ins was taken out intact, stained glass was found as well and all were carefully kept by the sexton James Buswell.

To some extent, these discoveries were expected, but the next certainly was not. In the first week of July 1889, whilst a grave was being dug, a large canoe-shaped pig of lead was found. Measuring 4ft 3½ins by 1ft 3½ins at its greatest breadth and 7½ins at its thickest, it weighed just over half a ton. In five places, it was marked with a stamp of an open crown and *"...a device resembling the broad arrow."* It was lying on the tiled floor of the priory and was soon identified as probably being part of the spoil of the priory roof. According to Mr Fretton of Coventry, it had been roughly cast in a hollow of loose sand. Fretton was of the opinion that the whole area should be subject to a proper excavation with relics removed and walls left as found, so that a plan could be made.

The news of the discoveries spread, articles appeared in newspapers, and archaeologists became regular visitors amongst the many sightseers. By August 1889, it was *"...possible to trace in a direct line the stone boundary wall of the old Priory, partly to the hospice or guest house. In another portion of the churchyard an arched passage, with mullioned stone walls and well preserved finials, has been laid open. A chamber of square dimensions, which was found some time ago, has been railed and affords a striking example of the skill and patience of the original builders."* By now, it had been decided to keep burials to another part of the churchyard and that excavations should be left to archaeologists. On the last Wednesday of October, the site was visited by Mr Hope, Honorary Secretary of the Royal Archaeology Society, and he made a tour accompanied by Reverend Alfred Binnie, Thomas Morris and W Jacks, the churchwardens William Evans and Joseph Roberts, and Mr Fretton. He suggested the sinking of shafts along the wall lines to find their extent and the ban on interments was extended to these areas. Mr Hope agreed as to the source of the block of lead and mentioned that it was the second found there; another found on the site previously was preserved at Stoneyhurst. It was expected to start a fund to finance future work.

It was becoming obvious that a more scientific

and organised excavation was needed and to this end, a meeting was held on 1st March 1890 at which the vicar, many members of the Board and other interested parties attended. The Society of Antiquaries Secretary, Mr W H St.John Hope, had by now prepared an extensive report. As several interments had already taken place, it was now impossible to open up the whole of the site, so Hope suggested removing all the debris down to the floor level of the Abbey and continuing burials under the well-preserved original floor tiling. He further suggested that all interesting stones found should be stored in the old gatehouse along with the remarkable pig of lead. The vicar announced that the Bishop had no objections to the area being excavated provided no damage was done to any of the remains. Replying to a question from Thomas Hawley, he also suggested that the cost of excavations should be met by public subscription. The meeting was adjourned so that more details of likely costs, and how the scheme would be carried out, could be ascertained.

In the meantime, some work continued under Fretton. The west and south walls of the abbey had been cleared down to the base "...the tiled floor being found nearly perfect." The western door had been cleared from earth six feet deep, and a stone bench ran along the exposed walls. The lack of Vestry or Board funds to finance the venture was lamented. It was also remarked that even more interesting remains were likely outside the churchyard wall and were untouched.

Test excavations continued in an attempt to discover the layout of the buildings. It was also decided that the tender for the excavation proper should be let locally and these were duly invited from Edward Smith and Son and William Ball, and were to include all fencing. Plans and specifications for the excavating were drawn up by T W Whitley, architect and surveyor of Coventry. He had already estimated that about 3,000 cartloads of material would have to be removed. In the event, Ball declined the invitation leaving the way clear for Smith who submitted two tenders, one of which included his own suggestion of putting 3ft-high fencing onto the existing wall to prevent vandalism during the excavations and to the churchyard afterwards. This was suggested as an alternative to the proposed temporary fence around the digging.

The removal of relics prompted some honest observations: "If the halls of the county and the homes of Kenilworth and the outhouses for ten miles around gave up their relics, the monastery might comfortably be rebuilt. A hundred and fifty years ago the main walls were standing very much in the condition that Kirkstall Abbey presents today." "In more recent years the curios dug up have been quietly appropriated by the digger whose cottage has the nucleus of a small museum." "The pavement of the Augustinian Priory would in time have graced the rockeries of the town in company with maimed teapots and stucco statues."

It was suggested that the building used as a stable and cowhouse should be turned into a museum, it "...already contains the old ducking stool stored away on an unreachable ledge." "Its first relic is ready, the lead coffin or coffer or what not discovered a month or two ago and not yet opened."

Another writer gave this account: "A few weeks ago, the sexton whilst digging a grave unearthed an arched doorway, which he thought was a drain, and it would have been bricked up but for the intervention of a passer by. A few days later the base of a column was unearthed but this time the burial took place. The sexton dug into some crypts some years ago and turned them into a vault."

The final decision to go ahead and accept Joseph Smith's tender for £140 was made at a parish room meeting on 9th May with Reverend Alfred Binnie taking the chair. It was perhaps apt that Smith was to undertake the task, as it was the burial of his father that uncovered stone-work that excited so much interest. It was agreed "To carry out an excavation scheme embracing all the most interesting portions of the discoveries and leaving the largest available space for burials, also the erection of a railing running from the vicarage garden to the entrance and bounding the newly enclosed part of the yard." Once formally passed, William Pears immediately pointed out some of the difficulties that would be involved. Firstly there would be the removal of the newly-estimated 1,000 cartloads of soil which would mean either leaving in one direction and going up a hill or in the other and risk damaging the Board's recently laid asphalt path. He also pointed out that the scheme included the laying out of a road through the churchyard sufficiently wide to carry out funerals. William Pears was also appointed treasurer to handle the subscriptions, which were now invited. A good start was made with the vicar promising £20, Pears and William Evans £10 each, and F Stanger-Leathes, F Wyer and Thomas Hawley £5 each.

"It is proposed to excavate the site of the church and the north cloister and a considerable part of the conventual buildings down to the floor level thus exposing the walls and pillars; to remove and preserve the tiles, to erect retaining walls to support the graves and parts of the churchyard already used for burials; to make good and cement the old walls and pillars; to spread the soil obtained by excavation over the lower part of the churchyard so as to make it on a proper level, and to construct an iron fence to preserve the runs from depredation and the churchyard from trespass, with a gate to afford access to the churchyard."

Part of the area of the churchyard excavated by Edward Smith and Son in 1890.

By June, the fund being collected by Thomas Morris at the Birmingham and Midland bank had reached

£128, almost entirely from Kenilworth people. It soon reached £147 and Smith announced he was to start work on Monday 16th June. He had taken on "...*a large number of hands...*", and the gravedigger confidently predicted that they would have "...*a very troublesome task.*"

Work began with the erection of notices warning against the theft of relics, and as expected, several were found very quickly. A stone head was amongst the first, as were several tiles with lettering on. Also disturbed was a wasp's nest, which was smoked out using burning straw, one man was badly stung twice. By August the excavation was nearing completion. Now exposed were the entrance and porch, north and south transepts, part of the chapel and annex, part of the south cloisters and north cloister walk, the nave and columns of the tower. It had proved necessary to dig at greater depths than expected. Many of the relics had been locked in the Tantara gate but were visible through the barred windows. The churchyard was by now being levelled, and old hollows in-filled. The boundary walls with palisades were under construction and some turf was being laid in completed areas. Smith was praised for the speedy and careful manner in which the work was done, there was not a single case of damage being done to the remains.

The excavated soil was used to raise the new area of the churchyard and a retaining wall was built. It was suggested that the adjacent barn could house the discovered relics.

There were large numbers of visitors to see the excavations and all local antiquities became of great interest. One of them was the contraption known as the ducking-stool, which had been stored in the rafters of the barn near the church "*for centuries*" and the tenant, Joseph Roberts, was only too pleased to show it to visitors, even though it was twenty feet off the ground. Quite unexpectedly, despite its location, it went missing; it was last seen on 31st July 1890, and the police began an investigation. Suspicion soon fell upon William Muddiman (44) of Little Virginia, and rumours were soon around that he had stolen it. A month after the stool was last seen he was forced to write a letter to the newspaper to explain that he had removed it to a safer place, the Local Board's offices on Rosemary Hill, upon the orders of his foreman. Muddiman worked on the roads so his foreman would have been Road Surveyor William Evans. It was a cause of concern that members of the Local Board must have known about the removal, but not one had taken the trouble to explain, leaving

Muddiman at the mercy of the rumourmongers.

Another curious antiquity was found in 1894 between the Castle and the golf-links. Strangely patterned sandstone, in which white squares were clearly marked, became known as "Adam's Chessboard".

* * *

In September 1886, new arrangements for lighting in the town were announced. An extra lamp was to be put up in Borrow-well Lane between the old schoolhouse and the well itself and additional gas lamps were to be placed at "...*Mr Robbins Vine Cottage at Tainters Hill; Dr Bourne's house near the churchyard; the mound forming the junction of New Row, Castle Green and Millbrook Lane...*" as well as outside William Jacks office near the station, and at Clifton Terrace. In addition, the new lamp at one end of Oakley Road was to be moved to the other side of the road. A new agreement with the gas company ensured that the price of lighting each lamp was to come down to 36s a year. The following month a request was made to the Board by the residents of Henry Street for lighting their road. The reply was positive, provided the occupants paid for the appliances.

The problems surrounding the completion of Oakley Road were finally overcome in July 1888 by Henry Street agreeing to pay for the small piece of land and to have the road completed; by November, the work was finished. The same month it was decided to re-name Castle End south of Station Road (still referred to by its original name Clarendon Street) as Warwick Road and a set of nameplates was ordered.

The certificate of completion of Oakley Road was handed in in early December. The opening of Oakley Road was seen as being of great importance as a route to the station and opening up valuable building land. The Board decided to light the road in the same way as Priory Road and asked the gas company to lay mains, and so no sooner had the road finally been opened than the Board began to dig it up again. The Board had agreed with the gas company that if they laid mains down Oakley Road, they would repair the road themselves.

The last piece of land allowing Oakley Road to be joined to Station Road was finally paid for in January 1889, with Henry Street giving £25 1s, and Mr Hodges £5. Towards the end of the previous year, Henry Street had suggested a name change from Oakley Road to Waverley Road but this was vehemently opposed by the road's builder William Clarke as he had chosen the name of his "...*late and present wife...*", but Street had his way. Bertie Road, named after Clarke's son Hubert, remained.

Just as all the problems surrounding the new road were finally settled, the Board had its attention drawn to problems in an older part of the town in February 1889. Spring Lane had 25 houses but was unlit, and "...*its people are often obliged to have to recourse to lanterns when business calls them out at night...*" and the burgeoning Henry Street, with 36 houses, also had no light. Every tenant in the 61 houses contributed towards the lighting of the town. The situation was compared to Fieldgate Lane, which was well lit but had only a dozen houses, and Priory and Waverley Roads that had only six houses but were lit. Additionally, there were "...two streets in Kenilworth that contain nine houses but can boast a dozen lamps." Nine houses with twelve lamps, sixty houses with none!

Some of the dangers of a night-time walk down Spring Lane were described in a letter signed "Fiat Lux": "Having left the last gas lamp at the top of Albion Street I descended the hill and as I did it seemed I was about to enter some black tunnel. Arriving at the end of dark Henry-street, I had a narrow escape from running into a large timber wagon. Getting clear of this I came to the "ugly bend", turning too suddenly I walked straight to the well which is in a line with the sidewalk. By the merest chance, I escaped from having a cold water bath free of cost. Fortunately, a friendly light from a nearby cottage enabled me to gain the middle of the road. Once there the difficulty of getting to the high ground was not great. How anyone can rest satisfied to live in this gloomy neighbourhood, for the life of me, I cannot understand." Spring Lane was described as "...the most stupid, the most awkward, the most crooked, as well as the most dangerous thoroughfare in Kenilworth."

It was now 30 years since the first gas street lights were installed, and in all that time the residents of Spring Lane had contributed to the gaslight rate without receiving any benefit, and yet the new Waverley Road was being lit. In the late 1870s, a plan had been drawn up by the gas company for laying a gas main down Spring Lane and on it marked the position of three intended lamps, but nothing came of it. However, it was not just down to the gas company, the Board could have provided oil or paraffin lamps as it had in Southbank Road and Borrowell Lane. Sarcastically, a writer to the *Kenilworth Advertiser* was sure the situation would be rectified by the Board just as soon as "...the pleasure walks have been made, the Park laid out, the lake created, Electric Light introduced and one or two of our Board members have been Knighted."

In March 1889, the Board received a petition from the inhabitants of Spring Lane and Henry Street, of which there were about 250 in sixty houses (nine of which were unoccupied), on their "...matter of the greatest inconvenience. It is at considerable personal risk that we may venture out of doors unless assisted by lanterns. Permit us to have a share of that light for which we are obliged to pay." The petition was signed by forty one persons and ten others would have, but "...were afraid for fear of an extra rate." Thomas Hawley pointed out that Henry Street still had not been formally taken on by the Board due to the arguments over the width. The Board decided to await further discussions with the gas company to see if they would lay mains down both Spring Lane and Henry Street, but by July they had received no definite answer.

Then, in November, four new gas-lamps were pledged by the Board, three in Spring Lane and one at Washbrook, but the gas company turned down a liberal offer from the Board to light Spring Lane. This brought immediate criticism and comparison to the water company who had installed water mains along the whole length of Henry Street, several times longer than Spring Lane, just to supply the dozen homes that had asked for it.

The top of Spring Lane was a confusing place for visitors, with a footpath to the station, Albion Street and the road to Abbey Hill also meeting there. It was suggested that a signpost was needed "...particularly as there are no houses near at which to make enquiries." "If Albion Street, or as it is more commonly known Albion-row, may not be considered one of the fairest streets in Kenilworth it is certainly one of the finest, and may yet be honoured by becoming the high road to Coventry. It has many features, more or less worthy of notice. A place of worship as a spiritual sentinel guards each end. A modest looking, unpretending, but well-attended temple of Bacchus, hoists its wooden flag in the middle, and the police, in their loving care of its people, have for many years held their court in this locality. Nor is this all. Albion-street possesses one of the most lovely of flower gardens, which for its dazzling beauty, and the exquisite taste with which its floral beds are laid out, is second to none in the county. A visit to Verbena Cottage would verify this and amply repay miles of a journey for that purpose."

More observations were published in 1890: It was not just the lack of lighting that was a problem in Spring Lane, it had the "...ugliest sidewalk and most dangerous in the Parish..." and the road itself had "...the appearance of a dried up river bed." It was claimed that it had been thirty or forty years since any fresh gravel had been laid upon it.

Finally, the campaigning eventually paid off and in December 1890, Henry Street and Spring Lane were lit for the first time. Even then the road still caused problems due to the narrowing "...after you go pass Mr Whateley's greenhouses. It would be a great improvement if the trees, especially the old stump, could be removed so the road could be set back. It would be dangerous if a carriage going at full speed were to meet a load of bricks coming from the brick-yard."

*   *   *

The late 1880s was a period of instability for the *Kenilworth Advertiser;* first in 1885 the agency moved from Miss Richards, who appears to have sold her business, to William Riley's Post Office, half-a-dozen or so doors away, then in 1888 it moved again: "In future, the Kenilworth Advertiser will be published at its original home, The Library, Castle End, by Messrs Robertson and Gray." The pair published it "...for the proprietor, Thomas Burbidge of Coventry." They claimed that the *Advertiser* "...by neglect had been allowed to markedly depreciate..." and promised to "...report all meetings fairly and to do our utmost to promote the best interests of the historic town of Kenilworth and its inhabitants." Kenilworth-born Charles Robertson (35), and his wife and assistant, London-born Rosa Matilda, had three daughters.

In 1891, difficulties arose with the machine that the *Kenilworth Advertiser* was printed on and so a new one was ordered, a print of which appeared in the issue of 16th May. From the first issue of 1894, the agency moved back to William Riley. By 1895, the newspaper had a new outlet at the W H Smith bookstall at the station.

*   *   *

James Sloss was born in Dalmellington, Ayr, on 23rd September 1859. He came from a farming family with his brother and father being a farm manager and shepherd respectively, and James himself was a shepherd in his teenage years. He also had five sisters. In September 1879, he joined the 2nd Battalion of the Scots Guards and in 1881 was stationed at the Chelsea Bridge Road barracks in London. He was discharged from the Guards in July 1884, joined the London City Police force, and was discharged from there at Christmas 1885.

Sloss (26), married but with no children, moved to Leamington, joined the Warwickshire Constabulary on 4th January 1886. He had a most striking appearance being 6ft 3¾ins tall, of proportionate build, hazel eyes, brown hair, of fresh complexion and no distinguishing marks. His education was described as "inferior". He was allocated the divisional number 58 and in July 1887, he was promoted to First Class Constable.

Stationed in Kenilworth, just four months later he and PC Lines arrested William "Rambler" James for being drunk and disorderly in Spring Lane. Rambler became violent, kicking out at both constables. Once at the police station he became more violent, kicking and badly injuring Lines on the shins, Sloss had to manhandle James into the cells on his own. The court case was delayed a week due to Lines' injuries and even then he needed a stick to walk. James was jailed for three months with hard labour.

At this time, the police force in Kenilworth comprised four officers, but it was Sloss and Lines that were always in the news. In the same week in early 1888, Lines caught a man in Thickthorn Wood who was revealed to be "The King of The Poachers", whilst Sloss won praise for his "clever capture" of two would-be thieves. He had seen two suspicious characters walking up and down Castle End and watched quietly when one of them entered Hannah Riley's grocery shop at the Post Office. He noticed Hannah Riley was standing at the door and sensing a problem, he went in to find the man behind the counter in the act of plundering. Sloss arrested both men. The two constables were praised; "We in Kenilworth may be glad we have such Guardians of the peace..." but the sentence given to the poacher was criticised: "Twelve months for killing a few rabbits! And yet children are brutally treated by friends in human shape who are let off with a few months."

In February 1889 a fern-gatherer named Harry Sturch was following his occupation on the Common near The Gables when, fourteen feet from the top of the hill he pulled back a furze bush to reveal a sizable "cave". He saw a bag just inside and with a second look saw a foot. "Startled almost out of his wits..." Sturch went about his way and said nothing until that evening in the Coventry Cross, suggesting that Jack the Ripper, then at the height of his infamy, was hiding on the Common! He managed to induce half a dozen men to go with him to the spot, whereupon they pulled back the gorse and saw a dim light glowing inside. Squeezing through the small opening, they one by one found themselves inside a chamber about 5ft by 7ft, and in the company of two Kenilworth boys, Chaplin and Townshend. The boys had with them two shovels and buckets. The men turned the boys out and returned to the Coventry Cross to relate the tale, which caused much gossip in the town. One night after hours, about eight men returned to spend time drinking, smoking and playing cards, and drinking the health of the boys for providing such a snug retreat. The police soon closed off the cave for reasons of safety and PC Sloss pointed out to the boys the dangers of what they had done, but they said that all they wanted was a place "...free from intrusive onlookers for the purpose of smoking and seclusion."

On Easter weekend in 1889, a large gathering of Coventry youths assembled at the Queen and Castle and when they began to throw jugs and glasses around the coffee room, Augustine Styles summoned the police. PC Sloss, acting alone, attempted to arrest Harry Wilson, who gave the appearance of being the ring leader, who then shouted "Come on Coventry, he can't take any of us to the lock-up!" and the whole assemblage, now a hundred strong, gathered on Castle Green, still behaving in a disorderly manner. With several armed with ginger beer bottles, they headed for the Clarendon Arms and Sloss asked the landlord not to let them in. Wilson and a few others approached Sloss and dared him to lock them up, and struck him, at which point Sloss arrested him. Wilson started to kick and struggle, shouting, "Come on Coventry" and Sloss, now surrounded by a gang of over 300 failed to hang on to him. A second constable, PC Fletcher, arrived and together they finally took Wilson into custody. The bench "...took into consideration that it was holiday time..." and Wilson was fined £1 5s including costs.

The area around the Castle seems to have been Sloss's beat in 1889 and just a few weeks later, he was involved in a nasty accident. Coventry watchmaker Mr Marlow, his wife, and a young niece, drove in a trap towards Kenilworth for a day out. When they got to Crackley-lane, Marlow noticed that the bit was out the horse's mouth and so he stopped and climbed down to adjust it. The horse suddenly jumped, knocking Marlow down and started off, the trap wheels running over Marlow's head. The horse bolted along New Street and into High Street with the young girl screaming. At New Row, an alert PC Sloss warned playing children in its path to move and then made a valiant attempt to stop the runaway, but failed owing to the absence of the bridle. A collie was run over and killed. At Castle Green, the trap turned over, throwing out Mrs Marlow. The young girl escaped entirely unhurt. Mr Marlow was first attended to by some passing cyclists and was carried to the Abbey Hotel where he was treated by Dr Wynter but his injuries were not as serious as they could have been. Mrs Marlow was carried to a house in Clinton Lane where her head injuries were treated by Dr Clarke. In the evening, the party were taken back to their home.

A quite extraordinary occurrence involving a rabid dog took place in the summer of 1889. Police Sergeant Allcott had been alerted that a mad dog was at large, and armed with a "heavy stick" he was directed to the Park Road crossroads, right alongside the Police Station, where he found 12 year-old William Shelswell terribly bitten with a piece of flesh torn from his thigh. Constables Sloss and Wall immediately gave chase in the direction of Coventry Road and soon saw the dog, a collie-sheepdog cross breed, but had great difficulty in getting close to it. The dog made for the Common, then Stoneleigh Road and into School Lane where it lunged at, but missed, Allcott, who gave him a severe blow with his stick. Off again, this time to New Street, it bit 9 year-old Henry Newey, of the Red Lion Yard, on the thumb. By now, a gun had been sent for, and a double-barrelled weapon was in the hands of the pursuers now going along Priory Road, Waverley Road, Castle End, over Mr Ward's bridge and off towards Windy Arbour. It then ran back across cornfields to Castle End, briefly visited Mr Davis's slaughter yard, then back up to Abbey End where it was chased into a passage alongside Dr Bourne's surgery - Allcott closed the gate to trap it. Cornered, a good view could now be had. *"Standing as large or larger than a wolf, which it was not unlike in shape or ferocity, with hair almost erect, eyes ablaze, and snarling horribly."* Allcott, or according to one report Sloss, fired and hit the animal's side, it tried to attack him, but the second shot hit his head and the three hour chase was over. At its height, a crowd of 500 followed the chase, swelled after 8 o'clock when the churches emptied, and spectators continually got in the way of the police. The carcass was inspected in Leamington and it was confirmed the dog was *"quite mad"*, but that was of little comfort to the two bitten boys. Dr Wynter immediately and successfully raised subscriptions and within days, the boys were on their way to Paris accompanied by their headmaster, H J Stone, to be treated for the prevention of hydrophobia by Professor Pasteur. The police authorities immediately issued a notice stating that all dogs in Kenilworth should be muzzled for a month, as it was believed that at least three had been bitten by the rabid animal. Already, few dogs were now seen walking in town, and at least two owners were fined for not muzzling their animals.

The market gardens were an easy target for rogues and during the late 1880s there had been *"...a number of most annoying depredations."* One July 1890 day, four suspicious-looking men had been seen prowling the streets at around 5 o'clock. The following morning they were seen amongst the fruit gardens, mostly strawberries, on Lower Ladies Hill. They were spotted by plain-clothed Sgt Allcott, and he was joined by PC Sloss. Allcott managed to arrest two of the men and Sloss captured a third, but the fourth ran off across the strawberry beds. He was quickly overcome by Sloss's dog, which held onto him until Sloss had handcuffed his first prisoner and made his way across. By now, some of the strawberry-pickers had arrived for work and they gave the policemen a round of applause as they marched off with their four captives.

1890 had seen many complaints about over-loaded brakes, mostly from Coventry, coming to Kenilworth. Four-horse brakes had been seen with only three or two, and on one occasion a solitary, horse. PC Goodridge was brought in from Warwick specifically to help PC Sloss apprehend any such offenders in August and they did not have to wait long before they stopped a brake loaded with 36 passengers nearing the Abbey Hotel. Another brake pulled up behind and during remonstrations the driver of one refused to give Sloss his name or get down from the brake, so Sloss grabbed him and in doing so dislocated the brakeman's wrist.

The man was charged with using bad language and obstructing a police officer, but he claimed that Sloss used worse language than he did and that he assaulted him. He was fined £2 3s including costs.

Accommodation was provided for officers at the police station in Albion Street; in 1891, James Sloss lived there with his wife, as did Sgt Job Allcott with his wife and five children.

One late August day in 1891, labourer James Overton had already left his Henry Street home for work when his wife Jane rose at 6.30 a.m., and she too soon left for work at Leicester House leaving their 32 month-old son George in the care of daughter Alice, aged 14 or 15. Soon after her mother had left, Alice brought George downstairs and along with a 16 year-old brother, Percy a gardener, had breakfast. He too then left for work. Alice went upstairs to fetch George's clothes, leaving him sitting in a chair by the fire, but heard him call out *"Alice, I am all burnt now."* She rushed downstairs and found him covered by flames. She ripped off his nightshirt, wrapped him in a dress of their mother's, and ran to the back door to call for help. Mary Ann Gardiner, whose Albion Street house backed onto the Overton's, was the first to respond. She took the child from Alice, laid him on the sofa, and looked at his horrific injuries. By now other neighbours and PC Sloss had arrived, followed by Dr Bourne, and mother Jane. There was little they could do and George died at 5.15. On the floor were four or five struck matches. The inquest was held by Dr Wynter at the Police station two days later and the members of the jury were so touched by the death of George they donated their fees to the Overtons.

George Brewer, 30, was a single man employed by Joseph Murdoch at Crew Gardens and he lived with a brother and their father at Clayfields, a row of cottages alongside the Cherry Orchard brickworks, abutting Whitemoor Road. A relative, Tom Brewer, was licensee at the Cottage Inn. At 7.30 p.m. on Thursday 29th October 1891, a cousin of the same age, Reuben Rainbow of Wappenbury, drove over in a trap to see him and leaving the horses in charge of some small boys the two men chatted freely for some 20 minutes, sharing some food and drink. They decided to spend an hour at their cousin's pub and set off in the trap towards Leys Lane. At the junction, and without apparently saying a word, Rainbow produced a loaded six-chamber revolver and shot Brewer in the stomach. Brewer jumped out the trap and Rainbow drove off at a furious rate. The struggling Brewer managed to make his way back to his own house, about three hundred yards away, and, bleeding badly and exhausted, collapsed into his father's arms. The alarm was soon raised, Dr Clarke attended, assisted by Dr Morris.

An uncle, Jacob Walker, took a lantern along the road and at the junction found a hat from the victim and a mackintosh of the assailant. Sgt Allcott was informed and he at once set off in a conveyance for Wappenbury in pursuit of Rainbow. Rainbow had tied up his horse a mile from his home and walked to his house, gone up to his bedroom and shot himself in the temple. His family were at home and one went to fetch a local constable and met up with Allcott; the scale of the tragedy was now unveiled. The next day, the bullet was removed from Brewer but he was in a bad way, and he died later at his home. Rainbow had once been apprenticed to cabinetmaker James Jackson in Kenilworth, was a local prize-winning athlete, but had recently had a run of heavy gambling losses. He had also had his eyes on a young lady but she suddenly rejected his advances and this he had blamed on Brewer for spreading rumours about him. The two had fallen out about a year previously but it was thought the differences were settled, however it seems that Rainbow had been harbouring a grudge.

The scene of George Brewer's murder.

On 5th October 1892, William Eagles applied to have the licence of the White Lion transferred to himself from Joseph Franklin, as he had already been selling beer for a week in Franklin's absence. Magistrate Mr Stanger-Leathes said, *"Kenilworth publicans seem to think they can do what they like. There are too many houses in Kenilworth and these constant changes prove they did not pay."* The transfer could not happen without Franklin being able to attend and so Eagles was advised to close the White Lion down. The following week the licence was transferred temporarily; it transpired that Franklin had gone home to Coventry for a change of clothes and was taken ill.

However, this led to Eagles being prosecuted for selling beer without a licence, the date in question being 1st October. Several witnesses claimed that they were at a Caledonian Corks meeting in the club room and were supplied with beer, in jugs, by Franklin. Franklin stated that Eagles *"...took the whole of the beneficial interest from the house from September 29th..."* although the licence was not transferred until 12th October. Franklin further confused the issue by saying it was Mrs Eagles that helped draw the beer. On the night in question Eagles was initiated into the club and Sergeant(sic) Sloss claimed Eagles served drinks without a licence on that night, although he then admitted that he himself was in Scotland at the time. Eagles not only claimed that he did not draw any drinks that night but also that he did not even know how to get out of the room. Not surprisingly, the case was dismissed as there was no evidence to sustain a conviction.

Sgt Allcott had been in the force 17 years, the last 11 of them in Kenilworth, and in charge of the Kenilworth district for 8, when in early 1893 he was promoted to inspector and transferred to Bedworth. In January 1894, Sloss (37) was transferred to patrol the Estate at Stoneleigh. The announcement was greeted with sadness: *"We shall miss our tall policeman who has been a conspicuous figure in Kenilworth's streets for so long. The Scotchman has been a terror to small children and also to tramps, and has been a protector in general to the inhabitants. At holiday times he has frequently suffered at the hands of females, who had worshipped too ardently at the shrine of Bacchus, most of them hailing from the Black Country, but our friend never came off second best."*

Within weeks of his transfer, Sloss was back in the news. Whilst he was patrolling near Cloud Bridge in Stoneleigh at 1.00 a.m. on a Sunday morning, *"...six rough looking men sprung out of the hedgerow and commenced to beat him with heavy bludgeons. Sloss felled two men, and also a large dog which attempted to bite him, with his staff. Sloss at length was knocked to the ground. He regained his feet but the men had run away. Sloss gave chase but from weakness was unable to overtake his assailants who are believed to be poachers from Coventry. Sloss's helmet was smashed in and only the metal top saved him from serious, perhaps fatal, injuries."* Three weeks after the assault, Sloss was one of a number of people who were awarded certificates at the Technical Education classes at Abbey Hill school. These included students of agriculture and geometry, but Sloss's award was for passing his ambulance exam. On presenting him with a certificate, Lord Leigh raised a laugh by suggesting that his ambulance knowledge may have recently been of great use to him!

Towards the end of the year, Sloss was fined 5s for being drunk on duty and forfeited two days' pay whilst suspended, and 27 months later, he was fined £1 for repeating the offence.

*   *   *

With all the fuss still surrounding the Abbey Fields estate, in March 1890 the Board were offered another piece of land to use as a park. They were approached by the "promoters" about a triangular piece of land alongside Tainters Hill, next to the water tower, and asked if they would be interested in being given it as a gift for use as a park; all that the Board would be required to do was to keep it in proper repair, perhaps not as easy as it sounded: *"The land known as the Gravel Pits has for many years been an eyesore and a disgrace to our town."* It was *"...a very unsightly dust-heap."* Burbery reminded the Board that a similar offer was made several years previously and nothing came of it, but Dr Wynter suggested that the offer should be accepted, and it was. With the Board not in a position to spend money on the site, a public subscription fund was opened to pay for making it usable, and £42 was subscribed for clearing and levelling. *"The work in transforming our ancient home of rubbish of all kinds into a capital recreation ground is being carried on with great energy."*

It was intended that the area would be used for boys to play cricket, but another use was expected: *"I presume our first step to commemorate the unselfish generosity of the donors will be to...erect and maintain a suitable monument...to record the undying gratitude of the nurse maids of that district...in providing them with this rendezvous for themselves and babies."*

With the Abbey Fields still effectively closed to the public, the belief that the small triangle of land could be thought of as a park brought about a sarcastic editorial proclaiming its virtues in eloquent terms such as *"The grand gravel walk"*, *"Splendid and uninterrupted views of the whole park"*, *"The tower promenade"*, and *"The Local Board...has given us a park which, for its size, may not be compared with the finest in England."* The suggestion that Royalty should be invited to perform the opening ceremony was not taken up. In June came the time for the Board to formally take it over and the resolution was duly carried.

The one time eye-sore and rubbish dump, Tainters Hill Common, was levelled to allow boys to play cricket.

*　　*　　*

In January 1887, Charles Trepplin informed the Board that the gravel at Villiers Hill *"...was sinking and diminishing..."* and so he would have to make an increase in price. At the same time, Trepplin declared that the pump for emptying the tanks at the sewerage farm was dangerous and in need of repair. *"If the Board expects £40 per annum rent from me and demand the regular pumping out of sewerage, then the pump must be put into proper order."* In July 1889, Trepplin and the Board agreed upon another seven year lease for the sewerage farm at an annual rent of £32 starting from 25th March 1890.

In 1890 mushrooms were extensively grown both indoors and out at Ernest Trepplin's The Crewe, under the care of its manager Joseph Murdoch, who had worked as a gardener for Charles Trepplin in his days at Leek Wootton. The outdoor beds were spawned in winter and covered with litter, and produced a heavy and long-lasting crop. The indoor growing was in old pigsties, barns, an old silo and any other building that could be utilised. *"Everywhere are shoals of mushrooms without any artificial heat whatsoever."* Instead of the usual 3ft wide beds, Murdoch had his 4ft wide, rising to about 3ft high and about 1ft wide at the top. He prepared them in September using manure from local railway stables and put ordinary garden soil on top. These larger beds held the heat for longer and mushrooms started to show just 5 or 6 weeks after spawning. Heavy frosts during the winter of 1890-1 destroyed the crops despite them being

covered by a foot thickness of straw, but although being frozen to some depth the spawn survived and by the end of May a large crop was being gathered daily and continued to be throughout the whole summer. The *Journal of Horticulture* stated that Murdoch had shown that *"...the cultivation of mushrooms outdoors is easy."*

William Mitchell at Elmdene, seems to have become a minor agriculturist, putting his land to good use. In 1890 he won a prize at a major agricultural show after employing *"...the most recent improvements for the manufacture of butter."* His success was partially down to the rich pasture on which his cows fed. His business, though, was recorded as a fancy-paper manufacturer.

In 1890, Henry Street leased to Richard and Charles Whateley land fronting onto Stoneleigh Road (Dalehouse Lane); it was the last plot before Common Lane and started about halfway from the railway bridge. It included one half of the bed of Finham brook. The agreement was for 99 years at £25 a year. Street had bought the land in 1882. On 25th August 1900, it was taken over by fruit grower Richard Knight.

In Spring Lane, Henry Whateley had two large blocks of green-houses, each containing ten houses 103ft long, 12ft wide and reaching 6ft at the apex. One block was devoted to cucumbers of "Whateley's hybrid" variety, many thousands of which were continually cut. The other block was for tomatoes, each house contained 550 plants in three rows on each side of the pathway. Varieties grown were Old Large Red and Glamorgan. They were planted in old mushroom beds and some excellent mushrooms were gathered amongst the tomatoes. *"They are really Covent Garden supply houses, a style well known to London growers."* A visitor from *The Journal of Horticulture and Cottage Gardener* in May 1890 claimed the tomatoes were the finest cropped plants he had seen for the time of year.

By the mid-1890s, William James of Ivy Cottage Gardens was *"at the front"* of strawberry growing, he supplied the Countess of Warwick with berries for the visit of The Prince of Wales. Tons of fruit, cucumbers and tomatoes were sent away each week. He also grew potatoes, at one time advertising 80lbs for sale for 4s.

*　　*　　*

One of the difficulties facing Kenilworth in becoming an expansive town was outlined in a letter by Cherry Orchard market gardener Henry Clarke: *"Though we may not hope to see Kenilworth grow into a noisy, bustling, manufacturing locality, there is no reason why she should not become a prosperous well-to-do residential town."* He continued by praising the healthy air, scenic attractions and the sites for building which *"...bear comparison with any in England."* Clarke's solution was that an enterprising builder should erect a dozen roomy mansions with stabling and coach-houses, which he claimed would immediately be occupied and give *"...new blood, fresh energy and more wealth..."* to the town. *"The pretty villas around us...are too small for one class and too large for another...and the consequence is they are often empty."* The building of mansions would, claimed Clarke, *"...see our town become what nature intended - the paradise of Warwickshire."*

Perhaps to aid building investors, the Leamington, Warwick and South Warwickshire Permanent Benefit Building Society received a request in 1891 from several of its shareholders to carry out transactions in town, and as a result the company secretary arranged to be at Mr T Burt's premises for an hour once every four Tuesdays for transactions to take place.

*   *   *

The appalling weather of the 1890-1 winter again caused great distress to families; not just agricultural workers but bricklayers, painters and others did not work for five weeks. An annual gift of boots and blankets came from the Edmunds and Dentons Charity and was administered by the vicar and churchwardens, but the various regular schemes run and organised through the churches and charities were not coping, and a special effort was required. Not surprisingly, it was Dr Wynter who brought together an influential gathering to discuss what could be done, and before the meeting even started Wynter, Henry Street, F Wyer and George Turner donated 2 guineas each to start the fund. The meeting, held at the Institute, was full of offers of help; Mr Sutcliffe offered to make soup and Mrs Sarah Adams of the Kings Arms offered fires and coppers, but the major decision was to organise an immediate town-wide collection before any decision on a course of action was made.

Just two days later, the initial collection had been completed, amounting to more than £44, and the meeting re-convened at the Institute. Wynter stressed that the efforts of those present was to supplement the work of the churches, not to compete against or undermine them, and pointed out that the Reverend Alfred Jones of St.John's had made a personal donation and sent a message of encouragement. There were at least 60 families in need of help in addition to those that always struggled, Registrar and Relieving Officer Henry Thornett thought it may be more. Discussions then took place as to the best way to dispose of the funds. Henry Street caused laughter by saying that people did not take to soup too kindly as they thought it was made of odds and ends, an opinion shared by most of those gathered. Wynter dropped soup from the discussion and he, Street, Bagshaw and Wyer put together the idea that the most necessary of commodities, coal, bread and groceries, should be made available. Immediately Town Crier William Jeacock was sent out with the message, "Any able-bodied man or woman out of work and requiring assistance is invited to attend the Institute today at 6 o'clock and on every Monday and Thursday evening until further notice." Jeacock did his work well, at 6 o'clock that evening there were almost 100 applicants queuing at the Institute. One by one, they were issued with tickets equivalent to 1s for each adult and 6d for each child to be used to purchase goods from their usual sources.

The poor weather continued into the spring, the town was covered in a blanket of snow in mid-May.

With so many farms under the Trepplins, not all the farm houses themselves were needed and so those at Chase and Goodrest were in 1890 the first to be rented out. Other buildings were put to good use. In April 1891, the County Council organised a number of agricultural-based classes for anyone wishing to learn particular skills. The cheese-making class was to be taken by Miss Nevel at Trepplin's Pleasance Farm. The cost was 5s a week or 1s a day. The first class was a little disappointing with only one pupil, however within a month the classes were described as *"...meeting with great success."* The produce could be purchased by visitors, but Mr J Harrison of Pailton was unlikely to be one who took up the offer: *"Being interested in cheese-making, I thought I should see what they were doing at (the classes) so I went last Friday. When I got to Kenilworth, I found the school was two miles from the station. As I approached the farm premises, where the instruction was supposed to be going on, I was surprised and disgusted. I have been a cheese-maker all my life and have always considered that the first principles in dairying were that the surroundings should be perfectly free from bad smells. I found just the contrary. There was a good deal of ensilage about, which I could smell two hundred yards before I got to the premises. Just outside the dairy door, about seven or eight yards away, there were seven large tubs full of pig swill, standing in the sun with all manner of filth thrown in. A few yards further away they were boiling up a cow that had died, and the attendant told me they boiled up an old horse the week before that had been lying dead some days. If the County Council expect good dairy produce from such a tainted atmosphere I am afraid they will be sadly mistaken."* The Kenilworth Co-operative decided to sell produce from the agricultural schools, perhaps wisely choosing the butter made elsewhere and not the cheese. The quality of local dairy produce had often been questioned, such as in early 1888 when one dairyman supplied milk coloured blue on which *"...the cream floats - bottomwards..."*, and another that supplied a liquid which was proved to be 60% milk and 40% water.

The summer of 1891 saw another tragedy involving a farm boy. Arthur Fell, the thirteen year-old son of labourer John Fell, was driving a hay wagon with three horses across Pleasance Farm when it tipped over into a ditch crushing him beneath it. The one witness to the accident was 14 year-old Charles Heath. At the inquest Charles Bond, Trepplin's bailiff, said that they employed 15 or 16 boys but they *"...have men to start the wagon and the boys take it on."* Coroner Dr Wynter was very critical of the employment of boys who could barely reach the bridle on a team of horses which stood 16 hands high. Although the jury returned a verdict of accident, Wynter expressed the hope that the practice of boys in charge of horses would be immediately discontinued; Arthur was the second young boy killed this way on a Trepplin farm in nine years.

Probably due to a combination of a general agricultural slump, overstretching his resources, and having a reliance on livestock, Charles Trepplin was in financial trouble. Word spread, and Earl Clarendon's agent soon began to receive numerous applications to take over the tenancies on his Trepplin-held farms. In September 1892, Grounds and Pleasance Farms hosted the first sales of Trepplin's property; 661 shorthorn cattle,

91 draught and half-bred horses, over 1,000 ducks, geese and fowl, agricultural machinery, steam engines, milk carts etc., drew prospective buyers from miles around. Initially set for 20th, 21st, 22nd and 27th September, the sale overran and had to be continued into another week.

The problems Trepplin was having had side effects, not the least of which was for those trying to play golf at Castle Farm in October 1892: *"Owing to the misfortune of Mr Trepplin, the grass is rather long."*

The depressed state of agriculture caused a major meeting to be held in Warwick near the end of 1892, but the problems continued into the next year. By May a drought was having a major impact on prices; sheep were sold for 20s, two year-old cattle were sold for as little as £5, yearlings half that, and straw was up to £4 a ton, higher than the price of wheat. Crops in general were expected to have a poor year and again there were major concerns about the winter food stocks for livestock. Despite the difficulties, the first of the new tenants were moving into to the farms vacated by Trepplin, 38 year-old Edwin Gee moved into Castle Farm in the summer of 1893, and George Bostock, in his mid-40s, took on Fern Hill, Oaks and Rouncil farms. Two of the Snelson family took on Chase House and Camp farms.

By August 1893, Charles Frederick Trepplin, then living at Villiers Hill farm, announced his decision to leave town and to return to his native Germany. He also still had Crew Farm but shortly gave up both, and additionally agreed to move all his property from the sewerage farm by the end of October. The final sale at Villiers Hill Farm took place in October 1893 with the sale of 17 fat cows and 31 horses, which fetched ridiculously low prices due to the shortage of winter food available to livestock. Also sold were eight acres of growing potatoes at £5 or £6 an acre, swedes and mangolds at £7 to £9 an acre, and 200 head of poultry for as little as 3s a couple. Some of Trepplin's former employees stayed on, including Charles Bond at High House and Joseph Murdoch at The Crew.

After leaving Kenilworth, Charles Trepplin, now in his mid-70s, embarked upon a world tour. Such was his attachment to Kenilworth he sent back regular despatches telling of his experiences in Honolulu, Japan and China. For a while, Ernest stayed in town, living in Leyes Lane, before he too moved on, first to Wiltshire and then to Somerset, working as an Estate Agent for Viscount Portman.

The prospects remained bad for livestock farmers. A hot 1893 summer had resulted in little grass growth and what hay there was would only suffice for perhaps half the local stock. Good store beasts were fetching only £5 at market, half their price six months earlier. It was feared many agriculturists *"...will be unable to cope for want of means..."* during the approaching winter. One such man was John Pittaway (62), a farmer and dairyman who suffered heavy losses, and in March 1894, he took his own life at Rosa Villa opposite St.John's Church; he was found hanging in an outhouse. An investigation into his finances later revealed he had misjudged his financial position and he was in fact solvent. He had farmed at Woodlands since the mid-1860s and was one-time licensee of the Malt Shovel Inn.

Within a month of his death, the situation had changed: *"The rains have worked miracles. The grass and grain crops are making very rapid growth. Vegetation has made wonderful progress and the quantity of fruit blossom is enormous. Mushrooms have been gathered in the week in the fields. The cattle are selling better having gone up in price in the last few days as much as £4 a head while sheep too are more in demand. With a continuance of the genial rains (the farmer) may hope to recoup some of his losses of the past dry season."* Unpredictable weather soon returned; in early August a frost followed by a hail storm then hot sunshine on the same day left crops laid low. Workers were paid £1 an acre for gathering it up. A new law for those under 18 years of age, particularly valuable for farm boys, now limited their working week to a maximum 74 hours.

The variety of produce ensured that not all suffered problems. One grower sent 30cwt of cucumbers in one despatch, whilst bee-keepers had successful yields of honey. The power of the local agricultural unionists was on the wane; an 1894 meeting at Abbey Hill School saw an attendance of just twelve. In 1895 the number of milk-carts in town was commented upon, and Kenilworth milk travelled well enough to be sold in London.

The new occupant of the Castle gatehouse, in residence by 1891, for the first time was not a farmer but a businessman, William Gambier Middleton. Five years later his daughter Helen married Herbert Hands, late of Flint Hall, Newbold Pacey, and her wedding party was reputedly the first to leave from the Castle since *"the days of Oliver Cromwell."* The reception was held at the Castle and the couple moved into The Hollies in New Street.

Joseph Holland Burbery died at Montague House on Friday 25th March 1892 in his 85th year. A well-known, leading agriculturist, he was for many years the Chairman of Warwick Board of Guardians and was the first Chairman of Kenilworth Local Board, and President of the Kenilworth Liberal Association from its inception. He was a member of Unitarian Church. One of the Chase farms which he farmed was said to have been in his family for a century and Burbery successfully bred Warwickshire long-horned cattle and won many prizes. When not participating, he was a judge at such events. A friend of Lord Leigh and other gentry, he was warm-hearted and benevolent to the poor. He was a quiet and unobtrusive man of *"essentially beautiful character."* His funeral, on March 30th at the Rosemary Hill chapel, was attended by Joseph Stone Burbery, his only son, and the whole of the Local Board. Edward Smith and Son carried out the arrangements. Just six weeks later, his widow Emma died aged 66.

Burbery's estate was sold by public auction at the Abbey Hotel that August. His dairy farms, two at Rowington and one at Meer End, were sold for over £7,000. Montague House was sold to William Mitchell of Elmdene for £1,775, and four acres of building land in the Abbey Fields to Henry Street for £500. Another Kenilworth residence, Prescott House, was sold by private treaty to its occupier, Miss Lyon, for £1,000. Burbery's possessions at Montague House were sold off, and included three cows kept on the premises.

Driving cattle to a slaughterhouse was not without its hazards, as an incident in High Street in January 1892 demonstrates: *"A bullock was being driven to Mr Roberts' slaughterhouse when the animal became restive and attempted to enter Mr Emery's shop door opposite. Mr Emery in trying to prevent the unwelcome visitor gaining access, defended the entrance with an umbrella and was immediately knocked down and gored by the beast. He was much bruised and knocked about."* Six months later, Emery retired from business and moved to Stourbridge. He had been in Kenilworth for nearly 50 years, trading as a hatter, draper, outfitter and undertaker. He never pursued debts through courts and was much respected for it.

Thomas Emery's drapery; the bull was beaten back at the front door.

The annual event know as the Cattle or May fair had all but ended. In 1894 it was reported that one cow and one calf was offered for sale in The Square *"about fifteen years ago"*, but there were a few children in town with may-poles. One horse, belonging to coal-dealer Mr Nadin, was decorated with a ribbon.

*   *   *

In the year ending June 1888, the water company made 28 new connections to houses and had a subsequent increase in takings of £72, to total almost £400, but the annual report declared that "Due to the continued depression in the building trade, revenue has not increased as anticipated." Shareholder Mr Banks of Coventry asked if there was a chance of property increasing to which Henry Street replied, *"They build and build, there are the houses but not the tenants."* During the year, the company had sufficient funds to allow £400 to be invested in the Coventry Gas Company, but there were misgivings and only 1½% dividend was paid. The cost of Kenilworth gas to the water company was 4s 6d per 1,000 cu ft, compared to just 2s 9d supplied in Coventry. Henry Street explained that the company hoped that gas would cost less in a year but they were looking at ways of making their own. There was a patent whereby gas suitable for power, but not light, could be made and unless a reduction in the price of gas was forthcoming, the company intended to invest in it. By

rotation, James Whittendale was up for re-election but could not attend due to his father's illness. The Coventry surveyor Edward J Purnell jnr offered himself as a Director and he was duly elected.

By the AGM of October 1889, the company had indeed avoided the cost of Kenilworth gas by installing a gas-making plant of the Dowson principle, which was expected to give a great saving in fuel costs of about 60% in the coming year. Mr Bagshaw had visited Wellington and found that the Dowson plant there cost £3 in maintenance in three years. Possibly in connection with this, Mr Marriott built a new shed for the works. He was also the company's plumber. Dr Bourne chaired the meeting and declared a dividend of 2%, leaving just £29 in hand after it was paid.

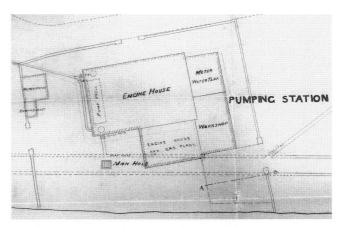

The gas-making plant was at the rear of the pump-house.
(County Records Office CR 2487/109)

The following year, shareholders were paid a 2½% dividend on an increased income of £41 from the water rates. John Bagshaw and Dr Thomas Bourne were retiring members up for re-election; the latter voluntarily stepped down from being both Chairman and Director as he regularly missed three or four meetings a year due to other commitments. A new member was added in his place, George Turner who described his only business as *"hunting"*.

During a time of heavy frost, January 1891, Colonel Harrison, presumably a Water Company director, contacted the Local Board to ask to borrow the water-carts to help deliver water to its consumers as pipes had frozen. The severe frost also committed the Company to numerous repairs and so a dividend was not paid that year. E J Purnell's position in the company was strengthened; he was now the company secretary and manager.

The end of year meeting in 1893 revealed a handsome £233 profit and a dividend to pay of 3%; it would have been more but for a £70 outlay on tools etc. Wages had increased to £130 against £113 the previous year but this was put down to extra work during the winter. George Beard raised the question as to whether it was still cheaper to make the gas through the Dowson method than to pay for town gas and it was generally agreed that it was. The company was justifiably proud of its contribution to local development: director John Bagshaw was right in stating *"If the company had not come forward and supplied Kenilworth with good water, the town would not be what it is today...",* but the company was about to have problems.

The drought of 1893 was not followed by a wet enough winter to replenish the water supply. By mid-1894 only half the amount of water of the previous year was being pumped, and to offset any future problems the water company investigated ways of increasing the supply. Geological information was supplied by Mr Andrews FGS, and after consultations with their own engineer, Edward Purnell jnr, it was decided to sink another borehole a little to the west of the existing one. Messrs Tilly and Son of Southwark, London, were entrusted with the work and in late 1894 boring began. Water was found in soft red sandstone at a depth of 106ft, but it was insufficient and so boring continued, mostly through marl. At 198ft, water was found in live sand and in sufficient quantities. The borehole was 12ins wide to a depth of 80ft narrowing to 7ins below that. In an experiment, 63,000 gallons of water were pumped in ten hours without the head of water being lowered. When pumping ceased the water rose rapidly up the borehole, 11ft in 13 minutes. The source was at 205ft, but boring was continued to 226ft. At one time, the water rose under its own pressure almost to the top of the hole and as a test it was decided to pump the hole out but such was the flow the level could only be lowered by less than five feet. The water was much softer than the earlier supply, but could not be used until the proper pumps had been installed. The water was analysed by Mr Bostockhill and he reported it to be of good domestic quality and free of organic matter. The new pump-well, pumps, boiler and engine-house works were carried out by Liggins and Strong of Coventry, with the boiler and pump supplied by J Hatton also of Coventry. The work was completed by early 1895 and the cost was estimated as between £500 and £600, which was largely offset by the issuing of 70 un-allotted £5 shares that were worth about £7 10s each.

The new boring gave a supply suitable for a town of twice the size. It was thought that a reservoir may be needed but, as *"..the gas and steam engine works with so much ease as not to require repairs during a lifetime...",* this was decided against. It was remarked that Kenilworth would soon have a water famine if it were not for the works, as many of the springs seemed to be failing.

Whilst this new work was continuing, the Company had a contrasting problem, another severe winter. In February 1895 the river was frozen, allowing skating from Blackdown Mill to Ashow where curling was an attraction. One adventurous gentleman was even seen riding his bicycle under the bridge at Chesford! At Kenilworth golf club, one player's ball landed on a frozen pond, and as he moved to play it, the ice collapsed. Despite a gallant effort to continue, the player retired after a few more holes. This was the last golf played for five weeks. The problem the Water Company faced was the damage caused by the severe frost to pipes laid at a depth of just 2ft 6ins and £575 was spent on repairs and laying them at a greater depth of 4ft. Despite all this expenditure, the company returned a profit for the year of £237, partly boosted by its extra supply, and paid a small dividend. Henry Street was the Company chairman, and George Turner, John Bagshaw, James Whittendale and Thomas Hawley the other listed directors.

The weather was so severe that the Assistance Committee of 1891 was re-formed and at its first sitting coal, meat and groceries were distributed to 83 men, 84 women and 176 children. By its second sitting on 11th February this had risen to 105 men, 107 women and 195 children - ten per cent of the town's population. The cost of the distribution was £28, which emptied the available funds, and so appeals were made for help and the London and Midland Bank received donations; more than forty persons were listed giving over £30. A small group, with James Whittendales's son Edgar, and Mrs Whittendale prominent, organised themselves into performing a concert to raise funds. Mr Evans of The Spring generously gave 25 tons of coal to the poor. *"It would be well for the poor of all towns if they were as well cared for as the poor of Kenilworth."*

At the time of the third distribution at 3.00 p.m. Monday 18th February at the Institute, 80 families were helped, but a sad case of overcrowding came to the Committee's attention; two men and their wives and a total of six children were all sleeping in just one room. The Council were criticised for not *"...extinguishing this focus of moral and physical disease."* Three times a week the vicar of St.Nicholas gave away 140 quarts of good soup, and a loaf of bread with each quart, whilst at St.John's soup was being sold for 1d a quart. Mr and Mrs Cay of Woodside found work for as many men as they could in wood-chopping and other tasks and there were other more localised benefactors. William Holland, a tailor living in Albion Street, distributed 150 2lb loaves at the top of Spring Lane. They had been made for him by Mr Liggins.

Perhaps surprisingly amongst all the hardship, the tradesmen of the town still held their annual supper at the Queen and Castle, which was attended by its largest gathering for years. The Chairman was Joseph Roberts and the hostess Mrs Styles who provided an excellent spread. The toast drunk in her honour was responded to by her son Frederick. The participants then provided their own musical entertainment, which included humorous songs.

*　　*　　*

The appointment of Lord Fielding, son of the Earl of Denbigh, as the local Parliamentary candidate, produced rapid strides in the popularity of the Conservative party. Two of the leading Conservatives in town, Dr Wynter and George Beard, held a meeting of 50 or 60 working men at the Coffee Tavern on Monday 25th November 1889, with the view of forming a permanent club. A List of 94 intending members had already been received and the two named gentlemen each subscribed five guineas. In addition, Wynter donated a bagatelle table, chess and draught sets, books and a framed portrait of Queen Victoria. James Whittendale gave an engraving of Lord Beaconsfield's Cabinet. A sub-committee of fourteen was appointed to draw up rules. This was the town's first political club and was given the title "The Conservative Working Men's Club."

The official opening took place on 16th December with both Lord and Lady Fielding present; it was Lady Fielding who performed the ceremony. The club had the use of the entire first floor of the Coffee Tavern, and its approaches were tastefully decorated for the occasion. The committee of twenty and various other positions were filled, with Dr Wynter being elected as President.

The whole assemblage then retired to the Kings Arms to meet up with members of the Primrose League for a concert, but before it started Wynter took another swipe at Henry Street, calling lies some comments attributed to him. Lord Fielding too made a speech, and even sang a song. The evening concluded with a rousing song about the inauguration of the club and Fielding's expected victory against the Liberal Mr Cobb at the next election.

The first floor of the Priory Road Coffee Tavern was the home of Kenilworth's first political club.

The manager of the club was John Matthews, formerly of the White Lion, and present proprietor of the transport business based at the Kings Arms, who had recently taken over the Coffee Tavern. The club raised funds by holding smoking concerts, at least one of which was attended by Fielding, but no ale was allowed to be sold on the premises. More pictures were donated; Mrs Fielding presented a picture of herself, whilst William Jeacock of Henry Street hung a portrait of Lord Salisbury. By August 1890 a large sign had been erected to be clearly visible by those leaving the station, but there was *"a cloud hanging"* over the club, and perhaps its best days were already behind it. The lack of a beer licence was seen as a reason for its declining popularity.

The club struggled on into 1892 but the end was in sight. First the Secretary, H J Stone, resigned due to leaving the town, and he was replaced by H Thornett jnr. Then the Earl of Denbigh died, leading to Lord Fielding resigning his candidature. The summer election was lost, the club was *"in a state of collapse"* and at its final meeting to discuss the situation in September, only five persons attended. A final dinner was held on 20th September to use up the remaining funds; ten sat down *"...nearly the full strength of the ordinary members..."* and the final winding up happened a week later.

In the Spring of 1894, John Matthews was in financial difficulties. He was described as *"...coffee house keeper, Priory Road, livery stable keeper, Kings Arms Mews, and mineral water manufacturer..."* and his liabilities outstripped his assets by £400. Within months, his Kenilworth businesses were taken on by former North Warwickshire Hunt stud-groom George Burton. Later the same year, Burton was advertising running *"...buses with careful drivers..."* to theatres in Leamington on Thursday evenings for parties of eight or nine for a shilling each, including the return trip after the performance had finished.

On Thursday 6th July 1893, William Pears married Edward Woodcock's daughter Helen Frances, then living in Wigan. William was nephew to A H Pears and Frances was a grand-daughter of the same man. He was 58, she just 22. The ceremony was at Allesley. The bride wore a dress of *"...brown silk brocade, thrown up with silver gray, with hat to match."* Her sister Edith was her solitary bridesmaid.

The reception was held at Kenilworth Hall: *"The whole of the servants and friends were generously entertained."* An elaborate dinner was set at 2.00 p.m. after which the party engaged in bowls etc. on the lawn. This was followed by tea and further festivities that came to a close at 8.00 p.m. The servants gave Pears a handsome walking stick and his bride a silver-mounted smelling bottle. The couple honeymooned in Oxford. The marriage was a short one: Helen died just eight months later at Kenilworth Hall, despite the attention of Sir James Paget, the Queen's medical adviser. In accordance with the wishes of William, the funeral was a quiet affair.

Colonel John Woodcock had served in India and made his fortune with tea trading. He left Kenilworth, c1884, for Scotland and by 1893 designed and built Newbold House on the outskirts of Forres, 25 miles from Inverness. He and his wife had no children, and were "much in absence." They employed eight gardeners who looked after the seven acre estate. The Reverend Somerset Pennefather is known to have visited him.

Emily Heath, aged 40 and wife of bricklayer John of 12 Whites Row, was the mother of ten children, the eldest being 16. She was paralysed on her right side, her right arm being useless, her voice was impaired and generally, she was not a strong person. Her husband had plenty of work and they lived pretty comfortably. As it was a fine morning, around midday on Saturday 4th March 1893, she took three of her children, twins Joe and Mary aged 2 years and 10 months, and 13 month-old Jack, for a walk. Emily had worked out a way to carry Jack in her apron with a shawl wrapped around him to leave her one good arm free. Their walk took them along the muddy track beside St.John's church and over the railway at Dodson's bridge and onto the footpath beside fields at the rear of The Hermitage. Joe, as usual, lingered behind.

They had only gone a couple of hundred yards past the railway line when Mary asked "Mother, where's Joe?" Emily turned but could not see him. A little way back on a slight bend in the path, they had passed a pit containing eight or ten feet of water. As quick as she was able, Emily hurried back to it and saw Joe struggling in the water. Clinging on to baby Jack as best she could, Emily stooped down to try and reach Joe but slipped; she fell in headfirst and Jack slipped from her grasp; Mary had been holding onto her mother's dress and she too was pulled in. The four of them were in serious difficulty; Emily could not even scream for help but managed to *"make a noise."*

Nearby was William Hickman, a lad employed by Kertland the butcher. He thought that he heard someone calling out, a voice from the pond repeating *"Oh, Lord, Oh Lord"* but was too frightened to go there alone. He mentioned this to Arthur Hincks, a gardener employed by Miss Birch at the Hermitage, and told him that the voice sounded like a duck. Hincks suggested that it may have been frogs and the two went to investigate. They discovered the horrific sight of Emily Heath and her three young children helplessly struggling in the stagnant water. Young Hickman immediately slid down the bank and managed to grab Emily who was still near the edge and, except for her legs, dragged her clear of the water. Two of the children were in the middle of the pond, the other about three yards out. The closest was Mary and Hincks got hold of his rake and managed to get her out, then knocked the head of the rake off, tied a rope to it, and got to the two boys. Hickman then went to get help; Emily was completely exhausted, there were marks that showed that part of the bank had given way.

PC Welch was one of the first to arrive to find Emily lying beside the pond with her three children; Joe and Jack were dead. Dr Edmund Bourne arrived and carried one of the lifeless children into The Hermitage, Mr Oram carried the other, and attempted to restore life for 45 minutes without success. PC Welch had stayed with Emily and eventually managed to get her to stand; she too was taken to The Hermitage and was given a change of clothes.

Rumours quickly circulated that Emily Heath had murdered her children for the insurance money, amounting to 30s for each child, and this excited widespread interest. The inquest was held two days later at The Green Man, but this caused difficulties as the largest room was very narrow and only three press reporters were allowed in. Other reporters, including from daily papers, protested at their exclusion and it was suggested that a larger room needed to be found. Coroner Dr Wynter asked *"Where? The school is not available and I cannot hold an inquest in open air."* Eventually several more reporters were allowed in but had to stand. The telegraph at the Post Office was kept open so that news of the verdict could be immediately sent. The suggestion of Emily harming her children was put to several witnesses but none had anything but good words and praise for the way in which she brought up her offspring, her husband had not even heard her threaten them. It soon became clear that the malicious gossip was misplaced and the jury, given two options for a verdict, without hesitation returned one of "Accidentally drowned" in preference to murder.

The funeral took place on the Thursday, just four days after the tragedy, and was attended by a large crowd. The two little coffins were placed side by side in the same grave just inside the churchyard gates in one of the areas that had been recently archaeologically excavated. The mourners included the still very distressed parents, and two sisters who walked holding hands. *"The ceremony was carried out in a quiet manner, the crowd being unobtrusive and respectful in their desire not to intrude upon a sad and pathetic bereavement."*

The scene of the Heath tragedy; the pond was on the left behind the modern hedge.

The remains of Jack and Joe Heath's gravestone, just inside the churchyard gateway.

* * *

During mid-1893, Henry Whateley added another block of greenhouses at Spring Gardens, each 210ft long, and filled it almost entirely with cucumber and tomato plants. Whateley was now producing about two tons of produce weekly for despatch at the nearby railway station. He was also growing large amounts of mushrooms out of doors.

The industrialisation of the eastern part of Kenilworth produced problems; Croydon, Hawkes and Whateley were collectively approached requesting a reduction of smoke through their chimneys. This had little effect, as all three were warned again the following year.

In early 1895, William Roberts erected a wind pump at his market garden at Whitemoor. The uprights, just 9ft from his fence, were 15ft high and the twelve sails were about 6ft in diameter and made of wood with zinc fans. The mill and pump, which ran very quietly, was used for pumping water into greenhouses. Unfortunately, Police-Sergeant Hipwell was aware of a law prohibiting the erection of wind pumps within 50 yards of a road and Roberts found himself up in front of the magistrates who included Mr Stanger-Leathes in the chair. Like Roberts, he too admitted being unaware of the law. The mill had not proved a nuisance, nor was it likely to frighten horses, and the Magistrates rather sympathetically decided to take no action, provided the mill was moved at the end of the summer.

* * *

E.H.Lingen Barker...

...was an architect whose works were of a "novel and remarkable character", and he was "connected professionally" with Kenilworth for many years and at one time lived with his father at Dudley House on Abbey Hill. His father built Southbank Road. By 1876, he was living at Shrub Hill, Hereford. In 1887, he entered into a partnership with Ernest H Morris of Waverley House in Southbank Road.

In 1862, he had devised a scheme for relief bridges for the crowded London streets that was approved by the Metropolitan Police Commissioner and the First Commissioner of Works but ultimately it was not carried out, although his idea was adopted and used successfully in America. His plan for moving the Wellington Arch would have been carried out were it not for a fault discovered in the arch itself. In the mid-1860s he designed an illuminated fountain on a gigantic scale for St.Peters Square in Hereford that was eventually built by Sir Francis Bolton at the Colonial Exhibition. In 1880, he became adviser to the Diocese of Bath and Wells on the back of testimonials from no fewer than 21 counties. In 1886, his new Board School at Llanelli won an award, and he won another for his design of the General Hospital at Merthyr, beating 17 architects all of whom specialised in hospitals. His particular talent was for economy in construction, particularly schools and churches for poor districts. He built 28 schools at a cost of less than £5 a head, by far the least on record, and mission churches at Brynamman and Cae Gurwen

at £4 and £3 per sitting. In 1875, he was called in by the London School Board to help reduce the cost of their buildings and his "...practical and intelligent assistance has been instrumental towards introducing cheaper methods of construction of which London still feels the benefits." His design in red brick with stone dressings for the "Herefordshire and South Wales Eye and Ear Institution" was put into effect in 1888-9. Closer to Kenilworth, he designed structural alterations to St.Davids at Moreton-in-Marsh in 1891.

* * *

The summer of 1894 saw the licensees of several pubs in trouble. Thomas Brewer of the Cottage Inn was fined £1 11s 6d for cruelty to a lamb by allowing it to become infested with maggots. The lamb died as a result and when the inspector turned the carcass over "a quart" of maggots fell out. Following the death of George Whale in October 1893, Harriett Alderman had not long been running the Coventry Cross when she was accused of adding 21% more water to her brandy than was allowed. In her defence, she innocently claimed that she was just copying her predecessor. She failed to win sympathy and was fined. Thomas Brown of the Royal Oak was caught watering down a gallon of whiskey, that he bought from a customer for 14s, "by more than the law allows". It was only ten months since he was last fined for the same offence and so this time had to pay £4 11s 6d.

James Barr had reversed the trend of short-term licensees at The Earl of Clarendon in Warwick Road by remaining for fifteen years. Then, in 1895, his daughter, "in a state of excitement" due to having some items stolen, served a Mr Faxton with beer out of hours at 11.30 a.m. on Good Friday just as a policeman arrived to investigate the thefts. Barr pleaded not guilty in his absence due to illness but was fined £1. Within months, Barr had been replaced by Alfred Sage.

In January 1894, Dr John Clarke, medical officer for the district for over forty years, died suddenly of "failure of the heart's system" at his home on Abbey Hill. He was 69. He had been seeing patients during the day and died soon after going to bed at midnight. During his 50 years in Kenilworth he had been particularly caring for the poorer classes, "...attending them even when he knew they could make no pecuniary return." His funeral was attended by all the local gentry and notables. Clarke had not long taken on a partner, Dr Reginald Carlyon Tweedy, who took over his practice and position as Medical Officer.

Started by Miss Bird of Spring Cottage in 1848, the Ladies Club had become an "Old Woman's Club" and had not met for some time when in September 1894 they gathered for tea in the parish room. Mrs Tweedy was elected President, replacing Dr Clarke's widow, who had held the post for 29 years.

John Clarke's only son, John Grayson Clarke, had left town, and by 1898, his widow had fallen on hard times. She was living on just £40 a year and when this became public knowledge, a subscription list was started for her, organised by Dr Edmund Bourne, Dr William Growse and A W Ledbrook. Within five weeks there had been about a hundred donations, from Lord Leigh's 5 guineas to *"an old patient"* giving just 1s, in a total of almost £150.

The grave of Dr John Clarke, shared with his mother, Sarah.

John Henry Grayson Clarke...

...was the only son of surgeon Dr John Clarke and was born at Hyde House on 10th August 1869. His known places of education were Guys Cliffe College, Leamington, and Birmingham University. At the time of the 1891 census, his occupation was as an architects articled clerk. He was generally a sickly person and his health caused him to take up a position with photographer S A Walker of Regent Street, London, and from there he moved to Bournemouth and started his own photography business. His travels next took him to Lincolnshire where he was to spend the rest of his life, first in Scotter and then Brigg, where he made his living as a photographer, producing post-cards and family portraits. A photograph he took of Kenilworth Castle, viewed looking across Purlieau Lane, was published in The Gazetteer of Great Britain and Ireland, published by Cassell in 1896. He married twice and had one daughter by his first wife. He was known as Grayson Clarke - Master Photographer.

---

*   *   *

The 1888 cricket season saw two remarkable individual performances for the town club. Away to Harborne, Dr Edmund Bourne, having scored 17 out of 76 runs in his side's two innings, took 15 for 43 out of 19 wickets as the opposition scored 126 in theirs. Then, towards the end of the season, against Kings Heath at home, Mr Edlman first scored 121 not out in a total of 222, and then took seven wickets for six runs including

5 clean bowled. The season was notable for another reason, the club paid its way. The total income was £84 6s, including £8 from the annual concert and donations of over £30, and expenditure was just £73 16s. Percy Evans remained as captain, *"...there is not a keener cricketer in Kenilworth...",* he was 24 years-old.

One way in which the club raised a small income was by renting out the ground for sheep and lamb grazing, and this also had the effect of keeping the grass down. By now, water had been laid on at the ground. In January 1890, a concert was held in the Elizabethan gallery at the Queen and Castle for the benefit of the club and the Medical Charity fund. Dr Thomas S Bourne took the chair for an evening of songs, including well-received comic performances, and sketches performed mostly by Kenilworth residents including the Misses Prime and Latoix, Mr Baulcombe, Haggar, Hughes, Paxton etc., who were referred to as the Kenilworth Glee Company.

During the evening, host Augustine Styles became ill and was attended to by the Chairman Dr Bourne. The following morning it was announced that Styles had suffered a burst blood vessel and had lost a lot of blood and only faint hopes were held for his recovery. Despite the attentions of doctors Bourne and Wynter, Styles *"gradually sank"* and died at 4.00 p.m. that Saturday. He was 42. He had been a member of the fifth troop of the Warwickshire Yeomanry Cavalry, and a sergeant and ten men attended the funeral, as did members of the tennis club, the Oddfellows and of course tradesmen and Board members. Now three years after the event, he was still fondly remembered for providing all the food for the Jubilee celebrations that no-one else would undertake. His wife Annie (43) took on the license, and was helped by their only son Frederick (17). The hotel had been bought by the Lichfield Brewery for £2,450 in 1887.

Augustine Styles, right, was buried alongside Post Mistress and pianist, Hannah Riley.

During the 1890 season, there were further occasions when the umpire's performance was called into question and perhaps the most justifiable complaint came in May in a match against Smethwick: *"In the second innings, Wheeler played well for his 42 till the opponents, glad to get rid of him in any way, endeavoured to run him out from a ball which had gone to the boundary amongst the spectators. Their explanation for this action took up the remaining time left for play."* The incident was recorded as: *"Wheeler, not (run?) out, 42."* Fourteen matches were won during that season against thirteen defeats and four draws.

Club President Dr Thomas Bourne was absent from the end of season dinner at the Kings Arms in November 1890 due to ill health and so the chair was taken by Percy Evans. At the start of the season, Mr Combe had promised prizes for the better players and it was down to Secretary Dr Edmund Bourne to award them, but there was a large degree of manipulation in the awards. To qualify, players had to play at least half the matches. Dr Harvey Smith and Colonel Jervis actually topped the batting averages, but had not played sufficient games and so Dr Edmund Bourne won with an average of 12.9, but as he had won the previous season he handed it on; Thomas Mitchener averaged 10.9, but was overlooked as he won another prize and so the prize of a bat went to Mr Paxton, actually the fifth-ranked batsman, who averaged just 7.8. Dr Edmund Bourne also topped the bowling averages, 83 wickets at 7.6 runs a wicket, but as he was deemed to have "won" the batting averages, this too was handed on, the recipient of a pair of pads being Charles Robbins with 31 wickets at 11.3 runs a wicket. A pair of gloves was awarded to the best fielder and this was won by Mr Went. The prize that Mitchener received was a bat donated by the Reverend Alfred Binnie and was presented for the most catches. His tally was 16, Dr Edmund Bourne almost inevitably being second with 15. Secretary Bourne also had to decide which players merited being presented with the distinctive cap badge and these were awarded to Mitchener, Robbins, Hudson, Paxton, Edmunds, Stone and J Smith. The evening concluded with a number of songs performed by members.

This was Dr Edmund Bourne's last event as Secretary, he resigned due to other commitments; his father was in poor health and it was likely Edmund was taking more responsibility for the practice. In January 1890, Edmund had cancelled his membership of the fire brigade due to *"numerous professional duties"*, but he could not have been prepared for the sudden death of his wife just three months later. She had been visiting her sister in Weston-Super-Mare. In 1891, his father Thomas was taken seriously ill and quickly deteriorated, dying at his home at Abbey End on 8th June aged 67; the earlier death of his own wife had been a blow from which he never recovered. His bright smile and cheery words were always appreciated by friends and patients alike. He had had a busy life, being one time Chairman of the Water Company, Chairman of the old Parochial Show Society and for many years attached to the Institute and Convalescent Home, but he was perhaps most noted for his enthusiasm for the town cricket club, the current incarnation of which he was the first President, and had always encouraged others to become involved. He had

been in charge of his practice for thirty years and now his son Edmund formally took it over.

One occasional player in the 1890 season was the newly arrived in town, London born Henry Smith-Turberville-Smith (40), often referred to by variations of his name, including Harry as an alternative to Henry, who had made an appearance for the MCC against Derbyshire in May 1886, scoring 11 runs in his two innings. He lived with his wife, Emma (27), at The Gables, Crackley, and first made the news when a racehorse he owned gave Mill End blacksmith Walter Freeman a nasty kick. Smith-Turberville was to become involved in a variety of Kenilworth sporting circles.

In late 1890, a number of the local sporting types formed themselves into a golf club. Henry Smith-Turberville was secretary and Treasurer, and William Pears the President. Ernest Trepplin was approached for land for a course and a large area of Castle Farm was rented from him.

The course was laid out by an admitted expert on links design, Mr Burns, the Professional at the Warwickshire County Golf Club. Hedges were purposely introduced to act as hazards.

"The links are very fair specimens of inland greens. They abound in very good hazards such as hedges, ditches, pools &c., and altogether make a very sporting course, and reflect great credit on the professional who laid them out. An improvement might be made by bringing the home-hole opposite the clubhouse and placing the teeing ground for the first hole, so as to carry the hedge from the first drive off. It will never make an ideal golf course but it will improve with time, and there will be some very fair putting greens, but it will always be heavy going more or less, as rich pasture land is rather unfavourable to good golf, nor does good putting greens and hazards constitute the sum total of a golfer's happiness."

The course had nine holes, each of which was named, and these had to be completed twice for a round. To avoid complete repetition, the course was arranged so that several of the early holes were played from different tees:

From T1 to Fishponds	266 yds
From T2 to Flat	257 yds
From T3 to Meadow	221 yds
From T4 to Ridge	197 yds
From T5 to Far	255 yds
From T6 to Cart	244 yds
From T7 to Short	166 yds
From T8 to Castle	308 yds
From T9 to Home	191 yds
From T1 to Flat	292 yds
From T2 to Meadow	221 yds
From T3 to Fishponds	299 yds
From T4 to Ridge	375 yds

(There is an error here, T4 to Ridge is given as two different distances)

The course was then completed from T5 to Home as in the first round. The first nine holes totalled 2,105 yds, the second 2,351 yds.

The club was formally opened on Tuesday 17th February 1891 by Smith-Turberville with a neat and appropriate speech which brought a round of applause from the ladies and gentlemen present. A foursome match against Coventry had been arranged to mark the occasion, Mr Smith and Mr Hillman for the visitors played Dr Edmund Bourne and T Latham in the first game. Mr Latham as Captain of the club had the honour of driving the first ball *"...which he accomplished in a very creditable style, driving very clean and straight for hole number one."* The terrain of the course very quickly caught up with the opposition: *"Mr Hillman responding for Coventry also drove a good ball but landed into some wet clay, literally burying the ball. (His partner) made a very good attempt but effected only a few yards."* The first hole was won by Kenilworth, which produced loud cheers from the onlookers, but the advantage was lost on the next and the Coventry pair eventually won by 5 holes. A singles match between H Smith and Dr Bourne followed, and produced a memorable shot; at tee number 5, Smith drove his ball clean over a 50ft high tree some 150yds away, landing almost on the green, a feat that was expected to be unequalled for some time. The match was halved.

Members of the Coventry club returned for another match the following week. The hopes of the home team rose when the first Coventry player's ball *"...was seen to be approaching the mud around the first pit and even more so when this gentleman appeared to be regarding the roots of the first hedge with anger and suspicion."* The match was tied, both players scoring 93. The second match involved Mr Smith who made the extraordinary first day shot off the 5th tee. This time he saved his best for the last hole, winning his game by scoring two. Dr Bourne played Mr Hill during glorious afternoon weather and they allowed themselves *"...a little longer time for their rounds, investigating more closely the varieties which art and nature have placed on the links in the shape of hedges, water and mud."* The additional care favoured Mr Hill who won by one hole with a score of 120. Kenilworth lost but was not disgraced.

14th March was a "Red Letter Day" for the club on the occasion of the first Ladies competition. Dr Bourne carefully handicapped the participants and the player awarded the largest, 60, Miss Jones of St.John's Vicarage, won with a nett score of 72. Mrs Frank Smith had a gross score of 65, suggesting that perhaps the full course was not played, but had 10 strokes added to her score to put her in second place. Last was Mrs Carter with a round of 188 and a handicap of 35.

In May, William Pears presented a silver Challenge Cup to be played for by club members every six months. The first winner was the popular Dr Edmund Bourne with a round of 95 (89 nett) with Pears himself in second place with 116 (92). This was regarded as the first important competition at the club and it was seen as appropriate that a man who had put so much effort into its foundation should have won. On 2nd June, the lady members played a similar competition for a silver Challenge Cup donated by Emma Smith-Turberville. The winner was Nina Allen of Leamington with a score of 207 (117nett). Last was Mrs Carter with 221 (141

nett) - perhaps this time the full course had been played.

The fine summer weather saw less golf played, with tennis and cricket being more popular but the course remained open for the summer evenings. Amongst the arranged matches were mixed-team events against Leamington. The Smith-Turbervilles paired up, less obviously, widower Dr Bourne paired with Mrs Mitchell.

Despite the problems he encountered playing only the second-ever shot on the course, Mr Hillman, the Coventry Gold medallist, had recently joined the club. He was amongst other eminent players to make complimentary remarks upon the sporting nature of the course. As news of the new course spread, *The Post* included an article that erroneously stated that Kenilworth did not have a defined course and that enthusiasts were content to *"knock the ball over a succession of hedges"* and this, as one might expect, brought a reply from Smith-Turberville in the next issue, as he feared the remarks might have damaged the reputation of the rising club.

The last Monday of September saw the start of what was to become an annual event, Kenilworth Golf Week. The first event was the mixed foursomes, won by Miss Jepson partnering Mr E Jones of the Vicarage with a score of 155 (95 nett). The winners received a gold scarf pin and gold brooch manufactured by Robert Sawyers, goldsmith of Edinburgh. In second place was an interesting partnership of Dr Edmund Bourne and Miss Nina Allen of Leamington. The Smith-Turbervilles logged the second lowest score but finished fifth under the handicap system. On Tuesday the gentlemen lost by eight holes to a Coventry team and on Wednesday the ladies match for the Captaincy was won by Miss E Middleton with a round of 124 (96). After a Ladies v Gentlemen match the next day, the ladies proceeded to beat Leamington Ladies by 35 holes. In presenting the prizes at the conclusion of the week on Saturday, William Pears proposed a vote of thanks to Smith-Turberville for the assiduity and success with which he conducted the club, and this was *"accorded with acclamation."* Great credit was also due to Mitchener the groundsman - likely to be the same Mitchener who cared for the cricket pitch who was known to be a keen golfer.

On 14th November 1891 the first annual meeting of the club took place at the Institute. William Pears took the chair at a largely attended meeting. There were now upwards of 50 members and a balance in hand of £12 on the first year's accounts. Dr Edmund Bourne was elected President for the year, Smith-Turberville retained his position as Honorary Secretary with C G Irving of Lloyds Bank treasurer. William Pears, F Carter, Vincent Jepson, T Day, Mr Carey-Franklin, Mrs Mitchell, Miss Middleton and Miss L Sidebottom formed the Committee. A handicapping committee was formed, consisting of the President, Secretary and Mrs Mitchell. Honorary members fees were reduced from a guinea to 10s 6d. Mr Pears closed the meeting hoping that its harmonious manner would always be maintained.

Kenilworth's club members were successful at other courses, Mrs Smith-Turberville, for example, won the gold medal at the North Warwickshire Golf Club in May 1892. Two months later a cricket match was played between golfers and non-golfers at the cricket ground, and, not surprisingly, the golfers lost by 114 runs to 62. The summer of 1892 also saw the first marriage between two club members when Dr Edmund Bourne wed his earlier golfing partner Nina Allen of Leamington. She lived at Thornecliffe on the Kenilworth Road, which is where the reception was held.

In time for the autumn 1893 Golf Week, the club built for itself a clubhouse of corrugated iron at a cost of about £100. It was placed near the first tee and Home green and consisted of one large apartment and a gentlemen's room. By the time of the AGM in November, chaired by its President William Mitchell, the clubhouse had become a "...*well lighted and a cheery little place on an autumn evening.*" Lockers were now in place, and indeed, a fresh batch of them was positioned by the gentlemen players on the night of the AGM itself. "*Mr H. Smith-Turberville, the valued hon. Secretary whose election for another year was carried by acclamation...*" presented the balance sheet. Despite starting the year with a balance in hand and having an income of over £113, there was now "*something due on the other side*" and so a lengthy discussion ensued as to the raising or lowering of subscriptions. Vincent Jepson suggested raising them, Mr Day suggested the opposite. It was eventually decided to have the entrance fee as a guinea, a yearly subscription of 26s, a two-person family ticket at £2 12s 6d with each additional family member paying half a guinea, honorary members 10s 6d and visitors' subscriptions to be 2s 6d. However, the revised rates were not to come into force until the following October. There were now 75 members and it was hoped that each would bring in an additional member every year. Smith-Turberville said he always tried to get the results of matches won published, but was not too bothered about the ones lost, but Dr Bourne had kept a complete record of "...*the club's doings from the very beginning...*" and had to be much thanked for his efforts. The feeling was, though, that the general play of the club would not improve unless they could be taught by a professional, but the only local clubs they should lose to were Warwick and Coventry.

Smith-Turberville's comments were prophetic. When the club next met Coventry in February 1894, they were beaten 62-1. "*The uneven character of the match is striking. We believe that never before has such disparity been shown in the annals of either club.*" Smith-Turberville on this occasion made the effort to have the defeat published.

The golf club-house was built in time for the autumn 1893 Golf Week event.

Prior to the 1891 season, the Kenilworth Cricket Club formed a workable Second XI by the amalgamation of the Tannery and Mutual clubs. Tannery manager Obidiah Woods was appointed Captain.

Smith-Turberville played in nine matches in the 1891 season, topping the batting averages with 20.5, and finishing third in the bowling with 17 wickets at an average of 6.5. He was already popular enough to chair the end of season annual dinner, and was the subject of much praise: "*Mr Turberville has taken up cricket, golf, shooting and everything else that was good for men.*" "*A splendid cricketer and judge of the game. He has a style of bowling that the club had long required, a style which was held in great respect by our opponents, to whom it had been simply appalling!*"

A number of those involved with the cricket club played hockey in the winter. In early 1892, a match was arranged between the two town parishes; played on a very muddy pitch it ended in a 5-2 victory for St.John's "*...which would have been much more decisive but for the magnificent goalkeeping of that grand hockey player, Mr H. Smith Turberville.*" Both the goals for the losers were scored by Dr Edmund Bourne "*with his usual dash.*" Ludlow, Jepson, F R Hudson and Inwood Jones also came in for special praise. Hockey was beginning to take a firm hold on the Kenilworth public and it was hoped that a club could one day be formed.

At the Cricket Club AGM, prior to the 1892 season, it was no surprise that Smith-Turberville was elected captain. He was "*...highly popular as a leader of sport, cricket and golf throughout the town...*" and he was "*...confidently expected to have a very beneficial influence on the seasons play.*" In his first match as captain, a victory, he scored 16 out of 58 runs and took 5 wickets for 16. The following week in a victory over Sparkhill, Dr Bourne, still a notable performer in his less frequent appearances, took 6 wickets for 17 runs.

Despite being very popular and receiving donations from at least thirty people, 1892 was not a good year for the club. Not only did they lose twice as many matches as they won, the club also now had a debt of £35 and could expect an income for the coming year from subscriptions of just £45. At the annual dinner at the Kings Arms, Thomas Hawley, the club's landlord, agreed to drop the annual rent of the 6 acre field from £24 to £19 on the condition that Percy Evans also donated £5 to funds. This was agreed to and an impromptu collection, which raised an additional £23, was paid immediately into Lloyd's Bank against the debt. On the playing side, the club captain, Smith-Turberville, said that poor fielding, and in particular dropped catches, contributed to many of the poor results. He promised to arrange fielding practices for the coming season. One member at the club was Colonel Swinfin Jervis, who had been the captain of his regimental team for 23 years; he scored 40 runs in his five innings for Kenilworth, and performed three songs at the dinner. Undoubtedly the star of the previous season was again Dr Edmund Bourne; he topped the batting averages with 17, (Smith-Turberville with 10.2 was the only other in double figures) and was the leading wicket-taker with 79 at an average of less than 8 runs; F Paxton took 47 wickets.

By the start of the 1893 season the debt had been

reduced, but only to £31, and the income from subscriptions was only £40 5s. To boost funds the subscriptions were altered to one guinea for *"Playing gentlemen members..."*, 5s for working men with the privilege of being able to pay in instalments, and half a crown for those under 17 years of age. All subs now had to be paid before members were allowed to play. William Evans resigned as treasurer and was replaced by Mr Irving.

Before practise for the new season started *"30 yards of turf have been taken up and laid with ashes."* This was the central playing area; the ashes were used as a sub-soil and the turf re-laid and then *"watered artificially"* to keep it in condition. The pitch was described as being in its best-ever condition. The field had a hedge running along its south side that was considered an ideal place for some seating, and some camp-stools were donated to the club. In July and August a professional was temporarily engaged with money raised by subscription and he, W Jones, made a quick impression taking 7 wickets for 8 runs in one match and 104 not out in the next. Overall, it was another poor season, only two batsmen making double figures in the averages, and it was decided to engage a professional for the whole of the next. He was Mr Wheeler and he arranged weekly two-hour practices, helped Mitchener look after the ground, and sight-screen "sheets" were used for the first time. Wheeler made an impression on the field as well. In his first match, he took 6 wickets for 11 runs and then scored 17 not out of the meagre total required to win the match. The following week he produced an astonishing bowling performance of 5 wickets for 2 runs.

Over the 9th and 10th August 1894, the club played a match against Hampstead with Smith-Turberville playing for the opposition. Kenilworth had the best of a draw, scoring 177 and 124 for 4 declared, against 149 and 46 for 5 at the close with Hampstead still 106 runs adrift. Smith-Turberville scored only 9 runs in his two innings, E Matteson was Kenilworth's top scorer with 58 and 35 not out. The next week Wheeler and Smith-Turberville scored 70 between them out of a total of 154 against Leamington Early Closers, and Smith-Turberville took 8 wickets, the only wickets he took all season, as the opposition were bowled out for 34.

This was declared the club's best season in a long time *"beating the record for many years"* and it was largely due to Wheeler, although Mayfield was described as the backbone of the club. *"Not many clubs have such a charming ground as the Kenilworth Cricket Club. Out of 36 matches, 30 have been won, 12 lost and 4 drawn."* (sic). Wheeler topped the batting averages and Smith-Turberville the bowling, thanks to the one extraordinary performance.

During the winter of 1894-5, Henry Smith-Turberville toured the West Indies with *"Mr Lucas's English team"*, effectively an England amateur side. He played in only one of the tour games officially recognised as first class, scoring 14 and 6 against Trinidad at Queens Park, Port of Spain and took 1 wicket for 28 runs in 8 overs. He also played against the Combined Services on 31st January, scoring 16 in a total of 247, and returned a bowling analysis of *"24, 0, 23, 0, 0, 1"* as the Services

made 124 and 148. The Barbados Herald mis-spelled his name and referred to the Kenilworth star as *"the genial Tuberville."* After the match, Smith-Turberville attempted to return to the field with a colleague for some practice, only to be mobbed by the locals. *"They clustered around him and treated him in a most familiar way possible. Some linked their arms in his; some patted him on the back; some essayed to carry him along; they shouted and yelled in his honour; in fact they did him every kind of homage, but would not clear the way for him to have his practice. Mr Smith-Turberville, who towered above them like a goliath, implored in vain, the affection and admiration of the mob too deep-rooted."* He abandoned his attempt at a practice and returned to the pavilion to the applause and laughter of the other players. The Gymkhana races in Trinidad in March provided another spectacle, particularly the "Hurry Scurry" race that was for *"...ponies and batsmen. This was the most exciting race of the day, and Mr Turberville came in a fierce second. Nearly all the animals bolted after passing the post and went for some cross-country exercise on their own account."*

The present form of the Kenilworth Cricket Club had now existed for nine years. £200 had been spent on levelling the ground and £40 on the pavilion. £24 a year was spent on rent and rates, but £5 was retrieved by allowing grazing. Bats, balls and other equipment came to about £15 or £16 a year.

* * *

On 28th November 1884, the St.Nicholas Mission Room on the corner of Park Hill and Albion Street was opened. Made of corrugated iron it measured 50ft by 25ft and could seat up to 250 persons. It was very neatly surrounded by an area of turf and gravelling which was enclosed with ornamental iron palisading. It cost £310 to build, of which £250 had been raised by the time of the opening, and was built on ground owned by Thomas Hawley who had made the land available on easy terms. The building work was done by William Henry Lawrence. During the first week, services were conducted every evening culminating in a *"...most enthusiastic temperance meeting at which over 100 put on the blue ribbon."* Closely involved was John Bagshaw who had for a long time been involved with services held at the Co-operative room nearby, and he conducted the Sunday evening services in the new Mission Room. In 1885, John Bagshaw was responsible for starting the Young Men's Mutual Improvement Society in conjunction with St.Nicholas church.

In late 1886, it was lamented that no football club had been organised for the coming year but one reason given was that the best sportsmen, the cricketers, were on *"...the shady side of thirty."* One of them had said that he hoped to play cricket for ten years more, but football not ten minutes more. *"Football, as played today, is rough and there is nothing particularly elevating about it."*

The Young Men's Mutual Improvement Society began to add the physical to their spiritual needs. In 1890 they formed their own cricket team, playing matches against St.John's, the Tannery and Crackley. There were a number of short-lived and occasional teams at this time; another was the Kenilworth Incapables. The YMMIS cricket team lasted until March 1891 when it merged with the Tannery team to form a Second XI for the Town club, but the lack of their own sporting club was short-lived as in October 1891, the YMMIS formed an Association Football team, a "...*long felt want in Kenilworth.*" The new club called itself Kenilworth Mutual FC and St.Nicholas' curate, Reverend William Bissett, was its President. Percy Evans and the ever-involved Dr Edmund Bourne were vice-presidents, Mr W Hiorns treasurer, and Mr E B Jeffcott secretary. On the playing side, J Moore was appointed captain and F Spires vice captain. Practices and matches took place on Saturday afternoons in a field on the Coventry Road lent by J Smith.

It was not until early February the following year that Mutual played their first match. It was at Woodcote Park against Leek Wootton, and it is probable that Mutual's faith was severely tested in a 14-0 defeat. The club's first team was Woods in goal; Lawrence and Brown full-backs; Drane, Nixon and F Whateley half-backs; College, Whateley, Moore, Penn and Spires, forwards. Three weeks later, a home match was arranged against Leamington Town. For half an hour the play was even, but the visitors scored twice to lead 2-0 at half time. "*In spite of the efforts of the Kenilworth team, their opponents were able to score six goals in the second half. Despite the result, the Kenilworth team showed a decided improvement.*" The team had changed: Ensall; Went, Welch; Lawrence, Woods, Paxton; Faulks, Whateley, Moore, Spires and Penn. The next match was also at home and the team had a notable change, with William Welch in goal. Playing downhill in the first half, Mutual restricted the opposition to one goal and in a tight second half there was only a single shot; a failed attempt after a long run by Kenilworth's Whateley. The following week saw another 8-0 defeat, this one at the hands of Coventry Olympic.

19th March saw the return match against local rivals Leek Wootton and another drubbing was expected, but Mutual now had "...*the services of a capable and experienced centre forward...*" in the form of the Reverend A Winter. A good crowd saw half-time reached without a goal. "*The Mutual forwards now began to assume an aggressive attitude and playing a long passing game carried the ball toward their opponent's goal. After a struggle, Colledge centred from the left and Whateley neatly put the ball through the posts. Wootton claimed offside but the point was allowed by the referee.*" Winger Spires soon added a second and Mutual had their first victory "...*brought about in a great measure by the resolute tackling of the half-backs.*"

In April, the return against Leamington brought a much closer game than the first. but still a defeat, 4-1, and then on Easter Monday, after the Parochial Sports on the field behind the Vicarage, a crowd of 500 saw Mutual beat a Reverend Winter XI 5-2. As well as himself, Winter also picked Dr Growse. Quickly becoming the star of Mutual was the goalkeeper Welch. Poor performances by the rest of the team obviously

gave him the chance to shine; he made "...*one or two brilliant saves...*" in a 5-0 defeat by Lord Street.

On Thursday 18th August at 8.30 p.m., the club held its first general meeting at the Mission Room. R V Butt was elected Treasurer and A College as secretary. Dencer, Bowen and Thomas Sherwin (who chaired the meeting) were elected as a committee. Several new players had enrolled and so an improvement on the first season's record of 3 wins, 5 defeats and 2 abandonments, was hoped for. A new pitch had been arranged in a field belonging to William Holmes adjoining Crackley Lane.

The opening match of the new, 1892-3, season, at the new ground, was between Mutual and the Kenilworth Stars, ending in a 2-1 win for Mutual. The Stars were a new club, their only other notable match had been five months earlier when they drew 0-0 with High Street Swifts at rugby-playing Kenilworth Albion's ground at The Spring, but they had now arranged a good number of matches for the coming season and had found a ground of their own, at Park Hill with an end-to-end slope. A home match in October ended in a 2-2 draw against Priory Villa of Coventry. The Stars were "...*the much heavier team, much faster but had less combination.*" The team was Heritage; Ingram, Moss; Batter, Garlick, Marriott; Whateley, Overton, Kelsey, Liddington and Hancox. The following month saw another home game, this time against Warwick Northgate Albion. The score was 1-1 at half time, thanks to goalkeeper Heritage who had to "...*negotiate a hot shot which he cleared in fine style.*" With Stars playing downhill after the interval, goalkeeper Heritage had little to do and spent much of his time "...*playing just behind the forwards for most of the second half...*" and they won 3-1. The following week they drew 0-0 against Coventry New Stars and followed this with another home win, 3-1 against Coventry Globe. In December, and then again in January (1893), Stars played host to another new team, St.John's Rovers. The Stars won both matches, at Park Hill, 7-1 and 5-0. In between these games, Rovers lost a game against Mutual in which goal-keeper Welch did not have a single shot to save.

These good results were not sustained by Stars in the new year, February and March saw an 8-0 defeat to Leek Wootton, 4-2 and 3-0 home defeats by Coventry Psycho, and a 3-3 draw against St.Mark's. Still not twelve months-old, The Stars put in a good performance and got off to a fine start against Coventry Gosford Street Bible Class who were considered strong opponents. "*A good kick by one of the backs enabled Batter to get possession, who after a good run, centred to Harris who opened the Stars account within two minutes from the start.*" But grand play by the opposition saw them win 3-1. This was considered one of the Stars' best performances of the season. St.John's Rovers on the other hand, playing on their own ground at Windy Arbour, showed a marked improvement by beating Coventry Rovers 1-0 and 4-0, and Unity Villa 9-1, but they lost 5-1 to Coventry Trafalgar.

With a pitch established at William Holmes's Springfield, it was not to be long before its own occasional team was formed. Kenilworth Springfield played a game in early March 1893 against "*Victoria*" and won 1-0 with a goal "...*scored in a squabble.*" The opposition was likely to have been Kenilworth Victoria, as the sides met at the same ground on Easter Saturday with the game finishing 1-1. It is worth remembering who owned the ground when looking at the Springfield team: A Warner; J Sumner, B Wood; T Wringrose, Fred Holmes, Frank Holmes, T Penn, H Holmes, E Roads, H Bennett and W Wringrose. The Victoria comprised Hornidge; A Leddington, A Hobbins; E Swain, G Webb, H Garlick; B Penn, A Hancox, E Hancox, A Batter, F Swain. Many of the players were mid-teenagers.

In a match in October 1892 against Bablake Old Boys, Mutual showed *"...more speed than combination...the reverse may be said of the Old Boys (who) played a much more scientific game than their opponents. Had Welch not kept goal in an admirable manner, the Old Boys would have doubled their score."* In the 4-2 defeat, Mutual's highlight was their second goal *"...a beautiful long shot from the right wing at an extreme angle by Moore."* In loosing 8-0 the following week *"Welch effected several really brilliant saves..."* and the next match, a 7-1 home defeat by Coventry All Saints, would have been worse had it not again been for the excellent keeping by Welch. *"Too much praise cannot be heaped upon his goal-keeping, his handling and punching being exceptionally good."* Leamington Town were the strongest of the local sides and Mutual played against their reserve side, managing a creditable 2-2 draw. The fullbacks' and halfbacks' tackling was praised, but the latter's kicking was *"...rather uncertain. The forwards continued to improve in combination."*

A match in January 1893 against Rotherham's United was played in slippery conditions. It was impossible to pass accurately, but Mutual won 2-1 *"...chiefly by the dash and vigour which the Mutual infused in their play."* The same approach the following week, *"...more energy and dash than combination...",* produced a 1-1 draw with Unity Villa, a side to which they lost 2-1 just three weeks earlier. The new year produced a change in the team's fortunes. Bablake Old Boys were beaten 2-1, but this was followed with another defeat, 2-0, but the pitch was to blame: *"The ground was very soft and muddy rendering correct play impracticable."* This was followed by an exciting home match against Coventry side St.John's Albion. 3-1 down at half time, Mutual came storming back to win 5-4. In April, the team was strengthened with three players from Coventry and this produced a 6-1 win against Leek Wootton and a 7-1 victory against New Star Rangers with a Smith hat-trick and two goals each for Moore and Hales.

The season ended at Easter weekend with a 3-1 victory over St.John's Rovers on the Saturday and on Easter Monday the annual match after the Parochial Sports. This time Reverend Spurrell chose the opposition, which lost 5-0.

At Mutual's end of season meeting at the clubroom, the Mission Room, on 24th April 1893, several resolutions were passed unanimously, the most notable of which was that the club was to be renamed Kenilworth Town Association Football Club, and that a reserve side was to be started. A College resigned his position as secretary and F Spires took his place. There were particular thanks to William Holmes for the use of his

field at Springfield. It was also decided to enter the Midland Daily Telegraph Cup competition the following season. The club's first end-of-season dinner was held in May at the Royal Oak and about 30 attended. Although the season had started badly, results had improved and the overall record of 10 wins, 2 draws and 13 defeats, scoring 49 and conceding 71 was described as satisfactory.

At a general meeting in August it was announced that the club had a deficiency of 2s 2d and that the following season they would continue to play on the pitch adjoining Crackley Lane. Further arrangements for the club continued to be made throughout the summer; in an attempt to collect all the best players from the town into one strong club, the Kenilworth Stars disbanded and the better players formed the basis of Kenilworth Town Reserves.

The Albion Street Mission-room where the decision was made to form Kenilworth Town Football Club.

In September 1893, the first match as Kenilworth Town, at home to Leamington Rovers, got off to a tremendous start with W Holmes scoring with a *"capital shot"* after five minutes. *"Within three more minutes a second goal was claimed by Town but the Rovers refused to play if the goal was allowed, claiming off-side. The referee eventually decided in Rovers favour."* It made little difference, Smith scored two more for Town before half-time. In the second half *"...the play became somewhat rough and the referee cautioned one or two players."* The referee in question was J T Holmes, head master of Kenilworth's National School. Smith completed his hat-trick, Bowen and Moore also scored in a fine 6-0 win. *"The brilliant goalkeeping (of the Rovers) was much applauded, no less than about twenty warm shots being fisted out..."* whilst for Town *"...the passing was conspicuous for its unselfishness, which added greatly to the victory. We express our belief that with constant practise they are destined to occupy an honourable position in local football circles."* This first Kenilworth Town side was W Welch in goal; A Colledge and B Penn full back; F Faulks, J Mayfield (captain), F Whateley half backs; J Moore, W Smith, A Bowen, W Holmes and J Bale forwards.

The good form continued the following week with a 3-0 win at Allesley; *"Welsh's services were not called into requisition once during the whole game."*

The next home match started much the same as the first, Bowen scoring after just two minutes with the opposition, Leamington Town Reserves, claiming offside. This time the goal was allowed. With the score at 2-1 in the second half, some hesitation by R Ensall in goal allowed an equaliser, but in the closing minutes Town forced a corner, well taken by Bale: *"A scrimmage took place in front of goal, and the ball partly cleared, but Whateley came up from half-back and sharply returned the ball, which was eventually forced through."* Another win, 3-2.

Despite a solitary defeat, narrowly 3-2 by All Saints, the good run of results continued including 5-2 away to Leek Wootton, a thrilling 4-4 draw against Warwick United Reserves at Emscote in front of 400 spectators (a game which goalkeeper Welch missed), and a 5-1 win against Leamington Brewery. Town were now to play away to Warwick United in a cup tie and came away with a creditable draw, 2-2, only to loose the replay 4-0. After losing a closely fought return against Leamington Rovers 1-0, winning ways returned just after Christmas when, with only nine men, they beat Leamington Town Reserves 1-0.

Victories were being logged by the reserves as well; 2-0, 6-1, 6-1 again, and 2-0 at home to Eagle Works in front of 50 spectators at Crackley, before coming down to earth when being knocked out of the Hospital Cup 16-0. Such was the interest in the club that a third team was started and they got off to a good start by beating Leamington United Reserves 2-1 at Crackley.

The start of the new year saw a downturn in the club's fortunes. The first week in January saw an 8-man Town beaten 7-0 by Townend in their first appearance in the Hospital Cup and this was followed by a 5-1 defeat at Allesley - the heroics of young Welch were not enough! A number of players were missing games through illness and another defeat, 7-1, led to the observation that the players needed to practise passing. Welch missed the next game, Ensall taking his place for a 6-2 victory over Leamington Brewery, and in fact, Welch had played his last game; the team were stunned in early March when he died just days after his 21st birthday. He had been an *"...estimable and quiet young gentleman..."*, the son of a blacksmith, and worked for J and T Dickenson. Mrs Pears died same week, there was a flu epidemic in town.

The first match after Welch's death was at home to Stoke. *"The wind was too high for accurate play. At half-time the score was 2-1 in favour of the home team. After that the wind increased in strength and in the last ten minutes the Stoke team increased their score by 6 goals."* The return against Stoke brought Town's biggest defeat, 9-0. A 3-0 home win against Coventry Pneumatic saw *"...Smith make one of the best runs down the right wing that has been seen on the Kenilworth ground all season, finishing with a splendid shot..."* adding to two goals by Woods. This was the final goal in a season that saw Town win eleven and loose eight, drawing two, scoring 57 goals against 51. The reserves had difficulty fielding a team at times towards the end of the season and used several players from St.John's Rovers to fulfil fixtures. They played only 18 of their arranged 27 matches, and won just 7. It seems the third team was short-lived.

The establishment of organised football clubs obviously increased interest in the game, but this caused its own problems with youths playing in the streets. *"Complaints have been made on several occasions that pedestrians are greatly annoyed by this street rowdyism, and frequently receive rude shoves from intrusive boys rushing madly to kick the ball. Boys must be taught to keep within proper bounds. It would be well too to remind some of the boys of Kenilworth that there are six days of the week that a game of football can be played without breaking the Sabbath."* *"I am sorry to see boys practising on the Common on Sundays, on the level piece on the east side of the railway, in their shirt sleeves using their coats to indicate the goals and playing as if it were an ordinary weekday."* Youths playing football on Castle Green were turning the grass *"...the same colour as the road..."*; there was an additional nuisance here as residents also hung their washing out to dry on the green. Visitor numbers to the Castle were greatly reduced at Easter 1894 and this was attributed to the many midlanders who preferred to stay at home and watch their local football team. The charge for entering the Castle had also just increased to 6d to successfully *"...keep the rowdy element out. One can now walk across the Castle grounds without being offended by swearing or offensive language of any kind."*

Such was the level of enthusiasm and expectation at the Kenilworth Town club, its members decided that for the 1894-5 season they should join the first division of the new North Warwickshire League. The AGM held at the Royal Oak in August discussed a couple of the rules; the team was compelled to provide a full team and linesman for each game, and for home matches they had to pay the referee 2s 6d and his return railway fare. The club had received in the previous season £18 3s 2d in subscriptions, but were now in debt to the extent of 11s 2d. Sherwin, the playing Secretary, announced that the club was looking for a new field for the coming season as they considered the one at Crackley was too far from the town; the Local Board had been approached but at this time, a decision had not been made. Deputations had been made to St. Johns Rovers with the intention of amalgamating the two clubs, but on a vote, this was not proceeded with. Already 16 had signed to play the following season and a further 20 had promised to.

By the start of their first league season, Kenilworth Town had managed to find a new pitch closer to the town centre. It was to the west side of, and sloping down towards, the railway station. A public way went across the field but some distance from the pitch. Courtesy of Mr Dance, the club was allowed to use a room at the Abbey Hotel for its committee meetings and all correspondence was addressed there. The season got off to a bad start in a friendly at home to Coventry West Orchard. Town were loosing 3-0 after only fifteen minutes, Bowen scored to pull one back but it was 5-1 at half time and finished 6-2. *"Two of the victor's goals, according to spectators, were off-side but allowed."* Another reason for the poor performance was the playing conditions: *"It would have been a different match, more in favour of the homesters, had the ground been in better order."* Unfortunately, a clause in the lease for the field restricted the *"taking of crops"* to just once a year and so the grass was far too long: *"Occasionally, the ball could scarcely be seen."* Worst was to come as the club's first ever league fixture ended in a 10-0 defeat. More were to follow; Town lost 4-1 to Singer Reserves despite being the better team, and a 13-1 thrashing provided the excuse that several goals were offside; *"What was the umpire doing?"* In October, the left wing partnership of Smith and Holmes was split to play one on each wing against Foleshill; 4-0 down at half-time Town reverted to their original formation and rallied to loose 6-3 leading to claims that the team would have won but for the re-arrangement. As a result, Captain Lester, full-back, resigned and Smith took his place. The following week saw a friendly against Leamington Brewery abandoned at half time due to the weather with Town leading 1-0. The result, according to a reporter, was *"A draw in favour of Kenilworth."*

By the second week of November, the grass had at last been cut and *"...the dribblers will now be able to show some finer play."* The next visitors were West Orchard from Coventry and *"...the partisanship of the visiting spectators was exhibited very prominently."* With one of the best crowds of the season, and playing uphill in the first half, the unexpected happened: *"Bowen passing to Whateley, he dodged and passed to Smith when some sharp exchanges between right wing and centre resulted in Smith scoring the first goal for Town."* In the second half, Smith set up centre-forward Williams to make it 2-0, West Orchard pulled a goal back but *"...Town quickly raised their score to four, Williams rushing the last two through."* A league victory at last, 4-1, but West Orchard did have only nine players. Unfortunately, defeats remained the norm; 2-1 at Nuneaton Town, with Sherwin scoring a brilliant goal, was followed by a 5-1 loss.

On Boxing Day, a friendly against Leek Wootton was arranged and it drew a crowd approaching 400, £1 4s was taken at the gate. The reserves, however, had collapsed, most had moved on to play for St.Nicholas Stars. The first league match of the New Year saw an embarrassing 9-0 home defeat by second in the table Great Heath. The pitch being *"very slippery, no remedy having been applied"* was the first attempt to explain the result followed by *"...the goals the visitors scored were by no means good shots."* With the score at 5-0 *"...at last the home custodian was fairly beaten..."* to make it 6-0 and *"...after this the visitors had it all their own way, scoring again and again."* Things were about to get worse. The following week, and with a fair degree of inevitability, a nine-man Town *"...at last have got to the bottom of the league..."* after an 11-1 thrashing away to Rudge Reserves in Coventry, a team who had themselves won only three matches all season. A victory against Hatton was secured by using no fewer than 6 players from St.John's Rovers who used the same pitch; it was again suggested an amalgamation might result.

After a refreshingly easy 10-0 friendly victory over Leamington Brewery, the next league game was to be against Warwick United, a side that at that point had won every match they had played that season. Fortunately, the appalling weather and frozen pitch caused a postponement. *"It would be lucky for the homesters if they could get out of the match altogether for a heavy defeat is certain."* When the teams did eventually meet in April, Warwick won 8-1, but *"...did not give as good a performance as expected."*

Of the 29 matches played in the season, 10 were won and 18 lost, with 56 goals scored and 118 conceded. At the AGM at the Virgins Inn, it was declared that as *"...this is really only the fourth birthday of football in Kenilworth, very good progress has been made."* It was decided to stay in the league, which was being reduced from ten to eight teams. Due to a higher rent than previous years there was a deficit of 16s 11d in the funds which Dr Growse offered to pay off. Musgrove, the new goalkeeper, was elected captain for the coming year and there was a discussion about which colours to wear but no decision was made. Club Chairman Edwin Podmore closed the evening by singing the National Anthem.

Not many years before, Mr Stuart who lived in the end house in New Street ran the only team in town, a Saturday afternoon team - now there were seven, including reserve sides.

*   *   *

In 1893 rumours began to circulate around the town that a company was trying to find a suitable site to build a new much-needed manufactory in town, a paper-mill. Sites alongside Finham Brook were investigated, but it was claimed that the proprietors could not obtain the land. There was much criticism of the Board and its members at this time, particularly the degree of borrowing money for projects, and it was insinuated that Board members, a number of whom owned land, did not want another industry in a town noted for its *"salubrity."* William Pears, who owned the land from the Abbey Fields to Mill End, refuted this, publicly stating that he would give up the land between Washbrook and his mill should the paper-mill proprietors wish to build there, but after this no more was heard of the scheme.

The days of the Local Board were numbered. Under the Local Government Act of 1894, it was to be replaced by an Urban District Council that would number twelve, with a Chairman elected from inside or outside its number. Eligible to vote would be all persons on the Parliamentary or Local Government registers and for the first time women would be allowed to vote *"...including married women who would be entitled to vote as single women."* This in itself caused confusion and later had to be qualified: *"A woman shall not be disqualified by marriage from being on any Local Government register of election, or from being an elector of any local authority, provided that a husband and wife shall not both be qualified in respect to the same property..."* clarified the situation. It was also to be the first local body in which party politics played a part.

Such was the likely confusion surrounding the new arrangements that a parish meeting was held to explain them, and just a month before the election there was, not surprisingly, a very crowded attendance at the Abbey Hill Chapel School. Joseph Roberts suggested that a committee should be formed to select candidates who would represent all sections of the town, a resolution carried by 50 votes to 39. It was agreed that politics should be kept away; the best men for the job were wanted. The committee selected twelve *"fit and proper"* candidates to stand and these included six members of the Local Board *"...so as to rid the election as far as possible of the character of a party struggle."*

This was a vain hope. After a series of meetings, mostly held in the same room as the parish meeting, the Kenilworth Liberal Association had already decided to nominate eight candidates. The Parish Committee tried and failed to get the Liberals to withdraw four of them. The Liberal Association had made their final choice of eight from twelve nominations at a meeting chaired by A J McMillan in late October. Without doubt, the leading party member was Henry Street who had just reached his 70th birthday and he received a rousing reception as he entered the room. Conveniently, the meeting room was alongside his back garden. There were 70 or more present, including six or seven ladies. The meeting also had to choose two representatives for the Board of Guardians and putting herself forward *"...because there was no other woman with pluck enough..."* was Caroline James, the wife of William James, who did indeed become the first female Guardian. The Association published a list of its views on local matters and this included encouraging new and more industry to the town, securing land for allotments, an investigation into the town charities, opening up the Abbey Fields to the public, the building of the swimming baths and the finding of temporary and useful labour in times of distress; all of which would be carried out *"with due regard to economy."*

The meeting room, the Abbey Hill schoolroom, was conveniently alongside Henry Street's back garden.

For the election, there was a total of 29 candidates. Two people, independent of any organisation, also published their thoughts, William Holmes, and D Liddington of Albion Street who intended to *"...watch over the interests of my fellow working man..."* with a particular intention of not adding to the already heavy burden of the rates.

The last undertaking completed by the Board was an improvement to the road layout just outside the station. In an agreement with Mr Whittendale, the landowner, a small piece of land on the corner between Station Road and Priory Road was bought for £80 to round it off and improve access to the station. This led to the demolition of Walter Lockhart's coal office. Whittendale had to modify his plans for a house and offices to a new building line, which had been staked out, and these were approved at the last monthly meeting.

The election result was published just prior to Christmas 1894:

Reverend G Field *(2)*	357
J E Jackson *(2)*	333
Henry Street *(1) (2)*	323
William James *(2)*	312
J Welsh *(1) (3)*	294
R Knight *(2)*	285
George H Church *(3)*	277
William Riley (High Street) *(2)*	276
Obidiah Woods *(2)*	276
Joseph Murdoch *(2)*	274
Dr Edmund Kemp Bourne	246
E P Hodges *(3)*	239
(all the above elected)	
Thomas Hawley *(1) (3)*	230
G Page *(1) (3)*	219
Henry T Smith-Turberville *(1) (3)*	218
J Satchwell *(3)*	213
W G Middleton *(3)*	208
F Wyer *(1) (3)*	186
George M Turner *(1) (3)*	179
H Hood *(3)*	171
William Holmes	136
J Brown	90
H G Brittain	72
E Lee	72
W Arnold	68
D Lillington	36
George Burton	23

(Local Board members *(1)*, Liberal Association *(2)*, Parish Committee *(3)*. Dr Growse withdrew, along with another).

All eight of the Liberal Association candidates were elected and only two of the Local Board survived. Dr Kemp Bourne was the only other who had any previous experience of representing the town, nine Council members were entirely new to the responsibility. *"How far will the efficient and economical policy of the Local Board be modified by the infusion of members without governing experience?"* With so many years experience, despite his advancing years, it was no surprise that Henry Street was elected the Council's first Chairman.

*   *   *

On the night of 21st December 1894, a ferocious storm lashed the Midlands and the town centre had a fortunate escape when at about 4.30 in the morning the top 140ft of the tannery chimney fell. With many dwelling houses nearby, it fell "safely" in an easterly direction across the yard, wrecking a fleshing shed, a clerk's office and some outbuildings. Had it fallen in a different direction, or several hours later with the men at work, the town could have had a major catastrophe. As it was, the only casualties were a couple of pigs. A number of dressed skins were damaged. The chimney's appearance was "...as though it had jumped straight from its base into the yard." About 60 or 80ft of the chimney was left standing but the top 25ft or so of that was "fractured" and another storm would have brought it down. A smaller office chimney in the yard also fell. The damage was estimated at £1,200. As news of the incident spread, the following day, a Sunday, "...as clear and calm a day as ever experienced in mid-winter..." crowds of people flocked from Coventry, Warwick and Leamington to have a look at the sight. Apart from fallen branches and some slates and tiles, there was little damage elsewhere, one other casualty being Mr Day's greenhouse in the field opposite the tannery. The same storm wrecked Mr Pollard's new greenhouse at Whitemoor.

The still standing part of the tannery chimney was in a precarious condition with several fissures and "a big rent on the station side." This was all carefully watched as the tannery workforce, boosted by eight or nine extra men, set about clearing the debris. It was another two weeks before work began to remove the dangerous part of the chimney and the same method of access was used as when a lightning conductor was fixed - ladders were fitted into sockets. Hammers and chisels were used to free the brickwork and one very large portion came down with a huge crash. Started on Tuesday 15th January, the work was completed the next day. Its replacement, completed in April, was not so inspiring. "Our famous chimney is no longer a stack of much interest or distinction of its own. The reconstruction is completed but it will never again be a guide." "Our landmark has been removed...it has not been again built up to its towering proportions."

At around this time, work at the tannery was "brisk" and sizeable despatches went to the north-east and Scotland, but the premises generally had been allowed to fall into a ruinous condition and the constantly recurring repairs brought heavy expenses. The fall of the chimney and the severe winter of 1894-5, which included a whole week when the men, on half pay, were frozen out and no work was done at all, added to the problems. With the lease set for renewal, the shareholders had a difficult decision to make, and it was decided that unless a buyer for the company as a going concern could be found by Christmas 1895, the company would work out the entire stock. With few exceptions, the staff had worked constantly since Thomas Day took over and there was much sympathy for the men and the position they found themselves in, particularly as they had earned a reputation for a high-quality product. There was also of course the worry of the knock-on effect, as felt before, by the town's traders.

However, another closure was averted and in January 1896, managing director Thomas Day left Kenilworth for a new undertaking in Bromyard, Hereford. He gave a farewell dinner at his home, The Limes, at which he was presented with a meerschaum pipe and an engraved cigar case. Obidiah Woods proposed the toast wishing Day success. "The tannery company is proceeding as a going concern by the same firm and the work is now being conducted under the superintendence of Mr Woods and Mr Parkes, chief clerk."

In 1894, a *Kenilworth Advertiser* correspondent visited the Whitemoor Brickworks and reported what he saw: "Three or four men are employed all day in filling small trucks with lumps of clay, which are run up a tramway to a height of about 20 feet. They are then broken up into smaller pieces and sent through an aperture which admits them to the grinding apparatus. Here they are ground between three sets of rollers into fine clay, emerging into a trough fitted up with a cutter something like a sausage machine, whence forced into a mould and sent out in long slices the width of an ordinary brick and cut into lengths of about 27 to 29 inches. These are carried onto a shelf of iron, and again cut by wires into nine bricks. Four or five men are continually employed in carrying away these pieces of brick-shaped clay on to the drying ground, close around the machine. All bricks, other than common, such as

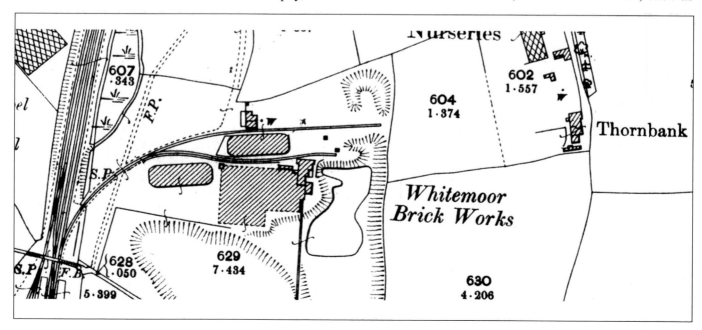

The Whitemoor brickworks of Henry Hawkes at about the time of the Kenilworth Advertiser report.

facing and ornamental bricks, have to be moulded and pressed into desired shapes and patterns and this is done with lever presses. The motive power in driving the machine in manufacturing the clay consists of two boilers, equivalent to 60 horse power. The water to feed them is raised from the water which collects in the clay hole, the waste water being taken away through pipes to the brook running alongside the railway." The machinery was built by Wootten of Coalville. About thirty men were now employed at the works and the bricks were largely sought after and were often specified in building plans.

In July 1894, Henry Hawkes gave a dinner to his workforce to mark his son's 21st birthday. The occasion though was less memorable for its meal than its conclusion when *"pugilism reigned."* In the summer of 1895, Bolton Joberns left Kenilworth to go and manage his father's brick-yard. Mr Hawkes jnr gave a dinner for the workforce to mark the occasion and 37 sat down at the Assembly Room. Being their Deputy Captain, the fire brigade staged a similar event two weeks later at which Joberns was presented with a silver-mounted umbrella. This occasion also marked the "starting of the new fire alarm."

The brickworks were probably the most dangerous place to work in Kenilworth as two accidents late in 1898 demonstrate. At the Cherry Orchard, it was usual to loosen large banks of clay with dynamite, but on one particular occasion, a charge did not explode. A workman named Job Carter picked it up to examine it, just as it exploded removing three fingers and part of the thumb of his left hand. Charles Moseley (28) was the son of former brickwork engine driver John, and as a child, was part of a family who suffered from typhoid at the time that neighbour Annie Constable died in 1882. Moseley worked at the top of a shed at Hawkes brickworks feeding a machine called a kibbler, which grinds the clay. Clay was brought up from the pits on small trucks hauled by machinery on a gangway, and then tipped into the kibbler through an aperture eight or nine inches square. On the day in question, Moseley went away to trim a lamp, leaving the operation to 15 year-old William Overton and he was successful in tipping the first truck load of clay over. It was thought that he then inadvertently stood over the aperture where the clay goes - the machine was fitted with revolving knives. They caught hold of his leg tearing away the flesh and then the bone. His cries were heard by a man named Barber who ran up the gangway to be confronted with the horrific sight of Overton's leg. Barber stopped the machine, which then had to be partly dismantled to release him. Dr Tweedy soon arrived and bound up the leg and Overton was taken to Warneford hospital, accompanied by a railway porter with first-aid training. His leg was amputated nearly to the thigh. Early the next year the Church Lads Club performed a concert for William Overton's benefit, raising £4.

Mill End too had its dangers. In 1890, Alfred Satchwell jnr, of the firm Satchwell Brothers was working on the steam saw-mill when the wood slipped and he caught his hand on the revolving blade. His right hand was *"fearfully cut and torn"* and despite the huge loss of blood it was thought that amputation was not

necessary. In August 1896, the son of Murcott Webb was one of several children playing on a crane in the fellmonger's yard. He got his hand caught in the mechanism and it was badly crushed, requiring the amputation of two fingers. The operation was carried out by Doctors Growse and Tweedy and the boy made good progress in his recovery.

Joseph Smith's quarry at Love Lane also had its share of accidents. In September 1888 a man was levering a rock when it gave way and he fell down an embankment. At the same place the following July, Joseph Ball of New Street suffered a broken leg when a rock fall *"crushed him."* Joseph Smith's mother and Edward's widow, Rebecca, remained in business until early 1896 when she moved into the house next door on Rosemary Hill. After a long and painful illness she died in the summer of 1897 aged 69. At the time of her retirement she was the oldest tradesman in Kenilworth.

In May 1893, Kenilworth's carpenters approached their employers for a pay rise of 1d an hour on top of the 6½d they received. On being turned down, they collectively decided to strike and did so on the first Monday in May, bringing building operations to an almost complete standstill. The following day the carpenters and employers met in an *"amicable spirit"* and their demands were fully met. It was thought to have been the first such strike in town. *"One of the men who offered to resume work prior to the new agreement was heartily jeered by his comrades."* The following year the carpenters and joiners had a meeting at The Globe to form their own society.

The cost and availability of coal became a problem in late 1893 due to a strike by coal workers in the Bedworth area, and so only coal from Worcestershire and Staffordshire was available. Prices had doubled in five years, 25s bought a ton of *"the cheapest and poorest quality."* The difficulties led to a *Kenilworth Advertiser* editorial asserting that someday coal would be found beneath Kenilworth giving employment and that the first piece dug out would be housed in a museum.

The following spring, after the strike had ended, "Frugal" wrote a letter complaining that the cost of Warwickshire cobbles had increased in price from 12s 6d to 17s 6d a ton in just two years; he normally kept five house fires and one for his greenhouse burning all winter, but had had to reduce this to just three. Employees of coal merchants remained on low wages; one employed by Charles Holland at Mill End was on 17s a week.

Taking unusual loads by railway always caused a spectacle and in August 1894 Kenilworth station, and doubtless dozens of sightseers, was witness to one when a 12ft length of a thousand year-old oak with a 30ft circumference was loaded, on its way from Stoneleigh Park to Birmingham.

*   *   *

At its eighth anniversary meeting in February 1886, the trustees of the Convalescent Home were overwhelmed with gratitude at the announcement that

Jane Woodcock had given them the premises as a gift. A fund had also been started to rebuild the older part of the home and this was boosted by several donations totalling hundreds of pounds from three out-of-town benefactors. The intention was to increase the number of patients at any one time from 16 to 20; in the previous year, 206 had been accommodated. The expenditure for the year was £493, £23 below income.

The home had to be closed for the first three months of 1887 whilst the work was being carried out. Two cottages next door were purchased for £200 and the successful tender to build the extension was that of John Fell for £809 7s 6d. The total raised for the project during the year was over £1,000 ensuring financial problems were avoided. The "*comfortable, commodious and handsome building*" was formally opened on the last Saturday of March 1887 by Lord and Lady Leigh. Excluding the building work, the receipts for that year were more than £50 above expenditure but the number of patients fell to 155 due to the temporary closure. Despite the extensions, the number of patients did not increase as expected, just 177 were treated in the following twelve months. The home was dealt another blow as many of the regular donors were victims of the Greenways' bank collapse and so it was decided once more to hold a concert.

In 1887, the Convalescent Home was extended into the two adjoining cottages.

At Christmas 1889, the patients were given a hamper containing turkeys, plum puddings and mince pies. The Matron, Miss Scace, did her energetic best to see to the patients' needs and in the evening the "*...customary indoor games were indulged in.*" The wards and other rooms were decorated and some were left in place into the new year.

John Gulson of Coventry presided at the AGM in early 1889, which was attended by Lord and Lady Leigh and their daughter Cordelia, Francis Stanger-Leathes of Parkfield, Dr Bourne, and Mr Willes of Leamington amongst many others. The home had provided respite for 219 patients in the year but there were concerns that rule five covering the permissible ailments of patients was not being strictly adhered to, there had been a number of admissions of those in "*the advanced stages of phthisis*" who should have been turned away. Financially, the home was in a healthy state. The running costs of about £500 a year were met by general donations but, in addition, the home had received

a number of larger bequests, the largest this particular year being £500 from the late David Spencer. This was invested in Great Western Railway Consolidated Stock which brought to £1,862 8s 9d the amount invested. Mrs Trepplin was amongst those now serving on the Committee and, despite her absence through illness, Jane Woodcock retained her position, but just a few weeks later, she died aged 57.

The year between the Annual General Meetings of 1893 and 1894 was an eventful one. Two extra beds were installed, bringing the total to 27, and running hot water was installed throughout the building, which was then entirely redecorated. The number of patients rose to 359, encouraged by the reduction in fees from 4s to 3s a week. The Matron resigned and her replacement, picked from 86 candidates, was Miss Beamish, fresh from eight years work as a ward sister at Bristol Hospital. Despite all this expense, £118 was carried forward into the next year. Dr Clarke had been Honorary Medical Officer since the home opened, and Dr Tweedy accepted an invitation to be his successor. The last few weeks of 1896 saw the home close once more for further improvements, this time to increase the number of beds to 30.

*   *   *

As it was so regularly used by members of the Kenilworth Swimming Club, it must have been generally thought that the area near Chesford was safe for bathing. It was locally known, however, to be very dangerous in parts due to varying water temperatures and having a mass of weeds which could entangle the unwary. In August 1893, Annesley Denham and Henry Hull (25), both engineers for the London and North Western Railway, and William Charles Sinclair Davies (25), a Southam Solicitor, went together on a bicycle ride from Southam to Kenilworth. Upon arrival at Chesford at around 4 o'clock, they agreed to bathe about 200 yards from the bridge and entered the water going down a shallow cut at the side of the river. After about five minutes, they all got out only to find that they were covered in mud and so re-entered the water to clean up. Several boys nearby pointed out to the trio an easier landing place and as Denham was making for it, Hull shouted to him that Davies was in trouble. The two of them tried to reach him but could not due to the weeds and became entangled; Davies disappeared and could not be reached. Denham and Hull had great trouble extricating themselves; the water was at least 15ft deep and had cold undercurrents, which made the task even more difficult. The rescue attempts became hopeless, William Davies drowned. Attempts to retrieve his body were begun as early as 4 o'clock the next morning with PC Fletcher from Leek Wootton, who had acquired a boat in order to drag for the body, and Sergeant Hipwell and PC Eagles from Kenilworth all involved. Eagles, and Mr Jordan from Blackdown Mills, had dived to try and find the body, and after dragging for some hours diving began again at 8.30. The Reverend Spurrell and Mr Maffield assisted in diving. PC Eagles at one point was trapped in the weeds. Eventually Eagles waded out from the bank and found Davies just six or seven yards out lying in about five feet of water, on his back, completely embedded in mud except for his head. Assisted by Fletcher he got the body to the bank and onto a vehicle provided by Mr Dormer, it was taken to the Green Man. The inquest held at St.John's School was a forgone conclusion, William Davies accidentally drowned whilst swimming. He was buried at St.Nicholas.

In March 1895 the KUDC, on the back of election promises made by its eight Liberal members, took the first major step to look into the financial and practical aspects of building a swimming baths by forming a Bathing Committee consisting of Henry Street as "Ex-Officio", Reverend G Field, Dr Edmund Bourne, E P Hodges, J E Jackson, George Church and William Riley. Within a week, four of the committee, three of whom were smoking pipes, were seen in the Abbey Field rented from the Council by Joseph Roberts, "...the one where the skating was..." near to the iron bridge. Their eagerly-awaited report and designs were made public at the KUDC meeting in May 1895. It was unanimous that the best site for the bath was indeed at the spot they had been seen investigating, but there was a difficulty with the water supply. This could be overcome by having a small sluice or weir in the stream near the bath, which would be filled from the up-side of it. The discharge would be effected by a drainpipe running into a back drain seven yards away, finally emptying itself in the tail water at Townpool bridge. The pool itself was to be 75 to 80 feet in length and vary in depth from 2ft 6ins to 5 ft. The sides, varying in thickness from 14ins to 18ins, would be of hard-pressed bricks and topped with blue coping bricks. The bottom would be a foot thickness of concrete covered with an inch of asphalte. Around the bath would be a mound made from the excavation material that would be planted to act as a screen. At one end of the bath, next to the brook, a dressing room was to be provided made from "thin boards or corrugated iron." The bath would be excavated by Council employees, after which contractors would be used for the brickwork and concrete. The cost was estimated as between £150 and £200. Joseph Roberts' permission was also obviously required. The designs appear to be that of a Mr Wilmshurst. Not everyone was over-impressed with the plans: "It is an open bath, may we expect a swarm of Kenilworth lasses with an appeal for a closed bath for them?"

There seems little doubt that ironmonger and tobacconist of High Street, Councillor Riley, was a driving force behind the scheme; he built an ingenious model from lead piping and tin to demonstrate the operation of the water system and this saved "...the ratepayers an expensive surveyor's plan which very few would have understood. A tin trench is made to represent the river flowing, and in the real thing a weir is to be made of stone, which can and will be made to look very pretty. A pipe conveys the water into a receiving chamber, where it percolates through different meshed sieves, entering the bath proper at the shallow end. A pipe at the deep end takes the surplus water back into the brook. A pipe at the bottom of the deep end will take the sediment off into a dumb well, which will have to be pumped out occasionally. There will always be clear and fresh water in the bath. Of course in flood time measures will be taken to keep out the flood water." In mid-May 1895, Councillor Riley was given the honour of cutting the first sod.

Within a month, the excavations were well underway. A quantity of sandstone was found which proved useful for building walls. Much of the excavation work was done in very hot weather and at an early stage it was suggested that the diggers should receive encouragement by the promise of a meal when the pool was completed. It was decided that only local builders should be allowed to tender for the building work and the three submitted were from E Lee for £103, E Marriott for £80, and the accepted bid from Edward Smith and Son, now in the hands of Joseph Smith, for £72. The brickwork was started almost immediately, while the excavations were still in progress, and needed to be if "the bath is to be any use to us this season." The weir for diverting the water into the bath was also an early part of the construction.

There were still some difficulties to overcome. Joseph Roberts not only asked for a proportional reduction in rent for the loss of part of the field, but an additional reduction for the encroachment of the public using the paths to it. There was also the possibility of problems being caused by taking water away from the millstream. William Pears owned the mill, leased by John George Eagles, at Mill End, and he had rights to the stream and so his permission was required to build the weir. Pears was assured that there would be no loss of water except at times when the bath was cleaned, and this would be done when there was plenty of water. There was also the question of financing the project. Added to the funds was the £56 from the earlier scheme, which had just arrived from the Reverend Somerset Pennefather, and further donations were being made; it was hoped that the Council could meet any shortfall without having to resort to taking out a loan.

Despite the election promise that the baths would be built to relieve the unemployed, the excavation work was carried out by Council employees working under the Road Surveyor, Mr Evans. It was perhaps no surprise that the excavations revealed historical remains. Of particular interest was a cannon ball and "two very large posts" which were taken to the Council offices. It was hoped a small museum could be provided to house them.

The contract for the "shed" was completed for £39 as soon as August 1895. It was 25ft long and 7ft 6ins wide and split into three compartments, one of which was private. There was a 4ft wide path in front with a step up into it. There was "an entrance gate at the back and a hoarding" which it was soon suggested could be used for advertisements to increase the Council's income. It was belatedly suggested that perhaps instead of the cheap boarding on the church side it would have been possible to extend the wall from the churchyard.

With all going well, the scheme hit a major problem in September 1895 when it was revealed that the required written permission had not been obtained from William Pears or John Eagles for the use of the stream water, Pears had only given verbal consent to Dr Bourne. The law was quite stringent on this and the Clerk had even told the bathing committee that they had no right to build the weir without this written consent. Eagles had already complained of serious damage to the workings of the mill by the dam and other works, and asked for the dam to be removed. He was against any extraction of water that interfered with the operation of the mill and was quite prepared to take legal proceedings to compel the removal of the dam and to recover damages through loss. Pears backed his tenant. The Council suggested a meeting with Pears and Eagles but Pears said such a meeting would not be of use. He demanded that the weir was taken down and then he would be happy to visit and to discuss other ideas "...provided such schemes were properly prepared and submitted in detail and did not effect in any way the working of the mill." The road surveyor was instructed to remove the weir and it was announced that town water was to be used instead. Mr Welch had made protestations throughout the scheme and again stated that no work should have commenced without it being approved by the Local Government Board, and this was finally granted in September on provision of a solution to the water supply problem.

In an attempt to solve the water supply problem, Joseph Smith, at his own expense, had by now surveyed the fields to the west with the intention of filling the bath from the stream by gravity, with an intake near Millbrook Lane.

In December 1895, with the bath "nearly completed", the Council realised it had to borrow £200 to finance the construction, and this decision meant that it had to follow proper procedures to put its case to the necessary inquiry. Purnell had to prepare plans for all possible methods of filling the bath and, with Dr Bourne, visited Pears for official discussions. The surveys of Joseph Smith for filling the bath by gravity appeared to be the solution.

Before the inquiry could even begin, another hurdle had to be overcome; the Local Government Board had to decide if the baths should have been built at all, as the fields were covered by a covenant preventing the erection of buildings and maintaining their use as pleasure grounds. When the inquiry opened at the Council offices on 12th December, Mr Wyer immediately raised this question but Mr Tulloch, who was in the chair, stated that the inquiry would not have been granted by the Local Government Board if those terms had been contravened, although no evidence was offered that it had even been discussed. Wyer then claimed that there was no need for a bath, an argument easily rebuked by Henry Street who had been involved in discussions for almost twenty years. But Wyer did make one incontestable point - the current application should have been made before work commenced.

The circumstances of the water supply were outlined by Street. There were three potential sources; the brook, the town water and a nearby spring. The mill owner, Pears, had consented to do all that he could to help, but a verbal arrangement with the mill leaseholder Eagles, had fallen through. If an agreement with Eagles could not be found, the cost of filling the 50,000-gallon pool from town water alone was 25s, but it was intended to supplement this with spring-water to the tune of 1,000 gallons a day to ensure fresh and clean water circulated.

The bath was to be emptied and re-filled twice yearly. The pool had been built just ten yards from where it was planned under the old Board. With Street stating that the Council would use half an acre of its own land and lose 25s a year in rent, the inquiry closed.

The Local Government Board delayed their verdict until they knew the chosen method of the water supply. The decision, made in February 1896, was not surprisingly in favour of that designed by Joseph Smith to lay pipes from near the ford at Millbrook Lane and under land leased by Mrs Draper. However, Mrs Draper asked for the work to be postponed until after haymaking time and it was agreed to honour her wishes even though it would mean delaying the opening of the baths, unless an alternative method of filling could be found. The 6ins glazed pipes required for filling the bath were ordered in any case. The Bathing Committee also looked into purchasing a pump needed to empty the bath.

The slow progress was beginning to irritate Councillor Knight: "I cannot quite see what the baths committee are doing. Here we are going on month after month and when summer arrives we shall have no bath. Month after month we are being diddle-daddled. The best thing to do is to put our pipes in and fill the bath and take the consequences. If we have to go into litigation we must fight our battle. We have given way in every shape and form and now permission is not granted. We ought to let it be known that we are not children and we intend to do the work."

Councillor Jackson proposed that they wrote to Pears to get an agreement, and finally, two months later, a letter of agreement with Pears to use the brook water was approved. Six Councillors voted in favour, none against, and this agreement was sealed and sent to the Local Government Board for approval. But, due to the agreement with Mrs Draper, using brook water was some time away and so a decision was made to initially fill the bath with town water, just to get the baths open. The Bathing Committee thus decided that "...on or about 1st June the bath is filled from the town main and that on or about the 8th bathing commences." It was also clear that until the gravity system was operational the water would have to be partly replenished from the same source "...once or twice at most."

The pool needed to be completely filled to check for leaks and it was going to cost 25s to do this from the town's main, which was considered a low price. In May, Mr Hodges suggested that the fire brigade hoses could be used and this was agreed, as the only alternative was 200 journeys with the 300 gallon water-carts.

The first filling of the bath was a scene of considerable interest. It was filled from a standpipe on Abbey Hill, using nearly all the fire brigade hosepipes, and was full by Thursday morning of 21st May - filling was slow, the 60,000 gallons took 20 hours. The water was very clear.

Arrangements to employ a caretaker had to be made, and rules for operation drawn up. The man at the pool would need to be young and active in case he had to jump in and rescue someone and Arthur Newey, one of the Council's workmen and likely to have been involved in the excavations, was appointed caretaker at 18s a week. "In the event of the baths being used by females Mrs

Newey be requested to act as attendant." "The caretakers are at liberty to make a charge not exceeding 1d for the use of a clean towel or a pair of bathing drawers." A WC was now installed at the baths and a blind fitted at the front of the females' dressing room.

All was well and it was now decided that the bath was to be opened a week earlier than originally expected on Monday 1st June. The ceremony was conducted by KUDC Chairman Henry Street in delightful weather. Standing at the entrance, he made a brief speech saying the bath was a long-felt need and he hoped the public would help preserve and look after it. He was handed the key by Councillor Riley and unlocked the door. Town Crier William Jeacock, with his bell, announced the event and about 60 bathers took advantage of the new facility in the first two hours. A dinner to mark the event was held in the picture gallery at the Queen and Castle and included as guests of the Council, as suggested early on in the excavations, were all those involved in the construction. Songs were sung during the evening. Councillor Jackson had taken his first-ever dip that day; he was amongst 128 first day bathers; nine of them were boys and apparently none of them were ladies. The second day saw 131 bathers, and Wednesday was Ladies' day, but an attendance of nil was recorded. *"On Wednesday three ladies presented themselves but were too late for admission."* On Thursday there were 128 customers but on Friday the baths were much cooler, following rain, and only six braved the chilly water.

Up to Sunday 7th June, 619 persons paid for admission. An earth closet was also now available, suggesting a greater attendance than expected, and the fence at the southwest was extended 9ft and barbed wire was put on top to stop trespass. A small tool house was needed at the back of dressing room. The pool's popularity continued. By the end of the second week, 1,217 had swum and on the second Saturday, the *"...caretaker was severely taxed at times issuing tickets"*. Even Sunday saw 85 swimmers in the three hours it was open.

Two weeks after the bath opened, the Local Government Board finally approved the loan for its construction. As the cost had exceeded the initial expectations, Councillor Hodges amusingly suggested the passing of a bye-law that every man woman and child should bathe three times a week, to ensure the baths would soon pay for themselves!

Until the gravitation scheme could be completed, arrangements had been made to pump water from the brook into the bath. As much water as required could be pumped at a cost of 15s a week payable to Eagles. This was cheaper than using the mains water and it was thought that the brook water was better suited for the baths. Had this arrangement not been made, the baths would have had to close again until the gravitational scheme was completed. Each Saturday after 6.00 p.m., a little water was run off and replenished from the brook.

Finally, seven weeks after the bath was opened, the gravitation scheme was completed and was used for the first time on 24th July. An abundant supply of fresh water now passed continually through the baths. The number of bathers was already claimed to be past the 3,000 mark, which was a considerable surprise and passed all expectations. The official figures published in the first week of September showed that since the bath opened 2,779 adults and 865 children, a total of 3,644, had paid for admission, and this was deemed very satisfactory, particularly as the bath was "not in proper working order until the end of July" and had also been closed for a week for cleaning. With the season coming to an end, it was decided to keep the bath open for only three days a week; males were allocated Saturday 9 till dusk, Tuesday from 2 till dusk, and Sunday 7 to 9.30 a.m. Females had use of the bath only on Tuesday from 8 until 1 p.m.

With the baths finally opened, the Council were under pressure to open up the fields to the public, and the bathing committee had the rest of the Abbey Fields added to their responsibilities. They acted swiftly: "Your committee having fully considered the questions of the tenancies of the Abbey Fields referred to them by the Council at its last meeting, recommend that the Council take over on 29th September the part of the public lands numbered 46 and 47 upon the Abbey Fields estate plan and that they also give notice to the other tenants that after 29th September the public lands will be let by public tender." It was adopted.

The two fields in question were those north of the brook alongside Bridge Street, with a western boundary of the swimming pool and churchyard. Improvements to the area were soon under way. In January 1897, it was agreed to remove the shed on one side and the short wall on the other of the old stone building used as barn. "The removal of these structures would open out the old building, the interior of which might be utilized at some future date for the preservation of objects of local interest." Half the shed was re-erected in the upper corner of the field. A footpath needed to be built from Bridge Street to the swimming bath. The obvious route was along the line of a hedge. A ditch running through the field was filled in and drainage pipes substituted. Work on the path was well under way in February. The ground where the hedge had been "grubbed up" was filled and the path laid with ashes. The area in front of the barn was also tidied up, work being done by the roadmen. Church Abbey Field, once let to Mr Roberts for £28 a year, was now let to Mr Wringrose for the grazing of sheep only, for the sum of £10 a year, and included the proviso that the Council horses could graze in the field during the summer months.

A footpath of ashes was made to the swimming bath along the line of a "grubbed up" hedgerow.

Rules needed to be drawn up for the portion of the Abbey Fields used as park, and it was decided in May 1897 that these should be enforced by a "watchman or caretaker", who in the summer months would be same person who attended to the baths. Remembering that the major reason for purchasing the fields was to provide recreational grounds, rule 13 was particularly frowned upon: "A person shall not play or take part in any game of football, golf, quoits, hockey or cricket or any other game the Council may prohibit." It was suggested that it should be amended to include the phrase "...nobody over the age of 14." This led to a heated discussion; getting children to stop playing in the streets was a priority, but allowing them to play "dangerous and boisterous games" could stop others from using the park. Unhelpfully, Mr Hodges observed "...*they might just as well be killed in the streets as fatally struck by a cricket ball.*" The age amendment was included, but this led to the Kenilworth United Cricket Club, who had recently lost the use of its regular ground, to apply for use of an area of the park claiming it would be no more dangerous for them to play cricket than 14 year-olds, but they were turned down. It was hoped that better sporting facilities could be provided at a later date. Rule 4 was equally unpopular: "No wheeled vehicle such as a perambulator or cycle shall be taken onto the grass."

Later in the year, two wych elms were planted in the public area and another had a dangerous branch cut, as it was a hazard to climbing children. Other trees were added. Towards the end of 1897 at the Tantara gateway, the top rail of the "movable style" was repaired, a dangerous stone taken down and accumulated rubbish removed. The key to the gatehouse was given to the surveyor. In addition, all the graveyard tools and other implements were removed from the old barn and it was locked. A decision on its future was to be made later.

Trees were soon planted in the area of the fields that had been designated a park.

In early 1897 the Council tidied up the finances of the bath construction. The borrowed money had been used first and this left a residue of over £27 from public donations; this was simply added to the Council's General Account. For the 1897 season starting 1st June, Mr Newey was again appointed Baths Superintendent, and was awarded a 2s pay rise, giving him £1 a week, and Mrs Newey again had to attend on the days set aside

for ladies at 2s a week. As agreed, Eagles was paid about £3 a month for the taking of water from the brook. The opening season was short, just four months, closing at the end of September. The sale of tickets from the 4th June to 4th September came to a total of £11 10s. The busiest weeks were the last of July and the first of August, which were the only times the receipts for a week was over £1, thus covering the cost of the caretaker. Most weeks about 10s or 15s was taken. Sales dropped alarmingly during September, the most taken in a week being 1s 8d, the lowest just 11d. Adding on the cost of the water payable to John Eagles and of repaying the loan, the bath was running at a notable loss. At the end of August, the expenditure had amounted to £18 14s 10d which, after deducting the income, left a deficiency if £11 10s 10d with a month's wages still due. Jackson said it was never expected that the bath would pay but it was seen as an education and he knew of several youngsters who had learned to swim - one in particular he had watched swim 30 lengths when the year before he could not swim 30 inches. Mr James remarked that attendance may have been affected by it being a wet summer. Far worse was the loss of income due to the Council opening up some of the fields as a pleasure ground; rents had dropped from over £153 to £111, but it was generally agreed that they had done the right thing by providing the park and bath.

* * *

The grave of William Mander and his wife Mary. Fires at his Oaks Farm were largely responsible for Kenilworth starting its own volunteer fire brigade.

William Mander moved to St.John's View. In the summer of 1891, he was yet again the victim of a fire, this time children playing with matches set fire to a hovel on his land at St.John's. The brigade dealt with it by using three hoses, two from the water mains and one from a nearby pit. He received another blow seven months later when his wife, Mary Jane, died aged 55 after a long and painful illness.

In late 1894, William Mander jnr, who was involved in the breach of promise case brought by Annie Steel, died aged 32. In 1895, the wine and spirit business became Mander and Co suggesting that William Mander snr was involving his surviving children, four daughters and his son Albert Edward (born 1874), who was also a coal merchant. William then retired, and he died at his home on 26th May 1899.

* * *

By 1892, Richard Knight had been the manager of the Co-operative Society for eight years and Mr Kimberley, heavily involved with the allotment association, had replaced William James as secretary. Henry Walmsley was treasurer. For the first time annual sales passed £10,000, another annual increase of over 10%, and the membership had reached a new milestone too, 502. Such was the optimism that opening a second store, in Warwick Road, was contemplated. Flushed with success the society held its own tea and entertainment in its hall.

At the AGM in January 1893 came the first signs that all was not so well with the society. Richard Knight had resigned, membership was down to 449 and income had fallen by about £500. *"Notwithstanding the recent depression amongst the agricultural and labouring classes (the Society) had fairly held their own...giving them the benefit of the very lowest prices..."* but twenty three members had been *"paid out"* and the accounts showed that over £840 was owing to the Society from members. The Chairman John Everitt however stated, *"There was not the slightest fear of the Society going bankrupt."*

In the third quarter, despite there being six new members, another 21 had been paid out and membership was down to 440. So many members had withdrawn their shares that by early 1894 the society was overdrawn at the bank to the tune of £1,120, an increase of £320 over the previous quarter. The rush upon withdrawals was apparently caused by *"...misrepresentations by a former member."* Henry Street chaired the February 1894 meeting, and pleaded with members not to withdraw any more, otherwise *"...the Society will fall to the ground."* In addition to this problem, the society was not in a position to produce a balance sheet for the quarter due to blatant inaccuracies in the stocktaking. It was unanimously decided to forgo a balance sheet for that quarter but ensure an accurate one was available for the next. It was also agreed to keep all the existing officers in place at least until then.

The full extent of the problems became apparent at the quarterly and annual meeting covering the year ending 2nd April. Not only had trade been declining, but goods had also been sold at unprofitable prices. There were also cases of members taking coal, bread etc., on credit, further undermining the finances. Due to *"incompetent persons"* the stock levels were inaccurate, a situation which had now been corrected. £1 shares were now worth 13s. At the meeting, the four retiring, but unnamed, committeemen were all replaced and the secretary was to be replaced by Mr Skutt in July, but treasurer Mr Walmsley kept his position. Fifty four members had been paid off in the previous year against fifteen new or re-admitted members. Membership was now down to 401.

On 10th May, an extraordinary meeting was called, as in *"...consequence of its liabilities the society was unable to trade..."*, and to devise a plan to avoid liquidation. John Everett presided but the press were excluded. The difficulties had not arisen due to creditors but by the members themselves *"...draining the life blood of the society by taking their capital away..."* which was unfair on those who had not. The first positive step from the meeting was that those who had given notice to withdraw their shares would not do so for a year, provided no one else did either. There was also a new commitment towards buying the stores own produce. It was then unanimously agreed to stop all withdrawals for a year. Also to be undertaken was the complete re-organisation of each department and to pay commission instead of fixed wages to its *"servants"*. The once lucrative coal business was abandoned as *"a great drawback to the society"*, (this was around the time of coal strike in Bedworth), and a mortgage was to be raised on all the property to clear the debt at the bank.

The next quarterly meeting, on 26th July, was obviously going to be of great significance, and promisingly there were already signs of improvement. The mortgage had been obtained with a local building society and the receipts for the quarter, £2,762 5s 3d, showed a small profit of £7 13s. *"The result would have been even more favourable if the coal trade had been disposed of earlier. Much more attention can be given to the stores and bakery..."* now the coal business had gone. The appointment of George Dainton as manager was also a key factor. The new secretary, Mr Skutt, urged members to work for the society and to try to introduce new members to add to the four that had recently joined.

By the 97th quarterly meeting in May 1898, trading profits were £43 and a dividend of 1s 2d was paid. Membership was now only 353, but the Society had survived the crisis.

* * *

John Davis's departure after ten years at The Globe, in July 1888, began a succession of transfers of the licence when it moved first to Henry Butler, and on to Thomas King, in just a few years. In March 1892 the licence was first temporarily, and a month later permanently, transferred from Thomas King to Jeanette Broughton of Birmingham, but her stay too was to be brief. Messrs Beard of Burton bought the inn from Mr Agg Gardiner of Cheltenham, and they wished to install Horatio Fletcher as licensee. He was willing to take on the inn at a yearly rental of £78; previously it had been just £65. Inspector Moth was against the transfer, claiming that there were six other public houses in a street just half a mile long which was considered three too many. It had long been considered that there were far too many public houses in Kenilworth and this was seen as an opportunity to close one. A temporary licence was issued until the matter could be discussed more fully in mid-September.

The main objection was that no necessity existed for the premises and that it was failing to attract custom, as demonstrated by four changes of licence holder in as many years and that it had actually been closed for several weeks earlier in the year. However, a recent case in the House of Lords gave a warning against Justices arbitrarily closing premises and so the application had to be dealt with carefully by the three magistrates. Sergeant Allcott stated that there was a public house for every 245 persons in town and with six others in the space of 842 yards, there was no necessity for this one, and he thought it would die a natural death in any case. However, cross-examined he had to admit that it was the best-conducted house doing a respectable trade, and held the oldest licence. G Barton, agent to the owners, stated that they had paid £900 for the house, £300 for fixtures and £100 on decorations, and if no licence was granted it would all be lost. The final and probably persuading argument came from Horatio Fletcher himself when stating it was as much for food as drink that excursionists came to the inn. The licence was granted, but with a warning that if another application was brought forward within a year or two the conclusion would be that the Inn was not required.

It was to be four years, in 1896, before the licence holder changed again, the new man being Fred Kings. In the grounds at the rear of his hotel, Kings set up the Kenilworth Zoological Gardens and listed an enticing collection of exhibits. "*A large collection of live Foreign birds and animals including a tame American Ant Bear, African Leopard Cat, Australian Kangaroo Fox, Brazilian Porcupine, Indian Mongoose, Snake killers, Scotch Silver Badgers, Foxes, Monkeys, American Racoon, Pigeons, Bantams, Canaries, Golden Silver Amherst, Reeves, Swinhoe, and Chinese Pheasants. The finest free sight in the Midlands.*" The gardens were open from 8 a.m. until dusk. Not content with his collection, the following year Kings added an Indian "*spotted paradoxure*" which he bought from Regents Park Zoo, who themselves kept the only other one in the country. By now, Kings also had a pair of Siberian Wolves, African Cape Jackals and a pair of Golden Eagles. In early 1898, the licence was transferred, initially temporarily, from James King to James Meredith, and it is assumed that Kings took his animals with him.

*　*　*

A Needlework Guild was started in late 1888. On the last Friday of September 1889, the Needlework Guild's produce was on display for two hours. The sixty one members had made 124 garments, but with other donations by members 165 were available for dispersal. The clothes were to be distributed amongst the poor of both parishes and some to the Convalescent Home. The members now had to start again; the target for the coming year was to make "*...two new garments, plainly made, suitable for poor parishes.*" There was also a plea for more members of any age. The club was organised by the secretaries Mrs Twistleton and Mrs Ffowkes-Taylor.

The welfare of less fortunate children was the subject of a special service held at St.Nicholas in the summer of 1891. The collection went towards the Children's Holiday Fund, which paid for twenty or more children of St.Pancras parish in London to have a holiday in the countryside. A similar service was held the following year, which also saw an appeal to give generously by Percy Bagnall Evans of The Spring, who explained that it cost between 8s and 10s to pay for one child to have a week's holiday.

In the summer of 1893, a meeting of children was held at local schools to start a Kenilworth branch of the Ministering Children's League, a movement started in 1885 by Lady Meath, and Miss Frances Pears (18) of Kenilworth Hall was elected secretary. The League aimed to promote kindness and unselfishness amongst children and create a desire in them to help the poor and needy, and the new branch was to help local children as well as those from further afield. Children were also encouraged to do one good deed every day. By the end of August, there were already over a hundred child members of the League branch and a weekly sewing bee had been started amongst the girl members. Ladies of the town contributed remnants and cast-off garments, the children themselves contributed cotton and odds and ends to the "basket" and the girls met each Saturday afternoon beneath the trees of the Common to make and repair children's clothes. Mrs Pounds helped by cutting and preparing garments, which were intended for the needy of the town. Tea was provided once a month at a cost of 1d. The Associate Members, adults who organised the branch, were short of gentlemen to help with unspecified boys' activities.

The Reverend Alfred Binnie had been associated with St.Nicholas church for about ten years when in 1891 he had resigned his position for a new posting in the Parish of St.Asaph's in Birmingham. In conjunction with Binnie, in the summer of 1893 three children from his new parish were in Kenilworth "*...recovering from serious illness...and they have benefited very much by Kenilworth air and the pint of milk apiece they consume daily.*"

Just prior to Christmas 1893, League members entertained 40 local poor children to a plum pudding supper at the Parish Room. By March 1894, there were 130 child members, paying 1d a quarter, and 30 associate members, paying 2s per annum. The same month saw the children of the League give a concert to a full Parish Room. All the members took part in the opening song "The Ministering Children" and it was mostly girls who performed solos and duets including the Misses L and B Robertson, G Chapman, K Butler, L Adcock and C Heatley; the only boys recorded being the Masters A Dyer, C Holmes and H Bennett, although the boys collectively performed two "*laughable dialogues.*" The concert raised just £3.

Following on from the successful rehabilitation of three children the previous summer, in 1894 the adult members began a scheme to regularly house needy youngsters from Birmingham who would benefit from "*three weeks in the invigorating air of Kenilworth.*" The first to arrive were three poor children again sent by the Reverend Binnie from the Parish of St.Asaph's and another from the Birmingham General Hospital where the Matron, Miss Margetts, was the sister of Dr Bourne's wife. Soon six more poor children of Birmingham were boarded out in Kenilworth for three weeks. They were supplied with some new clothes made by members of the League's sewing bee.

Activities for the young Kenilworth members continued throughout the summer. Frances Pears invited all the girl members of the sewing class to her home, Kenilworth Hall, each Saturday, and Henry Smith-Turberville of Crackley Gables arranged for the boys to play cricket and football matches in a field at his home on August Bank Holiday. Unfortunately, it rained most of the day. A report published in the autumn of 1894 revealed that there were then 180 members. During the summer a total of fourteen Birmingham children, eight from the General Hospital and six from St.Asaph's, stayed an average of three weeks each, with Mr Everitt, Mr Pratt, Mr Spiers, Mr Constance or Mr Satchwell providing accommodation. All the children went back much better for the change.

The sewing class was now held on Saturday afternoons at the St.Nicholas Mission-room and all the girl members were encouraged to attend. Donations of materials were invited and received.

At the National School in October 1895, Percy Evans gave an address and distributed prizes to deserving League members who had shown the greatest interest in the objects of the League. A similar sports and prize event was held in May 1897, this time at The Hall and naturally Frances Pears (22) again made the arrangements; she also distributed the prizes and made a major speech outlining the League's objectives. The Misses Riley, Hanning and Millar assisted. In August 1896, the League's annual sports were held at William Holmes's field at Crackley, again Frances Pears and others organised it. By the summer of 1897, the League had a cricket team that appears to have been a mixture of young and old members. In June they played against Abbey Hill Socials and bowled them out twice for 32 runs, and won with seven wickets to spare. The League team included a young schoolmaster Steven Hiscock and it is likely that some of his boarding school pupils were amongst the members.

The annual prize-giving had evolved into a sports and tea afternoon, this particular year it was held at Crackley and a large number of Kenilworth children took part. The sports consisted mostly of flat racing and hurdling and the prizes awarded included cricket bats, pocket-knives and fishing rods for the boys, and dolls, skipping ropes, books and Japanese cups and saucers for the girls. Mrs Evans of The Spring awarded the prizes, and all the arrangements were again made by the ever involved Frances Pears.

Just prior to Christmas the same year, a sale of work by members took place in the Parish room to raise funds for the branch. Stalls included woollen-ware and needlework, dolls and fancy goods, of which many had been made by the girls in the sewing class. Garments for men, women and children were available. A special stall for the benefit of the boy's recreation room included a display of *"...bent ironwork of various designs, specimen vases, candlesticks, &c."* A fully-furnished dolls house valued at £5 was raffled and won by six

year-old Nellie Knight, a draper's daughter. One particular attraction was provided by Frank Carter who for 1d demonstrated his phonograph whilst another attraction was *"an electric battery."* At the close, Mr H B Francis auctioned off many of the remaining items.

Despite the League successfully promoting good will amongst Kenilworth children, its chief object remained the welfare of all needy children. In 1897, seven Kenilworth children were sent away on a holiday, and 22 came from Birmingham, but the work was always limited by the help received and money raised. The girl's weekly sewing class continued to provide clothes for Kenilworth's and other poor children, and additional garments for sale. On the other hand *"...the boys have had games provided for them. We frankly confess, however, that the boys have been a little beyond our power."*

The League members also formed an occasional football team. In January 1898, it lost a home match 1-0 to Kenilworth Unity. In the summer of that year, the cricket team became quite active; having beaten a team called the Etceteras, they then took on and lost by 25 runs to 23, to the Abbey Hill Institute. The return match the following month saw a similarly low scoring game, 28-21, but the same victors.

In February 1899 the League was honoured to have as a guest speaker Mrs Arthur Phillips, the organising secretary of the League. It is noticeable that the men at the meeting, the Reverends Hanning and Berridge, and treasurer Percy Evans, were greatly outnumbered; the other 36 people listed were women. There were also a number of school pupils present. During the previous year, 60 children had benefited from the efforts of the Kenilworth League. Ten children had been sent away to the coast for a stay of at least a month whilst those who had come to Kenilworth had stays varying between three weeks and three months. Many of these had again been sent by Reverend and Mrs Binnie, from whom they had received many letters telling of the benefit the poor children had gained, and once more others had come from the Birmingham General Hospital. Mrs Phillips outlined some of the success of the League since it was started in 1885. It had now paid for a home for destitute children at Ottershaw and there were convalescent homes in Exmouth, Richmond, Scotland and Ireland. Work was now spreading abroad to France, Germany, Italy, Spain and Canada. Although Kenilworth was just a small part of the movement, neither of its two neighbours of Leamington and Coventry had a branch. The meeting adjourned to the new parochial room, which had been tastefully decorated by Frances Pears, and in the evening, a lantern show took place in the crowded room, with Percy Evans and the vicar operating the lantern.

The spring of 1899 saw another entertainment, this time a mixture of comedy and drama, organised by and starring Miss Nellie Pope, which raised another £16. By the end of the year, and with another sale of work raising £40, the League had £53 in hand. Frances Pears, Nellie Pope (who was now Mrs Morris) and Mrs Percy Evans continued to encourage adult subscribers, which now numbered 63.

*   *   *

During his time as an hotelier in Bangor and Cromer, W D Dance had been able to save £600 and in May 1892 took the Abbey Hotel from Mrs Humpage. It seems that Alfred Humpage had died. The valuation came to £1,600 exclusive of stock and so the furniture and effects were let to him under a hire purchase agreement with £400 down and £200 per annum. To meet all his financial commitments, Dance borrowed several sums totalling £700 from Fowler and Sons, but by early 1895, he was in severe difficulties and the subject of litigation with 23 claims totalling nearly £400 against him. He acknowledged that he did not keep proper books and simply admitted his expenditure far out-stretched his income. The situation was confused further by the expenses of Mrs Humpage and her daughter whilst staying at the Hotel being taken against the debt.

It seems that the Abbey Hotel was at that time in the hands of Slatter, Son and Gibbs, Solicitors of Stratford and in August 1895 Mr Gibbs of that company applied for a temporary licence transfer from Henry Hunt to Charles Edward Cleveley. It was granted, despite the fact that Cleveley had spent the last ten years as a "*draper's traveller*" and had not held a licence before, but he had a little experience in the trade some years previously. The following month the transfer was made permanent.

Cleveley charged 2½ guineas a week for full board, and for a weekend break from Saturday supper to Monday breakfast, 16s 6d, fully inclusive. Despite his inexperience, it was under Cleveley that the Abbey Hotel finally became a success and replaced the Kings Arms as the town's leading resort.

Kenilworth people continued to do well in cycling events, most notably Thomas Sherwin who in 1897 for example, finished second in the Humber 3-hour race, covering 70½ miles.

In the summer of 1899, Mr A Winter of Windy Arbour attempted to start another club, and initially to name it The Kenilworth Castle Cycle Club, but at a meeting in June, it was decided to drop "Castle" from the title. A badge, which was to be worn at all meetings, and runs were chosen and its officers were Winter, Captain; H Selman, sub-Captain; A Colledge, Secretary and Mr Peel, Bugler. Subscriptions were 5s a year, payable on 31st May, and the Queen and Castle was chosen as its headquarters, Frederick Styles was elected treasurer.

Runs were normally made on Thursday afternoons, early closing day, suggesting a number of tradesmen may have been involved. The Captain had control of all runs, leading, with the sub-Captain bringing up the rear, and no member was allowed to pass the Captain without permission. All had to abide by his orders. If a cyclist met with an accident to his machine whilst on a run, the club paid his return expenses. Although not a cyclist, Mr Margetts of Stone House was the club's president, and to show his enthusiasm he laid on a meal for them at the George Hotel in Solihull. Led by Captain Winter, thirteen members made the 12 or 13 mile trip and thoroughly enjoyed their tea.

Edward Farndon, whilst living in Castle End, "*...invented the spider wheel for bicycles.*" He was known as a clever inventor and had an article written about him in *The Million* magazine. By trade, he was a blacksmith and was employed by Lord Leigh for about 15 years, and was an engineer in the Stoneleigh fire brigade.

* * *

In what was possibly the only event of its kind, the week after the fire brigade's 1890 Annual Dinner, a tea was held at the Abbey Hotel for the wives and children of the brigade. The head of the table was given over to Selina Plumbe, as her husband was the longest serving member. Selina Plumbe herself was a grocer and toy dealer at Mill End, and in 1883 had become the first recorded person in Kenilworth to be issued a licence allowing the sale of fireworks.

Towards the end of 1891, word got around that Dr Atkinson was leaving Kenilworth to take up a practice in Leamington. This of course left the fire brigade without a Captain, but a very popular and experienced replacement was in the brigade, and Edward Paine Hodges was duly promoted, his position becoming official at the February 1992 Board meeting. His father Richard had been a brigade member before him, serving under the first Captain, Draper. Edward Hodges had been a brigade member since 1881 and had been Deputy Captain under both Trepplin and Atkinson. He had also been treasurer since 1882 and during the annual competitions, his 4- and 8-men teams were regular winners. He had always enjoyed great popularity within the brigade and his promotion was probably a foregone conclusion, but it did leave a problem - such was the gap he left behind, the choice of the new Deputy Captain had to be deferred. Hodges himself did have one reservation about his new position, he lived a long way out of town, farmimg Camp Farm. The engine itself, having completed 28 years service, had been extensively overhauled during the last year. A special drill was held to mark the departure of Atkinson and this was followed by a meal at the nearby Abbey Hotel. He was presented with a black marble clock, relieved in gold, supplied by Mr Whelan of The Square.

It was not until the AGM the following year (1893) that a Deputy Captain was finally appointed. Upon the recommendation of Captain Hodges, C Saunders of The Moorlands was unanimously elected to the post, even though he had been elected to the brigade for the first time just minutes before. Saunders had been just a short time in Kenilworth, but had proved to be very popular; he also had experience of being a volunteer fireman, as well as fire-fighting in India. It had been a quiet year for the brigade, having not been called to a single fire. Despite this, the brigade was in good order. Attendance at drills was good and the men particularly enjoyed the annual friendly competition. A new alarm bell had been bought for £5, but it was not an improvement on the old and so the manufacturers were called in. The brigade's uniforms though were now close to fifteen years old. New boots were estimated to cost 30s a pair, helmets 18s each, and tunics and overalls 50s, and so a fund was started for new outfits and the first donation was a generous £50 from the Board.

Just weeks later, in February, the brigade were deeply saddened by the death of fireman Thomas Plumbe (55), a member of twenty four years standing. For much of his service he had been an engineer responsible for the working of the engine. In business, he had been a blacksmith at Mill End since c1870. For his funeral the brigade Captain, secretary, four lieutenants and eleven brigade members formed up outside Plumbe's at Mill End and with six more members acting as bearers the coffin was loaded onto the fire engine. His coat, cap, belt and key were placed on top. The brigade walked in front as the cortège made its way to the Albion Baptist Chapel of which Plumbe was a trustee. Plumbe was also an Oddfellow, treasurer to the Hospital Saturday movement, a member of the Kenilworth Liberal Association and attended Salvation Army meetings. The funeral arrangements were made by fellow fireman James Jackson of New Street. Plumbe's was the first death of a serving brigade member.

The appeal for new uniforms continued with James and Mrs Whittendale putting on an entertainment which raised £10 6s. Tenders were received and the successful ones were from Leonard Keatley for 37s 6d for tunics and trousers, and William Bishop for boots at 24s 9d a pair. The new overalls and uniforms had blue tunics "...slightly decorated or relieved in red cord..." and to celebrate, a meal was held at the Queen and Castle, an evening during which Deputy Captain Saunders played his guitar. Soon after supplying the new uniforms, Leonard H Keatley (30) was appearing at the Official Receiver's office in Coventry with debts amounting to £117 against assets of £49. He had a debt of £20 to repay to Alice Harding and also owed to money lenders. The Official Receiver was intrigued by one item in the accounts, 5s a week, amounting to £12 a year, was allowed by Keatley for "amusements" and this along with illness was a major reason for his financial problems. Keatley explained he spent it on playing bagatelle or cards in pubs for the price of a beer.

In spring 1893, the brigade undertook a special drill at Albert Jones's residence, Rouncill, principally to test the mains water pressure at almost two miles distant from the tower and it was "found all that could be desired." There were three vacancies in the brigade and replacements were chosen by existing brigade members, each being allowed three votes. Ten applicants were put through a series of test drills, comprising ladder scaling and jumping into a sheet from a fixed height. Each candidate passed these tests and the new members elected were Hubert Lawrence, J Gardiner and W Holmes jnr.

At the monthly meeting in October 1893, Saunders resigned as deputy and his place was taken by Bolton Joberns, the brickmaker in partnership with Henry Hawkes at Whitemoor. Captain Hodges had always had a rapport with the brigade and this he showed at the 1893 annual meal when he said his firemen "would rather attend a good fire than a good meal any day!" The brigade was also indebted to their visiting counterparts from Coventry, the oldest brigade in the county, from whom the Kenilworth men received instruction in its early days.

The merry-go-rounds, swingboats, stalls etc.

returned to the Bear Field for the Statute Fair in September 1894, but continual rain spoiled the day. Despite the very muddy field, the fair continued into the next day when business was improved. As part of the general atmosphere of the fair, the fire brigade arranged a cricket match against the Kenilworth Amateur Minstrels. It was particularly notable for the brigade playing in uniform and the opposition in character! Unfortunately, only five brigade members turned up and "not many" of the minstrels and so the teams were made up from spectators. "The get up of Baulcombe as a clown and his comical antics caused much merriment. Hudson made a capital "nigger" and his running about with a lamp and bell was also diverting. The other get-ups were equally ludicrous." Of the brigade members, Lieutenants Cooke and Butcher, and Deputy Captain Joberns, managed just 3 runs between them in a total of 54, the Minstrels scored 70.

Captain Hodges' popularity amongst the brigade was doubtless helped by friendships built over a period of time. By 1895, Hodges had been in the brigade for 14 years and other long-serving members included Cooke (25 years), White (20 years) and John Heatley (19 years), but their experience was rarely needed as there had not been a fire for some years. Despite this, at the annual meal that year at the Kings Arms, attended by more than 75 members and friends of the brigade, the first mention was made that a steam-powered fire engine was now becoming a necessity, although the idea had first been minuted in 1892. For the next 15 months or so the desire for a new engine gathered momentum, but nothing of any significance actually happened.

Not all were convinced that a steam-engine was the first priority, fireman Bostin claimed a fire escape was needed. He had seen a fire in Hay Lane in Coventry he where saw one in action, and suggested that if there was a fire at the Abbey Hotel, the ladders might not bear the strain and break. An escape would cost £70-80, and Hodges agreed to include it in his annual report.

Early one November 1896 morning, a businessman saw distant flames and believed that, once more, there was a fire at Oaks Farm. A cycle messenger was despatched to summon the fire brigade, but it was soon discovered that the man was mistaken. He had seen "...flaring paraffin lamp illuminations cast by a travelling circus company who were busily engaged packing up for their departure from Kenilworth." Not surprisingly, he "...brought upon himself a considerable amount of good humoured chaff by his friends."

At the AGM in early 1897, it was revealed that an anonymous gentleman had promised £50 towards a steam engine, provided the rest of the money could be raised within a year. There was some discussion as to whether an escape was more necessary, but the impetus was in favour of the steam engine. Lieutenant Griffiths quickly became a key person; as the manager at the waterworks, he was well acquainted with engines and pumping equipment and he asserted that he could teach all brigade members how to operate the new machine in just three months. With the news of the promise out, it was not to be long before the generous benefactor was named, it was James C Stringer (34) a man of independent income living on Park Hill. It was quickly

169

established that more than £250 would be needed and accounts for donations were set up at both the Midland and Lloyds banks. It was Thomas Sherwin who set up the accounts, with permission from Hodges, and he promised to do all he could to raise subscriptions, even holding bazaars if need be.

By the time of the annual dinner in March, other contributions to the fund had been promised, the largest of which was £25 from George Beard. The manual engine was now over thirty years old and needed an astonishing 48 people to operate to its maximum, only 12 would be required for at least treble the performance from the steamer. A committee was formed with the sole purpose of purchasing the steamer. The first meeting of the steam engine committee was held at the Institute on 25th March 1897, and was chaired by Major-General Frederick Hadow (61) Royal Artillery retired, of Fieldgate. Also present was Lieutenant Colonel Edward Joynson, Dr Growse, and others such as Pears, Welch, Holmes, etc., and secretary Sherwin. By now, £125 had been promised towards the new estimate of £320. In addition, £30 would be needed for alterations to the engine shed and £10 a year for maintenance. Captain Hodges outlined the necessity of a new engine; *"The difficulty (I) have as Captain (I) had always found was that I had to employ 48 men for pumping, men who were always crying out for beer, and if we had a steamer we would be independent of that help."*

It emerged that the original initiative was all down to Sherwin who on his own began requesting donations, and it was he who instigated the original generous promise from Stringer. It was now down to Sherwin to visit other brigades to ascertain all the likely costs of running the engine. Although Sherwin made the arrangements, he was accompanied on the visits by Hodges and Griffiths, and Edward Joynson. Their conclusion was that annual maintenance would fall within £20. The need for urgency became greater when other local brigades from Leamington, Warwick and Coventry announced that they would no longer send their steam engines to assist in Kenilworth, as it would leave their own towns vulnerable.

Lieutenant Colonel Edward Joynson...

...of the 3rd battalion, South Lancashire regiment, was 41 years of age when he came to live at The Firs, after the death of Jane Woodcock in 1889.

He became involved in the Primrose League, becoming Ruling Councillor, and its fêtes in 1897 and 1898 were held in his grounds. He was elected to the KUDC in 1896 and served on the highways committee and it was due to him that the Council roadmen were allowed half an hour each morning for breakfast, but only in the winter. He was instrumental in getting the footways asphalted and was one time manager of the National Schools. He was married to Emily.

1897 was another quiet year for the brigade, which perhaps was just as well as there was little progress in purchasing a steamer. Due to this lack of action, Captain Hodges was rumoured to be on the verge of resigning his post, and this was confirmed late in the year when it was discovered that Dr Edmund Bourne had been lined up to replace him. Bourne was officially elected the Brigade's ninth Captain early the following year, and he was the fourth surgeon to hold the position.

A farewell dinner for Hodges was held in early 1898 at the Queen and Castle, at which he was presented with a medal by the oldest brigade member, fireman John Cooke, aged 47. The medal, made by Mr Brown of The Square, depicted the engine and appliances in gold on a silver background with "Kenilworth V.F.B." on the side. The reverse had the inscription "Presented to Captain E P Hodges by the members of the brigade on his retirement after 17 years service. December 1897." Hodges used the occasion to lament the lack of a steam fire engine and surprisingly claimed that with the high value of property on the outskirts of town, no-one had been willing to start a fund for one. Songs were sung in the evening, with accompaniment by William Riley jnr, the son of the Kenilworth Amateur Minstrel and his late piano-playing wife.

Such was the esteem in which Hodges was held, at the official time of resignation at the following week's AGM, he was appointed Honorary Captain and allowed to keep, and wear, his uniform. John Nelson of Crackley Hall was elected a fireman, and later Deputy Captain. The Captain, Edmund Bourne said he regretted ever leaving the brigade and in accepting the new post said *"...it was a common remark that the Kenilworth brigade was one of the smartest ever turned out of a small town."* Soon after the new appointments were made, the Whittendale family put on a show at the Assembly Rooms to raise a donation towards the steam engine. Also involved was Louis Schneider who had not long before opened a music shop in Station Road, near the station itself. His contribution to the show was the first appearance of the Orchestral Society, which he had assembled in just ten weeks. The concert raised £10.

Thomas Sherwin had meanwhile raised £260 and arranged for the Dunlop Volunteer Fire Brigade to bring over their steamer to give a public demonstration in Kenilworth, and the KUDC gave permission for it to take place in the Abbey Fields. It was hoped that the demonstration would give a fresh impetus to the fundraising. The Dunlop brigade got steam up outside town and made a thrilling sight entering the town with both a driver and postillion controlling the horses. Despite the *"wildness of the elements"* there was a large gathering, including of course the Kenilworth Brigade, to greet them. Quickly and impressively, the Dunlop engine was soon drawing water from the river and throwing it from three 50ft hoses connected to just one outlet. *"The Kenilworth brigade put their manual engine to work also and gave another object lesson - the impossibility of a manual coping with a large fire in anything like so satisfactory manner as a steamer. The spectators had an interesting afternoon."* The two brigades and dignitaries retired to a meal at the Coventry Cross, where it is assumed the two engines were taken and, as the Dunlop men made their way back to Coventry, a Steam Engine Committee meeting was held. Major General Frederick Hadow was elected Chairman and it was agreed that he and Lieutenant Colonel Edward Joynson, along with brigade members Captain Bourne, Engineer Heatley, Lieutenant Griffiths and Thomas

Sherwin were to inspect and report upon different makes of engines. On Wednesday 18th May 1898, a Committee meeting was held at the engine-house with most of the Brigade present. After hearing the sub-committee report, it was decided to order a Shand, Mason double vertical steam engine, capable of throwing 260 gallons of water in a minute. There was now £360 available in the fund.

While the new engine was awaited, practices had to continue. A special drill was held in June at Crackley Hall, residence of Deputy Captain Nelson. This was also the highest place at which mains water was available and its weak pressure meant that it had to be pumped. Nelson then provided a supper. A local topic of discussion was the potential name for the new engine, at an early stage it was thought an historical figure connected with the town would be most suitable.

It was at the June Council meeting that the formal acceptance of the engine was made, and at the fifth Horticultural Society show in the Castle grounds on 14th July, it made its first public appearance. Admired by all, including Lord Clarendon, it was announced that it was to be named "Queen Bess", particularly appropriate on the day as that queen's visit to the Castle had helped to make it so well-known. The engine looked *"very handsome"*.

It was the following Thursday, 21st July, at 5 o'clock that the official christening and trial took place. There was a huge gathering of the notables; all the members of the Council including Chairman Pears, the Steam Fire Engine Purchasing Committee including its Chairman Major-General Hadow and a spattering of wives and daughters. There were also deputations from other brigades, including those of Leamington and Dunlop. Also, of course, there was the entire Kenilworth Brigade; Captain Bourne, Deputy Captain Nelson, Honorary Captain Hodges, four Lieutenants and 16 men. At 5 o'clock precisely the wife of the purchasing committee's chairman, Eleanor Hadow (68), broke a bottle of wine on the engine and officially named her "Queen Bess". Unfortunately missing was Shand-Mason's engineer and so it was left to the Company agent Mr Elliott to get steam up and he managed 100lbs in exactly 8 minutes and 22 seconds. Three jets were started and the *"water was forced through at a tremendous rate."* One of the tests was to prove the flow capacity of the claimed 260 gallons in a minute - one of the Council's 350 gallon water-carts was used and at the first attempt it was filled in 1 minute 12 seconds, and a second test beat this by ten seconds, about a third faster than the manufacturer's statement. *"The height was the next test and a hose was laid from the brook to the wych elm in the park, a distance of somewhere about 200 yards, and the water was thrown above the elm to the height of about 135 feet."* This concluded the trial and Hadow announced he was quite satisfied, and the engine was formally handed over to William Pears. Coming in for particular praise were Sherwin for his perseverance, and Stringer for his generous donation that started the appeal. The opportunity was taken to present various members of the brigade with service medals; John Cooke for 27 years service, White for 22 years, John Heatley 21 years, ex-fireman F Heatley 19 years, Secretary Hughes 18 years, E Hodges 16 years, Lieutenant Jackson 17 years,

Butcher 11 years, Griffiths 11 years and Bostin 10 years. Fittingly, a supper was held at the Queen and Castle to celebrate the event. Those who were invited but did not attend included Lord Leigh who was in London, the Earl of Clarendon and the brigades of Hatton, Southam and Rugby.

The next day, Shand's engineer attended to instruct the brigade's engineer, fireman Griffiths, on how to raise steam. Griffiths was the ideal as engineer choice as he was manager of the water works and was used to steam pumps. *"No man has worked harder for the scheme and much of the success is due to him. As an engineer, his advice has been most valuable to the Committee and as a fireman he has offered to teach every man in the brigade the working of the engine."* 100lbs of steam was raised in 5 minutes 40 seconds, which was 45 seconds faster than the manufacturer's specification. The brigade was soon practising with their new engine and it was suggested that it could be used to water the streets, although the power of the jets was actually likely to cause damage to the gravel surface. Unfortunately alterations to the engine-house had not been completed and so, courtesy of Mrs Pitt, the engine was temporarily stored at Hill House, probably in the building that was the original engine-house in 1863. The contract, worth £20, to alter the engine-house was won by F Keatley. *"The engine-house which has been altered to take the new steamer looks very bright and clear inside, and the outside looks very smart, with its wooden oak-stained gable end."* A late donation to the fund was £10 from the London and North Western Railway Company.

After some years without a fire, the brigade only had to wait only about a month, until 8.15 p.m. on Wednesday 18th August, before it had the chance to use the steam engine in action. The brigade had just returned from a practice when news was received of a fire at Kingswood Farm and they set off immediately with some of the men following in a brake. A large straw-rick close to the farm buildings was ablaze, most of the brigade's efforts were in preventing the fire spreading, and little of the rick was saved. *"The new steamer worked admirably in the hands of the engineers Griffiths and Heatley."* The brigade returned to the engine-house at around midnight.

The nameplate carried by the steam fire engine.

In November, the Steam Fire Engine Committee met for the last time. £384 had been raised and £377 spent. Presentations of £2 each were made to Sherwin and Griffiths for all their efforts towards the engine, and £1 10s to James Heatley for his extra work. All papers and correspondence connected with the purchase were handed over to the Council.

As the steamer needed fewer firemen to operate it than did the manual, about half the brigade were trained in a new duty: *"A cycle corps is being organised. Ten men already to go to a fire, look out the best place for getting water and take the place of a salvage corps."* It must have been a curious sight for spectators: *"The fire brigade went down Warwick Road with their steamer, getting up steam, preceded by the cycle advance corps, for a practice looking ready for any emergency which might occur."*

* * *

In May 1893, a plan was drawn for a new bridge, to cost no more than £20, over the ford in Millbrook Lane. Nearby, the same year, New Row needed urgent and major attention: *"The thoroughfare is one of the most neglected in town and presents several ugly features."* It was in places very narrow and steep and, due to the heavy vehicles heading for the Castle that used it, was in a dangerous condition. To make the road 40ft wide throughout, an overgrown hedge and bank were removed as well as *"ancient thatched dilapidated cottages"* giving an extra 16ft width in places. The debris was used to fill in an old quarry.

It was suggested in November 1896 that roads could be rolled cheaper, and better, by the hiring of a steam road-roller. Glover and Sons of Warwick were contacted and they offered the hire of a roller at 30s a day from 7.30 a.m. to 5 p.m., or 22s a day if hired for a week or month. Included were a driver, fuel and water van, and it was decided to hire it for a week as a trial.

The work by the roller was declared "very satisfactory" at the next Council meeting, but no mention was made of the accident it caused. Miss Swift, of Warriors Lodge, was driving two female friends in her dog cart and upon reaching The Square her horse was frightened by the roller and bolted. Near Mr Prew's house, the wheels of the cart became trapped with the wheels of another and as they locked, the horse swerved round and fell to the ground. The three ladies jumped out none the worse for their mis-hap.

The roller was periodically hired, and incidents continued. In November 1898, its rear axle broke in Albion Street, and just three months later, it ran away, backwards, down Spring Lane! The horse-drawn roller used in between times fared little better; on a late September morning in 1898, it was being used to roll the footpath near the Wesleyan Chapel when, to avoid a lamppost, it was taken off the path. On turning to go back on it, the roller tipped over taking the horse with it. Some of Walter Lockhart's men were working nearby and were credited for the way in which they calmed the horse.

At the end of November 1900, Glover and Sons offered to sell the Council the road roller on terms which were well received and provisionally agreed to, but a final decision was postponed for twelve months after it was claimed that it would become a *"white elephant."* Not everyone was impressed by the methods by which the roads were repaired with a roller. John Welsh of Rudfen Manor wrote: *"The metal is applied in this way. The roads are first scored across with picks, the scores being from nine to twelve inches apart. A very light coating of metal is then given; and the coating is so light that after it has been rolled in the scores by the picks are still plainly to be seen, and during rain are filled with water. The Council are thus letting water into the roads and this rots and ruins them."* *"The metal is machine broken, and seems so brittle that by the time the steam-roller has done its work a considerable portion of it has been ground to powder. It is well known that machine-broken metal does not wear nearly so well as hand-broken. There is also the risk of getting inferior stone; and it is never broken to the proper shape. There are many men in Kenilworth now who can break road metal; why do they not get the chance of doing the work."*

Thomas Hawley had had plans for a new road out of Warwick Road opposite the tan-yard, passed as far back as 1884, and these he re-deposited in late 1897 to be re-assessed. By the end of the year, the scheme had been taken over by Mr Barrow and the 36ft wide road was again approved, subject to agreeing details about the cost of drainage connections to Warwick Road. In an attempt to get the road finished as quickly as possible, it was suggested at a Council meeting that Mr Barrow should not be burdened with the cost of the drainage connections, but this motion was defeated and Barrow duly paid £15 for the connections. In early 1900, the Council received a letter from Barrow saying the road was complete and ready for adoption. The new road was called Barrow Street after its promoter.

Later the same year another road to the west of Warwick Road was ready for adoption; built by Mr Bowen a Leamington builder along the course of the track-way leading to the cricket ground, it was named at a time of great patriotism during the Boer War as Queen's Road. At the Council meeting in early November, it was formally agreed to take over both roads.

In the summer of 1899, twenty three residents of Barrow-well Lane, petitioned the KUDC asking for the road name to be changed to Castle Road. The move was opposed both by the Post Office, who already had Castle End, Castle Green, Castle Terrace and Castle Grove to contend with, and by a petition organised by Mr Welch who could see no reason for altering a name which had existed since 1580.

Mr Gee provided a compromise - keeping the original name from The Square to the bridge over the brook and adopting the new name from there to the Castle thus doing away with Castle Grove, Castle Terrace and Castle Rest. His proposition was unanimously carried.

Just before Christmas 1896, the area suffered an earthquake: *"At Kenilworth the most severe shock appears to have taken place between 5 and 6 o'clock on the Ladies' Hills on the outskirts of town. The houses rocked violently and the inmates dressed amidst great alarm."* *"The contents of the houses, roof-tiles, chimney pots &c bore visible signs of the extraordinary vibration."*

Charles Whateley (23), married a minor who

was a ward in Chancery, in late 1889 in Chorlton, Lancashire. They then went on a tour to Brighton for 2 months, then Guernsey, Weymouth and London accumulating expenses of about £70 a month. Whilst in Brighton his wife was driving a landau when it was in collision with a pony chaise driven by a Mr Kay. She received head injuries. Whateley brought an action against Kay but lost it, costing him nearly £1,000.

Upon returning to Kenilworth, his wife, who had £3,000 when they married, lent him £740 of which he paid £700 on 27th August 1890 to his father for an equal partnership in his business. Up until then he had been working for his father. Charles made about £200 a year nett profit from the business. In October 1892, Richard Knight was admitted into the firm as an equal third and as his part of the deal, Charles received £269. But within months, on 6th January 1893, Charles filed a receiving order: he had been living well beyond his means. His wife was the major creditor, claiming back not only the money she lent him to join his father, but other amounts that did not go into the trade, totalling £990. In 1891, she also sold some property and he had some of the money. There were six other creditors totalling £309. His wife also had claims on their furniture, which had been left to her by her mother.

Even as proceedings against him progressed, Whateley's behaviour was poor. Just prior to making out the order, he bought a number of items, and the bailiffs called upon him to collect them. He refused them entry but eventually handed over six bottles of spirits, against the three or four dozen he had bought, and in place of £40 of jewellery handed over a watch with a damaged face. He was declared bankrupt.

In January 1897, Charles Whateley, described as a gardener, was in trouble for obtaining food and lodgings in Oxford, worth 5s, by false pretences. He was described as ill and erratic and was under the delusion that "...money awaited him wherever he went." He was ordered back to "...the Salvation Army farm colony with which he is connected."

In November 1896, another of Kenilworth's Societies held an event: "Birthnight supper: The anniversary supper held in connection with the Birthnight Society was held at the Virgins Inn and Castle Tavern on Saturday evening. There was a large company present and the chair was occupied by Mr W Holmes. A pair of photographs were presented, having been subscribed to by the whole of the members; these were companion likenesses of Mr T Mayes, a prominent member of the society. The portraits were excellent likenesses, framed neatly in oak, one of which was hung up amongst other worthy members of the society. And the other was presented by the chairman to Mr T Mayes who acknowledged the gift in suitable terms. The massive old china jug, with a capacity of twelve quarts and inscribed "May the trade of Kenilworth never fail" (1824), was then requisitioned and the usual loyal toasts were given interspersed with a capital programme of well-rendered songs. The health of the chairman, Mr T Mayes, host Prime, and the Misses Prime (acknowledging their efficient catering) were heartily received and a most successful and pleasant evening was passed."

The jug used during the Birthnight Society celebrations at The Virgins and Castle. (Courtesy of a private collection)

* * *

In 1893, Henry Street sold a little more of his land in Priory Road, this time the area that backed onto the railway station yard, and it was bought by James Whittendale who built four small cottages on it. James Whittendale had been in business in Kenilworth, with different partners, since about 1880, and had recently built for himself The Bungalow. He had been in poor health, and was thought to have recovered, but collapsed and died at his home on Saturday 7th November 1896. He was 60. His had married twice, each wife giving birth to three sons, and one of them, Edgar, had been involved with his father's business for some time. James was buried in Coventry.

Dr Wynter moved into one of four new cottages facing the coffee tavern.

Dr Daniel Wynter retired from his very public life before the formation of the KUDC, and began to live in seclusion, but continued his practice at Hyde House in Station Road. Financially he fell on hard times and on 14th October 1896, he sold off many of his possessions including over a thousand books, oil paintings and trophies and weapons, likely to be mementos of his father's time in India. With the money raised, he paid off some of his creditors and moved into one of the new houses *"...just around the Station corner of Priory Road, and facing the coffee tavern."* The house was called Brecon. He was known to be suffering from bronchitis and *"depression of spirits",* and was thought to be on the edge of a catastrophe unless someone came to his rescue.

On Monday 22nd February 1897, he appeared as well as usual, was cheerful, and the following day attended to his patients and went out for a short time. On Wednesday he did not get up; his housekeeper, Mrs Alice Smith went to his room and he got her to fetch some medicine from downstairs, she also gave him a brandy. He remained in bed all morning. On one visit to him, Alice was given a prescription by Wynter and she sent his other servant, a girl, to John Newton, Chemist, The Square, with it. Alice went back to Wynter's room at 2.15 and found him dead; he had taken his own life.

The inquest was held by Deputy Coroner W Ansell on Friday 26th at the Coffee Tavern, just across the road from Wynter's house. Alice Smith was visibly affected as she gave her evidence. She had been cook and housekeeper to Wynter for eight years. Some years before, he had had a bad attack of influenza and since then had complained about his heart. He had once told her that he had heart problem since he was a boy. He had money difficulties and bailiffs had been to the house as recently as Tuesday night and Wednesday. The Bailiffs were *"still in possession"* trying to recoup money for money lenders, but she did not know how much for. Wynter once told her that the money he owed was to pay debts to other money lenders and that he had no money of his own. He had told her several times, *"My trouble is more than I can bear; I have prayed to God to take me but he won't and I have a horror of committing suicide."* He was *"...worried and harassed in all directions about money matters and had difficulty in making both ends meet."* He cut down on expenses in every direction and did all he could to pay his creditors.

On the day he died, Alice went into his room and drew the blinds at 7 o'clock. He said he felt unwell and wrote a prescription at about mid-day. After the servant girl went out for medicine, he wrote two prescriptions for patients. John Newton had made up prescriptions for Wynter for 17 years. The prescription he received from the girl was, *"For self, 1oz prussic acid."* There was nothing unusual in supplying this to medical man, but Newton told the maid to be careful how she handled it and sent a message with the medicine to take care with it. Alice took the medicine to Wynter and he had a little brandy and water before she left him. About an hour later, she went to his room, knocked on the door but received no answer. She went in and asked, *"Do you feel any better now?"* There was no reply and upon feeling his hand found it quite cold and she realised he was dead.

Dr Tweedy saw the deceased at 2.30 on Wednesday, dead in bed. The bottle from the chemist was lying on the bed and contained rather less than 1/2 oz of prussic acid. There was a distinct smell of acid about the body and he assumed Wynter had taken the acid, and that death was caused by it. A *"drachm"* was sufficient to poison a person and death would have been practically instantaneous. He knew Wynter had heart disease from his general appearance and from what he had told him.

A bailiff, J P Smith of Coventry, was in the deceased's house at time of inquest and was sent for. The money lender in question was a Mr Gordon of Birmingham. The amount owed was not disclosed but described by Deputy Coroner Ansell as a *"very, very large sum."* In his summing up, Ansell said that with only one exception the case was without precedent as to one of Her Majesty's coroners ending his own life. He described Wynter as *"...an ornament, esteemed and regarded by everyone who knew him...driven to his wits end by his inability to meet the claims of some rapacious creditors. The deceased was practically irresponsible for his act."*

The remains of Dr Wynter's grave (foreground).

Wynter's funeral, on the Saturday following his death, saw hundreds of people attending. The cortège started from his home in Priory Road at 2.45 headed by the fire brigade, walking in pairs in order of seniority. Two members, Cooke and White, remained from the days when Wynter was the brigade's captain. There were three mourning coaches; the first carried the chief mourners, who were his brother-in-law Captain Very, and Mr Wyer of Ladies Hill. Daniel's brother Hugh was absent. In the second coach was his old sparring partner Henry Street and in the third his fellow doctors, Growse and Tweedy. Every curtain on the route was drawn, as were many others throughout the town. After the procession entered St.Nicholas church, there was "*unseemly crowding*" at the gateway. "*People were seen pushing and struggling with one another as though they had been fighting for the front seats at the doors of a theatre.*" "*The mortal remains of our good old Doctor were lowered into the grave with universal tokens of regret at this lamentable ending to a long and prominent public career.*" He was buried with his mother. Amongst the wreaths were those from the Noah's Ark Allotment Association of which Wynter was President, and his housekeeper.

A couple of weeks later, the sale of his remaining effects fetched good prices; it was generally thought that the buyers were collecting mementos of such a well-liked person. Despite being romantically linked in his early days in Kenilworth, the "*lady declined to complete the engagement*" and he reportedly never married. "*Extreme kindness and generosity endeared himself to the population.*" He was called Dan by those that knew him. Politically he was a Conservative, being a Ruling Councillor of the local Primrose League, but he remained popular with the Liberals.

*   *   *

Ten years after William Clarke's failed attempt, George and Ann Burton, as joint owners, made an application in August 1897 for a liquor license for the coffee tavern, now known as the Railway Refreshment Rooms, in Priory Road. It was claimed that traffic at the station had "*trebled in a few years*" and yet the railway company still had no refreshment facilities at their station. In fact, the railway company were the main objectors to the application, its representative saying that they were actually abandoning refreshment facilities at stations as "*...in many places they are a nuisance.*" There were none at Coventry either. The company also claimed that "*...the class of people carried were not those that would want to go into a public house. The first object was to get to Kenilworth Castle and enjoy themselves in a rational manner.*" The Abbey Hotel had recently been renovated and was conducted in a very orderly manner by Mr Cleveley, and he could provide any necessary refreshment. The town had 14 full licences, 3 beer-houses, 1 grocer's licence and 1 spirit licence. The application was refused.

The application became an annual event. In 1898, the opposition came from the Abbey Hotel, Bear and Ragged Staff and Earl of Clarendon inns, and another application in 1899 also failed. The following year the Burtons tried a different approach and applied instead for an off-licence. This time the railway company again provided most of the opposition saying that a nuisance would be created by excursionists leaving empty bottles and jugs in waiting rooms and trains. There was also an obvious additional danger that they could even be thrown from trains. Once more, the application failed.

Deputy Chief Constable Hannah surprisingly objected to the renewing of the licence for the Queen and Castle in August 1899 on the grounds that the premises were constructed so as to make proper police supervision impossible. "*Under the same roof...*" as the hotel was what was known as Leicester House, which was popular with excursionists, and Hannah claimed that if he went there and demanded admission he would be told that it was a private house. Annie Styles's representative pointed out that there had been no structural alteration for years, there had been no previous objection and no liquor was served in it. Hannah managed to have the hearing adjourned so that proper notice could be served. Leicester House was indeed a private house attached to the Hotel, Joshua Blackwell lived there when he was licensee and Annie Styles and her son Frederick lived there now, but Annie Styles agreed to certain structural alterations and the licence was granted.

From 1886, an anonymous donor paid for all fifteen Post Office staff to have a Christmas morning breakfast at 5.00 a.m. before they set off on their rounds. The food was prepared by Mrs Fancott and it became an annual event. At the end of 1887, there were 774 savings accounts open at the Kenilworth Post Office, with total deposits of £13,447 2s 9d, an average of less than £18 in each account.

Buying stamps in winter, traipsing up to half a mile through snow and mud to one of the two Post Offices, brought the suggestion in December 1889 of pillar and wall boxes having an "*...automatic arrangement, one slot for the penny and another for the still humbler brown.*" The only alternative was to buy stamps that were generally available in pubs, but at a cost of an extra penny. The following year stamp machines were installed near several of the collecting boxes.

The cost of providing the postal services to the town for 1892-3 was estimated at £735 with an additional £37 for telegraphs expenses. This was broken down as: Postmaster for postal work £115, for Telegraph work £5; 3 Sub-postmasters and Town Receivers for Postal work £32; 1 Clerk &c. for postal work £24 and for Telegraph £12; 7 stampers, Messengers, Postman &c., allowances for delivery &c., good conduct stripes and wages of the unestablished force - Postal £501, telegraph £2; other expenses £81. One of those who was on the payroll was former comb-maker William Letman who, at the age of 80 in 1892, still did a ten-mile post round before 10 o'clock each morning.

By the spring of 1894 wall boxes had been installed at Albion Street, Castle Green, Castle Grove, Field Gate, Clifton Terrace, Lady's Hill, Railway Station, St.John's, Rosemary Hill and Castle End, all of which were emptied five times daily between about 9.00 a.m. and 8.00 p.m. The last two boxes mentioned had additional collections at 5.45 a.m. These times were arranged to fit into the available rail despatches, and to facilitate the three daily town deliveries. There was just one collection on Sundays, in the evening, and it excluded the station.

Mr Morris always made the Post Office, and his house next door, look "*gay*" in the summer by decorating the outside with flowers. In early 1898, the Post Office staff was provided with new uniforms, and for the first time the bikes of the "*messengers*" and "*letter carriers*" were painted red. By now, possibly during the previous year, a new sub-Post Office had opened in Park Road.

In 1894, this wall-box at Field Gate was emptied daily at 9.15,10.35, 2.00, 5.50 and 7.40; and 6.45 p.m. on Sundays.

The site at Cherry Orchard continued as both a brickworks and market garden. Mr Douglas lost 10,000 tomato plants to severe frost damage in late May 1894 which cost him £100. In August 1896, Henry Clarke jnr, the son of the market gardener, died suddenly of heart disease in his father's woodshed. By 1897 the site had a third use, the KUDC having begun to use a clay pit at the brickworks for depositing rubbish, mostly ashes. Despite warnings not to, local children went there *"...to pick out any unconsidered trifle that falls in their way."* One of them was a young girl called Barnett, just two or three years old, who went there on her own - she slipped and rolled down the slope into the water and sank twice before anyone could get to her. A young man,

William Perks of Albion Street, went down the bank and grabbed her, but he became stuck in the very clayey and wet soil and himself was rescued by brickworks owner Percy Croydon. The girl quickly recovered from her ordeal. The dispersal of ashes was a major problem, often they were dumped anywhere and several times caused blockages to the brook between Spring Lane and Mill End.

On 6th September 1898, whilst Colonel Edward Joynson was striking an ordinary Bryant and May wood-match, a portion fell on the middle finger of his right hand. A small blister formed, then broke, and he covered it; an injury that was barely noticeable. Joynson was very well known for going about the town on his bicycle and, just four days after the incident with the match, he came off it, grazing his right knee and suffering other cuts and bruises. He was attended to by Dr Growse on the 12th, by which time his knee had become inflamed and he was ordered to rest. Two days later, due to pains in his right arm, the doctor was called again - he found blood poisoning extending through the whole arm from the small wound caused by the match. The poisoning took on a great intensity and despite the attentions of doctors from Leamington, and a small operation carried out by a Birmingham surgeon, Joynson's conditioned worsened, and he died on the 17th, aged 51. The carriage carrying his coffin was driven by his own coachman. Two hundred attended the funeral, with as many again in the churchyard. He left a widow, Emily (37) and one known child.

*   *   *

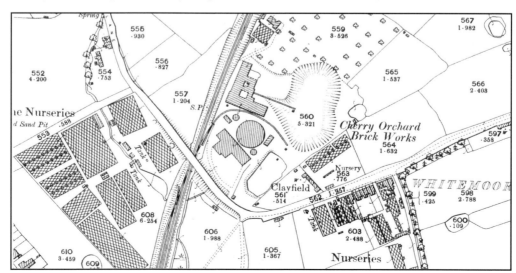

The Cherry Orchard Brickworks, already being used as a waste tip, was encircled by market gardens, including the original orchard on its northern boundary. Henry Street's original fellmonger works was in field 554.

The Kenilworth Pony and Galloway Races were first held in 1896 in a field on the Coventry Road near The Gables. The *"...races were well conducted and the crowd orderly, the promoters have every reason to be satisfied with the result."* In 1897 a card of seven races was organised, both flat and hurdles, with distances varying from one to two miles. The Kenilworth Tradesman's Stakes, over a mile, was won by Henry Whateley's 'Maid of the Mist' beating Thomas Brewer's 'Little Red Hat' into second place. Whateley collected £8 10s for the win. There was a nasty accident in the Kenilworth Stakes when 'Nettle' fell and broke its fetlock and had to be destroyed; its jockey at first appeared to be unhurt but later collapsed and was unconscious for some time.

There was a fairly large attendance, *"...the betting fraternity being abnormally represented..."*, but some races had very few contenders. As may be expected, amongst those involved in organising the meeting were Dr Edmund Bourne, Henry Smith-Turberville, E Boyce Podmore, J Stringer, F Smith and others involved with the cricket and golf clubs.

In early 1895 there were once more doubts as to whether the Kenilworth Cricket Club could continue. The debt was still at £30 and interest was waning, due largely to the growing popularity of golf, but once more the club managed to continue.

Kenilworth Mutual had reformed, and there was also a new club in town, Kenilworth United, and from the outset, membership was high enough to have a Second XI. The Seconds played in the Coventry and District Junior Cup and managed to reach the final against Emscote All Saints, played in mid-August on the Warwick Old Club's ground. United batted first and were soon in trouble at 13 for 5, but, thanks largely to G Daniels making 32 not out, they managed a total of 59. Emscote started just as poorly; Caldicott clean bowled four of the opening five batsmen in five balls. Only one batsman, scoring 27, managed to score more than two runs as they totalled 41. Caldicott finished with 7 wickets for 17. The trophy was presented to winning Captain J Hughes who also received a medal for the highest score in the competition, 39 in the semi-final. Caldicott topped the batting averages for the Second XI and in the season took 30 wickets for 84 runs, averaging 2.8, but was only second in the bowling; F Paxton took 11 wickets for 18 runs at an average of 1.63! Between them, the two club teams played 29 matches and won 23 of them.

The trophy was displayed in Mr Whelan's shop window in The Square and it was remarked how much cleaner it looked than when it was presented to the team. Joseph Whelan was a watchmaker, jeweller and optician. He sold eye glasses and spectacles from 1s to 10s 6d, and lady's and gentleman's sterling silver watches from a guinea. He also sold hall-marked silver spoons and brooches etc. as souvenirs of Kenilworth Castle.

This was to be the start of a great run in the competition for the team as they won the cup for four successive years, the final victory being a one-sided 100 to 28 win over Coventry Union Street. They then decided to withdraw from the competition.

Tannery manager Obidiah Woods was heavily involved with the Kenilworth United club and he was instrumental in securing a pitch in the Abbey Fields for the 1898 season. It was not in the "park" area but in a field alongside Forrest Road still privately owned on behalf of the town by William Evans. The first practice at the ground saw a presentation of a marble clock to H Went who had been club captain from the outset but now had to retire from playing. Woods was capable of producing some astonishing bowling performances; in one match in 1898, he took four wickets in successive balls, but this achievement simply brought back memories of an earlier game in which he took two hat-tricks in the same innings. In 1899 Harry Holmes, also a Kenilworth Town footballer, produced figures of 7 wickets for 3 runs as Leamington Athletic were bowled out for 13; Holmes had already top scored with 13 out of his team's 41 runs.

In June 1899, the town club made a return to Edgbaston, not this time to play the County side, but Birmingham. The defeat this time was narrower, 204 - 99. The end of the 1899 season was marked by a Ladies against Gentlemen's XI match at the Kenilworth Club ground; the Gentlemen were hampered by having to field one-handed and use toy bats. The top scorer of the 15 strong Ladies team was Miss M Gilbert with 34, six made ducks. The total recorded was 119 although the individual scores add up to only 109! In reply, R Loveitt top scored for the Gentlemen with 53. Amongst the recognised players in the team was J Mayfield, who was bowled by Mrs Mayfield for 9. The Gentlemen's total was 117.

The most prestigious match played at the ground was in July 1900 with the visit of the MCC team. Smith-Turberville, now 50 years old, turned out as opening batsman for the visitors and top scored with 40 runs out of 134. Kenilworth in reply could muster only 88; KUDC Chairman and Fire Brigade Captain Dr Edmund Bourne (40) was the victim of one of two catches Smith-Turberville held.

The golf clubhouse was protected with a spring-lock and each member had a key, but an open window provided an enticing entrance for would be villains - of any age. William Betts (11), was employed at the club as a caddie and between 15th and 19th October 1898, with several other lads, he went to the clubhouse. Albert Newey (10), Walter Sheepy (11) and Betts all climbed in through an unfastened window leaving William Smith (8) and Walter Hazle (8) outside. Those inside took some golf balls but the following night, using the same entrance, Newey and Betts returned and the latter took a club worth 5s, the property of Mary Carter of the Engine Inn. Betts sold on the *"head of the golf club"* to William Brewer for *"a penny and some Spanish juice"* but Mary Carter's husband Frank, made enquiries and managed to retrieve it. Mary Carter said that she did not wish to press the charge against Betts but just to use it as a warning to others. After pleading guilty, Betts received six strokes of the birch rod.

The Town football club were back in the position of looking for a field for the 1895-6 season. It needed to be secure, so that gate money could be taken, and they ended up back at William Holmes' field at Crackley. The season started dismally. Displaying a *"lamentable wont of pluck"* Town crashed to a 17-0 defeat to Lord Street of Coventry. In an attempt to boost performances, several players from Coventry were signed, but communication problems resulted in them failing to appear for a game until the last week of September when they were inspirational in a 5-2 victory in front of a small home crowd. However, the new stars brought problems with them as there were reports that they and their followers used *"...bad language. The language used in the field was such as should never be heard in a public place. I do not blame the club for this...if they want their matches to be well patronised they must take care that such scenes should be made impossible in the future."* By the time of the next home match, a 0-0 draw, notices stating "Bad Language Strictly Prohibited" had been pinned on trees around the pitch and *"...gentlemen wearing red ribbon may be seen walking about to prevent a breach of the very necessary regulation."* An area at one side of the pitch had been sectioned off for lady spectators and players. The team continued to struggle; starting a game with only 8 players due to late arrivals, they lost 8-0 in a match *"not remarkable for its gentleness."*

The strip for the club had been provided by Edward Boyce Podmore, an engineer who was involved in the North Warwickshire Hunt and lived at The Stone House. He was well known for running a coach to Stratford on summer weekends and on one occasion took the Kenilworth Town players to an away match at Hatton in it.

By December, the club's fortunes were turning and a return against Lord Street brought a 2-0 victory. By the end of the season, they had won as many as they had lost, eleven, scoring 47 and conceding 62, which after such a poor start was considered satisfactory. At the AGM in September at the Virgins and Castle, the decision was finally taken to amalgamate with St.John's Rovers.

The 1899-1900 season was to become a milestone season for Kenilworth Town. It started with a 0-0 draw with Leamington Celtic, but was followed with another complaint about swearing: *"I was horrified to find (the match) was accompanied by so much profane, blasphemous language, not only by both teams but by the spectators also. If the football club wishes to prosper it should modify its language and check such utterances, which no self-respecting man, much less lady, would care to stand by and hear."* The joint secretaries, H Holmes and S Hiscock, replied admitting *"polite astonishment"* at the accusation and enquiries found that no-one else had heard any. After another draw, the team began a run of impressive performances starting with a game against Berkswell, which was abandoned at half-time, due to rain, with Town 4-0 up. This was followed by 7-0, 4-1 and then 3-0 victories, the last against Milverton Loco, a team of railmen. Next were wins over Stoke 5-1, and Kenilworth United 10-0. A very one-sided match against Leamington Celtic followed, Celtic crossing the halfway line only once in the second half, but it was only a 1-0 win thanks to a *"beautiful shot"* from Fred Holmes. *"The Celtic would do better if they would play the game and*

not stop to argue with the referee every time he gives a decision against them."

Town entered the Warwick Charity Cup and in the first round were drawn away to Wilncote. In a fog-affected match it was 1-1 at half time. The fog thickened and as soon as the visitors took the lead, Aitken scoring his second goal *"...after a pretty run by the Town forwards...",* the referee abandoned the match. The replay was won 4-1. It was not until the second match of January that Town lost for the first time, 1-0, and this was due to having five players missing with illness. The following week, with four missing, they lost 3-2, and then 2-1 despite bombarding their opponent's goal and having one disallowed for offside. In mid-March, a benefit match was played against Rockliffe which enabled £2 5s to be added to the fund for Kenilworth Reservists.

The last day of March was the semi-final of the Warwick Charity Cup: *"Kenilworth Town gave their supporters a pleasant surprise on Saturday, when they went over to Warwick and easily defeated the Saint Nicholas by 4 goals to 0 on the Warwick United Ground."* Playing into the sun in the first half *"...the Town were rather lucky in clearing three free kicks which were given against them within twelve yards of the goal..."* but they soon had the advantage. After a splendid piece of combination play by the forwards, *"H.Holmes opened the scoring"* and Lees added a second before the break. In the second half H Holmes added a third and the opposition were rattled: *"The Saints now began to play roughly and the referee had to caution several of their players."* H Bennett sealed the victory with a goal from a Holmes corner. *"This is the first time that any Kenilworth team has ever entered into a final for a cup."* Town paid a price for their victory as the following week the team was *"...not fully represented owing to several of their players being badly bruised in the semi-final..."* and they lost to Leamington Parish 2-1.

The cup final was also played on Warwick United's ground, on a Wednesday evening, 2nd May, and the opposition was Leamington Victorias. *"The Town won the toss and started with the sun slightly in their favour. Both goals were visited frequently and the Town forwards missed some rather easy openings, but neither side could claim any advantage. At half-time the score was 1-1."* *"The game was full of excitement as both goals had some narrow escapes, and the winning goal (by the Victorias) was scored about five minutes from the finish. The Town goalkeeper Sewell had no chance with the goals that were scored and their defence was grand, but their forwards were not up to their usual form."*

Despite losing the first cup final that a Kenilworth football team had been in, it had been a good season for the club; they had won 20 matches, drawn 2 and lost 6, scoring 90 and conceding 28. At the AGM at The Globe, club President William Holmes praised the team for their efforts, saying that the players *"...had stuck to each other well and played their games with regard to good order. If any member had exhibited any trace of ill-behaviour he was quickly called to account."* Receipts for the season of just over £30 left a balance in hand of £6 and the club decided to return to league football, the Warwick and Stratford League, provided *"...not more than four clubs that enter are more than ten miles off."* The same field, leased from Mr Robbins, was to be retained for the following season - it seems the club had moved grounds again.

* * *

In the mid-1890s, a new form of transport started to appear on the roads and it was not to be long until it started to cause problems locally. The first was recorded in November 1896: *"As a large number of hunting people were returning from their sport to Kenilworth, they were met by a motorcar returning from Coventry to Kenilworth. An unusual amount of shouting caused the hunting contingent to pull up; ladies quickly got out of the way and gentlemen on restive horses quickly dismounted, as the motor car came on at a rapid pace. At Crackley Hill, however, there was a sudden stop, to the amusement of the company the motor fairly jibbed, and the driver had to dismount "non-plussed". A moment later, the car suddenly commenced its retreat and dashed backwards down the hill. It was sometime before the necessary repairs could be effected."*

Motoring offences soon made the news. In May the following year, Alphonse Deniot, an employee of the British Motor Company, was summonsed for driving his car above the regulation speed of 12mph down Rosemary Hill on the 18th of that month. John Wheatley and James Jackson were the witnesses who swore the car passed them going at a speed between 15 and 20mph. Deniot pleaded not guilty in his absence, he was in France, and Horace Knight, the car's only passenger, stated that the vehicle could not possibly have exceeded 12 mph, as the brake was applied the whole way down the hill. Unimpressed, the bench fined Deniot £5 with £2 10s costs. At the same hearing, he was fined a further £8 14s 6d including costs, for a similar offence in Leek Wootton.

The following February, Albert Davis was summonsed for not having the correct lights on a car he had parked outside the Coventry Cross at 11 p.m. A red light should have been lit at the rear of the vehicle but it was not. Davis had not arrived when proceedings against him started and he was fined £2 in his absence. Soon after the case had finished, Davis turned up explaining that he had driven his car to the hearing but the high wind had slowed him. He asked for the case to be heard again claiming that the rear light had been blown out by the wind and if he had a chance to explain fully the case would be seen entirely differently. The magistrate did not re-open the case.

It was inevitable that a collision between car and horse would eventually occur. In June 1898, Henry de Veulle was driving a car with passenger John Sharpe, an employee of the Coventry Motor Company, in a two-seat car from Coventry to Kenilworth. Coming down from Gibbett Hill, they approached a horse being ridden by Alfred Shuttleworth, coachman to Mr Stringer. They slowed and sounded the horn three times whereupon the horse became restless and kicked out, entangling its legs in one of the car's wheels. Shuttleworth had claimed the car was being driven at an excessive speed as it passed but it was easy to suggest that if it had been the

horse's leg would have been far more badly injured, perhaps severed. The horse was *"...one of a match pair, the permanent disfigurement consequent upon the injuries will of course be a serious matter."* Shuttleworth had not raised his hand requesting the car to stop, as was customary. The case, heard at Milverton Police Court, was not about the actual collision but the car's speed; *"The defendant was probably tempted to try the power of the car on a straight piece of road and the witness swore that the car was going between from 17 to 20 miles an hour."* The driver admitted that at the top of Gibbett Hill *"...the twelve miles an hour speed was put on..."* and so, the magistrates concluded, that speed must have been exceeded at some point. *"Before motor-cars came along, if there was an accident with which a horse was connected, it was always the animal that was in the wrong, but now it is always the motor-car."* The driver, Henry de Veulle, was fined £2 in his absence for exceeding 12mph.

These incidents prompted the Kenilworth Advertiser to comment: *"Dogs go mad in hot weather, and will run at terrific speed till they drop. Motor car drivers who go dashing and crashing about at fifteen or twenty miles per hour, to the danger of the public, must be mad also."*

John Sharpe was soon back in court, not this time as a witness but as the offender. Just a week after the collision with the horse, Sharpe was seen by PC Mellor driving a car at 11.30 p.m. up Abbey End without a rear red light. Sharpe stated that he had one when he left Leamington but gave it to a lady friend on a cycle, as she had no light at all. He also claimed that he was adequately lit as he had a 4 volt electric lamp *"in my buttonhole"* which was the equivalent to two cycle lamps. He was fined 20s.

In May 1899 The Automobile Club organised a rally of 30 vehicles at the Castle, but in the event only 8 or 10 turned up. A large one, a Lifu, had a dozen passengers. Most drivers avoided the ford as it was swollen but at least one attempted it and just a yard from reaching dry land stopped, its occupants having to get out and push. One observer was not impressed at this display of innovative machinery: *"So far as I can judge of motor cars they will be a very long time before they come into general use to the exclusion of horse flesh. They are not handsome and they do not seem to be reliable."*

On the return run, all the cars avoided the ford, returning to Leamington by way of New Row. As they climbed the hill, they passed a wagonette carrying Mr A Weetman and driven by two grooms, Mr Cooke, employed by Henry Whateley at Priory farm, and Harry Girling. They were breaking in a horse for Whateley. After the cars had passed, the horse became restive and once in Bridge Street it got beyond control. Weetman opened the door ready to get out but as he did so the *"...animal swerved, violently chucking him on to the kerbstone."* Girling jumped out and sprained his ankle, but Cooke stayed on board, the horse tried to jump a hedge but the wagonette became wedged and so the incident ended. Cooke and the horse were unharmed, but Weetman had broken his leg a few inches above his ankle. He was taken home on a stretcher fetched from the Police Station and was carried by Beck, W Riley, Councillor Jackson, C J Penn and PC Robinson. Mr Matthews-Bennett was telegraphed and the following day at Weetman's house he set the bones.

There were numerous incidents of horses being startled by cars. In a typical example, John Jenson, 64, a smith in New Street, who had for over thirty years specialised in making and repairing agricultural tools, was shoeing a horse when a car went past *"...sounding its siren..."*. The startled horse kicked out, throwing down Jenson and breaking his leg.

In July 1900, Harris Henry Eley, 33, a district manager to the National Telephone Company stationed at Ulverston, Barrow, went to Coventry specifically to buy a car for the Lonsdale Cycle Company to which he was a consulting engineer. He had some knowledge of cars, *"He had previously purchased one from the company but as it did not answer, orders were given for another one to be built which embodied some of his own suggestions."* The new car in question was "The Rapid", made by the Allard Cycle and Motor Manufacturing Company of Earlsdon. It was a 4-wheeled, 2-seater, standard type, geared for two speeds, one about 5 or 6mph and the other about 16mph. The weight of the machinery was unusually forward, totally in front of the front axle and in this respect differed to other cars. The company had turned out several cars practically identical to it but Eley made several modifications including alterations of a minor character to the electrical fittings, different steering wheel, etc,. The company had built cars for two years and had had no reports of any accidents.

Eley was a practical man, had seen the car during construction, and was present at its test when completed on Friday 13th July. The car had previously been tested and was in every way satisfactory. It had been put through 100 miles of road test.

On Sunday 22nd, Eley almost turned the car over by turning it too sharply, and on another occasion ran into a bank. Eley then loosened one of the wheels that had become tight. The following day, he was due to take the car for a run to Kenilworth, and at the suggestion of Mr Pilkington, the Allard manager, works manager James Montgomery (31) accompanied him on a motor-tricycle. Montgomery was certain that Eley understood the working of motor cars in every way, but perhaps Pilkington was not so convinced.

At a little before midday, they set out towards Kenilworth and as they approached the town, Montgomery was in front of Eley and going at about 10 or 12 mph. a suitable speed for the road. When they came to the decline, Montgomery looked round and saw Eley using both hands to adjust his hat, he gave him a warning and began the descent into New Street. At the bottom he heard a noise and looked round and *"...saw the car gradually rear up and topple over with (Eley) underneath."* Montgomery got off his own machine, ran back and lifted the car off Eley. There was little he could do; he was dead, with the back seat across his neck.

Montgomery found that a pin, which went through the joint of the rod connecting the two front wheels, was missing, but did not know if it came out before or after the accident. The pin may have been weakened in one

of earlier incidents, or even accidentally loosened by Eley when he adjusted the wheel. Inspector Parkinson was called to the scene and found the pin 105yds from the car. He reported, *"The Deceased's head was battered in, and the brain was protruding from the left temple."* Montgomery was of the opinion that Eley changed the speed of the car as it descended the hill, considered a dangerous practice for novices. Ambrose Valentine, of Croxton House, Leamington, had made a special study of motor cars ever since their invention. He was of the opinion that the pin came out, allowing the wheel to twist freely either left or right, and that the loose rod went through the wheel spokes; the whole weight being at the front, the car toppled over. Allard had been relieved of any responsibility as Eley did the repairs himself after *"the wrenches."* The jury at the inquest, held at the Police Station, returned a verdict of "accident" on Kenilworth's first motoring fatality.

The descent into New treet was the scene of Kenilworth's first motoring fatality.

The following week, the *Kenilworth Advertiser* carried a suggestion that all cars should carry numbers and be licensed so that any offenders could be easily recognised and traced. There was general opposition to this, as gentlemen would not want *"their carriages disfigured by labels"* and it placed their owners on a level with hackney carriages. Despite those being made in Coventry, car manufacturing was practically *"non-existent"* nation-wide and the import of foreign cars was on the increase: in January 1900, 25 came into the country, rising to 52 in June.

*   *   *

In August 1897, William Mitchell (45) had plans for a new, larger, house on his land approved. The name Elmdene was transferred to the new house, the original became Ivy Cottage.

With Spring Lane now lit, those who lived in its continuation at Whitemoor decided it was their turn to press for gas lighting. They were amongst the least provided for in town as they also had no mains water and no sewerage connection. In October 1899, the 60 residents put together a petition for lighting and the KUDC dutifully asked the gas company if they were willing to lay a main to Whitemoor. They were not. The solution was provided in the summer of 1900 when William Mitchell sought and received permission from the Council to erect three electric street lamps at his own expense and connect them to his private supply, and so on 15th October 1900 part of Whitemoor Road became the first area of the town to be lit with electricity. The work was completed by the following Saturday. Mitchell's generosity was not open-ended and he came to an agreement for the Council to pay for the power. Probably not coincidentally, the same week it was suggested that new incandescent gas lighting should be tried to improve the brightness in various parts of the town.

Richard Whateley...

...retired from the KUDC due to indifferent health and in the summer of 1899, he died in his 65th year at his home in Stoneleigh Road.

He had started his business in about 1854 and was the first to grow strawberries for market purposes. He was held in high esteem throughout the midlands as a horticulturist, prospering with strawberries, tomatoes and cucumbers. He and his son Henry *"...stood as unrivalled cultivators." "Many will miss his cheery words and kindly help."* He had a *"...most independent spirit..."* and received at his nurseries growers from all over the country seeking his advice. His knowledge was sought from as far away as Scotland, and he greeted all with a hearty welcome. He left a widow, five sons and three daughters.

The Common was considered a dangerous place, as sand and gravel was still being taken. The collecting of furze and gorse was still permitted, but it was the responsibility of Clarendon as Lord of the Manor, and he also had to make the decision, popularly suggested, as to whether it ought to be planted out and made *"ornamental."* The road across the Common was also becoming a problem as it was narrow and rutted. Perhaps due to this, instead of being kept to the horse-road, horse-carts were regularly driven down the footpaths in an area where a considerable number of children usually played. Besides annoyance to pedestrians, an accident was thought to be inevitable. This too had to be raised with Clarendon. Additionally, the area of the Common nearest the mill was regularly used for the dumping of rubbish, earthenware, ashes etc., whilst the behaviour of some boys regularly starting small fires gave worries to the future of the heather enjoyed by those walking.

Despite a warning by Joseph Roberts of the dangerous state of the unfenced gravel pits as long ago as 1882, no-one seemed concerned about the obvious danger. Just to the left as the Common was entered from Lower Ladies' Hill was a former quarry-working known as the sand-hole. Late one June 1894 evening, five boys, William Carter (11), Thomas Trunkfield (10), William Clarke (8 or 9), Frank Overton (10) and Harold Thelswell (8) were making holes in the sand by scooping it out when the inevitable happened and the sand above collapsed. Carter and Thelswell were buried up to their thighs, but Thomas Trunkfield was completely covered. The other two were free and tried to pull out the two they could see but could not move them and so ran for help. Fortunately, they ran straight into Mr Carter, Smith-

Turberville's coachman, who hurried to the rescue. As he began scraping the sand looking for Trunkfield, he sent the two boys off in search of help telling them to bring spades. Mr Dencer, a postman, was now on the scene helping and soon the boys returned with Trunkfield's father and some men. Thomas Trunkfield was found face downwards and unconscious having been buried for ten minutes; his father feared the worse but Dencer, a recent winner of a St.John's Ambulance Certificate, saw he was alive and helped him recover consciousness. The other two boys who were partly buried were freed, more frightened than hurt, once Trunkfield was safe. By next morning, Thomas had recovered sufficiently to walk about his house, his only injuries being severe bruising.

With a hot dry summer in 1899, there was a general concern that a major fire in town could be difficult to contain. In July a fire, which was thought to have been started deliberately, broke out on Mr Gee's Castle farm. It was at a place called Lingham's barn that included timbers from the Castle. Just next to it, two hay-ricks were on fire. The cycle brigade arrived and quickly located a pit, from which water could be drawn, but the brigade had difficulty getting 'Queen Bess' to the site; much of the way the horses had to be walked and it took half an hour from the time the alarm was raised for the engine to reach the fire. The ricks were by now too far gone to be saved and so the hoses were concentrated upon saving the barn, which was done successfully. Up to fifty tons of straw, hay and clover were destroyed, valued at between £120 and £150. There were hundreds of onlookers at this spectacular night-time fire, and all were careful not to tread down the growing crops.

The following month, a fire broke out on the Common and it quickly spread, threatening The Gables and Crackley Hall. 'Queen Bess' was soon at work laying 600yds of hose, both from the brook and the mains of the water company. Captain Bourne was in command, but in the absence of Engineer Heatley (missing a call out for the first time in twenty years), Superintendent Engineer Griffiths took charge of the engine on his own. The fire came within 30yds of The Gables. Hoses were played upon the fire for five hours before the engine was withdrawn at around 6.00 p.m. and five men with the hose cart were left behind for a further three hours. At around midnight, the fire broke out again and the full brigade once more attended; this time they stayed all night. Acres of underwood and gorse were destroyed, stretching across to the railway line.

During the following winter, the deliberate starting of fires on the Common was becoming a past-time for youths who were regularly seen starting and watching blazes. The gorse covering was slowly becoming completely destroyed and there were great concerns that no action was being taken.

In late 1899, the first examples of a new device, the telephone, were installed by subscribers and several telephone poles were in place by November. The fire brigade's Superintendent Engineer Griffiths was the first to see the potential and suggested that telephone subscribers should *"...allow their instruments to be used to convey news of a fire to the place where the horses are kept...",* in this way the horses should arrive and be attached to the engine before the brigade had mustered. In another attempt to improve communications, the cycle corps were issued with whistles.

The hiring of horses cost the brigade 10s for each drill, and their provider, Thomas Richards, was soon to leave the brigade.

*   *   *

In March 1894, Henry Street's works manager, William Henry Walmsley, died suddenly of a ruptured blood vessel to the brain. Despite being only aged 41, he had worked for Street for almost 30 years. At the funeral at the Chapel of Brethren on the corner of Spring Lane and Albion Street, Henry Street was *"...much affected, and many of the bystanders were moved to tears."* Soon after this sad event in his life, Henry Street leased his Mill End fellmongery jointly to his own nephew Arthur (30) and William Walmsley's son, also Arthur (17), for a low rent of £75 per annum "for life." With this arrangement, after 53 years, Henry effectively retired from business at the age of 69, but continued to serve on the KUDC.

Henry Street died, aged 74, on 10th October 1899 at his home on Abbey Hill. That evening was the monthly meeting of the KUDC, but not surprisingly, its business was adjourned after just a few minutes, all of which were spent paying tributes. *"He was one of the oldest and most respected of inhabitants."* *"No man in Kenilworth would be more missed than Henry Street."*

The funeral cortège assembled outside Street's house at 2.45 p.m. on Saturday 14th October. It included all the members of the Urban District Council, a large deputation of the Kenilworth Liberal Association, Captain Edmund Bourne and other members of the fire brigade that Street had help to establish and always supported, and representatives of the Midland Bank. Richards Brothers supplied the hearse and mourning coaches. House blinds on the short route to the church were all drawn as a mark of respect and the rest of Kenilworth's notables not in the cortège were present at the church, including George Turner, Richard and William Skutt, George Church, Edgar Whittendale, Charles Holland and Murcott Webb. Six of Street's workmen, witnessed by a large gathering, carried the coffin to the grave.

Living a full life, Street had been Chairman of the Kenilworth Liberal Association, Magistrate for Kenilworth Petty Sessional Division, one-time Chairman of the Water Company in which he was involved from its inception until his death, and Chairman of the Coventry Union Bank until it amalgamated with the London and Midland Bank. Most notably, he had served the town continuously from the days of the Vestry meetings, the entire duration of the Local Board, on the Kenilworth Urban District Council from its inception, and was elected once more just 18 months before he died.

An indefatigable businessman, clear-headed and industrious, fatigue was hardly known to him, he had been known to travel to London and back twice in a day. He was methodical in all his engagements, most abstemious in his personal habits and noted for his early rising.

The grave of Henry Street (foreground).

From the early 1880s, Walter Lockhart played the harmonium for the St.Nicholas Winter Singing Class which was regularly attended by 70-80 persons. After a number of years, the grateful singers presented Walter with a bound volume of Longfellow poems. In 1894, a bough on a tree near Mr Lockhart's Waterloo House had to be cut down, to the annoyance of many as it made an attractive approach to the nearby Old School House.

On new years day 1900, Walter Lockhart's wife Julia died of pneumonia at Waterloo House, she was 60. Walter was so overwhelmed at the number of letters and telegrams of sympathy he received that he could not reply to them all personally and so wrote a heartfelt letter of thanks to the *Kenilworth Advertiser*. His solitude was short-lived, as nine months later he married Ellen Piggott, likely to be a relative of his first wife, at Harpenden. His wedding gift to Ellen was a gold necklace, and in the evening the couple left for London en route to Southsea. Walter was 56. Nellie, as she was known, was 26.

*   *   *

On 7th December 1895 several contingents from the Warwickshire Volunteers under the command of Colonel Nesbit, including 97 from Coventry, 34 from Warwick, 50 from Leamington and two companies from Budbrooke Depot, mustered at 7 p.m. at Kenilworth Post Office in an exercise to carry out an attack on Kenilworth Castle, which was supposedly held by an enemy. *"After the officers had decided on the plan of attack, the party moved towards the Castle, the approach to which is well protected. The enemy were supposed to hold a very strong position behind a high mound near the Castle gates and the attacking party were divided into three sections. The Warwick and Leamington men made a detour to the right and when the charge was sounded, they attacked the mound from the top side; while the Coventry detachment cleared the ditch on the left and the Budbrooke companies scaled the face of the mound. The manoeuvre was very smartly executed, and Colonel Nesbit declared the position carried. The men then marched to the Abbey Hotel for refreshments."*

Two batteries of the Worcestershire and

Warwickshire Artillery, comprising 11 officers, 92 rank and file, and 80 horses, marched to Kenilworth from Coleshill in May 1899. There were four twenty-pound guns in each battery, with six ammunition and six transport wagons. The arrival was watched by a huge gathering, including visitors who had travelled and waited for hours. Cyclists acted as scouts, relaying information as to the progress of the warriors as they approached. The Council had given permission for the encampment to be set up in the Abbey Fields, but this was decided against as the firing of the guns could have damaged the church and surrounding buildings. The batteries marched into the field near Charles Bond's High House Farm, and the camp was laid out on the slope facing the Castle ruins. Guards and sentinels were placed, and a gun set off at sundown. The following morning was the Queen's birthday and a salute was fired in her honour. Volley practice was also engaged in. Rain was falling heavily and it interfered with the planned arrangements and due to the uncertainty, a smaller crowd than expected watched the rare event of a Royal salute being fired in Kenilworth. The march to their next encampment, at Knowle, did not start until 12.30.

Jonathan Prime died on 26th September 1899, aged 70, at his home on the Coventry Road having only just giving up as the licensee of the Virgins and Castle Inn. He was formerly a resident of Stoneleigh and was once House Steward for Lord Leigh. The new licensee was Thomas Slingsby.

The conflict in the Sudan saw two Kenilworth men in active service. One was Sydney Roberts, son of Joseph Roberts, the other was Harry Page, the son of George Page of the California area, who was serving in the Warwickshire Regiment. Harry kept in touch with home by writing letters, beginning in March 1898, addressed to "Fred" which were printed on a regular basis in the *Kenilworth Advertiser* alongside the latest reports of the war. He told of a life that was unlikely to be the envy of many. His first letter described his march to Berber, twenty miles a day mostly through sand up to his ankles, and of the rations of bread and tinned meat, with a dessert of locally-plucked dates, which could only be eaten in small quantities due to the risk of disease. A final march to reach the Atbara River was of 32 miles completed without a single pause or mouthful of food. Railway tracks were being laid behind them to provide a supply line. Harry was involved in the battle of Atbara, the conflict started with a final 20 mile march finishing at 5.00 a.m. and after a 30 minute pause, he witnessed the artillery bombardment of the enemy. At 7.45, they charged with fixed bayonets, *"...these were exciting moments...it was a great slaughter as the dervishes were shot and bayoneted down like rabbits."* The newspaper was grateful that *"this gallant young soldier has escaped injury."*

Another military family moved into Moorlands in the mid-1890s. Henry Townshend Boultbee (born 1827), was educated at the Royal Military College at Woolwich, progressed to Captain and became Deputy Lord Lieutenant of Warwickshire, and then High Sheriff in 1865. His son Charles was in the Kings Royal Rifles.

In late 1899, the Boer conflict in South Africa first came to the direct attention of Kenilworth with the wounding of Charles Boultbee (41), now Major. As the situation deteriorated there was a national call to arms and volunteers enlisted by the thousands. In Kenilworth, several appeals for funds were made. The Soldiers' and Sailors' Families Association was a national organisation, of which Emily Joynson of The Firs was the Kenilworth President. Applications to this were to be made to Major General Hadow of Fieldgate. There was also a fund started by John Heatley and Councillor William Holmes, which quickly raised over £17 specifically for the families of Kenilworth volunteers; major donors included William Pears, Mrs Cay, Dr Growse and William Riley. Acting upon a request from the Lord Lieutenant of Warwickshire, Lord Leigh, William Pears, in his capacity as Chairman of the KUDC, opened a county-wide fund. Pears himself donated ten guineas, as did Albert Cay and George Beard. This fund soon raised over £85. The publication of these appeals coincided with the siege of Kenilworth, a suburb of Kimberley.

The Convalescent Home put four beds at the disposal of the War Office, and Robertson and Gray arranged a concert to raise funds for the Kenilworth branch of the Soldiers' and Sailors' Families Association. It was a huge success, raising almost £30 and performed mostly by locals. Edgar and Claude Whittendale were prominent, as was Blanche Robertson who played a mandolin solo and was greatly involved in the arrangements. The "glee party", all members of St.Nicholas church choir, were called back for an encore. Additional funds were raised by "*...gaily attired young ladies handing around their decorated tambourines for contributions to the Widows and Orphans fund...*" and this raised a further £4 8s 3d. One highlight of the evening was Mr Hughes displaying his recent acquisition; "*So popular are the soldiers that when Mr Hughes gramophone played Soldiers of the Queen those present joined in heartily in singing the last few verses, although silence is necessary when it is playing.*"

As 1899 closed, the Soldiers' and Sailors' Families Association had received seven applications for assistance, but it was found that grants could only be made in two of the cases. Major General F E Hadow suggested that the local fund, the first to be set up, should be amalgamated with the Soldiers' and Sailors' fund.

In the last week of the year, Sergeant Frank Jeacock, Royal Engineer and son of the town's popular bill-poster and town crier, sailed from Southampton on 'Tintagel Castle' for the front, having served three years at Sandhurst. There were also three volunteers of the Imperial Yeomanry: Chichester from Goodrest Farm, Joseph Selman of Warwick Road and Frank Whateley who had just returned from Rhodesia where he was a trooper in the Matabeleland mounted police. Such was the interest in the conflict, Thomas Morris put the war telegrams he received in the Post Office window for all to see the latest news.

A committee including Dr Bourne, Dormer, Weetman and E Payne arranged for a farewell meal to be provided for the Kenilworth members of the Warwickshire Yeomanry and this was held at the Kings

Arms in the last week of January 1900. The Yeoman present were Quartermaster Hunt, Sergeant Wright, Privates Seymour, Chichester, Moncriefe, Passman, Bewley, Johnson, Crook, Tyler, Valentine, Tebitts, Cooke, Golby, Harvey, Deacon, Carter, Selman, Hollick, Whateley, Kingzett, Page and Brewster. Some of these were from the surrounding area. The room was decorated with union jacks and the Royal Standard, and guests wore tri-coloured ribbons in their button-holes. The meal provided by manageress Miss Tiso was excellent. Patriotic speech followed patriotic speech and the Yeomen were wished a safe return. A number of them provided songs, and one observed that "...*if his fighting is no better than his singing, then God help them all.*" The farewell dinner cost £37 2s for 72 people; all was raised by donation or tickets for guests.

There were not only appeals for money, but also for clothing. Emily Joynson was central in collecting specific garments to send to the army and Kenilworth's second despatch in February included 136 pairs of socks, 26 helmets, 31 shirts, 9 woollen mufflers, 8 handkerchiefs, 6 pairs of gloves, 17 pin-cushions, 7 doyleys, 6 pillows, 1 vest and a bundle of clothes for refugee children. A concert in aid of the Local Reserve Fund was held at the Assembly Rooms in February. The first half was mostly performances by Leamington gentlemen, but the second was given over to eleven members of the Kenilworth Amateur Minstrels and as always, they gave a highly enjoyable performance. It raised £12.

Letters began to appear in the local newspapers from the forces. One was from Warwickshire Imperial Yeoman W Martin on 'Lake Erie' of the Elder Dempster Lines. It was carrying 570 men and 500 horses and "...*this being a new ship it has all the latest inventions on board...*" and Martin was particularly impressed with a large refrigerator, but some traditional sources of food remained, as live sheep and fowl were carried.

There were already a number of Kenilworth people at the front: Sydney Roberts with the 9th Lancers, Horton and Hall with the Durham Light Infantry, Harry Roberts and King with the Royal Rifles, J Ashford with the 28th Battery Royal Artillery and Sgt Jeacock with the Royal Engineers. The whereabouts of others was unknown. Another about to leave was E B Jeffcoat who was to fill an important post as shorthand writer and typist on the staff of Commander-in-Chief Lord Roberts.

Another concert was arranged in early March, for the Daily Telegraph War Pension Fund, and Robertson and Gray obtained the services of the Imperial Concert Party who were "...*talented artistes which seldom visit so small a town as Kenilworth.*"

News of the war was eagerly awaited and the Post Office with its telegraph connection was often where it arrived, and since space inside was limited the nearby Virgins and Castle was as good a place as any for people to congregate. As soon as news of the relief of Ladysmith arrived a telegram was despatched to the Queen: "*We your majesty's loyal and devoted subjects, assembled at the Virgins and Castle Hotel, Kenilworth, send our congratulations to your Majesty upon the receipt of the splendid news of the relief of Ladysmith. Signed - Slingsby.*" A reply of thanks was received from

Sir Arthur Biggs, Her Majesty's Private Secretary. The news prompted immediate celebrations. The Council House displayed its standard, the Chairman's house had several flags, and streamers were hung across roads between business premises. Dr Growse decorated his house with streamers, the church bells were rung and jubilant faces were everywhere; children were seen carrying small flags. "*It was the exception not to see a flag displayed at every house. Not since the diamond jubilee has such a general display been seen.*" Great excitement was everywhere but "...*underneath was a thankfulness that our brave soldiers had an end put to their sufferings.*" Then came news of a Kenilworth casualty: Private H Roberts King's Own Rifles, who worked at a brick-yard, had been wounded at Ladysmith. Roberts, son of Joseph Roberts of High Street but living in St. John's Street, was wounded in the arm at Pieter's Hill but recovered. Roberts at one time had come across Kenilworth's Heritage of the Guards "...*beat dead from fatigue, asleep in a wagon.*" Horton was also slightly wounded.

Just days after the celebrations, on Monday 5th March, three men, Joseph Selman, Frank Whateley and Cyril Swain, left Kenilworth for Oxford to join up with the Oxfordshire Hussar Yeomanry and sailed for South Africa two days later.

Letters continued to arrive from the front but were often months out of date by the time they were published. Private J Harris wrote to his friends in town telling of his journey out from Liverpool at Christmas aboard 'HMS Majestic' and the action he had seen. At Frere he had met up with fellow townsmen Harwood, Horton, Overton and Watson of the Durham Light Infantry who all came through "*the scrap on the 15th of December.*" He also ran in to "*our old pal, H Roberts.*" J Ashford of 28th Field Battery also wrote home from Springfield; he had had some rough times, in action all day and marching all night. "*It is a fine country, but awfully hard to get about with artillery. I have not been shot so far, although a few shells and bullets have hummed around me.*"

The letters from the front no doubt prompted this one to be written by 13 year-old Charles Holmes soon after the relief of Ladysmith: "*Dear Sir, - We the boys of the regiment called "The Kenilworth Death or Glory Boys" are sorry to tell you that our captain, W.Burton, fell down and broke his thigh while playing on the Common. About twenty boys for this last week have met on the gravel pits, Coventry Road, to drill. On Thursday and Friday, they marched from there to the Common and on Friday had a sham fight. Some of the boys represented the officers of the English and Boer armies. On reaching the old stone quarry, the Boers took one hill and called it Spion Kop. The English charged and drove the Boers off. They returned and charged the English who retreated. As the British were retreating their leader fell and hurt his leg. He was carried home by some of the boys. Dr Bourne was called in and said his thigh was broken. Willie was taken to Warneford Hospital and had his thigh set the same night.*" Twelve year-old Willie Burton had been personifying his hero Commander-in-Chief, Lord Roberts (although Roberts was not involved in the actual Spion Kop action) and, presumably through townsman E B Jeffcott, Lord Roberts got to hear about his accident and remarkably sent him a letter: *"I am sorry to hear that in a sham fight which recently took place at Kenilworth you had the misfortune to break your leg. I hope that by the time this reaches you, you will have recovered and that when you grow up you will be a soldier, and perhaps some day rise to command our troops in a real battle. Please tell the other boys in the National School how glad I am to hear of the pleasant sham fights they have been having recently. Yours very truly - Roberts."* Lord Roberts had lost his own son early in the conflict.

Willie was still in Warneford Hospital when the letter was received. His recovery went well; his leg was out of plaster after just a few weeks. *"Willie is a very taking boy, ready at any time to break out into a smile as full of fun as possible and with a martial spirit strong within him."* He was a great favourite in the hospital and was escorted home in a coach by four nurses. Willie was a choirboy and on his return home, Charles Holmes presented him with a bugle on behalf of the choir. The story had reached the London papers and he had presents sent to him including a bound copy of 'The Life Of Lord Roberts', a sword, helmets, a khaki suit and a cord for the bugle. He became known as "Lord Bob" and his school friends as "Lord Bob's Brigade". Willie was the son of Mr Burton of Clifton Terrace.

At midnight, 19th May, carrier Mr Goode brought to town the news from Leamington that the rumours were true, Mafeking had been relieved. He had a flag out as soon as he got home, by 6 o'clock flags were out in The Square and by 10 they were all over the town, Albion Street alone had a hundred, and even Barrow-street had streamers from its only two houses. Flags and streamers criss-crossed High Street from the vicarage to the convalescent home, the Parish Room to Mr Tipson's, and "God Bless our Queen" was hung between Mr Knights and the almshouses. Another hung from the Bank across to Mr Roberts, and from Mr Church's to Major-General Hadow's house, Fieldgate. *"Mill End was gay with bunting."* In anticipation, Mr and Mrs Dickenson of The Square had been making streamers all the previous day (Friday) and now five stretched from the trees in The Square to the Post Office.

The bells rang all day; colours were worn by everyone, perambulators had flags attached, as did bicycles and traps. An impromptu parade was hastily arranged to start from the fire engine-house at 7 in the evening. The route was Abbey Hill, Castle End, Waverley Road, Priory Road, Albion Row, New Street, High Street, the Castle, Forrest Road, Abbey Hill, Rosemary Hill and into the park, where after singing the national anthem it dispersed. The parade was led by Chairman of the Council and Captain of the Fire Brigade Dr Bourne, in his uniform and riding a decorated bicycle. He was followed by the town-crier, the cycle fire brigade, the town band, the steam fire engine and a dozen ladies on their decorated bicycles and gentlemen on theirs. Captain A Winter and sub Captain H Selman led the Bicycle Club in Khaki outfits. The manual fire engine followed and members of the brigade carried on a stretcher a dummy man that they used to practise rescues from burning buildings. Finally, and by no means least, was the hero of the town, "Lord Bob", wearing a general's uniform but needing to be pushed in a bath-chair as his leg was still recovering. About 40 or 50 of his "Brigade" followed dressed in helmets and carrying swords and guns, and these heroes of the now nationally famous Spion Kop sham battle on the Common were cheered well. At night, some twenty men paraded in the town singing, finishing with the National Anthem.

Despite the celebrations, the war was far from over and letters continued to arrive from the front. W S Horton, of the First Durham Light Infantry, had suffered a small flesh wound and then an attack of dysentery and was convalescing 100 miles from his regiment. From 10th January to 4th March, he had slept under canvas just four times.

The next landmark victory was the fall of Pretoria. Unlike the previous impromptu celebrations, in early June it was decided this time to organise a parade a week in advance. Councillor Jackson was the chairman of the hastily convened committee, with Doctor Growse and Councillor Bostock to the fore.

At six o'clock on Thursday 14th, the assemblage set off from Abbey Hill. Bostock and the marshals led and were followed by the town crier, in full uniform, on horseback. Then came the town band, decorated bicycles including an *"ancient"* boneshaker ridden by William Lake and a solid-tyred trike ridden by H Glenn. The Cycle Club led by its Captain Winter were well represented. A collection of war characters followed and then came a brougham carrying representatives of the London and North Western Railway including Stationmaster Heatley. Next came a tableau of wounded soldiers and their attendants and Field Marshal Roberts inevitably portrayed by young William Burton, still suffering his wounds and carried in Mr Butcher's van and in the charge of nurse Petty. A collection of patriotic and military tableaux was ended with *"...an exact representation of the 4.7 gun from HMS Powerful which played so important a part in the defence of Ladysmith..."* mounted on a carriage. This had been lent by Willans and Robinson of Rugby and had been copied from drawings and photographs. It was attended by a dozen "naval" men who were mostly from the tannery and were "captained" by Obidiah Woods. Both fire engines followed and the Kenilworth Orchestral Society played music in decorated brakes. The St.John's Ambulance and various Oddfellow societies brought up the rear. The streets were lined with residents and visitors, every house had a flag, *"Few had expected so imposing a spectacle."* The day concluded with a hundred strong torchlight procession and a bonfire, burning Kruger's effigy, at Castle Green.

"Meantime, the war drags its slow and wearisome length along..."

Perhaps not surprisingly, the Parochial Trip that year was to Portsmouth to see the battleships. The party, largely organised by Arthur Street, was in the dockyard town by 9.00 a.m.

In July the wounded Harry Roberts returned to town and the Town Band paraded and made a collection of £4 7s 4¾d for him. Henry Heritage was another who had been invalided out and he was present at one of several Smoking Concerts, held at the Coventry Cross and Albion Tavern, arranged to boost the funds for Kenilworth Reservists' families organised by Charles Heatley. About £87 had been collected and now there was just £4 left in the account and with £1 17s a week being paid out, all such fundraising events were very necessary. One regular contributor was Miss Anderson of Abbey View, High Street who donated 2s every week. A wife was paid 5s a week and an extra 1s was given for each child.

An event at the Kings Arms in October raised £3 and the following month another was held at the Virgins and Castle Hotel. In between there was another homecoming, Sergeant Chichester of the Warwickshire Imperial Yeomanry had been invalided out due to suffering sunstroke. He had been with Major Orr-Ewing's company when he was killed. His journey home had been through very rough weather that delayed his ship, 'The Britannic'. His arrival home was not generally known but about a hundred gathered to meet him at the station at 9.40 p.m. on the last Monday of October. A dozen fog signals had been placed on the line to announce his arrival, much to the alarm of those not aware of the circumstances. His arrival was met with great cheers and he stopped a while on the platform chatting to his friends before they made a passage for him to a waiting carriage. Chichester was thinner and in need of a good rest. With the exception of Corporal Wright of Ashow, all those who left Kenilworth for the war were pretty well unharmed.

Despite the home-comings, fresh volunteers were occasionally leaving. Footballer Harry Holmes left in mid-December and his absence *"considerably weakened"* the Town side and they lost their next match 3-0.

*   *   *

On Sunday 30th December 1900 torrential rain fell all day and kept on until early on Monday morning. In the space of a few hours, floodwaters began to rise and all the lower areas of the town became inundated.

The fields for a mile or two outside Kenilworth, towards Haseley and Rouncill Lane, were soon under water, and before long, streams and brooks began to swell. The bridge leading from Mr Weetman's East Close on to the Birmingham Road was broken, as was the one from Mr Bond's and Mr Eykin's over the Purley Brook on the same stream. The water at the ford by the Castle overflowed for sixty yards on both sides, the footbridge became completely covered and was impassable. The house in the field on north side of bridge was flooded. *"The water rushing through the bridge in Castle Road and meeting with an opposing wind looked like a miniature sea." "The water on the park looked like the long projected lake was in existence."* The iron railings in the Abbey Fields were completely covered.

At the bottom of Warwick Road, from Mr Keartlands land to Mr Thompson's garden at St.John's Lodge, the water lay some 4 or 5 feet deep. *"Mrs Beck's house was unreachable but by boat or cart or getting wet up to one's middle."* Her cellar had been full of water

since 10 o'clock. The lower end of Rawlins Row was under water and Mrs Edwards and Mrs Horton were amongst those who were provisioned through their bedroom window and were not liberated until midday. The area from Waverley Road to the railway line was flooded and the station house surrounded, but the line itself stayed clear due to a culvert at the side taking the water away.

But the real problems were at Mill End. The stream at the back of the Engine Inn overflowed and the lower floor of the inn was a completely wrecked. The windows of the bar were forced out and water five or six feet high came pouring out into the street. The Engine Inn occupants had to be rescued. The houses adjoining were swamped and the furniture floated about, houses reaching almost up to the Cottage Inn were affected. Water rose to bedrooms or in some cases higher, residents spent most of Sunday night taking belongings upstairs. The majority of the residents worked at the mill or fellmongers.

The windows of The Engine were forced out by flood-waters at least 5ft deep.

Occupants of the houses opposite the mill were trapped and needed rescuing. The fire brigade was soon on hand and Mrs Muddiman was taken from her bedroom window by Lieutenant Heatley and Engineer Griffiths. *"One man was found hanging to the highest rafters of his cottage and was asked how long could he hold on? He replied "half an hour if the water does not rise much." It rose however and in answer to his call a young friend swam to his assistance and is actually stated to have brought the man safely away, swimming with his burden upon his shoulders."* This was likely to be a young man named James Lancaster rescuing Mr Dencer from a shanty at the back of Mr Trunkfield's house alongside the blacksmith's. He went there at 3.00 a.m. and then again at 7 and succeeded in getting him out. Afterwards Lancaster swam down to the Mill House to warn people.

The house of Mr Elmore, the Mill manager, was under water and he lost a lot of valuable fowls and dogs. Mr James had one of his two pigs drowned, and the other was missing presumably washed away downstream. James also lost a number of fowls. The next two houses were occupied by two old persons, Mrs Shaw, a nurse who was away from home at the time, and a man named Jones who had two pigs drowned, and much of the furniture in these houses near the mill was spoiled, remaining under water for several hours.

The blacksmith's shop was under four or five feet of water, and in the cottages next to it the water was up to the ceiling and had it not receded quickly there was a danger of several old people drowning. The house immediately next to it was occupied by Mr Trunkfield, who was employed at the water works, and he left the house by a window, as did his wife later in the day. The next nine or ten houses were flooded and the furniture ruined. Mrs Hall, a laundress had a load of newly washed garments on her line muddied and lost a *"pig of ten score"* which was in a sty at the rear of the garden. Five or six houses further up, Mr Smith lost two pigs of 14 score each. He led some *"store pigs"* from the same sty into his house but then had to take them upstairs as the water rose. He then went back for the larger ones, but they had drowned in that short space of time. The field in which the pig sties were, Woodmill Meadow between the fellmongers, brook and mill, was under about seven feet of water. Mr Lawrence, of Fern Cottage, took his pigs out of their sty and barricaded them into an entry at the side of his house, but as the water rose the pressure of the pigs against it broke the barricade and they swam across to some higher ground towards the railway line. Estimates of damage, excluding the loss of pigs, was estimated to vary between £5 and £15 a house.

Mr Eagles' mill was flooded, machinery damaged and produce of meal and oilcake lost. The most accurate estimate of cost was between £200 and £300.

By far the worst hit was Street and Walmsley's fellmongers causing damage estimated between £1,000 and £2,000. Bales of wool and skins were floating about in great numbers, a drying stove was flooded, a great deal of wool washed away. The wool store shed was protected by a wall and corrugated roof, strengthened by massive buttresses and pillars, but the wall was washed down and about a score of bales worth £15 to £20 each were washed away. Other wooden buildings were smashed up like matchwood. Walmsley had taken the horses out of the stables on Sunday night, otherwise they would have drowned. Footbridges over the stream were broken and the expensive machinery was flooded and needed much attention before being fit for use. Mr Walmsley's house, situated in the yard, was flooded and one of the floors sank six inches by the action of the water.

The havoc at the fellmongers had to be seen to be believed. Heavy bales of wool weighing 7cwt each were washed away downstream and the banks for a mile or so were strewn with wool and pelts. Street employed 10 or 12 hands to recover goods from as far away as Stoneleigh.

The vicars Hanning, Berridge and Bancroft distributed coal and food to the cottagers through the upper stories of their homes. Miss Hanning was busy with soup. Captain Stringer supplied tins of roast beef, cheese and bread. By midday the waters were receding, and clearing up begun. The bridge at the Castle, though damaged was passable once more. Ten men of the fire brigade under Lieutenant Heatley, who had helped to get people out of their homes, were now using 'Queen Bess', operated by Griffiths and Faxon, to pump water out of cellars. On Monday morning, the engine was employed pumping water out of the Engine Inn. Considerable sympathy was directed to the hostess Mrs Carter, especially as her husband was in South Africa with the Warwickshire Imperial Yeomanry. *"The damage to the house is considerable and presents a very pitiful sight."* The landlords, Hunt, Edmunds and Co of Banbury, later sent a message of thanks and a donation to the fire brigade funds.

The debris brought in by the flooding made a deplorable mess. When the water subsided, everything was deposited in a layer of mud. *"One is struck with sorrow to see the furniture wrecked, the little knick-knacks lying heaped up as thrown by the water, broken and mud covered."* It was the worst flood in Kenilworth since that of 1834, which had seriously damaged Townpool Bridge. It was thought that damage this time would have been greater had the brook through the Common not been straightened in connection with the sewer works some twenty years previously, but the narrow banks from the mill to the Common Lane bridge contributed.

A fund to relieve the immediate want was set up by Dr Edmund Bourne with Reverend Hanning, Reverend Harrington Lees, Reverend G Field, Captain Stringer, J E Jackson and Arthur Street assisting on the committee. Donations had to be paid to either Thomas S Morris at London, City and Midland Bank, or to Mr Bishop at Lloyds, and £40 was quickly raised, and within weeks this doubled. Herr Schneider offered to give a concert in aid of the flood fund. It was not just Kenilworth that suffered, there was severe flooding in Warwick, Leamington and Coventry where lives were lost.

It was expected to be a long time before some of the houses were again fit for human habitation. *"The people of Kenilworth must...make it impossible for a dangerous flood ever to occur again. It can be done and it must be done. The course of the brook must be inspected from one end to the other. The matter seems to me to be so important that it ought to be considered by a parish meeting..."* said John Welsh of Rudfen manor, and indeed it was announced that a committee was to be formed to inspect the brook to see if a repeat could be permanently prevented.

*   *   *

Lord Roberts was replaced by Lord Kitchener to fight what was now a guerrilla war in South Africa. Roberts returned home a hero and had an audience with Queen Victoria at Osborne House. A couple of weeks later, his staff member Corporal Jeffcott returned to Kenilworth, looking thinner and having suffered a bout of enteric, but otherwise healthy. By serving on Lord Roberts's staff, he had had many experiences, which he did not want to repeat. He arrived at the station wearing a bandolier, still full of cartridges tipped with poison, that he had taken from a live Boer. With his return, national pride and patriotism was once more to the fore, but the focal point of this fervour, Queen Victoria, was ill. The same week that Jeffcott returned, Lord Roberts had another audience with the Queen but this was to be her last engagement.

On 22nd January, a telegram was received at the sub-Post Office in Warwick Road at 5.30 p.m. to say Her Majesty was fading. People went to the main Post Office in High Street where many telegrams relaying the Queen's condition were arriving. At 7.30, the streets previously quiet became astir with people trying to find if the news was true, Her Majesty had died. By 8.00 o'clock, there was a muffled peel at St.Nicholas. *"The town is plunged in grief too deep for mere words to express."* *"Most women of all classes showed their sorrow in tears without restraint."* Blinds were lowered and all events cancelled.

"The Queen was regarded in Kenilworth with the greatest devotion and her death causes as much grief as though we had all lost a dear friend. It is now over 42 years since she passed through the streets of Kenilworth on her way to Stoneleigh Abbey; the Prince Consort was then with her."

"The tradesmen in The Square have boards in front of their shop windows in token of regret at the Queen's death. On the day of the funeral, we may expect to see much display of sorrow. Many of us have never seen Her Majesty, yet her personality has filled us all with love to her, and while she was living, we all felt great sympathy with her in all her troubles.

The Queen is dead, long live the King!"

The Victorian era was at an end.

Appendix

The death of Dr Wynter reveals a mystery. It was clearly stated in his obituary that he never married and no Mrs Wynter is ever mentioned - and yet at Kings Norton Register Office on 17th October 1888, Dr Daniel Wynter, 49, Surgeon of Hyde House, Kenilworth, married Sarah Ann Bromley of Edgbaston. Sarah was born in Wilncote and at the time of the 1881 census she was working as a cook at the Kings Arms, just a couple of hundred yards from Wynter's home, Hyde House. The 1891 census, just three years after the marriage, records Wynter as neither married nor widowed, but "single". It is easy to speculate that this is in some way connected with his financial downfall and eventual suicide, but I have found nothing to suggest it. Why his brother Hugh, then living in Somerset, did not attend Daniel's funeral is also a mystery.

Ewan Christian (1814-1895), the architect of both St.John's church and school, designed over 50 churches and 200 parsonages in his lifetime. He was also involved in the restoration of more than 150 churches. In 1850 he was appointed as architect to the Ecclesiastical Commissioners for England, hence his involvement with St.John's, and subsequently as a consultant in which capacity he commented upon over 220 designs each year. He is known to have crossed paths with one-time Kenilworth resident, Edwin H L Barker, over the designs for a parsonage in Hereford. He was not restricted to religious buildings, other work included country houses, schools and business premises, and perhaps his most appreciated design is the National Portrait Gallery. He was a Manxman by descent.

A noteworthy event in the life of famed trade unionist, George Potter, came in the early 1860's when *"...he led his fellow-men to give welcome to Garibaldi, and rode on horseback by the side of Garibaldi's carriage through one of the greatest multitudes ever seen in the streets of London."* Garibaldi's visit was commemorated by the creation of a new biscuit, which still carries his name. At the time of his appearance in Kenilworth in support of the farm labourers uprising, George Potter was at the height of his powers, but just six years later he was declared bankrupt, due largely to the expense of circulating *The Beehive*. Several attempts to be elected to the House of Commons as a Liberal candidate failed, his last such effort being in 1886. He addressed a number of meetings in Kenilworth in support of Mr Cobb, its Liberal representative. George Potter died from *"paralysis of the brain"* at his home in Clapham on 3rd June 1893, aged 61.

The gravestone of his father, Edmund, can be found in the grounds of the former Baptist Church on the corner of Spring Lane and Albion Street. Nearby are those of fireman Thomas Plumbe, fellmonger and close associate of Henry Street, William Walmsley, and brickmaker Edward Kimberley. The stones have been re-sited from their original location in the grounds.

Kenilworth-born owner of Derby winner 'Caractacus', Charles Snewing, had no success as a race-horse breeder but still made some £30,000 from racing. Despite his travels, Snewing never forgot Kenilworth; *"His charity to the town was unabounded."* Upon his death aged 69 at Holywell, near Watford, on 23rd December 1886, he was returned to his hometown to be buried with his wife at St.Nicholas; his parents share a grave nearby.

The gravestone of Charles and Maria Snewing.

Charles Boultbee recovered from his Boer War wounds and later served in India, gaining a reputation as a dashing soldier. He died in 1939 without marrying. After his mother died in 1885, his father Henry re-married; the only child from this second marriage was Harold (born when Henry was 62) who as a youngster lived at Moorlands. Harold's life was at sea, first in merchant shipping and then in the Navy. He eventually settled in Australia and two of his sons became World War Two pilots. Based in Britain, both were decorated and survived the conflict. Harold died in 1950, his descendants today still live in Western Australia.

George Beard died on Wednesday 18th July 1906, he would have been 90 on the 27th. Beard went out for a drive with his nurse on the Monday but suffered a stroke. He was described as being a great friend to St.John's church and school and had paid £220 for *"Hot air apparatus"* at the church. His funeral was in Solihull.

Coal merchant's son Thomas Hardy Hall, who was lost with HMS Atalanta, is remembered on a memorial plaque at St.Ann's Church, Portsmouth, along with his 280 shipmates.

Anthony McMillan snr died in 1893 after a 16 week stay in hospital. His son Alfred took on South Hurst Farm but in early 1898 he gave it up and joined his brother Anthony jnr in British Columbia.

The life and achievements of Kenilworth-born

photographer John Henry Grayson Clarke is told in full in John and Valerie's Holland's excellent book, *From Scotter to Brigg*. It includes several hundred of his photographs, mostly of Lincolnshire, and three modern pictures of his Kenilworth homes.

In 1894 John Fell, who built Kenilworth's sewerage system, a number of houses in Waverley Road (and the road itself) and whose brick company once owned the Whitemoor works, continued to prove his versatility by building Cairo's first tram system. He also built Leamington's Town Hall.

PC James Sloss was transferred to the Atherstone division in September 1900. Within a year he was found under the influence of drink at a "conference point" and fined £1. Two years later he was again fined £1 for a similar offence. In 1908 he was fined 5s for parading in front of a Government Inspector with a dirty lamp, and in 1910 fined £1 for once more being under the influence of drink. His list of offences required an additional sheet of paper to be attached to his page in the record book. He left the force on 5th January 1911, aged 51, and received an annual pension of £47 2s 11d.

In Kansas, John Boddington's career progressed. He became Assistant Master Mechanic in what was by then, through amalgamation, the Union Pacific Railroad. He was at one time a Councillor in Old Wyandotte City and, described as a "Pioneer resident", became an American citizen in 1902. He died on 14th March 1922 and is buried in Woodlawn Cemetery, Kansas. One of his grandsons, Edward, perhaps named after his own grandfather, died in 1982. There are still Boddingtons listed in the Kansas City phonebook. The Wyandotte Inn was to be the last pub built in Kenilworth for almost a century.

The man who found the young boys' den on the Common whilst collecting ferns, was probably acting under the enclosure act of 1755: the poor were allowed to make such collections.

The road onto which Clarendon Terrace fronts eventually became Clarendon Road, but not until the early 20th century, after the name Clarendon Street had been completely superseded by Station Road.

The cricket ground at the back of the Bowling Green Inn was also the earliest identified site where organised football was played in town. Today, part of this field remains as the upper playing field at St.Nicholas School. Football and other games are still played upon it. The cricket ground that was accessed by the driveway which became Queen's Road, in 1901 became the first home of the Kenilworth Lawn Tennis and Croquet Club. During the Second World War cricket returned - it was the first home of the Kenilworth Wardens club. Today the site is covered by Queens Close and Faircroft.

The Institute maintained its lethargic existence until in November 1915 it was decided to close at the end of year for the duration of the First World War. It did not re-open.

The swimming pool continued to run at a loss. By 1901, costs were being cut; the baths opened on 1st June as usual but the caretaker was appointed at only 10s a week. "It was resolved that the bath be kept open from 6 a.m. till dusk and that no females should be admitted." It may be that so few females used the baths the cost of a female attendant, just 2s a week, was prohibitive.

Thomas Pope's (later Turner, Webb and Pace) comb factory was at the rear of what became 5 and 5a The Square. Anstey's the grocers became A J Cookes and Mander's the wine merchant was eventually owned by Mitchells & Butler. Some of the buildings survived, just, the WW2 land mine explosion but were demolished to make way for the re-development of Abbey End in the 1960s. Today, a furniture sale-room is roughly on the site of the comb factory.

There is virtually no trace left of Kenilworth's major Victorian industrial sites:
The gas works site is now The Deer Leap.
The tannery site is now Talisman Square.
The mill site is now Forge Road.
Henry Street's fellmongery is now Woodmill Meadow.
Whitemoor brickworks' site is now Ebourne Close.
Cherry Orchard brickworks site is now Piper's Lane and a re-cycling centre.
Edward Smith's brickworks at Crackley is the tennis and squash club.
The original pump-house of the water works remains on the Common, but the extraction system is "mothballed", Kenilworth's water has come from other sources for over a decade.
Builder Edward Smith's School Lane stores and offices that were built in 1886, were incorporated in the development Rosemary Mews in the 1990s.

The new Bowling Green Hotel, later the Abbey Hotel, was converted into apartments in the 1980's, but remains as Kenilworth's most impressive Victorian building. The hotel it replaced as the town's leading hostelry, the Kings Arms, was demolished in the same decade but a new structure of very similar appearance replaced it. The original railway station stonework was renovated. Today, however, the premises are empty and their future uncertain.

Montague House, the home of William Boddington and Joseph Holland Burbery for at least 20 years each, became the home for the new Working Men's Club, which had earlier occupied a house in Albion Street. Today it is known as a sports and social club. Construction work on land at the rear recently revealed some remains of Kenilworth's workhouse.

Southbank House in Hereford, the home of Reverend Joseph Barker and his family after which Southbank Road was named, was demolished as recently as 2004.

Despite the calls in 1901 to take measures to stop a repeat of the regular Mill End flooding, such occurrences continued throughout the 20th century. The re-development of Henry Street's fellmongers site coincided with another serious flood, reaching bar-level in The Engine, and this instigated a major re-assessment of Kenilworth's drainage system, resulting in an extensive reconstruction that is continuing at the time of publication.

After leaving Kenilworth, Ernest Trepplin had an interesting life, becoming the land agent for Lord Portman. He also became friendly with Robert Walpole (the Earl of Orford) and at the age of 59 finally married - his wife being the widow of Major-General Sir Frederick Carrington. Ernest was a member of the Somerset Archaeological and Natural History Society, and due to this, his extensive collection of brass candlesticks is on permanent display at Taunton Castle Museum. A photograph of Ernest in 1879 appears on the Oxford University Athletic Club website. Ernest and his parents are interred in the churchyard of the parish church of Salcombe Regis, Devon. The Trepplins' first home locally, Green Hayes, is today named Wootton Court. For a reference to a full account of the life of the Trepplin family, refer to the Bibliography.

The Trepplin tomb in Salcombe Regis.

The rest of the Abbey Fields, those not opened as a park in late 1896, continued to be let to farmers for grazing their animals. The last left in the early 1960s. The stone building used as a barn, which it was suggested could be "...utilized at some future date for the preservation of objects of local interest..." was used by the Association of Friends of Kenilworth Abbey for an exhibition in 1937. The display lasted about three years. The Kenilworth History and Archaeology Society organised a permanent exhibition in 1974 that includes the curio known as "the ducking stool" which had been stored in the building's rafters "for centuries."

William Evans, at one time the driving force of the Local Board, died on 22nd July 1907, aged 81. His daughter Gertrude later conveyed to the KUDC two areas of the Abbey Fields, alongside Forrest Road and High Street, originally bought by William and the other members of the syndicate, Luke Heynes, Samuel Forrest and Joseph Holland Burbery.

The family grave includes the remains of William Evans, his son Percy and daughter Gertrude.

The author believes that it would be a fitting tribute to name the Abbey Fields footpaths after Evans, Burbery and Heynes (to compliment Forrest Road) as permanent recognition, and a show of gratitude, for buying the Abbey Fields for us all. Without their personal investment of about £10,000, and determination as Board member's, it is likely that many of the fields would not have been saved, and today would be covered with housing.

Index

The bracketed numbers denote the grave number as recorded in *Memorials in the Churchyard of St Nicholas*, published by the Kenilworth History and Archaeology Society. This has only been done in cases of certain identity - doubtless there are others. Specific identification of individuals has not always been possible, thus, for example, James, Mr and J E Jackson may be the same person. Conversely, entries for the same name may not be the same person as Christian names were often repeated within families. Small numbers in italics denote a positively identified second (or third) person with the same name. Page numbers in bold denote an illustration in addition to text. Although contemporary road-name spellings are used in the text, modern spellings are used here for convenience. In sporting circles, team members are only listed where they are of relevance. Teams and individuals from outside Kenilworth are not included.